Aś

AND THE DECLIN

Kālsi rock (east face). The Major Rock Edicts of Aśoka

Aśoka

AND THE DECLINE OF THE MAURYAS

WITH NEW AFTERWORD, BIBLIOGRAPHY AND INDEX

ROMILA THAPAR

OXFORD
UNIVERSITY PRESS

OXFORD
UNIVERSITY PRESS

YMCA Library Building, Jai Singh Road, New Delhi 110 001

Oxford University Press is a department of the University of Oxford. It furthers the University's objective of excellence in research scholarship and education by publishing worldwide in

Oxford New York

Auckland Cape Town Dar es Salaam Hong Kong Karachi Kuala Lumpur Madrid Melbourne Mexico City Nairobi New Delhi Shanghai Taipei Toronto

With offices in
Argentina Austria Brazil Chile Czech Republic France Greece Guatemala Hungary Italy Japan Poland Portugal Singapore South Korea Switzerland Thailand Turkey Ukraine Vietnam

Published in India
by Oxford University Press, New Delhi

First printed in India 1973
Second edition 1997
Oxford India Paperbacks 1998
Seventeenth impression 2010

ISBN-13: 978-0-19-564445-6
ISBN-10: 0-19-564445-X

Printed by Sapra Brothers, New Delhi 110092
Published by Oxford University Press
YMCA Library Building, Jai Singh Road, New Delhi 110 001

For

PROFESSOR A. L. BASHAM

PREFACE

THE reign of Aśoka began to attract the attention of historians well over a century ago. In 1837, James Prinsep first published his work on the Aśokan inscriptions in a series of papers. The first monograph on Aśoka did not however appear until 1901, when Vincent Smith considered the subject in greater detail.[1]

Repeated editions of Smith's monographs brought popularity to the subject, and in 1925 D. R. Bhandarkar published his Carmichael Lectures on the history of the reign of Aśoka. A small study by J. M. McPhail followed in 1926: 1928 saw a further study by R. K. Mookerji. Louis de la Vallée Poussin published a book on the Mauryas in 1930. From then until the 1950s there was no single monograph in English on Aśoka, except that of B. M. Barua in 1946. This is not to suggest that historians lost interest in this particular period of Indian history. On the contrary a considerable amount of research was being done, but it was largely confined to particular aspects of the Aśokan age, as for instance, Mauryan polity, numismatics, philological studies of the edicts, etc.; Barua's book was a compilation of all this research bringing the study up to date.

Nilakantha Sastri and his collaborators brought out an able study of the Nandas and Mauryas in 1952. In 1955, B. G. Gokhale brought out a study of Aśoka's relationship to Buddhism. 1956 saw an onrush of books on the subject, the most useful being by P. Eggermont. A study by F. Kern appeared in the same year. A small introductory study was published by A. C. Sen to celebrate the Buddha Jayanti, the 2,500th anniversary of the death of the Buddha. More recently, D. C. Sircar has published a work on the Aśokan inscriptions. Despite this formidable list of publications on the subject, I believe (for reasons which I have discussed in detail in the introductory chapter), that there is still scope for a reinterpretation of existing material. It is this reinterpretation that I have attempted in the present study.

The reader may find a lack of consistency in the use of diacritical marks in place names. I have tried as far as possible to transliterate the lesser known names from Sanskrit or Pāli, whichever is the more common form. But in the case of modern place names, I have retained the modern and more familiar spelling (even when this is not consistent with the use of diacritical marks), in order to make them easily recognizable. Sanchi, for

[1] For titles of these works, see Bibliography.

instance, spelt as Sānci, seems to me to be unduly pedantic. In the case of Sanskrit and Pāli words, I have kept largely to the original forms, without attempting to reduce all the words to one of the two languages.

Financial assistance in the form of scholarships and studentships from various institutions was primarily responsible for my being able to complete this study. I should like to express my appreciation for this to the International Federation of University Women (for the Crosby Hall Scholarship), the University of London (for the William Lincoln Shelley Studentship in History), and University College, London (for the Sir William Meyer Studentship).

I have been assisted during the course of my research by various scholars and colleagues, both in discussions and in the translation of certain source materials. I should like in particular to thank Dr. Allchin, Prof. Dave, Dr. Goodakumbara, and Dr. Marr. For reading through the typescript of the book and suggesting improvements, I should like to thank my parents, and my friends, Prof. J. D. Bernal, Dr. Sergei Horwitz, Dr. Anthony Michaelis and Mrs. Gertrude Wengraf. I am happy to thank Mr. J. F. Horrabin for drawing the maps in this book. My thanks are also due to the Librarian and Staff of the School of Oriental and African Studies, the Commonwealth Relations Office Library, and the British Museum Library. I wish to acknowledge my gratitude to Prof. A. L. Basham for his guidance and sympathetic help throughout the period of my writing this book.

R. THAPAR

London, 1960

CONTENTS

LIST OF PLATES x

ABBREVIATIONS xi

I. THE BACKGROUND AND THE SOURCES 1

II. EARLY LIFE, ACCESSION, AND CHRONOLOGY OF THE REIGN OF AŚOKA 20

III. SOCIETY AND ECONOMIC ACTIVITY 55

IV. INTERNAL ADMINISTRATION AND FOREIGN RELATIONS 94

V. THE POLICY OF *Dhamma* 137

VI. THE LATER MAURYAS 182

VII. THE DECLINE OF THE MAURYAS 197

CONCLUSION 213

APPENDICES

I. The Date of the *Arthaśāstra* 218

II. The Titles of Aśoka 226

III. The Geographical Locations of the Edicts 228

IV. Pottery and Coins of the Mauryan Period 239

V. A Translation of the Edicts of Aśoka 250

VI. Mauryan Art 267

AFTERWORD 271

BIBLIOGRAPHY 322

INDEX 333

LIST OF PLATES

I. Kālsi Rock (east face). The Major Rock Edicts of Aśoka. From *Corpus Inscriptionum Indicarum* edited by E. Hultzsch. Copyright, Department of Archaeology, Government of India — *Frontispiece*

II. Aśokan pillar with a single-lion capital at Lauriyā-Nandangarh. Copyright, Department of Archaeology, Government of India — *Facing page* 6

III. Ptolemy II Philadelphus of Egypt. Vatican Museum — ,, ,, 40

IV. Edicts from the Aśokan inscription at Shahbāzgarhi. From *Corpus Inscriptionum Indicarum* edited by E. Hultzsch. Copyright, Department of Archaeology, Government of India — ,, ,, 128

V. Kandahar bilingual inscription in Greek and Aramaic. By permission of the Editor, *East and West*, Rome — ,, ,, 260

VI. Dhauli. Elephant carved from the rock at the site of the Aśokan inscriptions. Copyright, Department of Archaeology, Government of India — ,, ,, 268

LIST OF MAPS

Areas to which Buddhist Missions were sent — 48

Routes of Trade and Communication between India and the West — 83

Tribal Peoples mentioned in the Aśokan edicts — 124

The Mauryan Period. Aśokan sites and important towns — *at end*

Sites of Aśokan edicts discovered since 1961 — *at end*

ABBREVIATIONS

ABORI	*Annals of the Bhandarkar Oriental Research Institute.*
AI	*Ancient India.*
AO	*Acta Orientalia.*
BSOAS	*Bulletin of the School of Oriental and African Studies.*
Ch.	Chapter.
CHI	*Cambridge History of India.*
CHQ	*Ceylon Historical Quarterly.*
CII	*Corpus Inscriptionum Indicarum.*
CR	*Calcutta Review.*
ed.	Edited by.
Ep. Ind.	*Epigraphia Indica.*
Ep. Zey.	*Epigraphia Zeylanica.*
HCIP	*History and Culture of the Indian People.*
Hist. Nat.	*Historia Naturalis.*
IA	*Indian Antiquary.*
IC	*Indian Culture.*
IG	*Imperial Gazetteer.*
IHQ	*Indian Historical Quarterly.*
Ind. Stud.	*Indische Studien.*
JA	*Journal Asiatique.*
JAOS	*Journal of the American Oriental Society.*
JASB	*Journal of the Asiatic Society of Bengal.*
JBBRAS	*Journal of the Bombay Branch of the Royal Asiatic Society.*
JBORS	*Journal of the Bihar and Orissa Research Society.*
JNSI	*Journal of the Numistic Society of India.*
JRAS	*Journal of the Royal Asiatic Society.*
P.E.	Pillar Edict.
P.T.S.	Pāli Text Society.
R.E.	Rock Edict.
S.E./S.R.E.	Separate Rock Edict.
ZDMG	*Zeitschrift der Deutschen Morganländischen Gesellschaft.*

I

THE BACKGROUND AND THE SOURCES

THROUGH the cross currents of activity and change which characterize Indian history in the five centuries before Christ, there emerges among the more outstanding figures, that of Aśoka. He appears to many people in many guises, a conqueror who forsook conquest when he saw the suffering it caused, a saint, a combination of monk and monarch, a political genius, a king with a rare understanding of human beings – and so the images can be multiplied. The picture we have of him is encrusted with legends, accumulating layer after layer through the centuries. Considerable care and sifting reveal something of the true contour.

It has been said on occasion that Aśoka was amongst those who stood in opposition to his age. This we believe to be a false view. He was, as we shall see, in many ways representative of his time. His greatest claim to recognition lies in the fact that he understood his age, and in terms of the Indian background, realized the requirements it demanded. He was not a narrow religious sectarian, as some have made him out to be, for his ultimate aims covered both the religious and secular aspects of life.

In reviewing earlier studies on Aśoka it may be said that on one aspect, his relationship to Buddhism, the general approach has been to depict him as having been suddenly converted to Buddhism as a result of his remorse at the cruelty inflicted on the people of Kaliṅga, during his campaign in that country in the eighth year of his reign. Conformity to Buddhist ethics then appears to become the sole concern of the king's life. Smith has described him as a monk and a monarch. Fritz Kern tries to analyse the inner springs of Aśoka's actions against the theological background of existence both in this world and the after-life, as well as of what he believes to be a widespread desire on the part of Indians at this period to become ascetics and to escape from life by other means. He depicts at great length the supposed conflict in the mind of the king who wishes to free himself of earthly ties, and yet is conscious of his responsibility as a king to society and to his subjects.

In our analysis of the subject we find that Aśoka was attracted to Buddhism, but his was not a case of a somewhat eccentric or unusual over-night conversion. We believe that in the context of society as it was then,

Buddhism was not just another religion. It was the result of a more widespread movement towards change which affected many aspects of life from personal beliefs to social ideas. It was a socio-intellectual movement with a large range of expression, making itself apparent in contemporary thought and life. A king with a policy only slightly more imaginative than usual, would have had to come to terms with such an important new development. As it was, it was an ideal tool for an ambitious ruler of Aśoka's calibre. Whatever his personal convictions may have been regarding the religion, it was eminently suitable for such a ruler who wished to use it to consolidate political and economic power.

One of the most difficult problems facing an historian concerned with a study of a personality belonging to an ancient period of history is that of distinguishing between the man in his private capacity and the same man in the role of a statesman. The two aspects which in some cases have been markedly different, judging from the biographies of statesmen dominating more recent history, can in the study of a remote age be hopelessly confused, owing to an arbitrary utilization of all the evidence available.

This confusion has frequently occurred in studies on the emperor Aśoka written during the last half-century. It is indeed unfortunate that, in reconstructing his life and activities, religious sources were regarded as reliable complementary evidence to that of his own inscriptions. The religious sources, mainly Buddhist, naturally wishing to take advantage of the fact of Aśoka having been a Buddhist himself, have, as has rightly been said, made him out to be a monster of piety — a picture which is not endorsed by his own edicts and inscriptions.

A careful study of the inscriptions reveals that they were of two kinds. The smaller group consists of the declarations of the king as a lay Buddhist to his church, the Buddhist *Saṃgha.* These describe his own acceptance of Buddhism and his relationship with the *Saṃgha.* Here the somewhat intolerant and wholly credulous believer appears, as in one inscription where he proclaims in no uncertain terms that dissident monks and nuns must be expelled from the order. A further inscription in a less fanatical vein speaks of the various scriptures with which all good Buddhists should be familiar.

By far the more important inscriptions are those of the larger group, which may be described as proclamations to the public at large. This group consists of the Major and Minor Rock Edicts and the Pillar Edicts. These define his famous policy of *Dhamma. Dhamma* is the Prākrit form of the Sanskrit word *dharma*, virtually untranslatable into English owing to its use in a peculiarly Indian context. It has been variously translated as morality, piety, righteousness, and so forth.[1] It was in the conception of this policy, regarded in the background of Mauryan India, that the true achievement of Aśoka lay.

In the past, historians have generally interpreted Aśoka's *Dhamma* almost as a synonym for Buddhism, suggesting thereby that Aśoka was concerned with making Buddhism the state religion. We propose to show that this was not his intention, although he himself, as a firm believer in Buddhism, was convinced that it was the only way to salvation. The policy of *Dhamma* was a policy rather of social responsibility than merely of demanding that the entire population should favour Buddhism. It was the building up of an attitude of mind in which social behaviour, the behaviour of one person towards another, was considered of great importance. It was a plea for the recognition of the dignity of man, and for a humanistic spirit in the activities of society.

In examining this policy we must of necessity analyse the conditions which gave rise to it. It was in part a policy which was nurtured in the mind of the king himself. But since it was seen by the king as largely a solution to existing problems, it is in the light of these problems and contemporary conditions that the value and importance of this contribution of Aśoka can be truly assessed.

Primarily there was the political situation arising out of the recent imposition of imperial control over an extensive area that had previously consisted of small kingdoms and republics. The imperial system of the Mauryas, started by Candragupta Maurya, the grandfather of Aśoka, roughly half a century before the accession of Aśoka, was a comparatively new feature in Indian politics. The dynasty previous to the Mauryas, the Nandas, had had an empire, but it was not nearly as extensive as that of the Mauryas, nor did it include such a variety of peoples and cultures. The Nanda empire had its nucleus in Magadha and included the people of the Ganges valley and its neighbourhood; culturally they either belonged to or were acquainted with the Aryan civilization. The Mauryan empire included far more diverse elements, some outside the area of Aryan India, thus creating many more political complications than in the earlier period.

By stressing these facts we are not suggesting that the personal factor in the development of the *Dhamma* can be ignored. Aśoka's private beliefs and his immediate environment must also have had their share in moulding the policy. As a family, the Mauryas were undoubtedly eclectic in their religious beliefs. Candragupta is said to have been a Jaina and Bindusāra,

[1] Our own translation would render it as Virtue, rather in the sense of the Greek ἀρετη. See Ch. V.

the father of Aśoka, favoured the Ājīvikas, both of which were non-orthodox sects, and if anything were antagonistic to brahmanical ideas. It is therefore not surprising that Aśoka himself did not conform to brahmanical theory and preferred to patronize the Buddhists. At least some Greek ideas must also have been noticed and possibly examined during this intellectual ferment.

The sixth century B.C. may almost be described as a century of universal questioning. Pythagoras in Greece, and Confucius in China had their counterparts in India. The existence of a variety of sects concerned both with religious belief and with philosophical speculation, testifies to a period of vigorous debate and discussion, when not only were the existing Aryan values questioned, but also each newly developed theory was put through a severe test of criticism. The materialism of the early *Cārvākas* vied with the more subtle metaphysics of the *Upaniṣads*. It was a period of doubts, when the brahmanical stronghold, gradually built up through the later Vedic period (from *c.* 900 B.C. onwards), was being attacked by the new forces. The privileges of the priests were being questioned, as well as the efficacy of the ceremonies and rituals which they performed. The caste system, which had begun to assume the features of its later rigidity during the Buddhist and post-Buddhist period, also came under attack, though often not in a direct way. Generally the less fortunate of the four castes tended to favour the new sects as against their previous allegiance to brahmanism. This was particularly the case with the third caste, the *vaiśyas*, who though technically included amongst the highly favoured twice-born or *dvija*,[1] in the practical matters of daily life tended to be excluded from the privileges by the first two castes, the brahmans and the *kṣatriyas*.

Thus, whereas on the one hand brahmanism was seeking to establish itself with all its rigidity in social ideas and all the emphasis on temporal control which it assumed later in the early centuries A.D., at the same time the dissident groups were trying to keep back this force. The spearhead of these groups was Buddhism. The conflict was not necessarily a violent one, since none of the dissidents had declared any sort of religious war. It would seem that usually the conflict took the form of social tensions and political opposition.

Nor were these religious and social trends isolated from certain economic changes of a fundamental nature which had occurred in the centuries immediately prior to the Mauryan period. Aryan economy had changed from what it was during the early Vedic period, a semi-nomadic pastoral economy, to a settled agrarian village economy with its necessary comple-

[1] i.e. the first time with their natural birth and the second time on their initiation.

ment of land-tax and rural administrators. Together with this the Buddhist period saw the opening up of extensive trade, and the increasing importance of that class of society associated with trade, the *vaiśyas*. Here again the material improvement of the *vaiśyas* through trade strengthened their antagonistic feelings towards the unjustified privileges that the brahmans and *kṣatriyas*, particularly the former, had taken to themselves. The establishment of guilds ushered in a new factor in urban society, a factor upon which city-life was dependent to a high degree. This introduced a new force with which the socially more favoured had now to contend in order to maintain their previous position.

Up to a point these economic changes forced the political pattern. The fact of the state being supported by an agrarian economy necessitated the development of a bureaucracy and a properly organized administration. Improvement in trade was brought about by a tendency towards the uniform administration of the country. The size and scope of the imperial structure entailed a strong, centralized control. The political pattern had therefore to place an overwhelming emphasis on governmental machinery and authority, if such a vast edifice was to be kept in working order.

We thus see Mauryan society in India as a multicultural society with the units at different levels of general development, and with economic, social, and religious forces counteracting each other. To any intelligent statesman of the period it must have been evident that some kind of binding factor was necessary in order to keep the empire intact and allow the movement of goods and services to continue. The policy of *Dhamma* with its emphasis on social responsibility was intended to provide this binding factor.

In a study of the Mauryan period a sudden flood of source material becomes available. Whereas with earlier periods of Indian history there is a frantic search to glean evidence from sources often far removed and scattered, with the Mauryan period there is a comparative abundance of information, from sources either contemporary or written at a later date.

This is particularly the case with the reign of Aśoka Maurya, since, apart from the unintentional evidence of sources such as religious literature, coins, etc., the edicts of the king himself, inscribed on rocks and pillars throughout the country, are available. These consist of fourteen major rock edicts located at Kālsi, Mānsehrā, Shahbāzgarhi, Girnār, Sopārā, Yeṟṟaguḍi, Dhauli, and Jaugaḍa; and a number of minor rock edicts and inscriptions at Bairāṭ, Rūpanāth, Sahasrām, Brahmagiri, Gāvimath, Jaṭiṅga-Rāmeshwar, Maski, Pālkīguṇḍu, Rajūla-Maṇḍagiri, Siddāpura, Yeṟṟaguḍi, Gujarra and Jhansi. Seven pillar edicts exist at Allahabad, Delhi-Toprā, Delhi-Meerut, Lauriyā-Ararāja, Lauriyā-Nandangarh, and Rāmpūrvā.

Other inscriptions have been found at the Barābar Caves (three inscriptions), Rummindei, Nigali-Sāgar, Allahabad, Sanchi, Sārnāth, and Bairāṭ. Recently a minor inscription in Greek and Aramaic was found at Kandahar.[1]

The importance of these inscriptions could not be appreciated until it was ascertained to whom the title 'Piyadassi' referred, since the edicts generally do not mention the name of any king; an exception to this being the Maski edict, which was not discovered until very much later in 1915. The earliest publication on this subject was by Prinsep, who was responsible for deciphering the edicts. At first Prinsep identified Devanampiya Piyadassi with a king of Ceylon, owing to the references to Buddhism. There were of course certain weaknesses in this identification, as for instance the question of how a king of Ceylon could order the digging of wells and the construction of roads in India, which the author of the edicts claims to have done. Later in the same year, 1837, the *Dīpavaṃsa* and the *Mahāvaṃsa*, two of the early chronicles of the history of Ceylon, composed by Buddhist monks, were studied in Ceylon, and Prinsep was informed of the title of Piyadassi given to Aśoka in those works. This provided the link for the new and correct identification of Aśoka as the author of the edicts.

These inscriptions were engraved in prominent places, either near towns, or on important trade and travel routes, or in the proximity of religious centres and places of religious importance. Their purpose was naturally to make public the edicts to as large a group of people as possible. The rock inscriptions of the major edicts usually cover a large rock face. The pillars may have commemorated events of some significance. Unfortunately some of the pillars have been removed from their place of origin. The Toprā and Meerut pillars were brought to Delhi in the reign of Firoz Shah Tughlak,[2] and were regarded as something of a curiosity since their inscriptions were by then undecipherable. The Allahabad pillar, it is believed, was originally at Kauśāmbī.[3] The Bairāṭ inscription was removed to Calcutta by Cunningham.[4] This prevents the study of the objects *in situ* and is to be regretted from the archaeological point of view.

Hsüan Tsang, a Chinese Buddhist pilgrim, travelling in India in the seventh century A.D. refers, in his memoirs, to pillars at Rājagṛha, Śrāvastī, and other places; of which some were of architectural importance and others carried the king's edicts, none of which have been discovered as yet.[5] Possibly there were other pillars too, which have not yet been discovered.

[1] A translation of these inscriptions is included in Appendix V, p. 250. The geographical identification of the sites may be found in Appendix III, p. 228.

[2] Elliot-Dowson, *History of India*, vol. iii, pp. 350 ff.

[3] *CII*, vol. i, p. xix.

[4] Ibid., p. xxv.

[5] *The Life of Hiuen Tsiang by the Shaman Hwui Li*, Book iii (trans. Beal, p. 93).

Aśokan pillar with a single-lion capital at Lauriyā-Nandangarh

Fa-hsien, another Chinese monk collecting Buddhist texts in India in the fourth century A.D. describes a pillar at Sankisā with a lion capital, and an inscribed pillar in the environs of Pāṭaliputra.[1] Neither of these has yet been discovered. Judging from the advisory purpose of the edicts it seems more than likely that, apart from stone, they were also inscribed on other materials of a more perishable nature, such as wood, and were sent to all parts of the Mauryan empire. Certainly many more copies must have existed on other surfaces, which are now lost.

The two northern major rock edicts at Mānsehrā and Shahbāzgarhi are inscribed in *Kharoṣṭhī*, a script derived from the Persian Aramaic; the most recently discovered inscription at Kandahar is bilingual, being inscribed in Greek and Aramaic; the rest, even those in the southern Deccan, are in *Brāhmī*, the earliest Indian script so far known to have been used for the writing of Sanskrit and Prākrit. The use of the local script clearly points to the wish on the part of the emperor that his edicts should be read by all his literate subjects. Except for the Kandahar inscription, the language used in each case is Aśokan Prākrit with regional variations, broadly speaking those between eastern and western Prākrit. Again it is interesting that Aśoka should have consistently used Prākrit, the language spoken by the people at large, and not Sanskrit, the language of culture.

Amongst the other inscriptions which are directly concerned with the Mauryan period and which are not necessarily those of Aśoka, may be mentioned the Priyadarśi inscription at Taxila.[2] This is an Aramaic inscription embedded in the wall of a house at Sirkap, a post-Mauryan level at Taxila. It was inscribed in honour of a high official Romēdōtē who owed his advancement to 'Priy . . . ' the viceroy or governor. There is no certainty of this being a reference to Aśoka, although the title given to the viceroy suggests the word Priyadarśi, the title used by Aśoka.[3]

A fragmentary inscription found at Lampaka or Laghman (on the northern bank of the Kabul river near Jalalabad), is generally thought to be part of an Aśokan edict.[4] It is written in Aramaic and this would fit in with Aśoka's policy of using the script of the region. The three phrases which survive indicate that most probably it was an Aśokan edict.

The Sohgaurā copper-plate inscription in Gorakhpur district, and the Mahāsthān inscription of Bogra district are both composed in Aśokan Prākrit and inscribed in the *Brāhmī* script of the third century B.C.[5] The contents of these inscriptions deal with relief measures to be adopted during

[1] Giles, *Travels of Fa-hsien*, pp. 25, 48.
[2] Marshall, *Taxila*, vol. i, p. 15.
[3] See Ch. II, pp. 21, 22, and App. II, p. 226.
[4] Henning, *BSOAS*, XIII, 1949, Part I, p. 80.
[5] Sircar, *Select Inscriptions*..., pp. 82, 85.

a famine. We believe these inscriptions to be early Mauryan, probably issued during the reign of Candragupta. The reference to a famine during his reign is corroborated by Jaina sources, and the symbols on the copper-plate at Sohgaurā tally exactly with the symbols on the punch-marked coins, usually attributed to the early Mauryas. Further inscriptions which can be used as source material for this period are the Nāgārjunī Hill Cave inscriptions of Daśaratha, the grandson of Aśoka, and the Junāgarh Rock inscription of Rudradāman dated *c.* A.D. 150 containing an incidental reference to the Mauryas. These will be discussed at length later in this book.

Of the evidence provided by religious sources, Buddhist literature is of chief importance. From among Indian Buddhist sources the *Jātakas* are useful not because they pertain directly to the Mauryan period, but because they reveal a general picture of social and economic conditions of the Buddhist period, which conditions continued as broad trends into the Mauryan period. Certain sections of the Buddhist scriptures such as the *Dīgha Nikāya* are of interest in determining the influence of Buddhist ideas in the political sphere, for example, the question of the concept of the *cakravartin* (universal emperor) as a political idea. This is a more complicated process than it appears to be, for it has constantly to be kept in mind that the dating of such sources is still uncertain. It is a debatable point whether the account of the *cakravartin* in the *Cakkavattisīhanāda-sutta* is pre-Aśokan, and therefore may have inspired him to imperial power, or whether conversely his political strength inspired the Buddhist thinkers to the idea of the *cakravartin*.[1]

The Ceylon chronicles, the *Dīpavaṃsa* and the *Mahāvaṃsa* in particular, may also be regarded as source materials, since they describe at great length the part played by Aśoka in the spreading of Buddhism, more particularly in the coming of Buddhism to Ceylon. Here again caution is necessary since these chronicles were written by Ceylonese Buddhist monks who depicted Aśoka from the orthodox Buddhist standpoint. The *Dīpavaṃsa* was compiled between the third century B.C. and the fourth century A.D. and the *Mahāvaṃsa*, a more polished work, is believed to have been written in the fifth century A.D.[2] A commentary on the *Mahāvaṃsa*, the *Vaṃsatthapakāsinī*, composed in about the tenth century A.D., contains many legends regarding the Mauryas which have been neglected by or have disappeared from other literature. Clearly, since none of these works are contemporary to our period, allowance must be made for changes in

[1] *Dīgha Nikāya*, iii, pp. 58 ff.

[2] Geiger, *The Dīpavaṃsa and Mahāvaṃsa*, pp. 26 ff.; Geiger, *Mahāvaṃsa*, p. xi.

ideas and form, though it may well be that, since these works deal with a foreign tradition, they may have preserved some of the early stories without the political or social need to tamper too much with them.

The *Divyāvadāna* and similar texts are a collection of legends built around the figure of Aśoka and preserved outside India mainly in Tibetan and Chinese Buddhist sources. Their evidence cannot be taken too literally, since the compilation once again was done by Buddhist monks and no doubt the stories were used on occasion to illustrate the impact of Buddhism on Aśoka. A further source in this particular class of literature is the history of Buddhism written by the Lama Tāranātha some time in the late sixteenth century. It contains a garbled version of some historical traditions associated with the Mauryas.

Of the secular literature on the period, the most important single source is the *Arthaśāstra* of Kauṭalya. It has been argued that the *Arthaśāstra* is a work of the third century A.D. and as such cannot be accepted as source material for the Mauryan period. But we believe that originally it was a Mauryan document.[1] The author was the prime minister or adviser to Candragupta Maurya. The main body of the treatise and certainly many of the earlier books were written during or about the time of Candragupta, though the book was edited and rewritten during the ensuing centuries.

It is now not so easy to sift the original from the later material but the similarities between terms used in the *Arthaśāstra* and in the Aśokan edicts would certainly suggest that the Mauryan rulers were acquainted with the book. Its importance lies in the fact that it gives a clear methodical analysis of economic and political thought current at that time, and, more than that, its application to existing conditions. In the administrative measures of Aśoka we can see a close similarity between the two.

Lists of the Mauryan kings are included in the *Purāṇas*. These are collections ot legends interspersed with religious teaching. The legends no doubt contain some old traditions, but the *Purāṇas* as a whole are fairly late, dating from about the fourth century A.D. With frequent transcriptions and interpolations, the sequence of rulers given in the king lists has become rather confused.

Of the remaining literary sources there are the accounts gathered from classical writings in Greek and Latin of the impressions of travellers who visited India, in and about this period. Foremost among these is the account of Megasthenes, the friend of Seleucus Nikator (the successor to Alexander who ruled in Persia and Babylon), who visited the court of Candragupta and remained at the capital Pāṭaliputra for some time.

[1] See Appendix I.

Unfortunately the original document has not survived and what remain are only quotations from it in various Classical texts. Megasthenes has been quoted by later Greek writers such as Strabo and Diodorus (both of the first century B.C.), and Arrian (of the second century A.D.). Pliny, writing in the first century A.D., used Megasthenes' account in his Latin works. This naturally detracts from the reliability of the account as found in the quotations, since some elements of the personal prejudices of the writers quoting from the original must no doubt have crept in.

While considering literary sources some comment must be made on the way in which they are to be handled. It must be kept in mind that many contemporary sources have either been destroyed in the course of time or have yet to be found. There are large gaps which can only be filled either by careful scholarship or by new discoveries. The literary style of some sources can create problems. For example the *Arthaśāstra* is composed in an aphoristic style; the minimum number of words are used, which naturally complicates the interpretation of the sentences.

Another problem common to all historians dealing with documents of an age well into the past, is that of the translation of specialized terms. The meaning of words varies according to the context, and the connotation of words changes from age to age and from society to society. By way of an example, there is no precise translation in English for the word *Dharma*, and furthermore the connotation of the word has changed considerably since the third century B.C.

The problem of the authenticity of a document is equally important. The philologist may in this case come to the historian's aid. Apart from this the only means that can be employed to obtain absolute certainty is cross-evidence from other sources. We may here cite the example of Megasthenes' description of the city of Pāṭaliputra in which he states that it was surrounded by a wooden palisade. Archaeological excavations near Patna have revealed the existence of this palisade. Where cross-evidence is not available, it is left to the historian to attempt by a critical study to sift the data which seem probably true from those which appear false.

More specifically the purpose of the document must be kept in mind. If it was written to propagate a particular view, then this function must not be neglected. Buddhist sources, in order to show Aśoka's adherence to Buddhism, would have us believe that he was completely in the hands of the *Saṃgha*.[1] His own edicts suggest otherwise.

[1] The literal meaning of *Saṃgha* is 'society'. It was the official title adopted for the Buddhist Order of monks. In its early history it was remarkably democratic in constitution.

With regard to the Greek sources it must be remembered that the authors were foreign to India, and therefore looked on the country and its customs with alien eyes. The undertone of awe and bewilderment that creeps into their writings cannot be taken too seriously. Owing to the alien character of the material they were handling it is possible that they may at times have confused the practical and theoretical aspects of a question. A case in point is Megasthenes' description of the seven castes in India.

Among the material remains of the Mauryan period, we have a considerable amount of numismatic evidence, some artifacts from archaeological excavations, and art objects. The first category consists largely of silver and copper punch-marked coins and silver bar coins, which appear to have been in circulation throughout the Mauryan period until the coming of the Bactrian Greeks. The area of circulation was largely north-west India, the Ganges basin, and the northern fringes of the Deccan plateau.[1] That these coins are the earliest surviving coinage in India and that the symbols were official marks can now be stated with a fair degree of certainty.

Over the last fifteen years many excavations have been conducted in north-west India and the Ganges basin, in addition to the earlier ones at Taxila. In most cases excavations were carried to a pre-Mauryan level. Pottery types which can be used among other things to determine cultural levels have revealed the interesting phenomenon of the northern black polished ware, which is widespread throughout the Mauryan empire with the exception of the southernmost areas.

Similar to archaeological evidence is the related material, termed by some historians 'art remains'. These are the animal capitals surmounting the pillars on some of which the edicts were inscribed. These consist of single lion capitals at Rāmpūrvā, Lauryā-Nandangarh, and the uninscribed pillar at Basāṛh; the single bull on another pillar at Rāmpūrvā, also uninscribed; the four lions at Sārnāth and Sanchi; and the single elephant which is thought to have been the capital of the pillar at Sankisā. The two elephant figures, one carved on a rock at Dhauli and the other engraved on the rock surface at Kālsi, are believed to be Aśokan.

With so much evidence of various kinds available, it is not to be wondered at that many historians have as it were been lured into writing on the Mauryan period. But this abundance of historical research should, we feel, not deter other historians from attempting new interpretations which may successfully answer the many questions on the Mauryan period which still remain unanswered. We believe that a reinterpretation of existing facts can still be made with every validity, owing to variations of historical

[1] Gupta, *A Bibliography of the Hoards of Punch-marked Coins in Ancient India.*

approach. These variations are not only possible but are indeed necessary because history is a living discipline and each new analysis is a furthering of knowledge on the subject, provided the analysis is borne out by evidence. Even within the confines of an historical system there can be a valid analysis with a difference in emphasis.

A reconstruction of the events prior to the coming of Aśoka would provide a useful background and would give continuity to the narrative. The Mauryas came on the scene after what the *Purāṇas* describe as the uprooting of the Nandas by the brahman Kauṭalya.[1] The rise of the Mauryas from what appears to have been a comparatively obscure and humble position has been the cause of a variety of traditions concerning their origin. One of these states that the name Maurya was derived from Murā, the wife of a Nanda king and the grandmother or mother of the first Maurya.[2] The *Purāṇas*, however, do not link the two dynasties, possibly because the Nandas were of *śūdra* origin, though the Mauryas are described in these texts as *śūdra-prāyāstv-adharmikāh*, 'mainly śūdras and unrighteous'.[3] This may merely refer to their unorthodox sympathies. Although the European classical writers describe Candragupta as being a man of humble origin, they do not connect him with Agrammes, the last of the Nandas, of whom they know.[4]

Buddhist writers have attempted to link the dynasty with the tribe of the Śākyas to which the Buddha belonged.[5] We are told that the region from which they came was full of peacocks (*mayūra* in Sanskrit and *mora* in Pāli), and even the stones resembled the necks of the peacocks. Hence they came to be known as the Moriyas (the Pāli form of Mauryas). This attempted link with the Śākyas is interesting in as much as it elevates the social class of Aśoka and his predecessors. Furthermore it provides a closer relationship between the Buddha and Mahinda, the supposed son of Aśoka and one of the early missionaries of Buddhism to Ceylon.

A suggestion has also been put forward that Candragupta was from the Uttarāpatha region, perhaps from Gandhāra if not from Taxila.[6] His early education, his military training and his alliances were largely connected with that region. The employment of *Kharoṣṭhī*-knowing scribes by the Mauryas and the artists working in the Achaemenid tradition are further indications of this connection. We are of the opinion that even if he was from the northern country, he must have had some close connec-

[1] Pargiter, *Dynasties of the Kali Age*, p. 26.

[2] Dhundirāja, commentary on the play *Mudrārākṣasa*.

[3] Pargiter, *Dynasties of the Kali Age*, p. 25.

[4] Justin, XV, 4.

[5] *Vaṃsatthapakāsinī*, vol. i, V, pp. 179, 180.

[6] Barua, *IC*, vol. x, p. 34.

tions in Magadha as well, to have been able to overthrow the Nandas so easily.

The Junāgarh Rock inscription of Rudradāman dated A.D. 150 mentions the *vaiśya* Puṣyagupta as the provincial governor of the Maurya king Candragupta.[1] It has also been suggested that there is a reference to Puṣyagupta being the brother-in-law of Candragupta.[2] It is quite feasible that Candragupta appointed his brother-in-law to govern the western province of his empire. This would imply that the Mauryas may have been of *vaiśya* origin, since the suffix *gupta* is known to have been used largely by the *vaiśya* caste, although brahman and *kṣatriya* names ending in *gupta* also occur. This would agree with the tradition of the Mauryas being of comparatively humble origin.

The *Purāṇas* state that Kauṭalya, also known as Cāṇakya, will annoint Candragupta as king of the realm.[3] We know from various sources that Kauṭalya who later became Candragupta's chief minister, was the motivating power behind Candragupta's early attempts at the throne of Magadha, and many legends have accumulated over the centuries on the role of Kauṭalya in this matter.[4] The emergence of Candragupta as a political figure is also linked with the invasion of Alexander. In Classical sources a meeting between the two is mentioned.[5] The disruption in north-west India which followed the withdrawal of Alexander enabled Candragupta to consolidate his position in that area both quickly and effectively.

The *Purāṇas* state that the Maurya dynasty will last for a total of 137 years. They list Candragupta as king for 24 years, Vindusāra for 25 years and Aśoka for 36 years, after which the list trails off into the names of a number of less important rulers.[6] The *Mahāvaṃsa* gives us the following king list, Candragupta 24 years, Bindusāra 28 years, an interregnum of four years, and then Aśoka 37 years.[7] The *Dīpavaṃsa* repeats this list.[8]

The chronology of the Mauryas hinges round the date of the Buddha's death, or the *Parinirvāṇa* as it is called in Buddhist literature. The Ceylon chronicles state that Aśoka came to the throne 218 years after the death of the Buddha.[9] There are three dates most widely supported for the Buddha's

[1] *Ep. Ind.*, vol. viii, pp. 42 ff.

[2] Kielhorn, *Ep. Ind.*, vol. vii, p. 46 n. 7.

[3] Pargiter, *Dynasties of the Kali Age*, p. 25.

[4] *Vaṃsatthapakāsinī*, vol. i, V, pp. 181 ff.

[5] Plutarch, *Life of Alexander*, lxii, p. 403. Tarn (*Alexander the Great*, p. 275) believes that this tradition is untrue. We believe that the meeting may have occurred, though not with any immediate significance.

[6] The Kashmir chronicle, the *Rājataraṅginī*, speaks of a Śakuni as the great-grandfather of Aśoka (I, 102). There is no corroboration of this in any other source. The chronicle has such a confused account of the early kings that it is difficult to accept the statement without further proof.

[7] V, 16.

[8] V, 97.

[9] *Mahāvaṃsa*, V, 21; *Dīpavaṃsa*, VI, 1.

Parinirvāṇa, 544, 486, 483 B.C. The first of these 544 B.C. is a later fabrication and does not tally with any other evidence. It was adopted by the Ceylon chroniclers in the eleventh century A.D.[1] Previous to this century the chroniclers had used one of the other two dates. Of these, 483 B.C. is generally more accepted although 486 B.C. agrees with the Dotted Record of Canton.[2] Fleet is of the opinion that the reckoning 483 B.C. is of Indian origin and became known in Ceylon through the arrival of Mahinda.[3] Dates other than these three have been suggested, but without sufficient evidence.

From our point of view 544 B.C. may well be disregarded. Calculating on the above evidence we would arrive at 382 B.C. for the date of Candragupta. This would make it impossible for him to have met Alexander, nor could there have been any relationship with Seleucus Nikator, of which relationship we have conclusive evidence. Moreover, the names of the Greek kings mentioned in the 13th Rock Edict of Aśoka would not tally. We are left, therefore, to calculate the chronology on the basis of the other two possible dates.

On the evidence from the Ceylon chronicles we arrive at the following dates for the Mauryas.[4] Candragupta began his reign in 321 B.C., he was followed by Bindusāra in 297 B.C.; and Aśoka's coronation took place in 265 B.C. after a four-year interregnum. This calculation is based on 483 B.C. as the year of the *Parinirvāṇa*. If we accept 486 B.C. as the year of the *Parinirvāṇa*, then we arrive at a date three years earlier in each case. Thus we are faced with two possible dates for the accession of Candragupta, 324 B.C. or 321 B.C.[5] This in turn gives us two alternative dates for Bindusāra, 300 or 297 B.C. But for the accession of Aśoka we have a variety of possible dates, since there is no agreement in the sources as to the length of Bindusāra's reign, and three alternatives are stated, 28, 27, and 25 years. Following from this and allowing for a four-year interregnum, we obtain as possible dates for Aśoka, 271, 269, 268, and 265 B.C.

The date 271 B.C. is invalidated because it would not synchronize with

[1] Fleet, *JRAS*, 1909, pp. 323 ff.

[2] It is said that a record was kept of the year of the Buddha's *Parinirvāṇa* by putting a dot at every anniversary of the event. The record was continued in Canton up to the year A.D. 489, when the number of dots added up to 975, thus giving 486 B.C. as the date of the *Parinirvāṇa* (History and Culture of the Indian People, vol. ii, *The Age of Imperial Unity*, p. 36).

[3] *JRAS*, 1909, pp. 324 ff.

[4] *Dīpavaṃsa*, V, 80–82.

[5] 313 B.C. has also been suggested on the basis of various Jaina sources, amongst them the *Pariśiṣṭaparvan* of Hemacandra, and from the evidence of Trogus, an historian of a later date. The Jaina reckoning is based on the statement that Candragupta came to the throne 155 years after the death of Mahāvīra, *Pariśiṣṭaparvan*, VIII, 339. Unfortunately the precise year of the latter event is not known. Furthermore, 313 B.C. as we shall see conflicts with other known evidence.

various events in the reign of Asóka, as for instance the evidence of the 13th Rock Edict mentioning the five Greek kings with whom Aśoka was in contact. While considering the others we have to keep in mind a new piece of evidence published by Eggermont in his recent book.[1] We are told in the *Divyāvadāna* that Aśoka went on a pilgrimage to the various places sacred to Buddhism, and that prior to the pilgrimage there was an eclipse of the sun.[2] From the Rummindei pillar inscription it is evident that the pilgrimage took place in his twenty-first year, since this was the year in which he visited Rummindei (Lumbinī), which is one of the specified places of pilgrimage for Buddhists. The date of the eclipse has been calculated to 249 B.C.[3] Thus the eclipse must have taken place a year or two before the pilgrimage, allowing for sufficient time in which to prepare for the royal pilgrimage. This evidence would definitely eliminate 266 and 265 B.C. as possible dates for Aśoka. It would seem, therefore, that the accession of Aśoka may be placed some time in 269–268 B.C.

We are now left with the following chronological sequences.

1. Assuming 486 to be the date of the *Parinirvāṇa.*

Candragupta	324 B.C.
Bindusāra	300 B.C. died 272 B.C. (28 regnal years)
Interregnum	4 years
Aśoka	269–268 B.C.
13th Rock Edict	256–255 B.C.
The eclipse	249 B.C.

2. Assuming 483 B.C. to be the date of the *Parinirvāṇa.*

Candragupta	321 B.C.
Bindusāra	297 B.C. died 272 B.C. (25 regnal years)
Interregnum	4 years
Aśoka	268 B.C.

Although the date 269–268 B.C. for the accession of Aśoka would synchronize with both chronological systems, if Aśoka came to the throne 218 years after the death of the Buddha, and we know from the above that Aśoka was crowned in 269–268 B.C., then 486 B.C. would be a more probable date for the *Parinirvāṇa* than 483 B.C. Furthermore on the basis of *Purāṇa* chronology, assuming that Bindusāra reigned for twenty-five years, we would still arrive at the date 321 B.C. for Candragupta even on the assumption of 486 B.C. as the year of the *Parinirvāṇa*. We may note that

[1] *The Chronology of the Reign of Asoka Moriya*, p. 165.

[2] XXVI, p. 380.

[3] See Ch. II.

the Purāṇic evidence makes no reference to the interregnum.[1] This is probably due to the fact that it gives the total number of years of the dynasty and the regnal years of individual rulers. Inter-regnal years are not listed. 321 B.C. seems a much more probable date for the accession of Candragupta, from the point of view of his career. He is supposed to have met Alexander in 326–325 B.C. and to have been a rebel against the Nanda king at this stage. It seems hardly possible that within a year he could have gathered enough forces to have established himself. Four to five years seems a far more probable period.

On the withdrawal of Alexander and certainly on his death in 323 B.C. the Greek control over the area along the Indus weakened considerably. This kept the interest of the northern kings confined to local politics, whilst Candragupta consolidated his position farther east. The continuing disintegration of the northern kingdoms must have provided the opportunity for him to conquer them and annexe their territories. From there it is likely that he moved southwards into central India and by 313 B.C. occupied the area around Avanti. 305 B.C. saw him moving to the north again, in the campaign against Seleucus, with the treaty of 303 B.C. concluding the war.

The actual process of acquiring Magadha began, it would seem, with a small-scale attack on the villages of the outlying areas. We are told the well-known story of the woman who scolded her child for eating from the middle of the dish first, instead of from the edges, which is said to have given Candragupta the idea that he should conquer the outlying parts of the Nanda kingdom first and then converge on the centre.[2] The empire was built and consolidated largely through strength of arms. Classical sources tell of the emphasis laid by Candragupta on the army, and mention staggering figures for the total strength of the Mauryan army. However, considering the purpose of that army, it is possible that it was a very large one. Certain areas in the north-west were acquired through the treaty with Seleucus. There is no absolute certainty as to which areas these were and it has been suggested that the territory ceded consisted of Gedrosia, Arachosia, Aria, and the Paropamisadae.[3]

To state, as some historians have done, that Candragupta set out to accomplish the unity of India is largely the result of a prejudice. Since there was no national consciousness then, involving the entire subcontinent, the only means of holding together such a unit depended on administrative and military strength. Candragupta was no doubt a man of

[1] Pargiter, *Dynasties of the Kali Age*, p. 27.

[2] *Pariśiṣṭaparvan*, VIII, 290–6.

[3] Smith, *Early History of India*, p. 159.

shrewd political intelligence, and he was fortunate in his ambition in that he was assisted by an adviser of exceptional intellectual ability and an abundance of common sense.

There appears to have been considerable contact with the West at the court of Candragupta. From the fact of the marriage alliance contained in the treaty of 303 B.C. with Seleucus, it is possible that the daughter of Seleucus was present at the court at Pāṭaliputra with her entourage, or else there must have been some Greek ladies present as wives of Mauryan officers. Apart from the visit of Megasthenes at Pāṭaliputra and possibly an exchange of envoys, there is reference to the frequent interchange of presents, including the sending of powerful aphrodisiacs.[1] The presence of a considerable number of foreigners is apparent from the special board among the city administrators in Pāṭaliputra which was responsible for the welfare of foreigners.

According to the tradition in the *Pariśiṣṭaparvan*, Candragupta was converted to Jainism in the latter part of his reign.[2] The same source mentions a famine in Magadha lasting for twelve years, which event appears to be corroborated by the Sohgaurā and Mahāsthān plates, both of which deal with famine precautions. The Jaina tradition further states that Candragupta abdicated in favour of his son Siṃhasena (probably an alternative name for Bindusāra), and went with Bhadrabāhu, the Jaina saint, to Śravaṇa-Belgola in Mysore, where he died in the orthodox Jaina way, mainly by slow starvation.

The name of Bindusāra, who on the death of his father succeeded to the Mauryan throne in 297 B.C., has given ample scope to the imagination of the Buddhist chroniclers, and we have a curious story about his birth, naturally with a play on the words making up his name. It is related that Kauṭalya made Candragupta immune from poison by putting minute quantities of it into his food each day.[3] One day the chief queen who was then pregnant took a morsel of food from Candragupta. Kauṭalya was too late in stopping her and realized that the only way in which the life of the child could be saved was to sever the head of the Queen, which he did. The embryo was then placed in the womb of a goat. When the child was born he was covered with spots and was therefore called Bindusāra (*Bindu* = spot, *Sāra* = essence or effusion).

In Classical sources Bindusāra is known as Amitrochates, which appears to be a Greek version of the Sanskrit *amitrakhāda* (eater of foes) or *amitraghāta* (slayer of foes).[4] Strabo refers to Deimachus being sent by

[1] Atheneus, I, 32, 18 D.
[2] VIII, pp. 415 ff. and p. lxxi.
[3] *Vaṃsatthapakāsinī*, I, v, p. 187.
[4] Strabo, II, Fragment 29, p. 70.

Antiochus I as his ambassador to Amitrochates the son of Sandrocottus. Pliny speaks of another envoy who was sent by the king of Egypt, Ptolemy II Philadelphus (285–247 B.C.).[1] This envoy was at the Mauryan court either during the reign of Bindusāra or during the reign of Aśoka. Atheneus of the third century A.D. writes that according to Hegesander, Amitrochates wrote to Antiochus I of Syria and asked for some sweet wine, dried figs, and a sophist to be sent to the Indian court.[2]

Early Buddhist sources do not have much to say on Bindusāra. This may have been due to the king's lack of enthusiasm about Buddhism. It would appear that Bindusāra was more interested in the Ājīvikas, since there was an Ājīvika fortune-teller resident at his court, who when Aśoka was born prophesied that he would become king.[3]

That Bindusāra was called a slayer of foes suggests a period of many campaigns. Since his reign is not documented we have to arrive at the extent of his conquests by a process of elimination. The date of the conquest of southern India by the Mauryas is uncertain. There is no reference in any source to Candragupta having campaigned in the south. Tamil literature refers to the conquest by the Mauryas of southern India but not to any particular king of that dynasty. There is a single quoted reference in an early Christian text, to the effect that Megasthenes saw some ascetics on the other side of the river Tagabena, identified by McCrindle as the Tungabhadra.[4] Even if this identification is correct it is not necessary to infer that Candragupta's empire extended so far. Megasthenes as a visitor probably travelled in areas outside the empire, as indeed did later travellers like Fa-hsien and Hsüan Tsang. Furthermore, in the case of Megasthenes an added attraction would be the strangeness of the ascetics, whom no doubt he was curious to see. It seems unlikely that with Candragupta's activities in the north he had time for southern conquests.

Aśoka has only mentioned one campaign in his edicts, the Kaliṅga War.[5] If there had been a campaign in the south he would have mentioned it. Yet his edicts extend as far south as modern Mysore. Tāranātha writes of Bindusāra conquering sixteen states and extending the empire from sea to sea.[6] This suggests that the upper part of the peninsula is meant. If the tradition of Candragupta abdicating and becoming a Jaina ascetic is true, it would be more than likely that he would travel outside his erstwhile

[1] *Hist. Nat.*, Book IV, c. 17, (21).

[2] Atheneus, III, 444 and XIV, 652–3.

[3] *Divyāvadāna*, XXVI, pp. 370 ff.

[4] Fragment LIV, Pseudo-Origen, *Philosophia*, 24. Quoted McCrindle, p. 120.

[5] XIII R.E. Bloch, *Les Inscriptions d'Asoka*, pp. 125 ff.

[6] *Geschichte des Buddhismus in Indien*, pp. 88–89.

dominions. His presence as a wandering ascetic within the empire might have been embarrassing to Bindusāra.

The period 273–272 B.C. saw the death of Bindusāra and the struggle for succession began among his sons. It lasted four years and in 269–268 B.C. Aśoka was crowned Bindusāra's successor.

II

EARLY LIFE, ACCESSION, AND CHRONOLOGY OF THE REIGN OF AŚOKA

AMONG the more romantic hypotheses regarding the birth of Aśoka, perhaps the one with the greatest possibilities is that which suggests that either his grandmother or his mother was a Greek princess. This is possible only if the clause regarding matrimony in the treaty between Seleucus and Candragupta was a *kedos* and not an *epigamia*.[1] Sylvain Lévi writes '[Seleucus] . . . concluded a matrimonial alliance with him [Candragupta] which no doubt introduced a Greek princess into the Mauryan harem'.[2] Greek sources speak of Sandrocottus and Amitrochates but do not mention Aśoka. However, if such a marriage alliance did take place there is still nothing to prove that Bindusāra was the son of the Greek princess and consequently that Aśoka was her grandson, or that Bindusāra married a Greek princess whose son was Aśoka. Nevertheless it is an interesting hypothesis particularly if we trace the facts further back and postulate that this princess might have been the child of Seleucus' own marriage to a Persian noblewoman.

In considering the possibility of such an alliance it is generally suggested that Seleucus provided a princess for the Maurya family. That the Mauryas may have provided a princess for the Seleucid house is equally possible. If either of these alliances did take place then we can trace a relationship between the Seleucid kings and Aśoka. Antiochus I who died in 261 B.C. would have been grand-uncle to Aśoka. If Aśoka's grandmother was roughly of the same age as her brother she may have been alive when Aśoka was still a boy and may have inspired him with stories of the exploits of Darius and Alexander. Antiochus II and Aśoka would have been second cousins. But Aśoka makes no mention of these relationships, and had they existed he would probably have done so, at least in the edicts, where he mentions the sending of a mission to Antiochus II,[3] or the Greek sources would have made some reference to them. The idea of this relationship has been dismissed by most historians, but we feel that the possibility of the relationship remains, although it may not have been as direct as has been suggested; it may account in a small part for the eclecticism of Aśoka.

[1] See Ch. I.

[2] *L'Inde Civilisatrice*, p. 48.

[3] XIII R.E.

More definite indications as to the identity of Aśoka's mother are given in the other sources, the *Aśokāvadāna*, the *Divyāvadāna*, and the *Vaṃsatthapakāsinī*. The *avadāna* sources mention her as Subhadrāṅgī and describe her as the daughter of a brahman of Campā.[1] It is said that she was kept away from the king by palace intrigue and that when at last she gained access to him and bore him a son, she said of the child, 'I am without sorrow', i.e. *Aśoka*. When she bore the king a second son she called him *Vītāśoka*, 'sorrow terminated'.

In a Ceylonese source the Queen is called Dharmā.[2] The *Divyāvadāna* version agrees largely with that of the *Aśokāvadāna*. She is called Janapadakalyāṇī, or in other versions described as Subhadrāṅgī, and is again said to be the daughter of a brahman of Campā.[3]

Legend has it that as a young man Aśoka was ungainly in appearance and disliked by his father. But obviously his father was impressed by his other qualities, because he appointed him as a young prince to the important post of viceroy at Ujjain. Since most accounts speak of him going directly from Ujjain to Pāṭaliputra, it would appear that his stay at Taxila was prior to his appointment as viceroy at Ujjain. His period in Taxila has in some sources been described as a viceregal appointment. The *Mahāvaṃsa* describes him as the viceroy at Ujjain while two other Buddhist texts, the *Aśokasūtra* and the *Kunālasūtra*, give him a high office in Gandhāra. We feel that he was sent to Taxila for a special purpose and after having completed his work there, he was then appointed to the viceroyalty at Ujjain in recognition of his work.

The *Aśokāvadāna* informs us that a revolt took place in Taxila during the reign of Bindusāra, when the citizens objected to the oppression of the higher officials.[4] This is perfectly feasible in view of the fact that Taxila had been comparatively independent until the coming of the Mauryas and therefore the control of Pāṭaliputra may have been irksome.[5] Culturally there was a close link with areas to the west and citizens of Iranian descent probably still looked to Iran for deliverance. Furthermore, in the process of centralization the Mauryas may well have been harsh in their treatment of outlying cities. The story continues that Aśoka was sent by his father to put an end to the revolt, which he did successfully and without arousing too great a resentment on the part of the citizens.

The only contributory evidence to the authenticity of this tradition so far known is the Aramaic inscription found embedded in a house at

[1] Przyluski, *La Legende de L'Empereur Açoka*, p. 320.

[2] *Vaṃsatthapakāsinī*, IV, p. 125; V, pp. 189, 193.

[3] XXVI, p. 369.

[4] Przyluski, *La Legende de L'Empereur Açoka*, p. 232.

[5] Marshall, *Taxila*, vol. i, p. 21.

Sirkap at Taxila.[1] The text has been read and relates to a high official Rōmēdōtē, who owed his advancement to Priyadarśi, the viceroy or governor. The reading 'Priyadarśi' is uncertain. There is a lacuna after the letters *prydr* . . . , which have been interpreted as Priyadarśi. Most scholars believe the inscription to be of the first half of the third century B.C.[2] That the inscription is in Aramaic, indicates that the impact of Iranian culture was still felt in this region, which once had had closer ties with Achaemenid Iran.

The very same story is told with reference to Kunāla, the son of Aśoka, and this has given rise to some doubt as to whether the event occurred in the reign of Bindusāra or Aśoka. If the word in the inscription is in fact Priyadarśi, as we believe it to be, then there can be little doubt that it referred to Aśoka, because we know that Priyadarśi was his name and was not used by any of the other Mauryas.[3] In this case the variant of the story which states that the events occurred during the reign of Aśoka, and that Kunāla was sent to Taxila, may be regarded as either a deliberate imitation of the story concerning Aśoka, or a confusion on the part of the author of the *Aśokāvadāna*.[4]

When the indignation of the citizens of Taxila had subsided, Aśoka may have spent a few months there before proceeding to Ujjain. Taxila at that period must have been a town of tremendous interest to a young man of Aśoka's character and tastes. It was not merely a political capital of strategic importance. It was on the main north-west highway, leading directly to the west, and a commercial centre with a cosmopolitan culture. Furthermore it was one of the major centres of learning.

We have considerable evidence from the Ceylonese sources on the viceroyalty of Aśoka at Ujjain. The information largely concerns his personal life. We are told that at Vidiśā he met the beautiful Devī, the daughter of a local merchant, with whom he fell in love.[5] There is no reference to a marriage in the *Dīpavaṃsa*, though it is said that two children were born, Mahinda and Saṃghamittā, both of whom are connected with the Buddhist mission to Ceylon. The tradition of Devī could well be true, since it does not interfere with the flow of events concerning the life of Aśoka.

In another Ceylonese source, Devī is referred to as Vidiśāmahādevī and a Śākyānī.[6] The same source also calls her Śākyākumārī, since she is described here as being the daughter of a member of the clan of Śākyas who had emigrated to the city of Vidiśā, and therefore she would also be related

[1] *Ep. Ind.*, vol. xix, pp. 251 ff.

[2] Sircar, *Select Inscriptions...*, p. 81.

[3] See Appendix II.

[4] Przyluski, *La Legende de L'Empereur Açoka*, p. 106.

[5] *Mahāvaṃsa*, XIII, 6–9; *Dīpavaṃsa*, VI, 15–16.

[6] *Mahābodhivaṃsa*, p. 116.

to the Buddha's family, as he also belonged to a clan of the Sākyas. This connection between Devī and the Śākyas was probably a fabrication on the part of the Ceylonese chroniclers, who naturally attempted to find some relationship between Mahinda, the first historically known missionary of Buddhism to Ceylon, and the family of the Buddha. It seems much more feasible to accept Devī merely as the daughter of a local merchant of Vidiśā, than to attempt to relate her to the Śākyas.

Tradition also has it that Devī preferred to stay at Vidiśā rather than move to Pāṭaliputra when Aśoka became king.[1] It has been suggested that this was because she was a pious Buddhist, and since by then Vidiśā had become a centre of Buddhism, she chose to remain there.[2] She is also supposed to have been instrumental in Aśoka's adoption of Buddhism and in Mahinda's becoming a monk. It is possible, however, to suggest other equally convincing reasons for her having stayed behind at Vidiśā. She was the daughter of a merchant and therefore her social position was not the same as that of the court circle. As she was not legally married to Aśoka she would have been debarred from performing the duties of the chief queen. On Aśoka's accession it would be expected that he would marry a princess of an appropriately high rank as his chief queen, which he may well have done when he married Asandhimittā. It is unlikely that the latter could be the official name of Devī, since the Ceylon chronicles would have mentioned it as such, particularly as they treat of Aśoka's relationship with Devī at some length.

Vidiśā figures as an important centre of Buddhism in literature pertaining to that period. It has been suggested that Devī was responsible for the construction of the *vihāra* at Vidiśāgiri, possibly the first of the many monuments to be built at Sanchi and Bhilsa.[3] Another opinion states that Aśoka took an added interest in Buddhist establishments in this region because of his associations with the area.[4]

The authenticity of Saṃghamittā, the daughter of Aśoka and Devī, is doubted by some historians.[5] The *Mahāvaṃsa* states that she was eighteen years old when she was ordained.[6] Certainly the story about her going to Ceylon so that a Ceylonese queen could be ordained appears to be something of an exaggeration. Saṃghamittā may have been Mahinda's sister and she may have been given this unusual name ('the friend of the Buddhist Order') owing to her mother's piety, but it is not necessary that she should also have become a Buddhist nun when her brother was ordained, and that

[1] The *Mahāvaṃsa* refers to Asandhimittā as his chief queen and not to Devī. V, 85.

[2] Sen, *Asoka*, p. 32.

[3] Mookerji, *Asoka*, p. 8.

[4] Sen, *Asoka*, p. 32.

[5] Smith, *Asoka*, p. 48.

[6] V, 205.

she should have played such an important role in the ordaining of the women of Ceylon. There is another tradition regarding Saṃghamittā, which states that she married Agnibrahma, a nephew of Aśoka, and that a son, Sumana, was born to them.[1] The child Sumana may have been named after his grand-uncle Sumana, the eldest brother of Aśoka. But in this case it is impossible that the daughter of Aśoka could have married her first cousin, unless she was not subject to the usual laws of exogamy forbidding the marriage of first cousins, because of her illegitimate birth. Agnibrahma could only be called Aśoka's nephew, therefore, in as much as he was the nephew of Aśoka's wife and thus no relative of Saṃghamittā. This evidence further proves that Devī was not Aśoka's queen. The story of Saṃghamittā's marriage appears to be a discrepancy, which invalidates the story of her going to Ceylon. We are told that she and her husband and her son were all three ordained. A few verses later it is stated that she was eighteen when she was ordained, so that she must have been married at the age of sixteen. It is unlikely that with so young a child she would have been allowed to become a nun.

There has been some controversy over the exact relationship of Mahinda to Aśoka. Whereas the Ceylon chronicles maintain that Mahinda was the illegitimate son of Aśoka, the Chinese pilgrim Hsüan Tsang states that he was Aśoka's younger brother, variously called Vītaśoka and Vigatāśoka.[2] Smith accepts the latter version and believes that the Ceylon tradition is another attempt on the part of the Ceylonese monks to give added prestige to Mahinda and thereby to Ceylon.[3] We are of the opinion, however, that the Ceylon tradition could well be true. Had Mahinda been the younger brother, the prestige involved in his leading the mission to Ceylon would have been much the same. There would thus have been little value in specially inventing a son. Being the illegitimate son of Aśoka it is quite likely that he preferred to join a religious order rather than be treated indifferently by the court at Pāṭaliputra. Sending him to Ceylon may well have been a gesture on the part of Aśoka towards Devānampiya Tissa, the king of Ceylon, whose admiration for the Indian king appears to have been great. In order to maintain if not increase the goodwill of Tissa, Aśoka sent his own son instead of sending an ordinary monk.

The story of Mahinda in the Ceylon chronicles gives us some indication of the number of years that Aśoka served as viceroy. The *Mahāvaṃsa* states that Mahinda was twenty years old when he was ordained and that

[1] *Mahāvaṃsa*, V, 170. If Agnibrahma was the son of Sumana the brother of Aśoka, then the child would be named after its grandfather.

[2] Watters, *On Yuan Chwang's Travels in India*, vol. ii, p. 93.

[3] *Asoka*, p. 50.

this event took place in the sixth year of Aśoka's reign.[1] Thus Mahinda was fourteen when Aśoka was crowned and ten when the struggle for succession among the princes began. It follows from this that Aśoka must have had a long period as viceroy. Assuming that Mahinda was born at the earliest when Aśoka was twenty, then the latter must have been thirty-four years old at least when he came to the throne. This agrees with the evidence that his father and grandfather had long reigns.

Concerning the actual accession there is general agreement on the point that Aśoka was not the crown prince, and that there was a struggle among the princes for the throne. The *Divyāvadāna* states that Bindusāra when dying wished to appoint his son Susīma as king, but his ministers placed Aśoka on the throne instead.[2] The legend suggests that Aśoka had the support of Rādhagupta, a minister of Bindusāra. We are told that when Bindusāra fell ill, Susīma who had been sent to quell a second revolt at Taxila, was recalled by the dying king and Aśoka was appointed instead.[3] Technically therefore Aśoka had superseded Susīma and at the time of Bindusāra's death held the equivalent status of a viceroy of Taxila, although not exactly in Taxila. Aśoka had the support of the ministers who conspired to set aside Susīma and make Aśoka the successor to Bindusāra. The *Mahāvaṃsa* states that Aśoka caused his eldest brother to be slain. Elsewhere in the same work and in the *Dīpavaṃsa* there is mention of his having killed his ninety-nine brothers, born of various wives to Bindusāra.[4]

In considering the above information the number of ninety-nine brothers can be dismissed as imaginary. What emerges as historical fact is that there was a struggle for the throne among the princes on the death of Bindusāra or a little prior to it, and that this involved Aśoka, who had to remove those of his brothers who were opposing him. This accounts for the interregnum of four years in which the issue of succession was being decided. It was not until 269 B.C. when Aśoka felt his position to be secure on the throne that he had himself formally crowned.

According to Tāranātha Aśoka had six of his brothers put to death.[5] The account contains a confused story of Nemita the king of Campāraṇa, who had six sons born of lawful wives, and Aśoka, who was apparently the natural son of his liaison with the daughter of a merchant. Aśoka defeated the people of Nepal and of Khāśya who had revolted against Nemita, and

[1] V, 204, 209.
[2] XXVI, pp. 372, 373.
[3] Susīma is the brother who is referred to as Sumana in the southern tradition. *Mahāvasṃa*, V, 150.
[4] Ibid., 20, 40; *Dīpavaṃsa*, VI, 21, 22.
[5] *Geschichte des Buddhismus in Indien*, VI, p. 28.

he received the principality of Pāṭaliputra as reward. Nemita died suddenly and the grandees of the kingdom raised Aśoka to the throne. The other brothers opposed this move, so Aśoka had them killed and seized their land. Obviously, six brothers is closer to the truth than ninety-nine. The Ceylon chronicles allow only the youngest brother Tissa to remain unhurt, the legend of whom we shall discuss later.[1]

The *Divyāvadāna* relates that when Bindusāra was alive the Ājīvika saint Piṅgalavatsa pronounced Aśoka as the most able of his sons and prophesied that he would succeed to the throne.[2] Aśoka appears also to have had the support of the ministers. I Tsing, the Chinese Buddhist pilgrim, records a story connected with an early Indian king, Bimbisāra of Magadha (who ruled almost three centuries prior to Aśoka).[3] Bimbisāra saw in a dream, a piece of cloth and a stick divided into eighteen fragments. The Buddha, who was a contemporary of the king, is said to have explained to him that these eighteen fragments represented the eighteen schools into which his philosophy would be divided after his death, and that well over a hundred years after his *Parinirvāṇa*, a king called Aśoka would come to the throne and would rule over the whole of Jambudvīpa,[4] and would unite the schools. Clearly this is a legend which became current in the Buddhist world some centuries after the death of Aśoka.

One of the Ceylonese sources embroiders the story of Aśoka's accession still further.[5] Bindusāra's wife, the mother of Aśoka, was the queen Dhammā.[6] When she was pregnant she expressed the desire to trample on the moon and the sun, to play with the stars, and to eat up the forests. The city elders were asked to attempt an interpretation of these signs. Dhammā being a devotee of the Ājīvika sect, it was perhaps natural that an Ājīvika ascetic succeeded in interpreting the meaning of her desires. He declared that her wish to trample on the sun and the moon indicated that her son would conquer the people of India, and rule over the entire territory. The other desires signified that this son would kill those of his brothers who displeased him. The text states that Aśoka had a hundred brothers and he killed all but one. The ascetic is also said to have predicted that Aśoka would destroy the ninety-six heretical sects and would associate himself actively with Buddhism.

[1] *Mahāvaṃsa*, V, 150.
[2] XXVI, p. 371.
[3] Takakusu edition (1896), pp. 13–14.
[4] Jambudvīpa, or 'the island of the rose-apple', was the name given to the southern continent of the earth in orthodox Hindu cosmology. This region had human inhabitants, and the southern part of it was India.
[5] *Vaṃsatthapakāsinī*, I, p. 189.
[6] The name of his mother Dhammā is interesting. It could well be that his own name Dhammasoka arose simply as a means of identifying him as the son of Dhammā, as in the case of names such as Sāriputta. It may not originally have had anything to do with his piety.

Obviously Aśoka realized his potentialities as a ruler through his ability in handling the revolt at Taxila, and his successful viceroyalty at Ujjain. This probably determined him to make an attempt for the throne. That he was not the rightful heir is obvious from the various legends, such as that of the Ājīvika saint foretelling his kingship, and the story of his mother Subhadrāṅgī being kept away from the king. Perhaps the killing of his elder brother or other brothers led to a palace revolution. This accounts for the story of fratricide in Buddhist literature. The exaggeration of numbers in the Buddhist sources is understandable, as they would attempt to describe him as a man who lacked all moral scruples until his conversion to Buddhism. In the 5th Rock Edict, Aśoka mentions officers who have amongst their other functions the superintending of the welfare of the families of his brothers, sisters, and other relatives.[1] This would suggest that he did have surviving brothers, though it has been argued that the reference is only to the families of such brothers. We feel that this is stretching the point unnecessarily.

The *Mahāvaṃsa* states that although he put ninety-nine brothers to death, Aśoka spared the life of the youngest of these, Tissa.[2] Tissa, his uterine brother, was later made vice-regent. In the Ceylonese sources he is called Tissa, but in the other sources he is called by various names, Vītāśoka, Vigatāśoka,[3] Sudatta and Sugatra.[4] He is said to have lived at first in great luxury, unconcerned with the world around him. In such circumstances it was incomprehensible to him why Buddhist teaching should lay such emphasis on the fear of death. In order to teach him a lesson Aśoka put him on the throne for a few days, and then accused him of trying to usurp the crown and sentenced him to die after seven days. It is related that during these seven days Tissa realized why Buddhist monks, being conscious of eventual death, forsook pleasure. He abandoned his erstwhile habits, left the palace, and became an *arhat*.[5] According to the *Mahāvaṃsa* Aśoka appointed his brother Tissa as an *uparāja* or vice-regent, but the latter retired to a life of religious devotion having come under the influence of the preacher Mahādhammarakkhita.[6] He was then known by the name of Ekavihārika. It is possible that this tradition is based on fact, although the real situation may not have been quite as simple as the story suggests.

[1] R.E. V (Shahbazgarhi version). Bloch, *Les Inscriptions d'Asoka*, p. 105.

[2] V, 33

[3] *Divyāvadāna*, XXVIII, p. 419 and XXVIII, p. 370.

[4] Przyluski, *La Legende de L'Empereur Açoka*, pp. 270 ff. The *A-yü-wang-chuan* refers to him as So-ta-to (Sudatta). The *Fen-pie-kung-te-hun* refers to him as Siu-ka-tu-lu (Sugatra).

[5] The literal meaning of the word is 'the worthy one'. In Buddhist terminology it came to signify the person who had achieved *Nirvāna* and was consequently free from the cycle of rebirth.

[6] *Mahāvaṃsa*, V, 161ff.

Younger brothers can often stand in the way of a king, particularly a king as individualistic as Aśoka. In this case the young brother may have realized that becoming a monk and renouncing all claims to the throne might spare him his life at the hands of Aśoka. The expedient of forcing such brothers to become monks is not unknown in other parts of the world.

The *Theragāthā commentary* has a variant on this story.[1] Vītāśoka, after leading a full and normal life, saw a grey hair on his head. Contemplating the coming of old age he retired to a monastery and eventually gained *arhat*hood. Stories identical to this are to be found in other Buddhist texts.[2] Fa-hsien, writing in the fourth century A.D., records another version of the story, and this version is repeated by his compatriot Hsüan Tsang, two centuries later.[3] The younger brother of Aśoka was Mahendra, and he is described as a dissolute young man. Aśoka, unable to tolerate his brother's behaviour, reprimanded him about it. The younger man, much ashamed, begged forgiveness and retired to meditate in a darkened cave, whereupon he became an *arhat*. Aśoka invited him to return and live with the family, but he preferred to live on a solitary hill. Consequently, Aśoka had a hill constructed for him at Pāṭaliputra, so that even when living in isolation he would still be close.

The *Aśokāvadāna* contains the account of still another event connected with the younger brother of Aśoka. The king ordered that all the *Nirgranthas*[5] in the Buddhist monasteries be killed because he considered them heretics. His younger brother being mistaken for one was also killed. This made Aśoka aware of the folly of his order and it was recalled. The incident is of interest even apart from the narrative. In an effort to portray the emperor's zeal for Buddhism, the chroniclers have indicated that he was intolerant of all but the orthodox Buddhists. This suspicion of deviationists on the part of Aśoka is not in keeping with his plea for tolerance as stressed in the edicts.

The desire to place his brother on the path to *Nirvāṇa* would appear to be a later development in Aśoka's character. The Buddhist sources would have us believe that as a young man he was an intensely wicked person.[6] We are told, for instance, that when the women of his harem told him that he was unpleasant to look at, he had all five hundred of them burnt, thus

[1] Colombo edition, 1918, pp. 295 ff.

[2] *Majjhima Nikāya*, II, 74.

[3] Giles, *Travels of Fa-hsien*, p. 45; Watters, *On Yuan Chwang's Travels in India*, vol. ii, p. 94.

[4] Przyluski, *La Legende de L'Empereur Açoka*, p. 278.

[5] Literally 'free from bonds'. Originally they were a pre-Jaina order of an ascetic nature. Later, the term was generally used for Jaina monks.

[6] Przyluski, *La Legende de L'Empereur Açoka*, p. 235.

earning the name of Caṇḍāśoka (Aśoka the cruel). Rādhagupta, his minister, advised him that he should employ a staff of people to perform such deeds, since it was unseemly that a king should do them himself. The idea of building a 'Hell' on earth, originated in this remark. A special area was marked out, and equipped with men and machines to trap innocent people and make them undergo the most fearsome tortures. Fa-hsien repeats the story and explains that Aśoka personally visited the infernal regions and studied their methods of torture before inventing his own.[1] Hsüan Tsang claims to have actually seen the pillar marking the site of Aśoka's 'Hell'.[2]

Tāranātha relates that Aśoka spent many years in pleasurable pursuits and was consequently called Kāmāśoka.[3] This was followed by a period of extreme wickedness, which earned him the name of Caṇḍāśoka. Finally his conversion to Buddhism and his subsequent piety led him to be called Dhammasoka. According to another source, the actual conversion to Buddhism was initiated by the act of a *bhikkhu* (monk) who, when tortured in the 'Hell', remained unperturbed, thereby arousing the interest of the king.[4] The *Rājataraṅginī* (a twelfth-century chronicle of Kashmir), does not relate any of these stories.[5] Here Aśoka is described simply as a follower of the doctrine of the Jina (i.e. the Buddha) and active in the building of *stūpas* and magnificent *caityas*.[6]

This portrayal of Aśoka as an extremely wicked man suddenly converted to a life of piety we may safely regard as a fabrication of the Buddhist authors. It naturally increased the value of his piety as a Buddhist if he could be described as a thoroughly unworthy man prior to his conversion. The incidents connected with the actual conversion do not tally from source to source. Furthermore if wickedness was so deeply ingrained in him as the monks would have us believe, there would surely have been some hint of it in the accounts of his early youth. The evil in him appears all at once with the story of his killing his ninety-nine brothers, making himself king, and building a place in which to torture the innocent. Equally suddenly he is converted and all trace of wickedness disappears.

Some members of the king's immediate family are mentioned in the

[1] Giles, *Travels of Fa-hsien*, p. 56.

[2] Watters, *On Yuan Chwang's Travels in India*, vol. ii, p. 89.

[3] *Geschichte des Buddhismus in Indien*, VI, p. 28.

[4] Przyluski, *La Legende de L'Empereur Açoka*, pp. 237 ff.

[5] I, 102–4.

[6] In the pre-Buddhist period, the *stūpa* was merely a funeral tumulus. On the death of the Buddha his relics were placed in such a tumulus, and consequently the mound came to be associated with the death of the Buddha and the various saintly personages. The *caitya* was a sacred enclosure, the term later being used for a hall of worship.

various sources. The chief queen for most of his reign was Asandhimittā who is well spoken of in the *Mahāvaṃsa*.[1] She died four years prior to the death of Aśoka, and on her death Tissarakkhā was raised to the rank of chief queen. Comments on the latter in Buddhist sources are not complimentary, since she was responsible for injuring the Bodhi-tree.[2] Aśoka's marriage to Tissarakkhā may have occurred late in his life, since he appears to have been considerably under her influence, judging by the *avadāna* stories.[3] A second queen, Kāruvākī is mentioned in the Queen's Edict inscribed on a pillar at Allahabad, in which her religious and charitable donations are referred to.[4] She is described as the mother of the prince Tīvara, the only one to be mentioned by name in the inscriptions. It is clear from its position on the pillar that this edict was issued towards the end of Aśoka's reign.[5] It ordered the *mahāmattas* (officers) to record whatever donations were made by Kāruvākī. It has been suggested that Kāruvākī was in fact the personal name of the queen Tissarakkhā, and that she assumed the latter name on becoming chief queen.[6] The reference to her being the second queen would agree with the fact that Tissarakkhā was the second chief queen. It would certainly fit the character of Tissarakkhā to demand that all her donations be recorded.

A third queen referred to in the *Divyāvadāna* as another wife of Aśoka was Padmāvatī.[7] Despite his enthusiasm for Buddhism, Aśoka did not forego the royal privilege of having many wives. Although Padmāvatī was never a chief queen, she was all the same the mother of the crown prince Kunāla, also called Dharmavivardhana. It would appear that Asandhimittā bore no children, hence the son of Padmāvatī was declared the crown prince. Fa-hsien speaks of Dharmavivardhana as the son of Aśoka who had been appointed viceroy of Gandhāra.[8] The *Rājataraṅginī* mentions Jalauka as another son of Aśoka, but his mother's name is not given.[9] Two of Aśoka's daughters are known to us. One was Saṃghamittā of the Ceylon chronicles, to whom we have already referred. The other was Cārūmatī, who is said to have married Devapāla the *kṣatriya*.[10] Of the grandsons of Aśoka, the two most frequently mentioned are Samprati, the son of Kunāla,[11] and Daśaratha.[12] At this point we merely list the members of

[1] V, 85; XX, 2.

[2] *Mahāvaṃsa*, XX, 3–6.

[3] Przyluski, *La Legende de L'Empereur Açoka*, p. 285.

[4] See the Queen's Edict.

[5] *Corpus Inscriptionum Indicarum*, vol. i (Cunningham ed.), p. 38 and Plate XXII.

[6] I am indebted to Prof. Basham for this suggestion.

[7] XXVII, p. 405.

[8] Giles, *Travels of Fa-hsien*, p. 12.

[9] I, 118–20.

[10] S. Lévi, *Le Népal*, vol. i, pp. 263, 331; vol. ii, pp. 1–3, 344.

[11] Przyluski, *La Legende de L'Empereur Açoka*, p. 297.

[12] *Viṣṇu Purāṇa*, XXIV; Sircar, *Select Inscriptions . . .*, p. 79.

his family known to us. Their identification and significance will be discussed at greater length, where it is more appropriate to the narrative.

It is indeed unfortunate that Aśokan chronology still remains uncertain. Here, as in some other periods of ancient history, the historian is justified in wishing that the emperor had been more explicit in the matter of dating. A preliminary question arises on the method adopted of dating the inscriptions, and determining whether the years mentioned were current years or expired years.

The formula for dating the inscriptions is usually contained in the phrase, *vasābhisitena*, 'anointed . . . years', which occurs in most of the edicts. For example, we have the complete phrase from the 3rd Rock Edict,

dbādasa vāssābhisittena mayā idam āñapitam . . .

'When I had been anointed twelve years, I commanded thus.'[1]

This may be taken to mean twelve complete years or the twelfth year current, eleven anniversaries of the original consecration having passed. The first alternative would seem the most logical interpretation but doubt has been raised by the fact that in the 5th Pillar Edict there is a statement which runs thus,

yāva saḍuvīsativassābhisittena me etāye aṃtalikāye paṃnavīsati baṃdhana-mokkhāni kaṭāni

This passage has generally been translated as,

'Until I had been anointed twenty-six years in this period the release of prisoners was ordered by me twenty-five times.'[2]

On the basis of the above translation it would appear that the twenty-five releases were spread over a period of twenty-five years running into the twenty-sixth year when the edict was issued. The term *vassābhisittena* therefore referred to 'the . . . year after the year of my consecration'. This led to the view held by some historians that the dating of the inscriptions was in current years.[3] It is argued that prisoners were released generally to commemorate some important event in the royal year such as the anniversary of the king's coronation or his birthday. Thus it would be reasonable to assume that by the twenty-sixth year of Aśoka's reign there would have been twenty-five occasions when prisoners were released.

[1] III R.E. Girnār. Bloch, *Les Inscriptions d'Asoka*, p. 95.

[2] V P.E. Bloch, *Les Inscriptions d'Asoka*, p. 167.

[3] Mookerji, *Asoka*, p. 184 n. 6; Eggermont, *The Chronology of the Reign of Asoka Moriya*, p. 64.

More recently, an alternative interpretation of this passage from the 5th Pillar Edict has been suggested, as follows,

'In the period [from my consecration] to [the anniversary on which] I had been consecrated twenty-six years, twenty-five releases of prisoners have been made.'[1]

The above translation is self-explanatory. It clarifies the point about the edict being issued after the twenty-sixth anniversary of his coronation. The number of releases being twenty-five was an arbitrary number.

This problem of whether the edicts were issued in current years or expired years, has been clarified and finally settled by the discovery of the bilingual edict at Kandahar. The Greek version of this edict begins with the sentence,

'Ten years being completed king Priyadarśin showed piety to men.'[2]

The Aramaic version of the same edict contains the identical sentence.[3] It is clear from this edict that Aśoka dated all his edicts in expired years.

In a detailed analysis of Aśokan chronology the first problem is that of the year of his coronation. This is naturally linked with the question of the reputed interregnum of four years between the death of Bindusāra and the accession of Aśoka. There is a conflict in the sources on this matter, in so far as the Ceylon chronicles state that there was such an interregnum whereas the *Purāṇas* are silent about it.[4]

If we accept the tradition that Aśoka was not the direct heir and that there was a struggle for the throne amongst him and his brothers on the death of Bindusāra, it seems quite logical for there to have been an interregnum. Four years would not be an unusually lengthy time for Aśoka to establish his position. We have stated earlier in this chapter our reasons for accepting the tradition of a struggle for succession among the sons of Bindusāra, although a number of historians have doubted the tradition and the need for an interregnum.[5]

The *Mahāvaṃsa* states that, 'Four years after the famous [Aśoka] had won for himself the sovereignty he consecrated himself as king of the city of Pāṭaliputra.'[6] This four-year delay has been contested by Eggermont, who uses as his main argument the idea that in the Ceylonese tradition the

[1] This translation was suggested to me by Prof. Basham.

[2] See Kandahar Inscription; *Journal Asiatique*, 1958, vol. ccxlvi, pp. 2–3.

[3] Ibid., p. 22.

[4] *Mahāvaṃsa*, V, 22; *Dīpavaṃsa*, VI, 21, 22; Pargiter, *Dynasties of the Kali Age*, pp. 27, 28.

[5] Smith accepts the interregnum but not the succession struggle. *Asoka*, p. 20.

Thomas doubts the interregnum altogether. *Cambridge History of India*, vol. i, pp. 502, 503.

[6] V, 22.

year 218 after the death of the Buddha had to be maintained at any cost as the coronation year of Aśoka. 'Owing to a number of manipulations such as the insertion of new names of kings and the increase and decrease of years of reign it became necessary to assign to Aśoka a four-year period of unanointed kingship, if the number 218 post Buddham mortuum was to be maintained.'[1]

If the Ceylon chronicles are to be accused of having had their dates tampered with in order to fit a pattern, the *Purāṇas* have not escaped from similar treatment either. If it was a matter merely of filling a gap of four years, this period of time could easily have been apportioned among other reigns in such a way as not to attract attention. We are of the opinion that the four-year interim period was inserted not simply to make the dates fit but rather as a regularly transmitted tradition, and its accuracy seems quite feasible in view of the circumstances of Aśoka's accession. Whether it was in fact three years and a few months or exactly four years is difficult to determine since the death of Bindusāra would not have taken place on the anniversary of his coronation, nor would the accession of Aśoka have occurred on the same day and month. According to our reckoning, the interregnum was a few months less than four years, and the tradition may well have been founded on historical fact. In the Introduction we have traced the chronology of the reigns of Candragupta Maurya and Bindusāra until the death of the latter, which took place in 272 B.C.[2] Thus allowing for the interregnum we arrive at the date 269–268 B.C. as the coronation year of Aśoka.

Much stress has been laid by historians on the question of the conversion of Aśoka to Buddhism. Some are of the opinion that it took place as a dramatic event soon after the Kaliṅga War, when the monarch was appalled by the suffering he had caused.[3] Eggermont has tried to show that the conversion took place before the Kaliṅga War.[4] The obvious doubt as regards the latter theory is whether as a recent convert to non-violent Buddhism Aśoka could have engaged in such a large-scale war. This view of Eggermont would suggest either that Aśoka had his own somewhat eccentric interpretation of the 'Middle Way', or else that his conversion to Buddhism was in fact not a conversion in the sense of a sudden change of heart involving a violent emotional upheaval.

To refer to a precise point during his reign as the moment of his conversion to Buddhism is to overstate what actually took place. Apart from the

[1] *The Chronology of the Reign of Asoka Moriya*, pp. 86, 144 ff., 161.

[2] See Ch. I.

[3] This is a generally held opinion. We quote here by way of an example *The Age of the Nandas and Mauryas*, p. 200.

[4] *The Chronology of the Reign of Asoka Moriya*, pp. 69 ff.

very prejudiced Buddhist accounts, which may well have been coloured by later conditions, we have no real evidence from this period of violent antagonisms between the various religious sects so strong that they would necessitate the disavowal of former beliefs on conversion to a new religion. Some antagonism between the Hindus and the Buddhists there must surely have been, but evidence shows that at the time in the history of India religious enmity may not have been so severe as it was to become on occasion in later times. The very fact that for the ordinary believer not wishing to enter the religious order there was no elaborate ritual pertaining to conversion in Buddhism as there is in Islam or Christianity would suggest that no great emphasis was laid on the actual act of conversion. For the layman, Buddhism involved in the main the general acceptance of the Buddhist attitude to life, and the support of Buddhist monks, which did not particularly restrict him in his religious activities.

An interesting point which emerges from the edicts is that Aśoka's fervour for Buddhism increased during his later years.[1] In the earlier edicts he does not give the impression of being a recent convert to a new religion. None of the fanaticism and bigotry usually associated with new converts is anywhere apparent. The earlier edicts have an individuality and a humanitarianism which are peculiar to the monarch himself and are not merely the tenets of Buddhism, even though they were issued after his 'conversion'.

Buddhist sources give two stories in connection with the 'conversion'. One of these is related in the Ceylon chronicles and centres around the personality of Nigrodha.[2] Nigrodha was the posthumous son of Sumana the eldest brother of Aśoka, whom Aśoka killed during the conflict for the throne. Nigrodha was born in the year of Aśoka's accession. At the age of seven he became a monk by special dispensation, and preached to the monarch, who was so impressed by the teaching of his nephew that he accepted Buddhism. As it appears, the story is obviously exaggerated. Eggermont has ingeniously suggested that the age of Nigrodha, seven years, is of significance; that it was meant to record the fact that Aśoka was converted seven years after his coronation.[3] However, as we have pointed out earlier, it is not necessary to date the conversion to a precise point in the history of Aśoka. If it was merely a question of recording the fact of Aśoka being converted in his seventh year, the chroniclers could have done that with even greater embroidery around the figure of Nigrodha. It seems

[1] Compare the Kaliṅga Edict with the Schism Edict. Bloch, *Les Inscriptions d'Asoka*, pp. 136–43, 152–53.

[2] *Mahāvaṃsa*, V, 37–72; *Dīpavaṃsa*, VI, 25–99.

[3] *The Chronology of the Reign of Asoka Moriya*, pp. 86 ff.

more plausible that this story records a reconciliation between Aśoka and his nephew. By his seventh year Aśoka was confident that there was no danger to his position on the throne from any male relatives. Restrictions may have been relaxed and Nigrodha made welcome in the royal household. Not being a direct heir the boy may in later years have become a Buddhist monk.

The *Divyāvadāna*[1] relates a different story of events leading to the conversion of Aśoka, and this story is repeated by Hsüan Tsang.[2] A prison was established by Aśoka at Pāṭaliputra under the direction of Girika, and the inmates were put to severe tortures. On one occasion Samudra, an ex-merchant from Śrāvastī who had become a monk, was put into the prison, but by his miraculous powers managed to save himself. Aśoka hearing of this visited the monk, and was so impressed by the series of miracles which he performed that the royal observer was soon a devotee of Buddhism. This story has all the ingredients of the usual conversion stories, previous wickedness, revelation through a series of miracles, and final conversion. Very little in the way of historical evidence can be gathered from it.

Further variations of the above stories occur in the *Aśokāvadāna*. In one section we are told that a twelve-year-old merchant's son was responsible for introducing Aśoka to Buddhism, and his name is given as Samudra.[3] This may be a confused version of two stories. Samudra was the *bhikkhu* who was unhurt by the tortures in Aśoka's 'Hell'.[4] His youth suggests the influence of the Nigrodha story. The tradition of the conversion as recorded in the *A-yü-wang-chuan* states that a *śramaṇa*[5] seven years old converted the king. One of the stories relates that the young *śramaṇa* devoured all the five hundred brahmans who were harassing Aśoka because of his interest in Buddhism. After this gargantuan meal, Aśoka was invited to visit the monastery Kukkuṭārāma, and there found all the five hundred brahmans now miraculously turned into *bhikkhus*.[6] The stories appear to have been influenced by local folk lore, since they all have an essentially legendary and fairy-tale quality about them.

The first major event of the reign of Aśoka which can be definitely dated was the Kaliṅga War and the conquest of Kaliṅga. The 13th Rock Edict states clearly that this event took place in the ninth year of Aśoka's reign, i.e. 260 B.C.[7] The tone of this edict, in which he mentions his regret and

[1] XXVI, pp. 374–82.

[2] Watters, *On Yuan Chwang's Travels in India*, vol. ii, p. 88.

[3] Przyluski, *La Legende de l'Empereur Açoka*, pp. 237 ff.

[4] Ibid., p. 154.

[5] The term used for Buddhist monks.

[6] Przyluski, *La Legende de l'Empereur Açoka*, pp. 413–18.

[7] Bloch, *Les Inscriptions d'Asoka*, pp. 125 ff.

remorse at the suffering in Kaliṅga, is not the regret of a man moved by a passing emotion, but the meaningful contrition of a man who was consciously aware of the sorrow he had caused.

The date of the Kaliṅga War is connected with the period when Aśoka became a Buddhist. Some historians place the latter event before the war and others after it. Eggermont upholds the former view and uses what he believes to be evidence from Tāranātha.[1] The Tibetan writer refers to the *nāgas* or the spirits of the sea stealing jewels from Aśoka and thus irritating him. Aśoka, after gaining sufficient merit, conquers them. Eggermont interprets the *nāgas* as the seafaring people of Kaliṅga, the gaining of sufficient merit on the part of Aśoka as his conversion to Buddhism, and the conquest of the *nāgas* as the Kaliṅga War. The reliability of this sequence of events is doubtful, since Tāranātha then goes on to state that Aśoka conquered the whole of Jambudvīpa during this war, whereas actually only the conquest of Kaliṅga took place. The equation of Aśoka gaining merit and his conversion to Buddhism is in any case rather exaggerated. At most it may be said that the Tibetan account hints at the real cause of the war, that Aśoka wished to control both the land and sea routes to south India, and any hostile power obstructing the route would have had to be conquered. Other historians such as, for example, Thomas are of the opinion that Aśoka's conversion to Buddhism took place soon after the Kaliṅga War, in this case in the ninth year of his reign, and furthermore that he became an active Buddhist at the end of the eleventh regnal year when he joined the Buddhist Order and travelled from place to place.[2] The period at the conclusion of the Kaliṅga War would certainly have been a most dramatic moment for the conversion. But it is fairly evident that it did not happen in such a manner, for if it had been so spectacular the Ceylonese monks would certainly have made much of it. However, there is no reference to the Kaliṅga War in the Ceylon chronicles.

The question of the conversion can be clarified by referring to the edicts of Aśoka. The Minor Rock Edict is often regarded as his confession to belonging to the Buddhist faith. The relevant portion of this edict reads,

. . . adhikāni aḍḍhātiyāni vassāni ya hakaṃ upāsake no tu kho bāḍhaṃ prakkaṃte husaṃ ekaṃ savaccharaṃ sātireke to kho saṃvacchare yaṃ mayā saṃghe upayite bāḍhaṃ ca me pakkaṃte . . . [3]

'. . . I have been a Buddhist layman for more than two and a half years,

[1] *The Chronology of the Reign of Asoka Moriya*, p. 88; *Geschichte des Buddhismus in Indien*, VI, pp. 31–33.

[2] *Cambridge History of India*, vol. i, pp. 495–6.

[3] Brahmagiri Minor Rock Edict. Bloch, *Les Inscriptions d'Asoka*, pp. 145–6.

but for a year I did not make much progress. Now for more than a year I have drawn close to the community [of monks] and have become more ardent . . . '

This edict confesses to a lack of fervour to begin with, which is quite contrary to the evidence of Tāranātha used by Eggermont. It confirms the idea which we have expressed earlier that Aśoka's conversion to Buddhism was a gradual process. If this conversion had taken place at a precise moment within three years after the Kaliṅga War, he would surely have mentioned it in the 13th Rock Edict. Drawing closer to the Order may have implied that the king took instruction from Buddhist priests on the principles of Buddhism. It must be kept in mind that Aśoka was sincerely interested in the mutual understanding between the various religious sects.

A far more direct avowal of Buddhist teaching is made in the Bhabra Edict.[1] Unfortunately it is not dated, but we believe it to belong to the latter period of his reign, issued perhaps at about the same time as the Schism Edict. In the Bhabra Edict he states his acceptance of the Buddhist creed, the faith in the Buddha, the *Dhamma* (in this case the teachings of the Buddha), and the *Saṃgha*. This edict was written specifically for the local Buddhist clergy and not for the population at large, nor was it an order to his administrators. He refers to himself as the 'King of Magadha', a title which he uses only on this occasion. In a study of his edicts it is of the greatest importance to distinguish between those which were meant for his subjects and those which were concerned solely with the *Saṃgha*. In the former he has the role of the king addressing his subjects, and the latter (to which category the Bhabra Edict belongs), are his personal religious manifestoes.

It is possible that the Buddhist clergy acknowledged him as their temporal head, referring to him as the king of Magadha in the same way as the Catholic clergy in Europe acknowledged the Holy Roman Emperor. In this case the emperor declares his faith in the creed and quotes specific parts of the scriptures with which he expects the clergy to be acquainted. We may therefore assume that his interest was more personal. The analogy with the Holy Roman Emperor is, however, limited, since Catholicism was the state religion in the European example, whereas Buddhism was not a state religion under Aśoka.

We are told that ten years after the coronation, i.e. in 259–258 B.C., he '. . . went to the *sambodhi* . . .'[2] The term *ayāya sambodhim* has been

[1] Ibid., p. 154.

[2] VIII R.E. Girnār. Ibid., p. 112.

interpreted either as referring to Aśoka having received enlightenment,[1] or as implying that he made a journey to the Bodhi-tree.[2] It has been pointed out in a recent work that the term *saṃbodhi* is used regularly in the *Dīpavaṃsa* to mean a Bodhi-tree, and this evidence confirms the latter interpretation of the term in the edict.[3] It is probable that Aśoka's visit to the Bodhi-tree was part of a larger country-wide tour which he made, and to which he refers in the same edict as the *Dhamma-yātā* (the journey made in connection with the Dhamma).

Closely connected with the interpretation of *ayāya saṃbodhiṃ* is the question of the significance of a 256-day journey mentioned in the Minor Rock Edict. Though in most of the versions of the Minor Rock Edict the figure 256 is given in an obscure manner, the Sahasram Edict makes it clear that the number can have no other significance except in reference to a journey or tour.

'... *iyaṃ ca savane vivutthena duve sapaṃnā lāttisatā vivutthā ti* 200 50 6 ...'[4]

'This announcement has been proclaimed while on tour; 256 nights have been spent on tour ...'

Some authorities maintain that the edict was issued after Aśoka had returned from the tour to his capital.[5] If that was the case there was not much point in indicating the precise number of days spent on tour. He could as well have said, 'When I returned from the tour.' The edict seems certainly to have been issued whilst he was actually on tour.

The figure 256 has caused much comment. Filliozat has explained the meaning of 256 nights by suggesting that Aśoka divided the year into three periods of four months each, as did the brahmans.[6] One of these periods, that of the *vassa* or season of the rains, was spent at home, while the other two periods of comparatively dry weather were spent in travelling. On the basis of the *Jyotiṣa-vedāṅga* a month is calculated as 27 days, 6 hours, 3 minutes, and 4 seconds.[7] Four months would therefore work out as 109 days, 12 minutes, and 16 seconds. This figure subtracted from the 360 days of the Hindu calendar, does not give us 256 days. Two-thirds of the year works out as 240 days and this leaves another 15 days for completing the

[1] de la Vallée Pussin, *L'Inde aux temps des Mauryas*, pp. 104 ff.

[2] Mookerji, *Asoka*, p. 294.

[3] Eggermont, *The Chronology of the Reign of Asoka Moriya*, p. 80; *Dīpavaṃsa*, XVI.

[4] Bloch, *Les Inscriptions d'Asoka*, p. 150.

[5] Ibid., p. 149.

[6] *Journal Asiatique*, 1949, pp. 143 ff. L'enigme des 256 nuits d'Asoka.

[7] *Jyotiṣa-vedāṅga* refers to the knowledge of astronomy as existing in India during the Vedic period until the Christian era.

period. If this number represents the days that a *bhikkhu* was supposed to travel and beg alms it seems strange that Aśoka did not wait another 15 days to complete the period as prescribed, before issuing the edict. If we calculate on the basis of a thirteen-month calendar we still do not arrive at 256 days forming two-thirds of the year, since 8 months on the basis of the length given in the *Jyotiṣa-vedāṅga* consist of 218 days, 24 minutes, and 32 seconds. This is roughly 36 days short of the journey made by Aśoka. Thus the 256 days would work out to a little above 9 months. Using a further basis of calculation, that of a calendar of a working year (omitting the intercalary months), of 354 days, we still do not arrive at 256 days representing two-thirds of the year. Finally since the number of days in a year are known to have varied from year to year we feel that to relate this figure to a prescribed period in Buddhist ritual is misleading.

Aśoka's journey was therefore not the wandering or pilgrimage of a royal *bhikkhu*.[1] Fleet's suggestion that it was Aśoka's final edict issued in the 256th year after the death of the Buddha, after Aśoka had abdicated and become a monk, has not sufficient evidence to give it credence.[2] We know from the evidence of the 7th Pillar Edict issued in the twenty-eighth year of his reign that Aśoka continued to reign for many years after the issuing of the Minor Rock Inscription. It is highly improbable that the king having turned monk would issue an edict in precisely the same tone as when he was king. As a monk he would hardly be in a position to address the officers of the region with any authority. That the number of days are connected with the number of years after the *Parinirvāṇa*, does not seem a feasible idea, since Aśoka would not have hesitated for a moment from drawing attention to the connection and probably calling it an auspicious one. We know from some of his other edicts that he was not exactly modest when it came to praising his own virtuous actions. It would seem therefore that the relevant phrase referring to the journey was a record of the fact that Aśoka had been on tour for 256 days and the number has no other significance.

The geographical locations of this edict are of interest. One group is found in the region of central India, and the other occurs at sites in the extreme south of the empire. The opening phrases refer to Suvarṇagiri and Isilā, which can be identified as Kanakāgiri near Maski and Siddāpura.[3]

[1] Kern in his work on Aśoka suggests that the 256 nights were spent in prayer for enlightenment. This is based on an incorrect interpretation of the word *vyutha*. We are of the opinion that Aśoka's interest in Buddhism was hardly of the sort that would lead him to spend 256 nights praying for enlightenment. Furthermore there was no necessity for him to have travelled all the way to Isilā in order to do so (*Asoka*, p. 38).

[2] *JRAS*, 1909, pp. 981 ff.

[3] See Appendix III.

The opening passage of the inscription reads thus,

suvaṃṇagirīte ayyaputtassa mahāmāttāṇaṃ ca vacanena isilassi mahāmāttā ārogiyaṃ vattaviyā . . . [1]

'From Suvarnagiri, on the order of the Āryaputra and the officers. Good health to the officers of Isilā . . . '

Had the edict been issued from Pāṭaliputra why should there have been this opening sentence? The mention of the *āryaputra*, who appears to be the local governor, and the good wishes to the officials of Isilā would point to the edict having been issued locally, probably when Aśoka was on tour in the southern regions of his empire. The existence of the same edict at places nearer Pāṭaliputra such as Sahasrām and Rūpanāth is explained by the fact that this was the area he was likely to travel through on his way to the south, and the edict was probably inscribed at all the important points which he touched on his tour. Thus 256 nights was the amount of time he had already spent on the tour. If this journey had had a purely religious purpose then surely Aśoka would have concentrated on places sacred to Buddhism alone and a version of this edict would have been found at Buddhist sites.[2]

The Kaliṅga War took place after he had been crowned for eight years. Assuming that his deepened interest in Buddhism began after the war, it took him two and a half years to become a zealous Buddhist on his own admission which brings us to the twelfth year of his reign. Thus we arrive at the date 257–256 B.C. for the Minor Rock Edict.

Among the more important sources of chronological evidence available on the reign of Aśoka is that from the 13th Rock Edict. Five Hellenic kings, all contemporaries of Aśoka, are mentioned in the edict and their identification provides evidence for dating the inscription. The relevant passage speaks of,

. . . *atta aṃtiyoge nāma yonalāja palaṃ cā tenā aṃtiyogenā cattāli* 4 *lajāne tulamaye nāma aṇtekine nāma makā nāma alikyaṣudale nāma* . . . [3]

'. . . where reigns the Greek king named Antiochus, and beyond [the realm of] that Antiochus [in the lands of the] four kings named Ptolemy, Antigonus, Magas and Alexander . . . '

It is possible to identify the first four kings as, Antiochus II Theos of Syria

[1] Bloch, *Les Inscriptions d'Asoka*, p. 145.

[2] The tour has been described as part of the *Dhamma-yātā* or tour of piety which Aśoka made in his tenth year (Eggermont, *The Chronology of the Reign of Asoka Moriya*, p. 81). But if he was attracted to Buddhism after the Kaliṅga War, he could not have made the tour in his tenth regnal year.

[3] XIII R.E. Kālsi. Bloch, *Les Inscriptions d'Asoka*, p. 130.

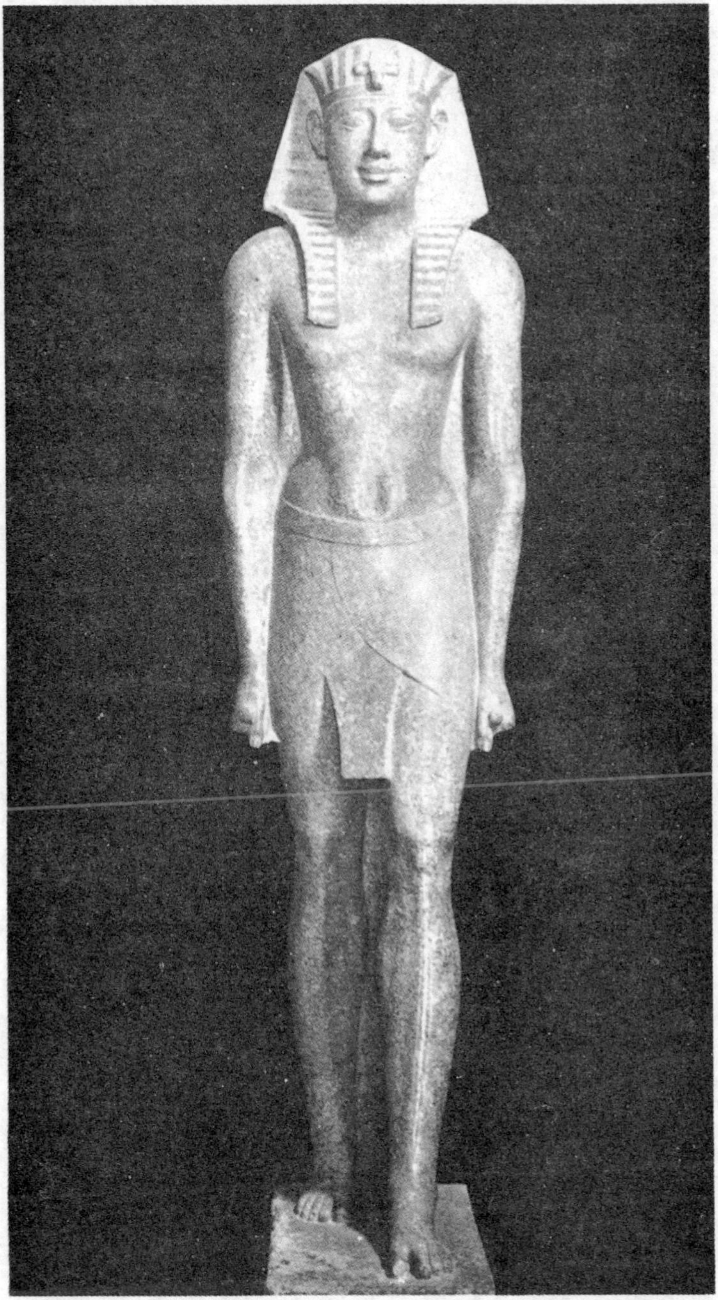

Ptolemy II Philadelphus of Egypt

(261–246 B.C.), the grandson of Seleucus Nikator; Ptolemy II Philadelphus of Egypt (285–247 B.C.); Antigonus Gonatas of Macedonia (276–239 B.C.); and Magas of Cyrene, the year of whose death has not been established, suggested dates ranging from *c.* 258 B.C. to 250 B.C.[1] The last-mentioned king, Alexander, can be either Alexander of Corinth (252–244 B.C.) or Alexander of Epirus (272–255 B.C.).[2]

We know from the 6th Pillar Edict that Aśoka began to issue his major edicts in his thirteenth regnal year. Judging by the style and content of the Major Rock Edicts, they appear to have been issued close upon each other. We may thus assume that the 13th Rock Edict was inscribed in about the fourteenth regnal year of Aśoka, i.e. in 256–255 B.C. Cross-dating can be provided by ascertaining the date of Magas, and determining to which of the two Alexanders the edict refers. It would appear that the edict was inscribed during the life-time of these kings. We can, however, allow for a year in which the news of the death of any one of them could have reached Aśoka.

The date 256–255 B.C. for the edict eliminates the possibility of Alexander of Corinth being the Alexander referred to, since he did not come to power until 252 B.C., and was therefore not known to Aśoka at the time when the inscription was issued. The dates of Alexander of Epirus would permit of his being known to Aśoka, since he ruled from 272–255 B.C. The news of his death may have arrived soon after the inscribing of the edict. We are of the opinion therefore that Alikyaṣudala was Alexander of Epirus.

The question of the date of Magas of Cyrene has been considered at great length by Eggermont.[3] He has proved fairly conclusively on the evidence of Catullus, Athenaeus, and contemporary coinage, that Magas' death took place in *c.* 252–250 B.C. and certainly not any earlier. Though this date has not been given the stamp of finality, we may assume that the first of the five kings to die was Alexander of Epirus in 255 B.C. Thus the latest date we can postulate for the edict is 254 B.C., although 256–255 B.C. in our opinion would be closer to the true date.

The Greek kings are mentioned in connection with the sending of envoys by Aśoka to countries outside his empire, with the purpose of preaching the *Dhamma*. The dispatch of these envoys, or missionaries as they are sometimes termed, presents a related question, that of Mahinda going to Ceylon on a similar mission and the date of this mission. But a preliminary event which needs investigation is the alleged Third Buddhist Council held at Pāṭaliputra. Two Buddhist Councils are said to have been held previous to

[1] 250 B.C. is suggested in *The Age of the Nandas and Mauryas*, p. 207; the earlier date is suggested by Bloch, in *Les Inscriptions d'Asoka*, p. 130 n. 23.

[2] *Corpus Inscriptionum Indiçarum*, vol. i, p. 48 n. 6; Lassen, *Indische Alterthumskunde*, vol. ii, p. 255.

[3] *Acta Orientalia*, 1940, pp. 103 ff.

the one at Pāṭaliputra. The first of these was held at Rājagṛiha, in Magadha, and was called in order to systematize and interpret the sermons of the Buddha as collected in the *Piṭakas*.[1] It was held fairly soon after the death of the Buddha, for it was at this Council that the Buddha's favourite disciple, Ānanda, was accused of unorthodox views, such as his plea that a separate order of Buddhist nuns should be permitted. The second council was said to have been held at Vaiśālī.[2]

The authenticity of the tradition of the Third Council is in doubt owing to the fact that only the Pāli sources mention it. According to these accounts Aśoka played a very important role in the calling of this Council and in the adopting of certain resolutions. Yet strangely enough Aśoka makes no mention of it in any of his inscriptions. The nearest we come to a possible reference to such an event is in the Schism Edict,[3] where he speaks emphatically of the continued unity of the *Saṃgha* and the expulsion of dissident monks and nuns. The fact that it was possible to distinguish between dissident members of the Order and the orthodox would suggest that some clarification on the point had taken place, and some rules of procedure adopted.

The story as related in the *Dīpavaṃsa* starts by explaining that the entry of non-orthodox sects into the Buddhist *vihāras* or monasteries led to a laxity of observances and beliefs.[4] This happened 236 years after the *Parinirvāṇa*, that is eighteen years after Aśoka's coronation. Eventually some of the orthodox Buddhists objected to the state of affairs. One of Aśoka's ministers who had ordered the revival of the *Pātimokkha* ceremony (a series of penances performed by the monks in order to further their emancipation), was so angered at some of the Elders of the monastery not performing it that it resulted in their being killed. The same story is explained at greater length in the *Mahāvaṃsa*.[5] Here the killing of the Elders comes to an end when Tissa, the king's brother, who appears to have been an orthodox Buddhist, was pained by this event and reported it to the king through another minister. Variations occur in the northern tradition where we are told that riots take place between the *Nirgranthas* and the Buddhists, resulting eventually in the death of the king's brother, a pious Buddhist. This brings about interference from the king and the pacification of the two sects.[6] The same story occurs in the *A-yü-wang-chuan*, but with the slight modification that Aśoka's brother is mistaken for a *Nirgrantha* and killed.[7]

[1] Dutt, *Early Monastic Buddhism*, vol. ii, p. 324.
[2] Hofinger, *Étude sur le Concile de Vaisali*, pp. 151 ff.
[3] Bloch, *Les Inscriptions d'Asoka*, p. 152.
[4] VII, 36–38, 49.
[5] V, 234–42.
[6] *Divyāvadāna*, XXVIII, p. 427.
[7] Przyluski, *La Legende de l'Empereur Açoka*, pp. 278–9.

The Pāli tradition incorporating the first two stories continues the narrative with the purge of the *Saṃgha*.[1] Aśoka sends for the revered Elder and saint of the Buddhist church, Moggaliputta Tissa, and gathers together all the *bhikkhus* in the famous monastery, the Aśokārāma. Only those believing in the *Vibhajja* doctrine are accepted as true Buddhists. The rest are expelled from the *Saṃgha*. After this purge the Third Buddhist Council is held at Pāṭaliputra with Moggaliputta Tissa presiding. The *Vibhajjavāda* is proclaimed as the true faith. The real difference between the two stories is that whereas in the Pāli version the conflict between Buddhists and non-Buddhists leads to the Third Council, and the purge of the latter from the *Saṃgha*, in the northern account it merely leads to the king guaranteeing the lives of all *śramaṇas*.[2]

The skeleton of these stories may well be authentic. We know from his edicts that Aśoka encouraged gatherings of various sects both Buddhist and non-Buddhist, so the presence of Ājīvikas and *Nirgranthas* in the Buddhist centres would not be out of order. It was a part of his policy of harmonious discussion. The possibility of conflicts and even riots under these circumstances cannot be ignored. Debates must have been heated enough, not to speak of the likelihood of friction between opposing religious communities living together at the same centre. It is equally possible that on a particular occasion when the debaters resorted to violence, Aśoka may have sent a minister to pacify the quarrelling groups. Aśoka would have realized the necessity of an amicable solution as soon as the rioting became serious. The death of the king's brother is therefore open to doubt, and seems a fictional addition to the story in order to give it pathos and increase its moral effect on an audience.

Dutt has suggested that since the non-Ceylonese sources do not give much prominence to these events, the conflict was a Ceylonese fabrication, based on disputes between the *Vibhajjavāda* and other sects in Ceylon, and intended to provide support for the former.[3] This may well be true.

Of all the events mentioned in the various sources, the only one that appears to be corroborated by the inscriptions of Aśoka is that of the purge of the *Saṃgha*. Here there seems to be some connection with the Schism Edict. The latter assumes that the purge has already taken place and that the *Saṃgha* is once more united. It threatens expulsion (wearing the white robe as against the yellow), to those monks and nuns who are accused of breaking up the *Saṃgha*. This edict does not prove the fact of a council

[1] *Mahāvaṃsa*, V, 268–71.

[2] *The Chronology of the Reign of Asoka Moriya*, p. 113.

[3] *Early Monastic Buddhism*, vol. ii, p .265.

having met before the purge. It merely states that the *Saṃgha* must be cleansed of dissident elements. The latter could easily have been a local matter carried out individually by each community of monks and nuns under a local council, no doubt with the knowledge of the *mahāmattas*. If Aśoka had actively assisted in the purge by calling a council at Pāṭaliputra, he would without doubt have mentioned it in one of his edicts.

It has been suggested that the Schism Edict was inscribed at the end of Aśoka's reign or in the latter years, because 'we easily find again the one hundred per cent Buddhist of the Ceylonese tradition'.[1] There is another perspective on the edict as well. It can also be interpreted from the point of view of the ruler, who is exasperated by the conflicts within the *Saṃgha*, and in which he, as the administrator, is being asked constantly to intervene. The first part of the edict in which he hopes that the unity of the *Saṃgha* may last, 'as long as the sun and the moon endure', is no doubt the utterance of a loyal Buddhist. But the second part threatening the expulsion of dissident members may be the reprimand of a ruler who sees religious bickerings as an obstacle to his work and that of his administrators. The pacification of religious sects has never been a happy task. The level at which Aśoka was taking Buddhism and the level of the interpretation of the teachings of the Buddha by the *Saṃgha*, must certainly have been very different.

The date of the edict remains uncertain. The Pāli chronicles state that the Council and the purge took place 236 years after the death of the Buddha.[2] On the basis of 486 B.C. as the date of the *Parinirvāṇa*, this would result in *c.* 250 B.C. as the date for the Council, i.e. in the nineteenth year of Aśoka's reign. A late date has been suggested for the edict on the basis of its position on the Allahabad pillar.[3] It is thought that this edict was issued some time after the 7th Pillar Edict which would place it after the twenty-eighth regnal year. The seven pillar edicts are engraved methodically, covering the girth of the pillar, and each letter is carefully cut and the whole evenly spaced. Below these edicts is the Schism Edict and farther down the Queen's Edict. If the Schism Edict had been inscribed before the pillar edicts it would most certainly have been placed at a higher level and probably would have been above the other edicts.[4]

Thus it would seem to have been inscribed in the latter years of Aśoka's reign. If the *Saṃgha* was in such a confused state as the Pāli chronicles would have us believe, with Buddhists and non-Buddhists living in

[1] Eggermont, *The Chronology of the Reign of Asoka Moriya*, p. 116.

[2] *Dīpavaṃsa*, VII, 36–38.

[3] *The Age of the Nandas and Mauryas*, p. 216.

[4] *Corpus Inscriptionum Indicarum*, vol. i ed. Cunningham, p. 38, Plate XXII.

discord in the various centres, it must have taken many years before the process of clarifying the situation could have achieved its purpose. The mere throwing out of dissident members was not enough. It is quite likely that this process did start in the nineteenth year of Aśoka's reign, and that it was not until another ten years or so that the *Saṃgha* was completely cleansed. The Schism Edict may have been issued when Aśoka felt that these religious conflicts had at last come to an end and some definite criterion of judging an orthodox Buddhist had been established. Thus the Schism Edict is not contrary to the spirit of tolerance demanded by Aśoka in his other proclamations, but is merely a record of the end of the conflict within the Buddhist church itself.

The historicity of the Council under the patronage of Aśoka remains doubtful. A local council at Pāṭaliputra may have been held under the direction of Moggaliputta Tissa, with which Aśoka had little or no connection. The decision to purge the *Saṃgha* in every part of the Buddhist world was the obvious solution to the problems raised by religious conflicts. It must have taken some years before this directive was put into practice in every local *Saṃgha*. The Council was not of great importance to Aśoka, who was at that time actively preaching tolerance. But it was of tremendous importance to theological dogma, hence it is given prominence in the Pāli chronicles. It was probably for the same reason that an attempt was made to connect Aśoka with it. Because of its importance to *Vibhajjavāda* Buddhism, this local council was given exaggerated importance.

Curiously enough Jaina theological history describes a similar council concerning various sects of the Jaina religion. Charpentier has collected the evidence and relates the following events.[1] At the end of the twelve-year famine, which took place during the reign of Candragupta Maurya, in *c.* 300 B.C., misfortune fell upon the Jaina church. It was divided into two conflicting sects, the *Śvetāmbaras* and the *Digambaras*. The monks who had travelled south during the famine had continued in their orthodox belief and on returning to Magadha, found that those monks who had stayed behind had become lax. The monks at Magadha therefore called a council at Pāṭaliputra to collect and revise the scriptures. The closeness of the two traditions would suggest that one may have borrowed from the other.

Linked with the Third Buddhist Council is the story of Mahinda's mission to Ceylon. We cannot overlook the idea that the Ceylon chroniclers would want to prove Mahinda a follower of the *Vibhajjavāda* sect. According to the Pāli chronicles Moggaliputta Tissa was responsible for the

[1] *Cambridge History of India*, vol. i, p. 165; *Pariśiṣṭaparvan*, IX, 55–76.

conversion of Mahinda.[1] This event took place when Mahinda was twenty years old in the sixth year of Aśoka's reign. After the Third Council was concluded, Buddhist missionaries were sent to various parts of the sub-continent and to the neighbouring countries. Allowing for a year in which the various missions were organized, we may assume that Mahinda was sent to Ceylon in the twentieth regnal year of Aśoka, in 249 B.C. and this is corroborated by the *Dīpavaṃsa*, which states that Mahinda came to Ceylon in the year 237 after the *Parinirvāṇa*.[2]

We know that previous to the sending of Mahinda there had been contact between Aśoka and Devānampiya Tissa, the king of Ceylon. The *Mahāvaṃsa* states that Tissa wanted to send jewels as a present to Aśoka, whom he refers to as 'my friend'.[3] The narrative continues, 'For the two monarchs already had been friends a long time, though they had never seen each other.' There are two references to Ceylon in the edicts, and both are prior to the Buddhist Council.[4]

A direct contact between Aśoka and Tissa is mentioned in the *Dīpavaṃsa*. Tissa was first crowned 236 years after the *Parinirvāṇa*, in the nineteenth year of Aśoka's reign.[5] Soon after this Tissa sent an embassy to Aśoka led by his nephew Ariṭṭha.[6] The journey took them from Ceylon to Tāmralipti and from there to Pātaliputra. After five weeks at the Mauryan capital the embassy returned to Ceylon with gifts for Tissa and also a message to the effect that Aśoka had become an *upāsaka* (lay-worshipper), and that Tissa should do the same. The message sounds highly suspect, for if in fact Aśoka had sent such a message it is surprising that he did not mention that he had been an *upāsaka* for at least nine years as would be the case judging from the evidence of the Minor Rock Edict. Tissa was consecrated a second time, soon after the return of his embassy, and Mahinda arrived in Ceylon a month later.[7] These events took place in 250 B.C. It might be suggested that the accounts of this embassy and Mahinda's mission reflect one and the same event. The envoy could well have been Mahinda, the king's son, an envoy of an appropriately high rank to honour the coronation of a friendly neighbour. In his capacity of a Buddhist monk he no doubt filled

[1] *Dīpavaṃsa*, VII, 14–20, 24.

[2] Ibid., XV, 71.

[3] XI, 18.

[4] II R.E., Girnār; and XIII R.E., Kālsi. We base this fact on the identification of Tāmrāparni with Ceylon. See Appendix III.

[5] *Dīpavaṃsa*, XVII, 78.

[6] *Mahāvaṃsa*, XI, 20.

[7] It is indeed strange that the chronicles should have mentioned that Tissa was crowned twice. There is no precise explanation for the second coronation. Since it closely followed Tissa's initiation into Buddhism, it may be assumed that from the point of view of the Buddhist monks it was the more important of the two, and was the one referred to in their king lists.

the dual purpose of preaching Buddhism to the king and his court, as well as serving as an ambassador.

Ariṭṭha, the nephew of Tissa appears again in the narrative.[1] On this occasion he is sent to Pāṭaliputra to fetch Saṃghamittā in order that the queen Anulā of Ceylon and the ladies of the court may be ordained. It was on this occasion too that Aśoka was supposed to have sent a branch of the Bodhi-tree to Ceylon. The historical certainty of the event is in doubt. The chronicles do not give any date for it. Fa-hsien in his memoirs mentions that a king of Ceylon had sent an envoy to India to obtain seeds of the Bodhi-tree, which were then planted in Ceylon.[2] The story of Saṃghamittā may well be just a pleasant anecdote attached to the main narrative, which gave the chronicler an excuse to indulge in imaginative passages, as the descriptions of the journey certainly are. It is unlikely that Tissa would have permitted Anulā to be ordained, she being already a queen. The story of the branch of the Bodhi-tree may contain some truth. It is possible that Tissa in his enthusiasm may have requested such a branch from Aśoka, who lost nothing by granting this request, but if anything gained Tissa's further goodwill.[3]

We are told that at the conclusion of the Third Buddhist Council, Buddhist monks of some repute were selected and sent as missionaries to various regions. Amongst these were, Majjhantika (who was sent to Kashmir and Gandhāra), Mahādeva (Mahiṣamaṇḍala), Rakkhita (Vanavāsi), Yona Dhammarakhita (Aparantaka), Mahādhammarakkhita (Mahārattha), Mahārakkhita (Yona), Majjhima (the Himalayan region), Sona and Uttara (Suvarṇabhūmi), Mahinda (Laṅkā).[4]

The mission to the Himalayan region was a large one and consisted of a team of four monks, Kassapagotta, Dhūndibhissara, Sahadeva, and Mūlakadeva. Some of the relic caskets from Sanchi contain a few of these names. The word Yona (generally used to indicate a Greek) preceding the name of Dhammarakkhita suggests a non-Indian monk, possibly Greek or Persian. But it seems strange that he should be sent to Aparantaka on the western coast of India, whilst Mahārakkhita was sent to the Yona area. Yona appears to refer to the Indo-Greek settlements of the north-west, though it would seem from the reference to Tuṣāspa in the Junāgarh inscription of Rudradāman that there may have been a foreign settlement of Persians or

[1] *Mahāvaṃsa*, XI, 18–42; XVIII; XIX. *Dīpavaṃsa*, XI, 25–40; XII, 1–7; XV, 74–95; XVI, 1–7, 38–41.

[2] Giles, *Travels of Fa-hsien*, p. 68.

[3] That this story spread beyond India and Ceylon can be seen in a place as distant as Tun-huang in the Gobi Desert. There is a fresco painting in one of the caves at this monastery, which is said to depict Aśoka sending an image of the Buddha and a branch of the Bodhi-tree to Ceylon. The fresco has been dated to the seventh century A.D.

[4] *Mahāvaṃsa*, XII, 1–8.

Greeks in western India.[1] The other possibility is that there was some textual confusion when the chronicle was being transcribed. It may be said that the names of these missionaries are so similar as to sound suspicious. It

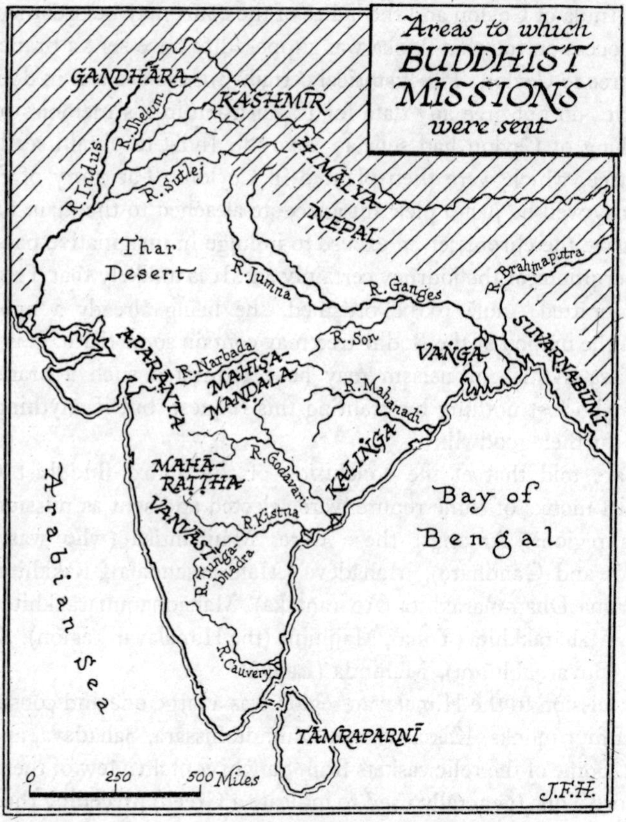

is possible, however, that these were the names adopted by the persons concerned when they entered the Order, a custom known to exist in Buddhist ritual as in the ritual of some other religions such as Christianity.[2]

The sending of these missionaries by the Buddhist Council has been associated with the *Dhammavijaya* (conquest through *Dhamma*) policy of Aśoka.[3] The 13th Rock Edict is quoted in support of this view, where Aśoka declares that true conquest is conquest by piety or virtue, and he claims such a conquest since he believed that his *Dhamma* policy had been

[1] Sircar, *Select Inscriptions...*, p. 169.
[2] Kern, *Manual of Buddhism*, p. 117.
[3] Nilakantha Sastri (ed.), *The Age of the Nandas and Mauryas*, p. 217.

accepted beyond the frontiers of his own kingdom.[1] But this is no basis for a necessary connection between the Buddhist missions and the embassies of Aśoka. The 13th Rock Edict was issued in 256–255 B.C. and the embassies must have been sent before this date. In the 5th Rock Edict Aśoka specifically mentions that in his fourteenth regnal year he started the institution of *dhamma-mahāmattas*.[2] This was a special body of officials whose work was concerned with the practice and spread of *Dhamma*.

If we can call this, missionary work on the part of Aśoka (on the assumption presumably that all diplomatic missions are missionaries of some cause or idea), then in any case he had a lead of at least five years if not more on the Buddhist missions. The Buddhist missions were purely religious in character and were sent out under the direction of the Buddhist Council and not under the direction of Aśoka. His own embassies were quite distinct from Buddhist missions, although they may have assisted the latter in some way.

It is noticeable that the Buddhist missions concentrated on areas either within the kingdom or on the borders of it. This is only natural since their primary concern was with communicating the decisions of the Council on purging the *Saṃgha*, and secondarily with making new converts. Most of the areas mentioned in the Buddhist sources had already received *dhamma-mahāmattas* from Aśoka.[3] Had the king been responsible for these missions he would have been far more keen on sending them farther afield, where he had not already sent his own embassies and officials.

It is important to remember when considering the evidence of the Buddhist chronicles that they were composed by a body of Buddhist monks. Although they give an account of some events in the reign of Aśoka they are primarily interested in the development of Buddhism during those years. Historical information is included only where it affects this development, and furthermore events of importance to the history of Buddhism are given prominence over all others. Aśoka is of importance to these chroniclers not because of his historical position but because of the role he played in the development of the religion. We must therefore be constantly aware of the distinction between those events which are largely of theological significance, and those which are connected with the politics of the king.

In the twenty-first year of his reign Aśoka visited the Lumbinī garden where the Buddha was born.[4] This event would date to 248 B.C. An inscrip-

[1] R.E. II. Bloch, *Les Inscriptions d'Asoka*, pp. 93 ff.
[2] Ibid.
[3] Ibid.
[4] The Rummindei Inscription. Bloch, *Les Inscriptions d'Asoka*, p. 157.

tion on the pillar recording the visit was ordered by the king. This visit has been linked by Eggermont in an ingenious and convincing manner with a pilgrimage made by the king after an eclipse in 248 B.C., and the event can be regarded as an important factor in the working out of Aśokan chronology.

There is a story in the *Divyāvadāna* that Aśoka wished to build 84,000 *stūpas* on the same day and at the same hour.[1] The *thera* Yaśas, who was informed of this, hid the sun with his hand, thus enabling the impossible to take place. The story with slight modifications occurs in other Buddhist sources as well.[2] The hiding of the sun has been correctly interpreted by Eggermont as the eclipse of the sun. The meaning is obvious and the passage cannot imply anything else. It is possible to calculate whether such an eclipse could have taken place during the reign of Aśoka. On the research of Fazy[3] and Sidersky[4] it was discovered that three eclipses of the sun occurred during the reign of Aśoka on the following dates, 4 May 249 B.C., 15 June 242 B.C. and 19 November 232 B.C. Having established that an eclipse of the sun did take place, we must now consider any cross-evidence which would suggest which of the three above eclipses is referred to in the *Divyāvadāna*.

The *Divyāvadāna* continues the story by narrating that after the erection of the *stūpas* and the eclipse of the sun, the *thera* allowed Aśoka a vision of the places sacred to Buddhism, and Aśoka had *stūpas* and *caityas* built at some of these sites. Among the latter, the birth-place of the Buddha is mentioned. Tāranātha bears out the fact that all these events followed in quick succession.[5] The vision of the sacred sites and the further building of *stūpas* and *caityas*, seems to refer to a pilgrimage or tour that Aśoka must have undertaken after the eclipse of the sun. How else, in practical terms could he have seen all these places? The three eclipses occurred in the twentieth, twenty-seventh, and thirty-seventh years of Aśoka's reign. Doubtless he may have been on tour or made a pilgrimage in any one of these years. But more specifically, the twentieth year seems the most appropriate, since the pillar inscription at Rummindei was issued in the following year.[6] The king states that he visited Lumbinī (Rummindei is the modern form of the ancient name Lumbinī), and worshipped there because it was the birth-place of the Buddha. For the same reason a sculptured horse and a pillar were set up to mark the spot.[7] The *Divyāvadāna*, as we have stated

[1] XXVI, p. 381.

[2] Watters, *On Yuan Chwang's Travels in India*, vol. ii, p. 91. *Dīpavaṃsa*, VII, 1–8.

[3] *JA*, 1930, vol. ccxvii, pp. 135, 136.

[4] *JA*, 1932, vol. ccxx, pp. 295–7.

[5] *Geschichte des Buddhismus in Indien*, p. 36.

[6] Bloch, *Les Inscriptions d'Asoka*, p. 157.

[7] It is strange that the animal should have been a horse. Usually the elephant is associated with the birth of the Buddha.

earlier, particularly mentions the honouring of Lumbinī. Furthermore the pilgrimage to Lumbinī is one of the four recommended pilgrimages which good Buddhists are expected to make. It was in the same year that Aśoka visited the *stūpa* of Konākamana. It would appear that he made the pilgrimage in his twenty-first regnal year, probably a few months after the eclipse.

The Ceylon chronicles date these events to the seventh year of Aśoka's reign, 262–261 B.C.[1] On the evidence of the eclipse this is a false date as there was no eclipse in that year. The pilgrimage in the twenty-first year is not directly mentioned. But, as has been pointed out, Aśoka must have made a journey in the region of the Ganges during that period, since we are told that he was present at some stage of the journey made by Moggaliputta Tissa down the Ganges by boat, after the Third Council had met at Pāṭaliputra.[2] Thus we may assume that the hiding of the sun was the eclipse of 4 May 249 B.C., and that in the following year Aśoka visited the sites sacred to Buddhism.

The issuing of pillar edicts was the next known event of Aśoka's reign, and these are dated to the twenty-seventh and twenty-eighth year. The first six edicts, concerned largely with the *Dhamma*, were engraved in his twenty-seventh year. The seventh and last, engraved in the following year, appears to be a survey of his work, particularly the development of the *Dhamma*. It is indeed strange that for the next years until his death in 232 B.C. there were no further major edicts. For a man so prolific in issuing edicts this silence of ten years is difficult to explain.

There are enough stories in the Buddhist religious sources to suggest that Aśoka in his later years began to lose the control that he had had over the government of the kingdom. The *Mahāvaṃsa* relates the following events concerning the last years of Aśoka. In the twenty-ninth year of his reign, his chief queen Asandhimittā died. In the fourth year after this, in 237 B.C. he raised Tissarakkhā to the rank of chief queen. Two years later, she, being jealous of the king's devotion to the Bodhi-tree, injured the tree by piercing it with a poisonous thorn, thereby causing it to wither away. Fa-hsien mentions the cutting down of the tree, intending its destruction, although he does not mention the name of the queen. He adds that Aśoka being extremely upset, prayed that the tree be saved and there was a miraculous revival of the root.[3] In 233–232 B.C., his thirty-seventh regnal year, the king died.

The comments of the chroniclers on these events are frank. Asandhi-

[1] *Mahāvaṃsa*, V, 173-6.

[2] Eggermont, *The Chronology of the Reign of Asoka Moriya*, p. 128.

[3] Giles, *Travels of Fa-hsien*, p. 58.

mittā was a good queen because she was friendly towards the *Saṃgha*. One has the impression of a thoughtful woman who sympathized with the ideas of her husband. Tissarakkhā is described as proud and foolish. She appears to have been a selfish woman who resented the many hours Aśoka spent on ideological matters and possibly also the attention he gave to Buddhist affairs. The story of her destroying the Bodhi-tree by having it pierced by a thorn is unacceptable in the light of modern botanical knowledge. However, she may have tried somehow to injure the tree, and to have shown her resentment in this and other ways. Evidently she was far less partial to the Buddhists than her predecessor. What is more probable is that the tree began to wither through natural causes, but the chroniclers associated it with Tissarakkhā's antipathy for Buddhism. The story hints at the idea that Aśoka in his later years succumbed to the influence and charm of his new queen, when he had lost the possibly more mature companionship of his previous wife, Asandhimittā.

This suggestion is corroborated in the stories of the *Aśokāvadāna* where Tissarakkhā (called Tiṣyarakṣitā in the Sanskrit sources), demonstrates her power in a devastating manner.[1] We are told that the prince Kunāla, the son of Queen Padmāvatī is born with particularly beautiful eyes. But it has been predicted that he will be blinded in later years. The prediction is proved true through the machinations of Tissarakkhā. Although already the wife of Aśoka, she is enamoured of Kunāla because of his beautiful eyes. He rejects her advances so she plans to harm him. Meanwhile Aśoka falls ill. Tissarakkhā by means of a strategem diagnoses the sickness and is able to cure him.[2] The king in gratitude grants her whatever she may wish, a promise of which she later makes use in a manner that ends tragically. There is a revolt in Taxila and Kunāla is sent to suppress it. The queen then sends an order to the officials at Taxila, sealed with Aśoka's seal (which she obtained as part of his promise to her), that Kunāla is to be blinded and put to death. The officials, much puzzled, carry out the first part of the order, but because of their affection for the young prince they refuse to kill him and permit him to leave Taxila. Kunāla wanders out from the city together with his favourite wife Kañcanamālā. He roams through the country playing the *vīṇā* and singing, and one day when he reaches the city of Pāṭaliputra, Aśoka recognizes his voice. On being told the whole story Aśoka is inconsolable. Tissarakkhā is punished by being burnt to death. Kunāla remarks that this is a punishment which he has to bear for some

[1] Przyluski, *La Legende de l'Empereur Açoka*, pp. 283 ff.

[2] The diagnosis was conducted by finding a similar condition in another person and then eliminating various possibilities by a variety of treatment, until the right antidote was found. This passage throws light on the medical analysis of the time.

sin in a previous life. Obviously some degree of moralizing had to be included in the story.

As it stands this legend appears largely to be the result of monkish imagination. The account of the revolt at Taxila follows the original story of a similar revolt at the end of Bindusāra's reign, when Aśoka was sent to suppress it, too closely to carry conviction. It is hardly likely that a precisely similar event would have occurred at the end of Aśoka's reign. It is possible that the story of the first revolt was confused by the editor of the *Aśokāvadāna* with a tradition of the sending of Kunāla to another part of the country, perhaps as vice-regent. As we have stated earlier, the historical exactness of the first revolt is more convincing, since there is complementary evidence from the Aramaic inscription at Sirkap. An alternative interpretation of this story is that towards the end of his reign Aśoka may have had to face minor revolts in various parts of his kingdom. This would not be entirely the result of his own lack of control, but rather of public opinion reacting against the more irksome aspects of the *Dhamma*, an idea which we shall consider at greater length in the final chapter.

The story of the sickness and the cure of Aśoka would suggest that there was some intrigue and interference from the lesser members of the royal family in matters of state. In the context of the whole narrative it was essential that Tissarakkhā should obtain a promise from Aśoka that he would grant her wish. The most obvious way of doing this would be by saving his life at a critical point. A comparatively simple way of achieving this would be by making him suffer from a seemingly incurable illness. The same legend appears in almost an identical form in other cultures. Whatever meagre historical data can be gathered from this legend would suggest that Aśoka may have been beset with trouble from his queen and family in his later years.

This is not the only legend contained in the *Aśokāvadāna* on the king's later years. A further story is connected with his inability to make donations to the *bhikkhus* towards the end of his reign.[1] Aśoka is said to have donated all his treasure to the monastery at Kukkuṭārāma. He declares the son of Kunāla, Samprati, to be the heir-apparent, and the latter is king in all but name. The source suggests that the prince was in the confidence of the ministers and that they were all conspiring against Aśoka because they disapproved of the latter's donations to the Buddhist order. One day a *bhikkhu* comes round asking for alms. The only thing which Aśoka can give to the *bhikkhu*, is his sole possession, half an āmalā. The story would suggest that the king died a sad and disappointed man, divested of all his power.

[1] Przyluski, *La Legende de l'Empereur Acoka*, pp. 296 ff.

These legends from Buddhist sources have led some historians to state that not only did Aśoka's power weaken considerably in his later years, but that the officials became oppressive and the princes who had been taught not to use force were incapable of governing the empire.[1] Some writers are of the opinion that Aśoka virtually retired from governing in his old age, delegating his authority to the heir and ministers, who appear to have conspired against the continuation of his policy.[2] The error in these views lies in the fact that they give too much credence to the Buddhist stories. That there was some weakening in the powers of Aśoka towards the end of his reign cannot be denied. The lack of unanimity in the various sources regarding the successor to Aśoka would point to some degree of confusion in his later years. But that there was a ministerial conspiracy against him seems unlikely, nor is it possible to believe that he donated all his possessions to the *Saṃgha* and was left with half an āmalā. In the legend the minister in question is called Rādhagupta. It is a little difficult to believe that Rādhagupta the minister of Bindusāra who assisted Aśoka in gaining the throne, would at the end of the latter's reign of thirty-six years still be powerful enough to conspire against him.

In considering the veracity of these legends we must keep in mind the purpose for which they were written. Furthermore they were not the work of a single man. The traditions were collected from various areas and were being continually revised and contaminated by the ideas current in different centuries and in the particular localities to which the tradition belonged. The traditions as they have come down to us today were worked over by Buddhist monks who no doubt changed them where necessary to suit Buddhist morals. The main purpose of each story was to illustrate, somewhat crudely, the truth of Buddhist attitudes, and the moral of the story was in conformity with Buddhist teaching. Thus Aśoka started life as a wicked, anti-religious man; he was converted to Buddhism and soon became an absolute paragon of Buddhist righteousness. Despite his piety, he ended his life in comparative sorrow, possessing only half a mango. Since suffering on earth is the lot of every man, even the pious Aśoka had to undergo his due share of suffering, which for him was all the greater since it came at the end of his reign, and in the eyes of his contemporaries may have declared him a failure.

[1] Raychaudhuri, *The Political History of Ancient India*, pp. 363 ff.

[2] Barua, *Aśoka and his Inscriptions*, p. 62.

III

SOCIETY AND ECONOMIC ACTIVITY

As we have already stated in the introductory chapter, a study of the social and economic conditions of Mauryan India is essential to a proper understanding of the policy of Aśoka. Furthermore the particular type of administration started and developed by the Mauryas, that of a centralized bureaucracy, was possible because of these conditions which helped to fashion this administrative system. The influence of social and economic factors upon each other is equally important. No single force is entirely responsible for the development of a society, be it a religious force, an economic system, or a philosophical movement. Each of these forces is interrelated and plays a significant part in the general development. Nevertheless the economic factor, because it is so closely associated at a primary level with the sheer physical fact of livelihood, can modify the form of a society. If the study of the history of a period aims at authenticity, it must of necessity take into consideration the role of various forces.

An analysis of the social factors moulding a society, and an examination of the economic forces, may often merge one into the other, since the two are closely related. That these two features of Mauryan life are of particular significance during this period is clear from the fact that the organization of the empire meant the acceptance of a new type of economy, which in turn affected the social order. In the pre-Mauryan period, the early pastoral economy had changed to a village economy based on agriculture. This was a natural step after the forests had been cleared, and agrarian village communities became the general pattern in the Ganges valley. Comparative permanence of settlement brought with it the organization of other facilities such as trade, to which again the Ganges was well suited since it provided river transport. The development of trade led to the establishment of the mercantile community through a system of guilds. These were a predominant factor in urban life, and consequently introduced a new force into existing society. Gradually as this change in the economy spread from the Ganges valley to other areas, it became possible to regard these areas as one unit. This in turn, once it was brought under a single political control, considerably facilitated the administrative system. Administrative ideas could be developed more easily since the same general pattern existed in most areas.

This is not to suggest that no other type of economy was possible once the agrarian economy became permanent. Variations on the economic structure continued to exist, but generally tended to be concentrated in areas where they were more advantageous. The expansion of the agrarian economy accelerated the realization that a single predominant economy facilitated the evaluation of taxes. For instance coastal areas dependent on maritime trade would continue the trade or increase it as the case may be, but nevertheless would be regarded as areas specifically devoted to one main economic pursuit and would be taxed accordingly. There was much to be gained by those governing a settled economy which would permit a near-permanent establishment of taxation systems and tax-rates. It is not surprising therefore that Kauṭalya, the theorist of the politico-economic basis of the Mauryan state, devotes an important part of the *Arthaśāstra* to the application of taxation.[1] The predictability of revenue in the form of taxes created a feeling of economic and social security. It also simplified the working of the administrative system, in so far as in its embryonic stages administration was largely a matter of collecting taxes. Social security led to the utopian desire to organize society, in such a way that it would function consistently and with advantage to its constituents.

Social organization had already begun in the Vedic period. Based on the organization of social labour, the system of dividing society into four castes had emerged. Until the Mauryan period the system tended to be fairly fluid and examples can be quoted of considerable social mobility.[2] The position of the first two castes for instance, the brahmans and the *kṣatriyas*, was interchangeable. The prince often appeared to be socially superior to the brahman who was regarded very much as a mere priest and was on occasion ridiculed. Buddhist literature frequently gives the list of the four castes as Khattiyas, Brahmaṇas, Vessas, and Suddas, suggesting thereby that in the time of the Buddha the brahmans had a position socially inferior to that of the *kṣatriyas*.[3] By the Mauryan period, it would appear that the brahmans had gained the upper hand. Although the later rigidity of the caste system was not prevalent in all its forms in Mauryan times, the process of crystallization had begun. Certain priorities and privileges for the brahmans were accepted as a matter of course.[4] The earlier indication in the *Brāhamaṇas* of the leading role of the *purohita* in matters relating to the state, is emphasized in the *Arthaśāstra*.[5] The theoretical aspect of the caste system had been fully accepted, as is evident from

[1] Book II.
[2] Rhys Davids, *Buddhist India*, p. 56.
[3] *Aṅguttara Nikāya*, III, pp. 362 ff.; *Jātakas*, III, 19; IV, 205.
[4] *Arthaśāstra*, II, 28.
[5] Ibid., I. 10.

Megasthenes' account of Indian society. Buddhism could have been a check on increasing brahman power, but it was never effectively used as an anti-brahmanical weapon. Once triumphant, brahmanical forces held fast to their position by all and every means, as is amply demonstrated by Manu, and the rigidity of the caste system became a permanent feature.

In considering social organization in ancient India, a useful approach is that of examining the reports made by contemporary visitors and foreign sources on the same subject. Greek and Latin sources for instance refer to the caste system in India, and the majority of these references may be traced largely to the account of Megasthenes. We intend to use the comments of Megasthenes as a basis for our discussion, not because we believe them to be more reliable than any other source, Indian or foreign, but because they take into consideration the more predominant features of Mauryan social life without any marked bias; they are meant largely to record and not to maintain a particular point of view.

Megasthenes states that Indian society was divided into seven classes. These he lists as philosophers, farmers, soldiers, herdsmen, artisans, magistrates, and councillors.[1] Arrian states that there are about seven but does not speak with certainty.[2] This observation of Megasthenes is only partially based on fact. The idea of society being divided into groups was no doubt a prevalent one, and the system must have been explained to him by local brahmans. But the number of classes and the categories must have become confused in his mind. His divisions appear to have been rather economic divisions than social. This is understandable because the system of the four *varṇas* or castes originated in an economic division, and it is possible that vestiges of this origin remained in Mauryan times. It is obvious that the divisions of Megasthenes could not follow rules of endogamy and restrict themselves to their own trade.[3] He appears to have confused his own observations with brahmanical theory. The numerical confusion may be due to the fact that in writing his account, possibly some years after his visit to India, he may have accidentally arrived at the number seven, forgetting the facts as given to him. We must also keep in mind that the fragments remaining to us are not the original accounts but are quotations from the original. Some of the inconsistencies may be explained by erroneous quoting on the part of later authors. Megasthenes may also have had in mind the description of Egyptian society as given by Herodotus, who enumerates seven social classes in Egypt.

[1] Diodorus, II, 40–41.
[2] *Indica*, XI.
[3] Timmer, *Megasthenes en de Indische Maatschappij*, p. 66.
[4] *Histories*, II, 164.

Amongst the general remarks Megasthenes makes about the various castes, he states that, 'No one is allowed to marry outside of his own caste or to exercise any calling or art except his own.'[1] But he adds elsewhere, 'and exception is made in favour of the philosopher who for his virtue is allowed this privilege'.[2] This passage is reminiscent of a later text, the *Dharmaśāstra* of Manu, where brahmans are permitted marriage with a lower caste.[3]

The first caste mentioned by Megasthenes is that of the philosophers. This group is generally believed to represent the brahmans. Before examining Megasthenes' comments on this group, its position in traditional literature may be considered. Fick is of the opinion that the brahmans are divided into two groups, and his suggestions based on near-contemporary literature are convincing.[4] The two categories consist of the *udicca* brahmans, the more orthodox ones who were the teachers and the priests, and the *satakalakkhana* brahmans who were the worldly ones, superstitious and ignorant. The latter practised fortune-telling and magic. Sacrifice was the stock remedy for all ills, and money was made by the brahman each time he conducted a sacrifice. Thus the ban on the killing of animals by Buddhists may have been resented by these brahmans, as also Aśoka's disapproval of *maṅgalas* and other ceremonies which he regarded as being valueless. The second group of brahmans was sometimes driven to non-brahmanic activity through economic necessity. For example a brahman living on the edge of a forest might take to carpentry if there was a surplus of priests in the area.[5] Thus it would seem that some degree of mobility within the caste was allowed provided it was the direct result of economic pressure. However, on the whole the laws of endogamy were strictly observed, and marriage within the brahman caste preserved the brahmanical birth; this prevented the brahmans from merging with the rest of the population.[6]

Fick makes particular mention of the *purohitas* who, it would seem, were not content with the occasional care of political affairs but were greedy for more permanent power.[7] This policy naturally had a disastrous effect on a weak or superstitious king who would find himself a pawn in the hands of the *purohita*. Although the *Jātakas* are certainly prejudiced against the brahmans, they nevertheless do present the other side of the story, a view of the brahman as he appeared to members of the lower order. Megasthenes'

[1] Diodorus, II, 40.
[2] Strabo, XV, 1, 48.
[3] III, 13.
[4] *The Social Organization in North-East India in Buddha's Time*, p. 212.
[5] *Jātaka*, IV, pp. 207 ff.
[6] Fick, *The Social Organization in North-East India in Buddha's Time*, p. 212.
[7] Ibid., pp. 174, 187.

description of the brahman is certainly more sympathetic than the one we find in the *Jātakas*.[1] His remarks on the philosophy of the brahmans suggest that in this instance he made some reliable observations. He mentions briefly at one point that the brahmans offer sacrifices and perform ceremonies for the dead and foretell the future. He adds that they are small in numbers but very powerful.

In another longer fragment he classifies the philosophers into two groups, the Brachmanes and the Sarmanes.[2] The Brachmanes undergo a severe training in a retreat and study there for thirty-seven years. This number is strikingly close to that given by Manu, who states that the maximum length of time that a man can spend as a *brahmacārin* is thirty-six years.[3] The Brachmanes then return to a family life. They eat meat but not the flesh of animals employed in labour, therefore they refrain from eating the flesh of cows, oxen, horses, and elephants. They are permitted many wives and consequently have many children. The children do most of the work since there are no slaves in Indian society. The women are kept in ignorance of philosophy. Megasthenes appears to have taken an interest in the philosophy of the Brachmanes since he adds that they believed that life was a dream-like illusion. This appears to be a reference to the doctrine of *Māyā* current in Indian thought. Death was not associated with fear and terror but was accepted with a certain anticipation, since they believed that dying was the real birth. He states that their ideas about physical phenomena were crude, but that they did hold some beliefs similar to the Greeks, for example some of their cosmological theories.

The Sarmanes he divides further into various smaller groups.[4] The *hylobioi* are the most respected of these, and they live as ascetics. The second group are the physicians and finally the diviners and sorcerers. This appears to be a confused description since it suggests the two categories of brahmans mentioned earlier, the ascetics and the more worldly brahmans, but it hardly agrees with the usual description of Buddhist and Jaina *śramaṇas*. Megasthenes must surely have known about Buddhists if he took an interest in religious ideas. It is possible that in later years he confused the two groups of brahmans, the *udicca* and the *satakalakkhana* and referred to the latter as the Sarmanes. Timmer believes that Megasthenes confused the Sarmanes with the *vānaprastha* stage of the four *āśramas* of orthodox

[1] Diodorus, II, 40.

[2] Strabo, XV, 1, 59.

[3] III, 1. *Brahmacārya*, was the first *āśrama* or stage of the four stages in the life of a Hindu. The first was the period of religious study and celibacy. This was followed by periods of being a householder, then learning to renounce the world, and becoming a hermit, and finally renunciation.

[4] Strabo, XV, 1, 59.

Hinduism.[1] In Hindu religious works they would not be regarded as true ascetics. The reference to their leaving their retreats after thirty-seven years and becoming householders would suggest that they were *brahmacārins*. The four stages were a theoretical sub-division and it is unlikely that they were rigidly adhered to by even the majority of the 'twice-born' Hindus. For all its physical deprivations the life of the ascetic was free from personal and social responsibility. It would not be incorrect, therefore, to suggest that for the majority of ascetics, their vocation may well have been an escape from the drudgery of daily life in organized society.

In another fragment there is an even more confused account of a group of philosophers again called Brachmanes.[2] The confusion is not surprising since the passage is quoted in an early Christian text, the Pseudo-Origen *Philosophia* which has been dated to the third or fourth century A.D. This group of brahmans is said to subsist on gathered and fallen fruit. They live in the region of the Tungabhadra river in southern India, but they wander about completely naked, as they believe that the body is merely a covering for the soul. Not surprisingly they are also said to be celibate. There follows a passage containing a very muddled account of the mysticism of the words used by this sect. References to God being very frequent amongst them it is possible that this may have been a colony of brahman ascetics. The description, however, tallies far more closely with that of Jainas living in southern India. The ban on eating food cooked by fire and living instead on fruit is quite in keeping with certain orthodox Jaina practices.[3] The location of the group at Tungabhadra again suggests the Jainas. We know that Candragupta Maurya went to south India with Bhadrabāhu and he may well have spent his last days in this region. Unfortunately Megasthenes does not state clearly whether he actually went as far as the Tungabhadra to see these ascetics, or whether this was a part of the Mauryan empire, and the life of these ascetics was reported to him. The fact of their nakedness agrees with the beliefs of the *digambara* sect of Jainas.

Megasthenes' comments on the privileges of the philosophers are interesting. Amongst them he mentions the exemption from taxation. Diodorus states that they were free from any kind of service,[4] but Arrian writes that they were free of all duties to the state except that of state sacrifices.[5] This freedom is granted to them on condition that their predictions to the state synod are correct. It is not clear whether those who did

[1] *Megasthenes en de Indische Maatschappij*, p. 105. The *vānaprastha* stage is the third stage, that of being a forest hermit.

[2] Pseudo-Origen, *Philosophia*, 24.

[3] Filliozat, *L'Inde Classique*, 2447–54.

[4] Diodorus, II, 40.

[5] *Indica*, XI.

not accurately forecast the future were made to pay. It is possible that the reference to duties and services to the state may have been forced labour or *viṣṭi* which was current in Mauryan times and which we shall discuss in detail later. Megasthenes also reports that philosophers who make incorrect predictions have to remain silent all their lives. Again it is not explicit whether this meant complete silence or only a prohibition on forecasting events. The fragment quoted by Diodorus states that philosophers are hereditary, but this disagrees with the fragment quoted by Arrian according to which anyone can be a philosopher, the only deterrent being that it is a hard life.

Timmer is of the opinion that it appears from these fragments that Megasthenes based his caste divisions on observation and not on information.[1] We feel, however, that he must have had some knowledge, although confused, of the Indian caste-system. His observations do present certain generally acceptable points. It is clear that the brahmans were a privileged section of society, despite the fact that they were numerically small. They were not expected to contribute their share in forced labour, and it would seem, were on the whole exempted from taxation. This in itself was a valuable right, singling them out immediately as a special body. Nor does this position change too radically judging from the information of Indian sources. It is clear from the frequent references to the brahmans and *śramaṇas* together in the Aśokan edicts and his constant exhortation to his subjects that they should be respected, that they were granted special treatment and were almost a pampered section of society, their religious merit being taken into account in place of productive labour.

With the growth of the agrarian economy the cultivator began to assume an increasingly important economic role. His social position was inferior but his economic position could not be ignored. According to Megasthenes the second class among the seven Indian castes was that of the farmer.[2] This class was numerically large and was devoted to the land. It was generally left unmolested by armies fighting in the neighbourhood.[3] He states further that all the land belonged to the king and was cultivated by the farmers for the king. The cultivators paid one-quarter of the produce in tax. In addition to the tax they paid a land tribute to the king. Strabo's quotation from Megasthenes is in agreement with the above except on the matter of taxation. Strabo maintains that the cultivators received one-

[1] *Megasthenes en de Indische Maatschappij*, pp. 66–69.

[2] Diodorus, II, 40.

[3] Cf. Breloer in *Grundeig*, p. 119. A Buddhist work, the *Abhidharmakośavākhya* (*IHQ*, II, No. 3, 1926, p. 656), states, 'Philosophers should follow logic in debate, even as kings allow peasants to go on working, even when enemy country is over-run'.

quarter of the produce from the king as payment.[1] The fragment in the writings of Arrian does not specify the amount when referring to taxation. He merely states that the husbandmen cultivate the soil and pay tribute to the kings and the independent cities.[2]

It would seem that the cultivators formed the majority of the Indian population, a situation which has not changed to this day. They were kept disarmed according to all accounts, and their sole task was the cultivation of the land. Some villages were exempt from taxation but this was only in lieu of providing soldiers.[3] Megasthenes maintains that the peasants were left untouched during a war. This no doubt was the theoretical ideal, but it is hardly likely that when hard-pressed in battle the king did not employ whatever man-power was available in the form of local peasants, or attack the villages in enemy territory. The figures quoted by Aśoka of the dead and wounded in the Kaliṅga War, even if they were exaggerated, could hardly refer only to army casualties.[4] Of the one hundred and fifty thousand people deported from Kaliṅga, a fair percentage must have been peasants who were probably made to clear forested regions and to cultivate virgin lands. The organization of the commissariat department of the army must have depended quite considerably on local supplies, and this must surely have led officially or unofficially to peasants being forced to surrender their own supplies.

In an effort to relate the castes as listed by Megasthenes and the traditional Indian division, it has been suggested that the cultivators were the *śūdras*,[5] and that new villages were built in the waste land by deported *śūdras* from over-populated cities and from conquered areas. They were kept unarmed and under state control and the state took their surplus wealth. The *śūdra* helot had come into his own under state control to make large-scale slavery unnecessary for food production. The *Arthaśāstra* suggests the formation of villages either by inducing foreigners to immigrate (*paradeśāpavāhanena*), or by causing the excessive population of the heavily populated centres to emigrate to the newly settled areas (*svadeśābhiṣyandavamanenavā*).[6] The foreigners referred to in this context were most probably people from conquered areas; *śūdras* may well have been deported from over-populated areas. Naturally the *śūdra* peasants would not be the only settlers to move to virgin lands. Members of other professions necessary for the establishment of a village would also be included, as for example carpenters and merchants. The distinction rested no doubt

[1] XV, 1, 40.
[2] *Indica*, XI.
[3] *Arthaśāstra*, II, 35.
[4] R.E. XIII, Kālsi. Bloch, *Les Inscriptions d'Asoka*, p. 125.
[5] Kosambi, *Introduction to the Study of Indian History*, pp. 185, 218.
[6] II, 1.

on *śūdras* being ordered to move and the others going voluntarily for improved economic prospects. Village economy under the Mauryas emphasized the collective efforts of each village.[1] The village tended to develop into a self-sufficient unit in so far as the everyday needs of the villagers were concerned. The overall authority was with the state and the economic integration of the village into a larger unit, the district, was supervised by the administrative officials of the state.

Megasthenes' statement that the land was owned by the king is open to debate and some historians are of the opinion that this was incorrect. In defence of the latter it has been stated that the various texts quoted on this matter should be interpreted as referring to the king as the protector of the land, and not as the owner.[2] The area of the Mauryan empire was so vast and at such dissimilar stages of development, that it is in fact impossible to maintain that one particular type of land ownership existed. In our discussion of the subject we shall restrict ourselves to the region of the Ganges plain, and more particularly Magadha, which area both Megasthenes and the Indian texts were most familiar with. The possibilities of land ownership in Mauryan society are five, the king, the state, large-scale land owners, communal ownership, and the cultivators. Nowhere in any of the sources is there even a hint of land being owned by the cultivators, and this is not surprising since most of them were *śūdras*. Communal ownership was a much later conception and did not become current until quite a few centuries after the Mauryan period.[3]

Fick draws attention to the frequent references to *gahapatis* and *gāma-bhojakas* in the *Jātakas*, both of whom appear to control large areas of land.[4] They are said to have employed hired labourers on the land, whose living conditions were poor but not nearly as bad as those of the *dāsa* (slave). The precise function of the *gahapati* during this period remains uncertain. Fick suggests two possibilities, that the term referred either to the land-owning gentry, or to the rich urban families. If the term referred to the former then it is strange that an extensive land-owning gentry did not produce a political system to incorporate its position, as was the case in later centuries in Mughal India, or in the feudalism of Europe. No known social category of Indian society of the period coincided with such a land-owning gentry. It is possible that the *gahapatis* were a class of entrepreneurs who were responsible for the development of villages in the new areas, and acted as financiers both to the cultivators and the tradesmen.

[1] Rhys Davids, *Buddhist India*, p. 49.

[2] Jayaswal, *Hindu Polity*, vol. ii, pp. 173–88.

[3] It is referred to in a medieval work, *Jaiminī nyāyāmālavistāra*, p. 358.

[4] *The Social Organization in North-East India in Buddha's Time*, pp. 253, 305.

Thus while they were strictly neither land owners nor tax-collectors, they did have a semi-official status. As wealthy merchants many may have acquired land of their own, apart from the state lands, and not sufficiently large as to form an independent source of income. The term *gāmabhojaka* also occurs widely in Pāli literature. Bose interprets it as a landlord, either in the sense of a man who has acquired territory and has had it confirmed by the king, or as a man who has been given a village as reward for services.[1] Here again, the implication was probably an emphasis on the revenue derived from the land rather than on the ownership of the land.

The question may be clarified further by examining a few of the terms and ideas prevalent in the Indian texts. Originally the king was not the owner of the land, which is apparent from the story of the king Viśvakarman Bhauvana who was rebuked by the earth when he treated the land as his private property.[2] But gradually the position changed. Later law books refer distinctly to the ownership of the land by the king. Kātyāyana for instance states that the king is the lord of the earth but not of any other wealth, and that he may take one-sixth of its fruit.[3] As one authority points out, there is a distinction in brahmanical law between the ownership of land and the enjoyment of land.[4] For the former the word *svam* (and its derivatives, *svatra*, *svāmya*, *svāmitra*) are used. For the latter the word *bhoga* is used. Thus there would be a difference between the land personally owned by the king, which he could dispose of as he wished, and the state lands, whose tax he received as the head of the state, and which he did not therefore own, but merely enjoyed their produce. Private donations of land to religious sects or to anyone to whom the king wished to make a private gift, would be made from the lands he owned in his personal capacity and not from the state lands.

Thus we have a reference in the *Arthaśāstra* to the crown lands.[5] These are the lands owned personally by the king, the income of which formed part of what would be termed in modern times the privy purse. The rest of the land theoretically would belong to the state. Here, however, usage complicates theory. Since the king is in fact by this time regarded as the state, it is extremely difficult to distinguish between the king in his personal capacity and the king as the head of the state. The same chapter of the *Arthaśāstra* dealing with the work of the superintendent of agriculture, treats of the administration of the land as if it was owned by the king, which it was, in his capacity as the head of the state. Since the conception of the

[1] *Social and Rural Economy of Northern India*, p. 38.

[2] *Śatapatha Brāhamaṇa*, XIII, 7, I, 15.

[3] Kane, *Kātyāyanasmṛtisaroddhara*, pp. 16–17.

[4] Ghoshal, *The Agrarian System in Ancient India*, p. 84.

[5] II, 24.

state in Indian political thought was not developed at this stage, this distinction in the power and position of the king was not made. The subtle and gradual change from the king not owning the land to the king as the sole land owner is apparent from the work of later theorists.[1] Arrian, maintaining that he is quoting from Megasthenes states that the same payment was made by the cultivators in the monarchies as in the republics. This would stress the point that in the monarchical lands the king, being the representative of the state, was regarded as the owner of the land.

A small section in the *Arthaśāstra* deals with the sale of land and buildings.[2] It appears that this category of land might be bought by those who were willing to bid for it. Timmer explains this passage by the fact that land was not completely and absolutely the property of the individual; the Indian idea of property being based on the just and fair use of a thing, as opposed to the Western idea which implies more absolute ownership.[3] The passage seems to treat this land as subsidiary to the buildings upon it. State ownership of land did not exclude individuals from owning small areas of cultivable land, which they could cultivate themselves with a little assistance. It merely means that small-scale ownership of land was not the dominant feature.

The distinction made by Diodorus between land tribute and the tax paid to the treasury, may be explained as implying a rent for the land distinct from the tax on its produce.[4] This appears to indicate a heavy total taxation. Since Diodorus alone refers to it, it is possible that there may have been some confusion regarding the interpretation of the source from which he obtained this evidence. Alternatively it is possible that in some areas, the tax of one-quarter of the produce applied only to certain crops, the land tribute being the basic revenue. Ghoshal has pointed out that later two types of revenue was obtained from the land. One was known as *bhāga*, based on the idea of the early Vedic tribute or *bali*, and the other was *hiraṇya*, that is, the cash tax on special classes of crops.[5] Thus it may have been possible under very special conditions to apply both types of revenue in one area.

Although Arrian does not mention the amount that was paid in tax, other writers quoting Megasthenes give the figure as one-quarter of the produce of the soil.[6] Strabo states that the cultivators receive one-quarter of the produce as their payment, the rest of the produce presumably going to

[1] Manu, *Dharmaśāstra*, VIII, 39.
[2] III, 9.
[3] *Megasthenes en de Indische Maatschappij*, p. 123.
[4] Diodorus, II, 40.
[5] *The Agrarian System in Ancient India*, p. 6.
[6] *Indica*, XI; Diodorus, II, 40; Strabo, XV, 1, 40.

the king. This discrepancy may have been due to an error on the part of Strabo or the source from which he took his information, and, instead of stating that the cultivators paid one-quarter of the produce to the king, he states that they received the same amount. The other possibility is that he is here referring to those cultivators who are working as labourers on the crown lands although he does not make this clear. They would receive one-quarter of the produce as their wages. The remaining three-quarters would go to the king, providing a substantial income for him. Such revenue is referred to in the *Arthaśāstra*.[1] The revenue being assessed at one-quarter was perhaps a general estimate or was applicable only in very fertile areas such as the region around Pāṭaliputra with which Megasthenes was most familiar. The precise amount must have varied according to local conditions. An example of such a variation in tax occurs in the *Arthaśāstra*, where the type of irrigation provided, changes the amount of tax on the water, this ranging from one-fifth to one-third.[2] The same must undoubtedly have been the case with land tax, but with possibly a smaller degree of variation. One-quarter of the produce is more than the normal amount suggested by most Indian texts, which is one-sixth.[3] Variations occur of one-eighth, one-tenth or even one-twelfth. The *Arthaśāstra* advises that in a period of emergency, the tax may be raised to one-third or one-quarter, or a system of double cropping may be adopted, but only in fertile areas irrigated by rain water.[4] Some historians have maintained that one-quarter was a high tax and consequently a heavy burden on the people, which could easily have led to a justified rebellion against the government.[5] Admittedly one-quarter as a regular tax was high, but later centuries saw worse, when during the reign of Akbar for example, one-third was the regular amount in tax.[6]

The Rummindei inscription is the only Aśokan inscription which makes a precise reference to taxation.[7] We are told that because the village of Lumbinī was the birth-place of the Buddha, the king exempted it from taxes, and it was paying only an eighth share of the produce. The word used for the first item is *udbalike*, which generally conveys the meaning of freeing from *bali* or tribute. This probably refers to the land tribute which every village had to pay. The *aṭṭhabhāgiye* or eighth share, no doubt refers to the produce of the soil.[8] It is uncertain whether this was a reduction from

[1] I, 6.
[2] II, 24.
[3] Ghoshal, *Contributions to the History of the Hindu Revenue System*, p. 58; Manu, *Dharmaśāstra*, VII, 130.
[4] V, 2.
[5] Raychaudhuri, *Political History of Ancient India*, pp. 363 ff.
[6] Moreland, *The Agrarian System of Moslem India*, p. 91.
[7] Bloch, *Les Inscriptions d'Asoka*, p. 157.
[8] Fleet, *JRAS*, 1908, p. 479.

the normal amount paid, which may have been a quarter or one-sixth, or whether it referred to the continuance of the usual amount of one-eighth. Had it been the latter there would have been no necessity for the king to have mentioned the tax. Since the village was now exempted from land tribute, it is more likely that the tax would be reduced by only a small amount and not by half. Thus the usual tax in this area must have been one-sixth. This would suggest that the assessment was lower in the area of Rummindei as compared to the tax of one-quarter in the region of Pāṭaliputra. This was probably due to the fact that the land as far north as Rummindei, was not as fertile as that nearer the Ganges. Variations in taxation must have been introduced as the settlements spread farther away from the fertile region of the Ganges basin. It is therefore possible that Megasthenes' statement of the assessment of revenue being one-quarter was based on the amount collected in the vicinity of the capital, which he assumed applied to the entire country.

Another interesting fact which emerges from the Rummindei inscription is that the king deals directly with the question of exemption from land tribute. If there had been any intermediary in the form of a land owner, the king would have had some difficulty in granting the exemption, since it would have affected the land owners' economic position. One of the possible ways of building up a system of landlords appears not to have been in use. Megasthenes mentions that military officers were paid in cash.[1] This eliminated the necessity of granting them land revenue by way of payment as was done by most later Indian governments both Hindu and Muslim. Land revenue given to religious sects did not imply a transfer of ownership but literally only the gift of the revenue, so that the members of the sect in question did not have to work for a living. Where the transfer of land ownership was involved, it was known as a *brahmadeya* gift.[2] Certain rights of the king listed in the *Arthaśāstra* imply that his ownership of the land was tacitly accepted even though it was not theoretically stated.[3] The fact that the king could demand a compulsory second crop in time of need is such a right.

It is clear that in the Mauryan period the state officials such as the revenue collectors made a direct assessment of the land under cultivation. The assessment was based not on the combined lands of the village as a whole, but considered the details regarding each cultivator and member of the village. The first step in the process of assessment was the subdivision

[1] Diodorus, II, 41.
[2] Bose, *Social and Rural Economy of Northern India*, p. 18.
[3] V, 2.
[4] *Arthaśāstra*, II, 35.

of the lands of the village into categories of high, middle, and low quality. The village was then listed under one of the following heads: villages that were exempted from taxation (*parihāraka*), those that supplied soldiers (*āyūdhīya*), those that paid their taxes in the form of grain, cattle, gold (*hiraṇya*) or raw material (*kupya*), and those that supplied free labour (*viṣṭi*) and dairy produce in lieu of taxes. It is thus amply clear that the administration took into consideration all local features before any assessment was made.

Megasthenes states that there were no famines in India,[1] which is something of an exaggeration, since Indian sources do mention their occurrence. Jaina tradition has it that there was a famine in the reign of Candragupta Maurya.[2] Evidence of such conditions may also be gathered from the two Mauryan inscriptions at Sohgaurā and Mahāsthān, which are concerned specifically with measures to ameliorate famine conditions in the Ganges valley.[3] Either Megasthenes was attempting to describe India in such glowing terms that he wished his readers to believe that it was a land of plenty which never suffered from famines, or, as is more likely, he left India just before any famine occurred.

Increased centralization under the Mauryas, more particularly during the reign of Aśoka, meant an increased control of the state over the economy. The administrative system was improved and developed and was made capable of examining and controlling even the minutiae of the economic structure. The king in turn, both controlling and co-ordinating this system, assumed a corresponding increase in power. The cultivator came into direct contact with the administration, which to him signified the state. The king became an even more remote symbol than before, and the immediate world of the cultivator was concerned with officials, a condition which was to remain current for many centuries.

The third caste listed by Megasthenes is described as that of shepherds and herdsmen.[4] They are said to be nomads and are the only group of people who are permitted to hunt animals. They were probably called in when an area had been cleared and they were needed to rid it of whatever wild animals remained. There is no confirmation in Indian sources of their existing as a major class, but the mention of the Ābhīra or Ahīr caste in later texts would suggest that they existed in smaller groups, probably as a sub-caste. Megasthenes adds that they paid tribute in cattle. It may be suggested that these were the remnants of the pastoral Aryans, who were

[1] Diodorus, II, 36.

[2] *Pariśiṣṭaparvan*, p. lxxi, VIII, pp. 415 ff.

[3] Sircar, *Select Inscriptions . . .*, pp. 82, 85.

[4] Diodorus, II, 40.

still nomads living on the waste lands and had not yet settled down in an agricultural occupation.

The *Arthaśāstra* does not pay much attention to herdsmen or shepherds. Its remarks on this subject are largely general, as for instance the statement that, 'the king shall make provision for pasture grounds on uncultivable tracts'.[1] That there was no particular caste whose work was the care of animals is confirmed by a lack of evidence to the contrary. Megasthenes looked on them as a caste because he was thinking in terms of economic divisions. In the hierarchy of the social order the shepherds may have been included among the *śūdras*. Although, as we have suggested above, they may have been of Aryan origin, nevertheless the nature of their occupation would relegate them to the lowest order. If they tended domestic animals then they were probably included with the cultivators. If they were huntsmen leading a nomadic life they would still be regarded as degenerate Aryans by those that were now living in settled communities.

Of the domestic animals reared and maintained by herdsmen cows, buffaloes, goats, sheep, asses, and camels are mentioned.[2] Horses and elephants were also maintained but they came under a different category and had their own superintendents, presumably because they were important for military purposes.[3] Draught oxen are also referred to,[4] so the wooden plough drawn by an ox must have been known to the cultivator. The cow is certainly the most important of these domestic animals. There is no reference to its being a sacred animal, but the value of the cow is appreciated. Dairy products and hide were regarded as the chief commodities for which the cow was bred. This is borne out by the statement in the *Arthaśāstra* that when a man rears a herd of cows he has to pay the owner a certain quantity of clarified butter per year, together with the branded hide of the cows that may have died during that year.[5] Although the cow was not killed for its meat, nevertheless cow's flesh was eaten. We are told that the cowherd may sell either the flesh or the dried flesh of the cow when it has died.[6] Another passage states, 'Cattle such as a calf, a bull or a milch cow shall not be slaughtered'.[7] The reason for this is obvious since they were animals of labour and provided dairy produce, and were consequently of considerable value. Presumably if cattle died a natural death then the flesh could be sold. With regard to Megasthenes' remark that the herdsmen paid tribute in cattle, it appears from the *Arthaśāstra* that the tribute was paid not in cattle but in dairy produce. A certain

[1] II, 2.
[2] *Arthaśāstra*, II, 29.
[3] Ibid., II, 30, 31.
[4] Ibid., 29.
[5] II, 29.
[6] Ibid.
[7] II, 26.

percentage or share of the produce is given either to the owner of the herd, or to the superintendent of cows.[1] The reference to the owner of the herd points to the fact of private ownership of cattle. Herds were not maintained only by the state but also by wealthy individuals. The work of the superintendent included the collecting of taxes, inquiring into the condition of the animals, and the work of the herdsmen.

Aśoka made repeated requests in his edicts that animals should be treated with kindness and care. At one point he mentions that arrangements have been made for the medical treatment of animals in his kingdom and also in neighbouring areas and countries.[2] Furthermore trees have been planted along the main highways, and wells have been dug, so that men and cattle may have access to water and may rest in the shade of the trees. In a further edict he calls upon his subjects to abstain from killing animals. He himself had reduced the number of animals killed daily in the royal kitchen to two peacocks and a deer and even the killing of these would not continue for long. With the same idea in mind, he discontinued the favourite pastime of earlier monarchs, the royal hunts.[3] This policy was no doubt prompted both by a genuine regard for animals and by the fear that indiscriminate killing would harm the country's live-stock. The sacrificing of animals was a particularly harmful custom, since, to propitiate the god fully, the best animal of the herd was selected as the victim. Had non-violence been Aśoka's only purpose in instituting this ban on the killing of animals, then surely by way of an example the royal kitchen would immediately have ceased to cook meat.

The 5th Pillar Edict contains a detailed list of animals that are not to be killed under any circumstances, and a further list of animals and creatures which are declared inviolable on certain days.[4] The superficially arbitrary nature of the first list has long been a great puzzle. Why geese, queen-ants, and iguanas should be declared inviolable seems hard to explain. The king concludes the list by stating that all quadrupeds which are neither useful nor edible should not be killed. This is a justifiable ban on unnecessarily killing animals. If this list of animals is compared with the names of animals mentioned in Book XIV of the *Arthaśāstra*, some connection can be traced. This section is devoted to the making of spells and poisons incorporating various parts of the bodies of a wide range of creatures. The lizard family occurs with great frequency, and as the iguana is also a member of the lizard family, we may postulate that some of these animals

[1] II, 29.
[2] II R.E. Girnār. Bloch, *Les Inscriptions d'Asoka*, p. 94.
[3] I, IV, VIII R.E. Girnār. Ibid., pp. 91, 98, 111.
[4] Ibid., p. 165.

were declared inviolable because they were used in the making of poisons and magic potions. Aśoka's disapproval of sacrifices and what he calls useless ceremonies and rituals is apparent from a number of edicts.[1] His objection to the use of certain animals in magical rites, may have resulted in this edict; this may have been a subtle attempt on his part to undermine the influence of sorcerers and magicians on the more gullible section of the population.

In the chapter dealing with the superintendent of the slaughter-house, there is a list of animals and birds that are to be protected from molestation.[2] Animals with a human form are included. This probably refers to monkeys. Fish of all kinds are mentioned in the list, and also the following birds: swans, geese, parrots, and *maināś*, which are included in the edict. Animals coming under the general description of 'other auspicious animals' are included in the edict. Unfortunately there is no explanation in the *Arthaśāstra* as to why these animals should be protected. The ban on catching certain fish can be explained on the basis of their being inedible.[3] The edict continues with the statement that she-goats, ewes, and sows which are with young or in milk, and young ones under six months are also inviolable. This statement hardly needs any explanation. Aśoka obviously considered it a heartless act to kill animals in such conditions, and furthermore they were all domesticated animals, bred for meat and subsidiary products.

Fish generally are prohibited from being caught and on certain days even the sale of fish is prohibited. The latter has been explained on the basis that the indiscriminate catching of fish interferes with their natural breeding habits.[4] Thus the ban on the sale of fish on certain days, mentioned in the edict, was a means of regulating the sale of fish evenly throughout the year. Fish were regarded as an important commodity in Mauryan times. A toll had to be paid on the capture of fish and birds which amounted to one-tenth of the catch.[5] Although in the *Arthaśāstra* fish is classed as edible food and the organization of fisheries was given much thought, it was also used for various other purposes. The value of fish manure for instance was known. The poisoning of fish in streams running into enemy territory was one of the many means of undermining enemy strength, and it would seem, therefore, that fish was commonly eaten.

[1] IX R.E. Girnār. Bloch, Ibid., p. 113.

[2] *Arthaśāstra*, II, 26.

[3] Hora, *Archives Internationales d'histoire des Sciences*, No. 15, 1951, pp. 405–12. The author states that the fish named in the edict are common to Gangetic waters, and are regarded as inedible even to this day. They were probably known to be inedible even in the third century B.C.

[4] Ibid.

[5] *Arthaśāstra*, II, 1; II, 2; II, 24; XIV, 1.

There is a curious reference in the Kandahār inscription to the hunters and fishermen of the king. It occurs in a sentence which reads as follows,

'... And the king refrains from [eating] living beings, and indeed other men and whosoever [were] the king's huntsmen and fishermen have ceased from hunting ...'[1]

It may be suggested that this refers to the hunters and fishermen employed by the king on his estates or for his private purpose. We know for instance that Aśoka stopped the royal hunts. But if fish was an important article of diet in Mauryan times it would have been impossible for the king to have banned the catching of fish. The wild forest areas must have needed the hunters to make the regions comparatively safe for travellers. It is hardly possible that all the hunters and fishermen throughout the empire had ceased to hunt and to fish.

One of the more important results of the political unification of India under the Mauryas, and the control of a strong centralized government, was the impetus given to the various crafts. With the improvement of administration, the organization of trade became easier and the crafts gradually assumed the shape of small-scale industries. Megasthenes refers to the artisans and craftsmen as the fourth class in his seven-fold division of Indian society. He writes of them that some pay tribute and render to the state certain prescribed services. Diodorus maintains that they were the armourers and implement makers. They were exempted from paying tax and instead were paid wages by the royal exchequer.[2] Arrian explains that most of the artisans and handicraftsmen paid a tax to the state. The exception were armourers and ship-builders who received wages from the state.[3] It would appear that certain members of the artisan class were exempted from tax, since they were employed directly by the state. In the case of armourers it is not surprising that they were state employees. Those that rendered the state certain services probably worked for the state for a fixed number of days per year. This would be regarded as service tax in addition to the regular tax.

It is apparent from remarks both in European and Indian sources that the artisans were systematically organized. For instance there is general agreement that finished products were not only taxed immediately, but were also stamped by a special officer with a particular stamp, in order to distinguish the new goods from the old unsold goods.[4] Such a high degree of organization on the administrative side meant that the producers of the

[1] *JA*, vol. ccxlvi, pp. 2–3.
[2] Diodorus, II, 41; Strabo, XV, 1, 46.
[3] *Indica*, XII.
[4] Strabo, XV, 1, 50; *Arthaśāstra*, II, 21.

commodity must have been organized into a working system as well. The sources frequently refer to the system of guilds which began in the early Buddhist period and continued through the Mauryan period. Fick, in tracing the history of the guilds suggests that topography aided their development, in as much as particular areas of a city were generally inhabited by all tradesmen of a certain craft.[1] Tradesmen's villages were also known, where one particular craft was centred, largely due to the easy availability of raw material.[2] The three chief requisites necessary for the rise of a guild system were in existence. Firstly, the localization of occupation was possible, secondly the hereditary character of professions was recognized, and lastly the idea of a guild leader or *jeṭṭhaka* was a widely accepted one.[3] The extension of trade in the Mauryan period must have helped considerably in developing and stabilizing the guilds, which at first were an intermediate step between a tribe and a caste. In later years they were dominated by strict rules, which resulted in some of them gradually becoming castes. Another early incentive to forming guilds must have been competition. Economically it was better to work in a body than to work individually, as a corporation would provide added social status, and when necessary, assistance could be sought from other members. By gradual stages guilds developed into the most important industrial bodies in their areas.

Having arrived at a point when the guilds controlled almost the entire manufactured output, they found that they had to meet greater demands than they could cater for by their own labour and that of their families; consequently they had to employ hired labour. This consisted of two categories, the *karmakaras* and the *bhṛtakas* who were regarded as free labourers working for a regular wage, and the *dāsas* who were slaves.[4] Aśoka refers to both categories in his edicts when he speaks of the *bhatakas* and the *dāsas*.[5] Thus by the Mauryan period the guilds had developed into fairly large-scale organizations, recognized at least in the northern half of the sub-continent if not throughout the country. It would seem that they were registered by local officials and had a recognized status, as there was a prohibition against any guilds other than the local co-operative ones entering the villages.[6] This suggests that a guild could not move from one area to another without official permission. Furthermore they must by now

[1] Fick, *The Social Organization in North-East India in Buddha's Time*, pp. 279, 280.

[2] e.g. the carpenters' village outside Banaras, which developed because of the forest near by. *Alīnacitta Jātaka*, II, 18.

[3] There are references in the *Jātakas* to the *jeṭṭhaka* or president of a particular craft. *Jarudpana Jātaka*, II, p. 295.

[4] *Arthaśāstra*, III, 13, 14.

[5] IX R.E. Girnār. Bloch, *Les Inscriptions d'Asoka*, p. 115.

[6] *Arthaśāstra*, II, 1.

have developed a social hierarchy within their class of artisans, based on their occupations. A chapter in the *Arthaśāstra* describing the buildings within the city throws some light on the social status of various professions; this varies according to their location and in relation to the parts of the city inhabited by their social superiors.[1]

Because of the guild organization individual members possessed certain rights. For example they were protected against injury and theft. If a craftsman was hurt, the person responsible was put to death.[2] Presumably this law only applied during the time he was actually working. A person accused of stealing articles belonging to an artisan had to pay a very heavy fine of 100 *paṇas*.[3] There were equally strict rules against deception by artisans. People were told to be cautious when trusting money to artisans, even when they belonged to guilds.[4] The fact of belonging to a guild must have acted as a check on fraudulent practices. If a particular artisan was caught in such an act it is unlikely that he would be permitted to continue as a member of the guild, and for an artisan to work independently appears to have been extremely difficult.

Wages were determined according to the quality of the work and the quantity produced. The wages of the weaver for instance, depended on whether the threads were spun fine, coarse, or of middle quality, and in proportion to the quantity woven.[5] The system of fixed wages for a given amount was also known. Further payment or reward was made for work done during holidays. Strict supervision and examination of the product was enforced. Fines and penalties for inferior or fraudulent work were very severe. Kauṭalya was of the opinion that wages were to be paid according to the amount of the work completed.[6] Thus if a commission was half-finished the artisan was to be paid only for the completed part. The whole payment would be made after the work was completed either by the artisan or a substitute, or else the artisan would have to compensate the man who commissioned it. This system was applicable both in the case of individual artisans and the guild as a unit.

It would seem that artisans' guilds were not the only ones in existence. The corporation of soldiers played an important part in the recruiting of an army.[7] It is clear that these were not regular soldiers who had formed themselves into guilds (*śreṇī*), but were more akin to the modern reserve force. The army, we are told, consisted of hereditary troops, hired troops, corporations of soldiers, troops belonging to an ally, and wild tribes. The

[1] *Arthaśāstra*, II, 4.
[2] Ibid., III, 19; Strabo, XV, 1, 54.
[3] *Arthaśāstra*, II, 13.
[4] Ibid., IV, 1.
[5] Ibid., II, 13.
[6] Ibid., III, 14.
[7] Ibid., IX, 2.

term hereditary troops undoubtedly refers to the standing army, which was directly employed by the state on a permanent basis. Hired troops were temporarily employed as and when they were needed. The remaining categories of soldiers, other than the corporation soldiers, were probably also employed only in time of need. Unlike the cultivators, the artisans were probably allowed to carry arms, and therefore could be called upon to serve in the army during a war. Those that were fit to be thus called up were perhaps listed and, in addition to their guild, belonged to a military corporation.[1] That they were not as efficient as the trained soldiers is clear from a further paragraph in the same chapter. Here it is explained that the soldiers belonging to a corporation and not to the regular army, can be put into action when the enemy's army consists of similar troops, suggesting thereby guerilla warfare rather than pitched battles.

The *Arthaśāstra* in discussing the work of administrative superintendents, relates it to the working of a number of guilds. Evidence of the products manufactured by these guilds is corroborated by European classical sources and by archaeological remains. Weapons manufactured by the armoury are listed in great detail.[2] Arrian mentions that Indian infantrymen carried bows, javelins, and swords, and each cavalryman was armed with two lances.[3] Excavations at Hastināpur have revealed the regular use of metal for domestic and military purposes showing a technological advance over the earlier period.[4] Barbed and socketed arrow-heads of iron were found amongst the weapons.

A wide range of metals was known and special characteristics as regards the mining and manufacture of these are noted. This knowledge extends both to utilitarian metals such as iron, copper, and lead, and to precious metals such as gold and silver. There are remains of copper antimony rods and nail-parers from Hastināpur and other copper and bronze objects from the Mauryan strata at Bhir Mound in Taxila.[5] The copper bolt found on the Aśokan pillar at Rāmpūrvā and the copper cast coins dated to the Mauryan period are further evidence of the use of this metal.[6] The demand for iron appears to have increased during the Mauryan period. Iron objects at the earlier levels at Bhir Mound consisted of adzes, knives, and scrapers. The later level shows a wider use of iron, including weapons, tools, agricultural implements, and household vessels.[7]

Precious metals such as gold and silver and precious stones of many

[1] A similar system prevailed in England during the Tudor and Stuart periods.
[2] *Arthaśāstra*, II, 18.
[3] *Indica*, XVI.
[4] Lal, *Ancient India*, 1954, vol. x, p. 16.
[5] Ibid.; Marshall, *Taxila*, vol. i, p. 103.
[6] Panchanan Neogi, *Copper in Ancient India*, pp. 18–20.
[7] Marshall, *Taxila*, vol. i, pp. 104, 107.

kinds were much in evidence during this period. Kauṭalya has a fair amount to say on the work of the superintendent of gold and the duties of the state goldsmith.[1] A further chapter is concerned entirely with the examining of gems that are brought to the royal treasury.[2] Strabo describes an Indian festive procession where royal attendants carry an abundance of objects made of gold or inlaid with precious stones.[3] Evidence of jewellery of various kinds was found at Hastināpur and at the site of Bhir Mound. It seems that the goldsmiths' and jewellers' guilds were kept busy with royal orders and commissions from the wealthy citizens.

The craft of stone cutting and working in stone needs no literary evidence to confirm the excellence of its quality. The Aśokan pillars with their capitals are sufficient evidence. How this degree of excellence was reached is still something of a puzzle, since no example of stone sculpture which can be dated with certainty to a pre-Mauryan period is extant. The extensive use of wood in pre-Mauryan times and the equally extensive use of stone in the post-Mauryan period, suggests that the Mauryan period itself was a period of transition in this matter.[4] It is fairly evident that most of the craftsmen responsible for the stone work of the Aśokan period which has survived were trained in the north-western part of the empire, probably at Taxila. The uniformity of workmanship certainly suggests a common centre. In a place like Taxila the Indian craftsmen would also be in contact with Iranian craftsmen who were already familiar with the medium of stone. Remains of Mathura and Chunar sandstone at Bhir Mound suggest a confirmation of this hypothesis.[5]

The guild of wood workers must also have been amongst the more active guilds. The *Arthaśāstra* suggests that cities were built largely of wood since the city superintendents had to pay special attention to precautions against fire.[6] Fire is listed as the first of the national calamities.[7] Although there are indications of brickwork and in fact archaeologists recognize a particular sized brick as Mauryan, wood must have been used fairly extensively.[8] It was probably a cheaper building material than stone since the clearing of the forests covering the waste lands must have provided ample supplies of timber. Pāṭaliputra had a wooden palisade surrounding it.[9] Associated with woodwork are craftsmen working in ivory and bone. Remains of ornamental objects in these two materials were found at Bhir Mound.[10] Art-historians have maintained that much of the

[1] II, 13, 14.
[2] II, 11.
[3] Strabo, XV, 1, 69.
[4] Cf. *Jātakas*, I, p. 470.
[5] Marshall, *Taxila*, vol. i, p. 103.
[6] II, 36.
[7] IV, 3.
[8] Lal, *Ancient India*, 1954, vol. x, p. 15.
[9] *ARASI*, 1912–13, pp. 53 ff.
[10] Marshall, *Taxila*, vol. i, p. 103.

low-relief carving on the gateways at Sanchi was based on ivory prototypes.[1]

Guilds of textile workers must also have been prominent during the Mauryan period. The *Arthaśāstra* mentions places specializing in certain textiles.[2] Cotton fabrics were made at Madhurā, Aparānta, Kaliṅga, Kāśī, Vaṅga, Vatsa, and Mahiṣa. Cotton manufactured at Aparānta may well have been exported from Broach to the west. Other varieties of fabrics are also mentioned. Among them are the *dukūla*, a white, soft textile, and the *kṣauma*, a type of linen. The manufacture of woollen blankets and other woollen fabrics was also known. Greek sources mention processions in which important persons appeared dressed in garments made of cloth embroidered and inter-woven with gold.[3]

Surprisingly enough Kauṭalya does not mention the potter's craft, beyond a brief mention of trade in earthenware pots. Considering the frequency with which pots and potsherds are found in Mauryan sites, the potters' guilds must have been flourishing ones. Earthenware pottery was common enough not to warrant special mention. But since the black polished ware was extensively used by the upper classes of Mauryan society, and was evidently a more exclusive type of pottery one would expect Kauṭalya to have given some description of it.[4] However, since he does not claim to mention every craft, but only those that are necessary to his general exposition, it is possible that the pottery makers were thus left out.

Trade regulations are carefully planned and suited to a well-organized system. The sale of merchandise is strictly supervised by the state. The superintendent of commerce, when valuing an article, takes into consideration the rise and fall of prices and the means of transportation.[5] The latter causes a difference in the price of the article, since transportation by water is cheaper than transportation by land. Merchants importing foreign goods can claim a remission of trade tax, so that they can derive a profit from the sale of goods from a foreign country. The trade tax was probably the same as the state dues. This consisted of one-fifth of the toll dues, and the toll tax was one-fifth of the value of the commodity. There was a control on prices as well, since it was the responsibility of the superintendent of commerce to prevent the merchant from making too great a profit such as would harm the people. The percentage of profit to the merchant was fixed and excess profits went to the treasury.[6] The amount consisted of 5 per cent

[1] *History and Culture of the Indian People*, vol. ii, p. 541.

[2] II, 11.

[3] Strabo, XV, 1, 69.

[4] See Appendix IV.

[5] *Arthaśāstra*, II, 16.

[6] Ibid., II, 22.

on local commodities and 10 per cent on foreign produce.[1] This beneficial control on prices was a boon during normal periods. However, in times of need, when the treasury required replenishing, the merchant was no doubt encouraged to ask for a high price, since that would result in a larger amount for the treasury as well. The general control over prices and profits extended even to regulating the earnings of the middleman.[2] It would seem that supply and demand were also regulated, both within a certain area and with regard to a particular commodity. But as it was not possible to calculate overall production and consumption, this measure could take effect only in a very superficial way. Since the process of controlling and diverting production was an extremely slow one in those times, crises in over-production of a particular commodity must surely have occurred. The sale or mortgage of old goods could only take place in the presence of the superintendent.[3] This rule was enforced largely to avoid deception, to prevent old ware being passed off for new.

The general tax levied on merchandise appears to have been one-tenth, although it probably varied with each commodity.[4] It ranged from one twenty-fifth, the tax on certain qualities of textiles, to one-sixth, the tax on flowers, vegetables, and so forth. Since all merchandise was taxed, it was a punishable offence to buy anything in the place where it was manufactured, i.e. before it had been taxed and priced. Commodities manufactured in the country were stamped in the place of manufacture, those that came from foreign parts were stamped at the toll-gates. Since the toll was based on the value of the commodity it was probably paid in money and not in kind. Although the tax on foreign goods might be remitted so as to encourage foreign trade, foreign traders were not particularly welcome. The artisan or the merchant was made responsible for the good behaviour of another member of his profession who came and resided in his home.[5] Thus a person known to the former would be vouched for, but a stranger would have no one to act as a referee for him. Any fraudulency with regard to weighing and measuring a commodity in order to fix the price was severely punished.[6] The degree of punishment for the degree of crime in this matter is stated in detail. Similarly the gaining of more than the specified profit is considered a punishable offence.

About the practice of usury, Megasthenes states that Indians neither put out money at usury, nor know how to borrow.[7] In view of the economic activity we have described above this seems hardly possible. From Buddhist

[1] *Arthaśāstra*, II, 21.
[2] Ibid., IV, 2.
[3] IV, 2.
[4] I, 13; II, 22.
[5] II, 36.
[6] IV, 2.
[7] Aelian, V, L, iv, 1.

literature it would appear that the commercial community of the time had a highly developed sense of business administration, judging by the way in which resources and fortunes were consolidated. An appropriate passage runs thus,

'The wise and moral man shines like a fire on a hilltop, making money like the bee which does not hurt the flower. Such a man makes his pile as an anthill, gradually. The man grown wealthy thus can help his family and firmly bind his friends to himself. He should divide his money in four parts: on one part he should live, with two expand his trade, and the fourth he should save against a rainy day.'[1]

It is unlikely that there was no system of private banking to assist a business man in his transactions. Kauṭalya deals with organized money lending in the *Arthaśāstra*. It would seem that there was no ban on such activity, since money could even be lent from the treasury on interest paid at fixed periods.[2] Details are given of the amount of interest that can be legitimately charged in certain situations.[3] Fifteen per cent per annum appears to have been the average rate of interest on borrowed money. A special commercial interest is mentioned (*vyāvahārikī*), and this works out at 60 per cent per annum. This high rate of interest was probably charged for commercial activities involving sea voyages or lengthy travels. It is possible that the rate of interest was controlled by the state and this may have given the impression of there being no usury.

Greek sources speak of tax evaders being sentenced to capital punishment (*kleptim totelos*).[4] It has been argued that this may not mean evading the tax, but stealing it from the collector.[5] In the *Arthaśāstra* there is no mention of capital punishment for such a crime.[6] The punishment is merely the confiscation of goods or the payment of a fine. As the latter source places considerable emphasis on the crime of stealing from the collector, it would seem that it was known and practised. It is probably more correct to treat the Greek phrase as a reference to this crime.

In consulting the *Arthaśāstra* for evidence of economic organization during the Mauryan period, and the administration of trade and commerce, it must be remembered that the picture presented by Kauṭalya is that of the ideal state. We cannot accept the belief that the Mauryan state was run along these lines in every detail. The *Arthaśāstra* suggested general policies and described various ways in which these policies could be implemented.

[1] *Dīgha Nikāya*, iii, p. 188 (trans. A. L. Basham).

[2] II, 8.

[3] III, 11.

[4] Strabo, XV, 1, 50.

[5] Timmer, *Megasthenes en de Indische Maatschappij*, p. 217.

[6] II, 8.

Undoubtedly the general policy of the *Arthaśāstra* and that of the Mauryan state were very similar and the administrative system of the Mauryas was largely inspired by the ideas in the *Arthaśāstra*. It is, however, reasonable to expect that there were discrepancies. Economic organization on such a detailed scale was a new feature in the politico-economic system of the country. The practical application of these ideas must certainly have resulted in a few lapses. It is difficult to believe for instance, that merchants importing goods from a foreign country or a distant area, with all its attendant risks, would be willing to accept so low a profit as the official rate of one-tenth which we have already discussed. It is more probable that the officers may have been bribed and the matter of profits privately settled between the superintendents and the merchant.

Trade routes during this period tended to follow the main highways and the navigable rivers. Sea trade was conducted both with the West and with the northern coast of Burma. There is an interesting discussion in the *Arthaśāstra* on the efficiency of land and water routes.[1] The water route is certainly cheaper but it is not a permanent route nor can it be defended in the same way as can a land route. A route that follows the coastline is preferred to a mid-ocean route, because the former may touch the various ports along the coast and thus perhaps enhance commerce. A navigable river is thought to be a fairly safe route. Of the land routes, those going northwards towards the Himalayas are said to be better than those going south. This was presumably because the northern region was better known and was better served with well-known roads than the southern region. The opening up of the south by northern traders was at that period a comparatively recent venture.

Kauṭalya, however, contradicts the above suggestion that the northern routes are better, because he evaluates the routes on the basis of the trade connections they provide. He decides that trade prospects in the south are more numerous and the commodities available are of greater value than in the north. It is suggested that of the routes leading to the south it is wiser to follow those traversing the mining areas as these are frequented by people. This would avoid the necessity of long distances of solitary travel and it would again allow an opportunity of trading en route with the people and habitations. A cart-track is preferred to a foot-path and a route which can be traversed by pack animals is naturally all to the good.

A list of the various routes in use in pre-Mauryan India has been compiled largely from Buddhist sources.[2] These routes must have continued in use during the Mauryan period. The more important of these

[1] VII, 12.

[2] Rhys Davids, *Buddhist India*, pp. 103 ff.

routes were the north to south-west route (from Śrāvastī to Pratiṣṭhāna), the north to south-east route (from Śrāvastī to Rājagṛha), and the east-west route which followed the river courses of the Ganges and the Yamunā. The desert of Rājasthāna was known. The port of Bhārukaccha (Broach) on the west coast was frequently mentioned, and Baveru (Babylon) was known as a trading centre in the west. These routes we may assume were frequently used by the Buddhists in the fifth and fourth centuries B.C. These were the nucleus of the communications which were later to spread across the extent of the Mauryan empire. The Buddhist emphasis on pilgrimage no doubt assisted in the care and maintenance of these routes. At the same time the development of commerce both along the Ganges and in the western part of the country made it imperative that good communications be maintained.

With the spread of the Mauryan empire from Pāṭaliputra outwards communications had naturally to be extended as far as the frontier or even farther. The development of bureaucratic administration contributed to the necessity for such communications, since the officials had constantly to be in touch with the capital cities. Thus, there were not only the main routes traversing the empire or radiating from Pāṭaliputra, but the provinces had also to be served with their own smaller network of routes. Mauryan administration seems to have employed a special group of officials whose concern was with the building and maintenance of roads. These are referred to by Megasthenes as *agoranomoi*, the literal meaning of the term being 'market commissioners'.[1] But their work was related to communications. They were responsible for the construction of roads. At every ten stadia signposts were erected recording distances, by-roads, and other such information. This remark is reminiscent of the 7th Pillar Edict where Aśoka states that he has had wells dug at every eight *kos* which is a distance of about nine miles.[2]

The Royal Highway from the north-west (in the region of Taxila) to Pāṭaliputra was considered the most important route; it has continued to be so through the centuries, being familiar today to modern Indians as the Grand Trunk Road. It has been described in some detail in a Latin

[1] Strabo, XV, 1, 50.

[2] Bloch, *Les Inscriptions d'Asoka*, p. 170. Bloch has translated the term *aḍḍhakosikya* as half a *kos*, but we prefer Hultzsch's reading based on Fleet's argument that the *aḍḍha* is derived from the Sanskrit *aṣṭam* (Hultzsch, *Corpus Inscriptionum Indicarum*, vol. i, p. 135 n. 1; *JRAS*, 1906, pp. 401 ff.). The precise length of a *kos* is difficult to ascertain, since the length of the *yojana* (4 *kos*) varied from five to nine miles. The digging of wells and the construction of rest houses at every half a mile would not have been necessary. The same every nine miles would be the right distance in view of the fact that travellers who walked for most of their journey would need to rest after a nine-mile walk.

source.[1] There was an extension eastwards which was said to have reached as far as Tāmluk or even farther to the mouth of the Ganges. It was equally important from both the commercial and the strategic point of view. Before the development of sea-trade it was the chief trade route with the west, Taxila being the point of exchange. Even for inland trade it was frequently used since there was considerable exchange of goods between the Ganges region and the north-west.[2]

Evidence of routes to south India is scanty. Journeys as far as the Vindhyas were probably not extraordinary events, but travelling farther south may have been something of an adventure. The sea route along the western coast from Broach and Kathiawar to ports on the south-western coastline and Ceylon, appears to have been in use. We are told for instance that Vijaya, the first king of Ceylon travelled from Sopārā on the west coast to Ceylon.[3] The east coast sea route appears to have had heavier traffic. Ships sailed from Tāmluk to various ports along the east coast, some going farther south to Ceylon.[4] The importance of Kaliṅga to the Mauryan empire was due largely to its strategic position. Lying between the Mahānadī and Godāvarī rivers it could control the sea traffic between Vaṅga and the south. Kaliṅga in hostile hands would thus be a perpetual danger to this route. Furthermore it obstructed the land routes to the south, since the easier routes following the river valleys were in the Kaliṅgan territory.

Land routes across the Deccan plateau would naturally tend to follow the river valleys as far as possible. One of the obvious routes to south India would be along the Son valley as far as Sahasrām, then over the plateau descending later to Tosalī in Kaliṅga, and along the coast to the Krishna delta. The road farther along the Krishna valley would lead to the Raichur area. The Tungabhadra valley leading off the Krishna would give access to northern Mysore. Another route from Pāṭaliputra following a more inland course would branch off at Rūpanāth and would meet a northern tributary of the Godāvarī in the Wainganga valley. At the mouth of the Godāvarī it would go south to the Krishna river and then follow the Krishna valley. Another route may have followed the west coast, from Pratiṣṭhāna to Sopārā and farther south.

The reasons for suggesting that the routes followed the river valleys are largely geographical. The height of the Deccan plateau is on an average 1,200 to 3,000 feet, which is certainly not too great a height over which to travel. The problem of crossing this plateau is that it rises sharply from low-lying areas, which would necessitate steep ascents and descents in the

[1] Pliny, *Historia Naturalis*, VI, 21.
[2] *Arthaśāstra*, II, 11.
[3] *Mahāvaṃsa*, VI, 46, 47.
[4] Ibid., XI, 38.

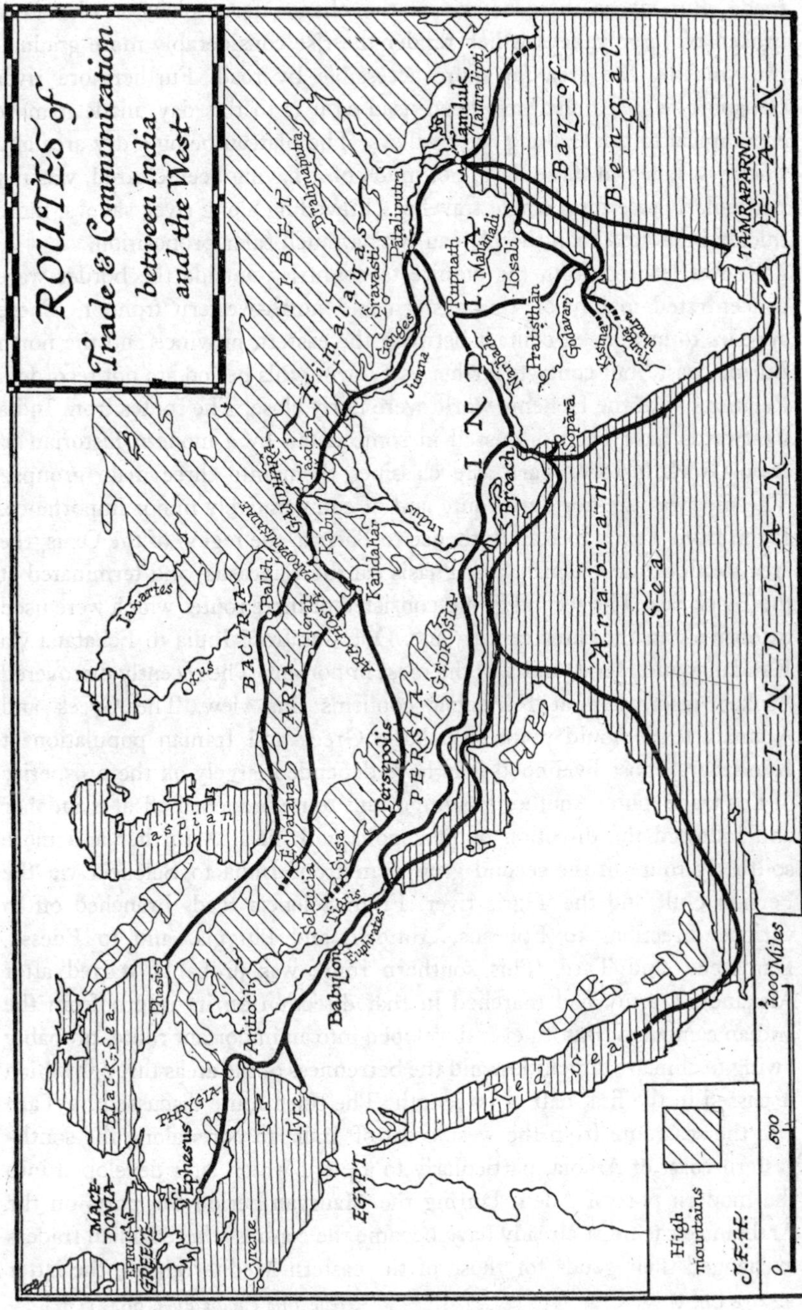
ROUTES of
Trade & Communication
between India
and the West
TIBET
Himalayas
Brahmaputra
Tamluk
(Tamralipti)
Bay of
Bengal
Pataliputra
Sravasti
Ganges
Jumna
Rupnath
Mahanadi
Tosali
INDIA
Pratisthan
Narbada
Godavari
Kistna
Tunga-bhadra
TAMRAPARNI
OCEAN
Sopara
Broach
Taxila
GANDHARA
PAROPANISADAE
Kabul
Indus
Kandahar
Arabian
Sea
INDIAN
Jaxartes
Oxus
BACTRIA
Balkh
Herat
ARIA
ARACHOSIA
GEDROSIA
PERSIA
Persepolis
Ecbatana
Caspian
Susa
Seleucia
Tigris
Euphrates
Babylon
Phasis
Black Sea
Antioch
PHRYGIA
Ephesus
Tyre
EGYPT
MACEDONIA
EPIRUS
GREECE
Cyrene
Red Sea
High mountains
0 500 1000 Miles
J.F.H.

roads. But where there are rivers the change from plain to plateau is broken by large valleys which render the rise considerably more gradual, thus making the area far more accessible by road. Furthermore river transport, which must have been used as it is to this day, made it more economical to travel along river valleys. The plateau being a dry area and thickly wooded in those days, not much of it having been cleared, was not particularly safe for a single traveller. Travelling along river valleys, more thickly inhabited than the plateau, was a much safer proposition.

Routes leading from the empire to countries outside the border were concentrated mainly on the western and north-western frontier. There appears to have been contact between the eastern province and the north Burma coast,[1] but contacts farther east during this period are not recorded. Relations with the Hellenic world were fairly close. The routes from India westwards have been discussed in some detail by a modern historian of Indo-Greek history, Tarn. He classifies them into three main groups.[2] The first was the northern route and of comparatively minor importance. It ran from Taxila to Kabul, thence to Bactria, the region of the Oxus, the area south of the Caspian Sea, Phasis (in the Caucasus) and terminated at the Black Sea. The second group consisted of three routes which were used extensively in the third century B.C. One was from India to Ecbatana via Kandahar and Herat, and was the most important. The recently discovered Aśokan inscription at Kandahar confirms this view. The Greek and Aramaic texts would point to a large Greek and Iranian population at Kandahar, whose livelihood may have depended largely on the prosperity of this trade route. Another less important route branched off at Kandahar and followed the direction of Persepolis and Susa. A further and more southerly route in the second group ran from India to Seleucia via the Persian Gulf and the Tigris river. From Seleucia roads branched off in various directions to Ephesus, Antioch, and Phrygia, and to Edessa, Damascus, and Tyre. This southern route was probably started after Alexander's army had marched in that direction on its return from the Indian campaign. But it never developed into an important route, probably owing to climatic difficulties, and the barrenness of the areas through which it passed in the first half of its length. The third route discussed by Tarn was the sea-route from the west coast of India to ports along the south-eastern coast of Arabia, particularly to a point which later developed into the modern port of Aden. During the Mauryan period the ports on the Arabian coasts must already have become the centres where Indian traders exchanged their goods for those of the eastern Mediterranean, the latter

[1] See Ch. II.

[2] *Hellenistic Civilization*, pp. 211 ff.

having been sent down the Red Sea, though undoubtedly the trade had not developed to the degree to which it did in later centuries.

References in Buddhist literature to merchants undertaking long journeys are very frequent.[1] These cross-country journeys were full of terror both imaginary and otherwise. If the fear of robbers and wild animals was not enough, the imagination was always ready to provide a host of demons. Desert journeys were particularly trying. These were conducted only at night, when the stars could be used as a guide.[2] Owing to the hazardous nature of these travels they were normally undertaken in the form of a large caravan. The *Jātakas* also contain references to sea voyages with some interesting remarks on navigation. For instance crows were used for piloting a vessel since they were known to fly in the direction of land.[3] It has been suggested that this practice was borrowed from the early Babylonians and Phoenicians.[4]

Ship-building was known to the Indians in the pre-Mauryan period. Arrian states that during Alexander's campaign, the Kathyioi, a tribe living in the Panjab, had large dock-yards and supplied galleys and transport vessels to the Greeks.[5] The tribes living along the banks of the Indus must have been acquainted with maritime traffic because there had been trade between this region and that of the Sabaeans at an earlier period.[6] Strabo writes that the Mauryas maintained ship-building as a state monopoly.[7] Ship-builders hired ships to merchants for use on rivers as well as on the seas. The state appears to have had a considerable control over the ship-building industry judging by the remarks of the *Arthaśāstra*.[8] Sea-going vessels and ships on rivers and lakes were in the charge of a special officer, the superintendent of ships. Pirates' ships or those bound for enemy country, or any ships disobeying the regulations were to be destroyed. Presumably this law was not taken too literally. Capturing such a ship would suffice. Merchandise coming by ship and damaged owing to sea conditions, could either be exempted from toll, or the toll in this case might be reduced.[9] This was a particularly helpful provision for maritime trade. The sailing ships of those days being what they were, it was hardly possible to take sufficient precautions against damage, as for example from sea spray.

Much of the small-scale trade must have consisted of the exchange of

[1] *Jātakas*, vol. ii, p. 248; vol. iii, p. 365.
[2] Ibid., vol. i, p. 107.
[3] Ibid., vol. iii, pp. 126–7, 267.
[4] Fick, *The Social Organization in North-East India in Buddha's Time*, p. 269.
[5] *Anabasis*, VI, 15.
[6] Warmington, *Commerce between the Roman Empire and India*, p. 64.
[7] Strabo, XV, 1, 46.
[8] II, 28.
[9] Ibid.

local products between neighbouring areas. Of the more expensive and adventurous trade we have some mention in the *Arthaśāstra*.[1] The northern areas exported blankets, skins, and horses, while from the south came conch shells, diamonds, and precious stones, pearls and gold. There is unfortunately no indication of the objects that were traded with the West during this period. This trade developed enormously in the next two centuries, when we do have information of the commodities that were traded. At this later period various sources mention that India sent to the West, pepper, cinnamon, and other spices, pearls, diamonds, carnelian, sard, agate, Indian cotton cloth, peacocks, parrots, and ivory work.[2] Among the merchandise imported from the West were horses, red coral, linen, and glass.[3] We may assume that much the same type of merchandise was traded in the earlier period under the Mauryas, but probably in smaller quantities. Even more important than the actual exchange of goods is the fact that this trade carried with it a transmission of ideas and practices. As the volume of trade increased, the areas within which the trade was conducted became more familiar, resulting in greater knowledge and understanding.

The last three classes listed by Megasthenes, that of the soldiers, the administrative officials, and the councillors will be discussed at length in the next chapter, dealing with the administration of the country.

The role of women in Mauryan society is of some significance. It was taken for granted that their position was subordinate to that of the men. This is particularly the case in the type of society envisaged by the *Arthaśāstra*. Brahmanical treatises were usually severe with women, who, in later works are regarded without equivocation as an inferior species. The Buddhists were much more humane in their attitude. The decision to allow nuns in the Buddhist Order was one of tremendous importance, whereas their brahmanical counterparts would not even admit of education for women. It has been suggested and with some justification, that for a woman life in Buddhist society was not so trying as life in brahmanical society, since she was not regarded primarily as a child-bearer.[4] The birth of a son was not necessary to Buddhist ritual as it was to Hindu ritual. Since Buddhist society accepted unmarried women, the women tended to be less concerned with finding husbands and consequently less subservient. All the same marriage was still regarded as the most suitable occupation for a woman. Working women were restricted in their work. The only pos-

[1] VII, 12.

[2] Warmington, *Commerce between the Roman Empire and India*, pp. 162, 167, 180, 210.

[3] Ibid., pp. 150, 263, 264.

[4] Horner, *Women in Primitive Buddhism*, pp. 22 ff.

sibilities seem to have been those of performing in circuses and plays, working as domestic slaves, either in private homes or in royal palaces, and as a last resort, setting themselves up as prostitutes and courtesans. At a later stage when Hindu ideas on this matter began to infiltrate into Buddhism the woman's importance even within the home, declined, and the older brahmanical attitudes were revived.

Megasthenes and Arrian in speaking of the manners of the Indians, mention the prevailing attitudes towards women and their place in Indian society. Megasthenes writes that Indians marry many wives.[1] There appears to have been a fixed bride-price consisting of a yoke of oxen to be exchanged for the bride. Probably most people who could afford it had a yoke of oxen for pulling carts and carriages. Those who did not possess the oxen must have paid the equivalent in value. The *Arthaśāstra* refers to the giving in marriage of a maiden for a couple of cows.[2] This practice is called *ārṣa-vivāha* and is described as an ancestral custom. It is also included as one of the eight types of possible marriages. It would seem that the two cows were symbolic and the equivalent in value would be equally acceptable. Megasthenes seems to suggest that some of the wives were solely concerned with bearing children whilst the others assisted their husbands in their work. The latter category would apply more to the cultivators than to any other class, since it is possible that women worked in the fields, but it is highly unlikely that they would be permitted to assist in any other kind of work, particularly in the towns. It is possible that Megasthenes was referring only to the domestic sphere, where, in well-to-do families, some of the wives would maintain and supervise the household, while others would look after the children.

The unchastity of Indian women is commented upon. Wives prostitute themselves unless they are compelled to be chaste. Arrian writes that for the gift of an elephant even the most chaste of Indian women would be willing to stray from virtue.[3] Apparently it was regarded as a great compliment since it meant that she was worth an elephant. Judging from the frequently repeated stories in Indian sources of the adventures of various Hindu gods with the daughters of high caste Hindus, there appears to have been considerable laxity in these matters. This is not surprising. With regard to sexual matters the Hindu moral code was, during this period, free from the guilt complexes which other religions have associated with sex, and consequently a far healthier attitude of mind was exhibited. However, even the Hindu attitude was not without blemish. Owing to the subordina-

[1] Strabo, XV, 1, 53–56.
[2] III, 2.
[3] *Indica*, XVII.

tion of women in society, it resulted in curious situations. For instance the state did not ban prostitution but in fact derived a tax from it.[1] Prostitutes were protected against being maltreated. They could also if necessary be called upon to act as spies for the state.

The women employed in the royal palace either worked in the harem,[2] or were responsible for looking after the king.[3] Those in the latter category were bought from their parents. Evidence of the king's personal attendants being women is confirmed by the *Arthaśāstra*, where the king is advised to maintain an armed bodyguard of women.[4] The king's hunting expeditions seem to have been very elaborate. Even on this occasion the king was encircled by armed women. These precautions may have originated in the idea that men, since they were not as subservient as women, would be more liable to corruption and might turn against the king; whereas women, knowing their weak and inferior position in society, would be only too glad of the prestige of serving the king and would therefore be meticulous in their care of him.

One occupation from which women are not debarred is that of weaving.[5] In fact the *Arthaśāstra* suggests that women of all ages can be gainfully employed by the superintendent of weaving. But this occupation is suggested largely for deformed women, widows, ageing prostitutes, or women compelled to work in default of paying fines. A married woman or an unmarried woman not belonging to any of these categories, if she had to seek such employment, would work at home. This chapter indirectly reveals social conventions with regard to women. For instance there are three main degrees in the segregation of women; the women who do not leave their houses (*aniṣkāsinyah*), those whose husbands have gone abroad, and those who are crippled and have to work in order to maintain themselves. It is suggested that where possible a maid-servant should act as the go-between when the woman has to send for yarn or return the woven material. Where this is not possible then the superintendent is permitted to deal directly with the woman, but she must visit the office only when the light is dim, so that he cannot see her clearly, and that he must restrict his conversation strictly to the work in question.

The *Arthaśāstra* further discusses the position of women in the chapters concerning marriage, and the relationship between husband and wife.[6] The social role of married women is still more flexible than in later centuries. The marriage of a widow outside the family of her in-laws is not

[1] *Arthaśāstra*, II, 27.
[2] Ibid., I, 20.
[3] Strabo, XV, 1, 53–56.
[4] I, 21.
[5] *Arthaśāstra*, II, 23.
[6] III, 2; III, 3.

unheard of; she must obtain the consent of her father-in-law. Divorce was permitted if both husband and wife wished it under certain circumstances, but this only applied to those marriages which were either voluntary unions or abductions, or contracted with a high bride-price. The types of marriage which were considered more respectable, were those held completely in accordance with social custom and these could not be dissolved. Here again we must remember that this section of the work was a theoretical discussion of possible situations. Whether in practice, social convention permitted the above-mentioned usages cannot be stated for certain. No doubt public opinion, then as now, must have influenced the day to day working of these laws.

Megasthenes has stated in his account that there were no slaves in India.[1] This remark has led to much debate, since the existence of slaves is mentioned in Indian sources, and in fact most of the labour power was supplied by slaves and hired labourers. It is possible that Megasthenes having the Greek conception of slavery in mind, did not recognize the Indian system which was different from that of the Greeks. If for instance Mauryan slavery was organized according to the system described in the *Arthaśāstra*, then Megasthenes was right. The Indian *dāsa* was not identical with the Greek *doulos*, since the former could own property and earn for himself.

Of the slaves and hired labourers employed to provide labour power, the latter were in a more elevated position than the slaves. They were paid wages in accordance with the amount of work they completed and were not owned by the employer. As we have noticed earlier, much hired labour was employed by the artisans. They were also used as agricultural and domestic labourers and are known to have worked on ships as well.[2] The social position of these labourers was extremely low and was almost on a par with the outcastes. The *Arthaśāstra* concerns itself with details about their wages, but does not suggest any action for the improvement of their condition. Wages were either fixed according to their work or there was a standard wage of one-tenth of their produce.[3] The system of hired labour is to be distinguished from forced labour or *viṣṭi*, which was in practice in Mauryan times. Megasthenes mentions that artisans worked for the state for a certain number of days in lieu of paying tax.[4] A similar system existed for land cultivators. The *Arthaśāstra* refers to it and warns against the tyrannical use of *viṣṭi*. The king is supposed to protect the cultivator from the oppressive infliction of forced labour by his subordinates.[5]

[1] Diodorus, II, 39.
[2] Bose, *Social and Rural Economy of Northern India*, p. 424.
[3] III, 13.
[4] Strabo, XV, 1, 46.
[5] II, 1.

Arrian writes that, 'all Indians are free and not one of them is a slave. The Lacedaemonians and the Indians here so far agree. The Lacedaemonians however hold the helots as slaves and these helots do servile labour; but the Indians do not even use aliens as slaves, and much less a countryman of their own.'[1] Strabo affirms that in India no man is a slave.[2] Diodorus quotes Megasthenes as saying that, 'the law ordains that no one among them shall under any circumstances be a slave, but that enjoying freedom they shall respect the equal right to it which all possess'.[3] The passage following this speaks of an equality of laws not excluding an inequality of possessions. This passage provides the clue to the above ideas. Following the textual emendation made by Timmer, the passage runs, 'for they who have learnt neither to stand over or under others, must have the best life in all conditions. It is foolish to make the laws the same for everybody and yet keep the status unequal.'[4] Timmer rightly sees in this passage an attempted criticism of the Greek system. Megasthenes is suggesting that the Greeks cannot see that an equality of laws and slavery are incompatible. The reference to slavery need not have been a description of Indian conditions. It may well have been an attempt at propaganda against slavery in Greece.[5] Agitation against slavery had begun with the attacks on the system made by Diogenes and the Cynics. Megasthenes either did not recognize the existence of slavery in India, or else used his account as a polemic on the debate regarding slavery in Greece. It is also possible that Arrian inserted the comparison with Sparta to the original statement of Megasthenes to give more point to the statement in the minds of his Greek readers.

It is possible that Megasthenes may have referred to it in his original text, but later editors may have deleted it and added their own comment believing the latter to be more correct. From Buddhist literature it appears that slaves were of three types, those that were inherited from one's father, those that were bought or were given as a gift, and those that were born in the house.[6] It must also have been the practice to make prisoners of war work as slaves. The 13th Rock Edict mentions the deportation of 150,000 people from Kaliṅga.[7] It is unlikely that the entire number were enslaved, but a certain percentage of them must have been employed as slaves. The majority were probably sent as settlers to newly cleared areas as the *Arthaśāstra* suggests.[8] By the time of Manu in the early centuries A.D., this

[1] *Indica*, X.
[2] XV, 1, 54.
[3] Diodorus, II, 39.
[4] *Megasthenes en de Indische Maatschappij*, p. 274.
[5] Ibid., pp. 274–6.
[6] *Vinaya Piṭaka: Bhikkhunīvibhaṅga Saṅghādisesa*, I, 2, 1.
[7] Bloch, *Les Inscriptions d'Asoka*, p. 125.
[8] II, 1,

practice had become a regular one.[1] Slavery as a result of punishment (*daṇḍadāsa*) is also known in the *Jātakas* and is referred to in the *Arthaśāstra*.[2] Domestic service in households was probably the most common work for slaves. They were used as personal attendants by their owners. Some may have worked as agricultural labourers, others among the artisans. It is also possible that a man owning many slaves may have on occasion, hired them out for general purposes.[3]

The *Arthaśāstra* describes another group of slaves which affirms the fact that slavery in India was not so severe as in Greece. It is said that in normal circumstances, an *Ārya* should not be subjugated to slavery, but it is possible that due to some misfortune, family troubles, or the necessity for earning more money than usual, an *Ārya* may temporarily work as a slave.[4] He can buy back his freedom when his term of agreement is over, and resume his normal life. This reference is of importance since it establishes the fact that even though a slave had no freedom, nevertheless he had a social position and was regarded as another category of labour force. The lowest order in the social scale of Mauryan society was not the slave but the outcaste, the person belonging to the despised classes. Thus the social degradation of being a slave was not as great in India as in Greece. To a casual Greek visitor of the period, slavery in India was of a better nature than it was in Greece, but he would at the same time fail to understand or recognize the condemnation of the outcastes by the rest of Indian society.

Both the *Jātakas* and the *Arthaśāstra* suggest a generally humane attitude towards the slaves.[5] The latter mentions various regulations for the protection of slaves. The children of a man who has sold himself as a slave shall not be slaves. A slave is permitted to own what he has earned and to inherit from his father and bequeath to his kinsmen. Proper treatment of female slaves is insisted upon. If a female slave has a child by her owner, both mother and child are immediately recognized as free. The king is expected to chastise those who do not give heed to the claims of their slaves.[6] Such were the prescribed regulations which no doubt were followed on the whole. But there must also have been lapses. Some *Jātaka* stories refer to the misery of slaves, who had to suffer beatings, imprisonment, and malnutrition at times.[7] In his edicts, Aśoka frequently appealed to his subjects to treat their slaves and labourers with kindness.[8]

[1] Manu, *Dharmaśāstra*, VIII, 415.

[2] *Kulavāka Jātaka: Jātakas*, vol. i, p. 200; III, 13.

[3] Bose, *Social and Rural Economy of Northern India*, p. 413.

[4] III, 13.

[5] e.g. *Nānacchanda Jātaka: Jātakas*, vol. ii, p. 428; III, 13.

[6] II, 1.

[7] *Jātakas*, vol. i, pp. 402, 451.

[8] IX, XI, XIII R.E.; VII P.E.

The main distinction between the slaves and the outcastes was, that the former could not be considered impure since they were in constant and close attendance on their masters.[1] They lived with the family and not in segregated parts of the town as did the outcastes. The despised classes or *hīnajāti* consisted of people in an assortment of occupations largely concerned with things that were considered unclean. There was complete social segregation between them and the rest of society, and they had no hope of being accepted in the main body of society.[2] The *Caṇḍālas* are an example of such outcastes. They were supposed to have originated as the result of a brahman-*śūdra* union and were therefore of very low caste.[3] The reference to *Caṇḍāla-bhāṣā* which occurs in a *Jātaka* story suggests an aboriginal speech.[4] They were restricted in their occupations to being public executioners, cleaning the cremation grounds, hunting and performing as acrobats and jugglers.[5] Leather workers were despised and because of this the *rathakāras* were also considered degraded, since their work involved handling leather. The *veṇa* caste were basket makers and flute makers and were probably also of aboriginal origin. The *nesāda* caste lived by hunting and fishing, and probably came from areas lying on the edge of the cultivated land.[6] To the settled cultivators the occupation of the *nesāda* was inferior. Potters, weavers, barbers, dancers, snake-charmers, and beggars were all grouped together as despised castes.[7] It is of some interest to notice that their caste names refer directly to their profession or work.

The outcastes accepted this position of social ostracism because they were numerically not strong enough in each area to take objection to it. They lived together with their families outside the towns or concentrated in a small area within, and were thus at a disadvantageous position in relation to the rest of the town. They were not banded into guilds which could act as organizing bodies. The fact that they were deliberately kept uneducated made their position even weaker.[8] The description of the despised classes in the *Jātakas* is borne out by the *Arthaśāstra*, particularly in connection with the *Caṇḍālas*. It is stated in no uncertain terms that 'heretics and *Caṇḍālas* shall live beyond the burial grounds', i.e. well outside the boundary of the city.[9]

Archaeological evidence reveals that towns were built according to a

[1] Fick, *The Social Organization in North-East India in Buddha's Time*, p. 312.

[2] Bose, *Social and Rural Economy of Northern India*, p. 435.

[3] Manu, *Dharmaśāstra*, X, 12.

[4] *Citta-sambhūta Jātaka*: *Jātakas*, vol. iv, p. 391.

[5] Bose, *Social and Rural Economy of Northern India*, p. 435.

[6] Ibid., pp. 447–55.

[7] Ibid., p. 483.

[8] *Citta-sambhūta Jātaka*: *Jātakas*, vol. iv, pp. 390 ff.

[9] II, 4.

plan and that houses were well constructed.[1] The house plan was generally a simple one, a central courtyard with rooms surrounding it. The rooms on the ground floor were often smaller than those above, and this, it has been suggested, was because in wealthy households the slaves and servants would live on the ground floor and the family upstairs. The lay-out of Mauryan cities improved considerably in the later Mauryan period and the Śunga period, when they were planned in a more regular and controlled pattern.[2] Municipal responsibilities such as the drainage system were evidently well organized even at the earliest period.

It would appear from literary and archaeological evidence that the Mauryan period was one of an expanding economy. New possibilities of the development of various crafts on a large scale were being realized, particularly in the context of increasing trade and all its attendant commercial advantages. The benefits of an agrarian economy were also revealed for the first time on an extensive scale and this type of economy assumed a degree of permanency. Together with this economic change social organization developed along a pattern which was to remain comparatively unchanged for many centuries.

[1] Marshall, *Taxila*, vol. i, pp. 91–101.

[2] Sharma, *Ancient India*, 1953, vol. ix, p. 168; Lal, *Ancient India*, 1954, vols. x–xi, pp. 5 ff.

IV

INTERNAL ADMINISTRATION AND FOREIGN RELATIONS

THE establishment of the Mauryan state ushered in a new form of government, that of a centralized empire. The usual pattern of kingdoms familiar to Indians until that period, was a confederation of smaller kingdoms and republics. The pattern changed under the Nandas, when an attempt was made at a centralized monarchy. This form developed into the centralized control of the Mauryan government over areas which gradually lost their independence and were included within an extensive political and economic system planned by this government. Kingdoms and autonomous states situated on the borders of the empire naturally maintained a looser relationship with the Mauryas. Areas lying within the empire were not confederated, but were regarded as subordinate to Mauryan rule. The Mauryan state was not composed of federal states, as has been suggested.[1] The relationship between the Mauryas and the state of Kaliṅga for instance speaks against this view. If the idea of federation was a current one during the Mauryan period, it might have provided the solution to the conflict with Kaliṅga. But Aśoka desired complete control over the state and hence had to go to war against it.

Since, however, this was the first occasion that a centralized empire had been established on such a vast scale in India, it is possible that some tribes, though within the empire, or on its border, still maintained their political organization. The *Arthaśāstra* mentions certain tribal republics such as the Kāmbojas who were governed by a corporation of warriors, and others such as the Licchavis, Vṛjjis, and the Pañcālas, which, though tribal republics, were governed by a titular *rājā*.[2] But these tribes were in no way federated to the Mauryan state, as there was no question of their being equal or near equal units. The fact that they were permitted to continue with their political organization was based largely on the practical consideration of this system facilitating administration. As long as these tribes did not disrupt the organization of the Mauryan empire they were permitted their political privileges. The free accessibility of these tribes to Mauryan agents, as is obvious from the *Arthaśāstra*, suggests that they were regarded as adjuncts to the empire. They were not given the importance that might be expected had they been confederate areas.

[1] Dikshitar, *Mauryan Polity*, p. 78. [2] Book XI.

The Mauryan empire indicates the triumph of monarchy as a political system over tribal republics.[1] This is demonstrated not only in the attitude adopted by Kauṭalya towards the tribal republics or *saṃghas*, but in fact in the entire conception of the *Arthaśāstra* itself. The treatise emphasizes the control of the central authority. Every detail of the organization of the kingdom is fitted into the administrative plan and is aimed at giving final control to the king. The king is expected to protect and maintain society, and such maintenance of the *status quo* facilitated administration. This in turn leads to a consistent inflow of revenue. The supremacy of the king's authority is asserted by the fact that he not only defends social usage according to the traditional concept of kingship, but can also make his own laws.[2] It is stated that where there is a conflict between traditional law *śāstra*, and the king's law *dharmanyāya*, the latter shall prevail. This was indeed a tremendous increase in the power of the king. Certain checks were imposed on this power, but nevertheless the king's authority was enhanced by such statements.

It was because of this increased power of the king that the Mauryan centralized monarchy became a paternal despotism under Aśoka. The previously held idea of the king being a protector, remote from the affairs of his subjects, gave way to the belief that he had complete control over all spheres of social and political life. This paternal attitude is expressed in the remark, 'All men are my children',[3] which almost becomes the motto of Aśoka in defining his attitude towards his subjects. He is concerned with the welfare of his people and rightly regards it as an important responsibility. The *Arthaśāstra* lays great stress on this welfare.[4] Aśoka's concern is such that he dictates to his subjects the course which is morally approved and that which is not, albeit in a fatherly way. He expresses a wish to be in personal contact with his subjects.[5] This in part accounts for his undertaking extensive tours throughout his empire. These tours were made possible largely through the existence of an efficient administrative system. Improved roads and communications also played an important part in assisting this new development in administration. New communications meant the opening up of new areas, and a greater freedom of movement and travel.

According to Indian thought on the subject, the chief function of the king was to maintain social order. The four castes and the four orders of religious life had to be made to adhere, as far as was possible, to their respective duties and occupations.[6] The authority of the king was linked

[1] *Age of the Nandas and Mauryas*, p. 172.
[2] III, 1.
[3] I S.E., Dhauli. Bloch, *Les Inscriptions d'Asoka*, p. 137.
[4] II, 1; IV, 3.
[5] VI P.E. Bloch, *Les Inscriptions d'Asoka*, p. 167.
[6] *Arthaśāstra*, I, 4.

with divine approval. At the level of daily functioning this connection was expressed by the important position of the brahmans, and more particularly of the *purohita*, the high priest of the palace. This importance can be seen, for instance, from the fact that the *purohita*, together with the prime minister, are present when the king is examining any of his other ministers.[1] Thus the role of the *purohita* is not restricted to religious functions in his relationship with the king but extends to the political sphere as well. The dependence of the king on the brahmans is more clearly indicated elsewhere in the work, where it is stated that the three factors which bring unqualified success to the king are, the support of the brahmans, the good advice of the ministerial council, and action in accordance with the *śāstras*.[2] Nowhere in his edicts does Aśoka make any mention of the *purohita*. It is possible that during his reign the *purohita* was excluded from interfering in political matters.

It has been stated that the use of the title *Devānampiya* by Aśoka was another indication that the king sought the support of the sacerdotal power.[3] But it would appear that it was more than an indication of his wish for priestly support. It was an attempt to emphasize the connection between kingship and divine power, perhaps even to the degree of excluding the intermediaries, the priests. It further assisted Aśoka in his propaganda. Such remarks, as his claim that Jambudvīpa was fit for the gods after the propagation of the policy of *Dhamma*,[4] would in the minds of the unsophisticated, be linked with his own title, thereby convincing them that he was indeed the beloved of the gods. Judging by his self-satisfaction with regard to the good which he had brought to his kingdom, as expressed in pillar edicts and elsewhere,[5] we may suggest that, in his later years at least, he believed in the literal application of this title.

The *Arthaśāstra* stresses the idea that the king must be accessible to his officials and his subjects at all times, and warns the king that his inaccessibility would cause confusion and disaffection and would make him a prey to his enemies.[6] This advice it would seem, was followed implicitly by the Mauryas. No doubt the pressure of work in governing the empire made it imperative. Megasthenes writes that the king is available for consultation even when he is being massaged.[7] Aśoka states in one of his edicts that his reporters are to have access to him no matter where he is; whether he is eating, relaxing in the harem or in the park. If any matter arising in the meeting of the ministerial council needs attention, it should be reported to

[1] *Arthaśāstra*, I, 10.
[2] Ibid., I, 9.
[3] *Age of the Nandas and Mauryas*, p. 175.
[4] Minor Rock Edict, Brahmagiri. Bloch, *Les Inscriptions d'Asoka*, p. 146.
[5] V R.E.; II P.E.
[6] I, 19.
[7] Strabo, XV, 1, 53–56.

him immediately.[1] Kauṭalya insists that the king can be successful only if he adopts three general practices. He must give equal attention to all matters, he must always remain active and ready to take action, and lastly he must never slacken in the discharge of his duties.[2] Obviously such an ideal could only be realized in a kingdom ably administered by an extensive network of officials.

Legislation in that period consisted largely of a confirmation of social usage. Decisions on individual issues were taken by reference to social customs. The king had the freedom to make these decisions. The king is advised to take into consideration the opinion of his councillors, but the final decision rests with him alone. The council of ministers or *mantrī-pariṣad* may have acted as a political check on the king. But it could only be effective where public opinion was against any policy made by the king. The council had no consistent political position within the framework of the government, as have modern bodies of a similar nature. No doubt its powers varied from time to time according to the strength of the king, and the calibre of its members. We have an example of ministerial power during Aśoka's accession. His coming to the throne was facilitated by the support he had from the minister Rādhagupta. Aśoka refers to the council in two of his edicts. On the first occasion, the council acts in a subordinate way, it being merely expected to order the *yuktas* to register certain new administrative measures adopted by Aśoka.[3] From this instance it would appear that the council was responsible for the enactment of the policy decided by the king. On the second occasion the council appears to have far more authority.[4] It can in the absence of the king discuss his policy and suggest amendments to it, or it may consider any emergent matter, the discussion of which the king may have left to the council. However, even in this case the opinion of the council has to be reported to the king immediately, wherever he may be. The final decision rests with the king and the council is regarded as an advisory body. It was probably in the interests of the king to consult the council on most matters, particularly during an emergency.[5]

[1] VI R.E., Girnār. Bloch, *Les Inscriptions d'Asoka*, p. 107.

[2] I, 19.

[3] III R.E., Girnār. Bloch, *Les Inscriptions d'Asoka*, p. 96.

[4] VI R.E., Girnār. Ibid., p. 107.

[5] Jayaswal has attempted to prove that the ministerial council had over-riding powers and could reject the policy of the king (*Hindu Polity*, pp. 275–80, 294–305). As Barua has pointed out (*Aśoka and his Inscriptions*, p. 213), Jayaswal's reading is based on an incorrect interpretation of the word *nijhati*. This word is not derived from *nikṣapti*, rejection, as Jayaswal believes, but from *nidhvapti*, which indicates an agreement resulting from deliberations. There is certainly no hint in the edict of Aśoka waiting anxiously for the acceptance of his policy by the council. If anything the tone is imperious. Besides if the council were so powerful, Aśoka would not make public his own weakness.

The king's control over the council was increased by the fact that the members of the council were personally selected by the king. The tendency would be for the king to select only those people who were in favour of his own policy. The *Arthaśāstra* gives a list of the qualities that a minister should possess, and stresses those of birth, integrity, and intelligence.[1] It further suggests that these qualities should be ascertained from a variety of sources. This is a most idealistic view on the selection of ministers and it is hardly likely that it was ever fully put into practice. Ways in which a king can test the loyalty of these ministers are also explained. Here he is assisted by the Chief Minister and the *purohita*.[2] Megasthenes states that the advisers to the king are selected from a particular caste, which he lists as the seventh caste.[3] This statement is correct only in so far as the councillors no doubt belonged to the brahman caste or were high caste *kṣatriyas*. It is unlikely that members of any other caste would be chosen as ministers.

There was no fixed number for the members of the council. It varied according to need. The Mauryans probably had a fairly large council. The *Arthaśāstra* lists the Chief Minister or the *mahāmantrī*, and also distinguishes between the ministers and the assembly of ministers (*mantrinomantripariṣadāṃca*).[4] It would seem that of the ministerial council or *mantripariṣad* a small group of perhaps three or four councillors, together with the Chief Minister, was selected to act as an inner council or a close advisory body. This may have been a permanent group or it may have been selected for consultation on particular issues similar to a modern committee. It is suggested that if the king wishes to be advised on any matter, he can consult privately with three or four ministers, or even collectively with a similarly small group.[5] Such consultations facilitate frankness of opinion, since ministers would be more liable to state their views openly when consulted privately by the king than in the midst of a large assembly. Furthermore such consultations permit of greater secrecy with regard to the matter discussed, and Kauṭalya urges the importance of secrecy in these matters.

The central administration was conducted through a number of offices largely relating to the control of revenue, and each under a particular officer. The treasurer (*sannidhātā*) was responsible for the storage of the royal treasure, and of the state income both in cash and kind, the latter chiefly in the form of grains, gems, etc. The storage of these was his particular charge.[6] This office worked in conjunction with that of the chief

[1] I, 9.
[2] I, 10.
[3] Diodorus, II, 41.
[4] I, 15.
[5] Ibid.
[6] II, 5.

collector (*samāhartā*) who was responsible for the collection of revenue from various parts of the kingdom.[1] Sources of revenue as listed in the *Arthaśāstra* include that of cities, land, mines, forests, roads, tolls, fines, licences, manufactured products, merchandise of various kinds, and precious stones. The chief collector was also concerned with matters of income and expenditure and supervised the accounts submitted by the accountant general. The latter kept the accounts both of the kingdom and the royal household.[2] He was assisted by a body of clerks (*kārmikas*). The *Arthaśāstra* states that all the ministers shall together report the accounts of each department. This suggests a system of joint responsibility, though no doubt in the case of fraud the individual minister or department was punished. Embezzlement of finances by government servants was apparently known.[3] Heavy fines are suggested as a punishment for such an offence. The fiscal year was from *Āṣāḍha* (July), and 354 working days were reckoned in each year. Work during the intercalary month was separately accounted for.

Expenditure was largely on salaries and public works. The maintenance of the royal court and the royal family required the use of part of the national revenue in addition to the revenue from the crown lands. Salaries of the officials were also paid with the money that came into the royal treasury.[4] One-fourth of the total revenue was kept for this purpose. Some of these salaries are listed. The minister, the *purohita* and the army commander received 48,000 *paṇas*. The chief collector and the treasurer were paid 24,000 *paṇas*. Members of the ministerial council received 12,000 *paṇas*. The staff of accountants and writers were paid 500 *paṇas*. Unfortunately we are not told the value of the *paṇa*, nor whether these salaries were yearly or monthly. The proportion of the wages paid to various officials is clear.

Expenditure on public works included the cost of building and maintaining roads, wells, and rest-houses, of building irrigation works such as the dam on the Sudarśan lake and the planting of medicinal herbs and trees. The cost of maintaining a large army must also have been a serious draw on the revenue. The outlay on state mines and manufactures and the wages of state-employed artisans would come from the treasury. It is not certain whether grants to religious bodies were made from the same source or from revenue obtained from the crown lands. The distinction between the national treasury and the privy purse is not made in the *Arthaśāstra*. Thus private benefactions made by the king would be paid from the

[1] II, 6.
[2] II, 7.
[3] II, 9.
[4] V, 3.

treasury. It is possible that Aśoka's endowment of the Buddhist Order with funds from the treasury antagonized both the civil administration and other religious bodies.

Kauṭalya devotes an entire section to the duties of various superintendents.[1] These officials supervised the revenue coming from particular sources and were also responsible for the administration of the departments concerned with these sources. They generally worked at local centres and made their reports to the administration at the capital. They were in turn assisted by committees and under-officers and therefore formed a link between the capital and the local administration. Those mentioned in the text are the superintendents of gold and goldsmiths, the store-house, commerce, forest produce, armoury, weights and measures, tolls, weaving, agriculture, liquor, the slaughter-house, prostitutes, ships, cows, horses, elephants, chariots, infantry, passports, and the city superintendents.

Provincial administration was under the immediate control of a prince or a member of the royal family. The terms used in the edicts are *kumāra* and *āryaputra*. The former may have been the title of the sons of the king, and the latter may have referred to other close relatives.[2] They were generally viceroys or governors of the provinces of the empire. The empire during the reign of Aśoka was divided into four major provinces, as four provincial capitals are mentioned in the edicts. Taxila was the capital of the northern province, Ujjain of the west, Tosalī of the east, and Suvarṇagiri of the south.[3] These provinces were administrative divisions and were placed under viceroys. The appointment of princes as viceroys served the practical purpose of training them as administrators. Where the relationship between the king and the prince was good, there was the added advantage that the prince as viceroy would conform to the king's policy. There would be less likelihood of an insurrection under a prince loyal to the king. But the disadvantages were also known and warned against by the theorists. A period of viceroyalty could be used to advantage by a prince, in order to establish his own position in opposition to the king. The *Arthaśāstra* warns that the prince can be a source of danger, and to give him complete control over a province can lead to irresponsible action on his part.[4] As provincial viceroys there must have been considerable competition between princes who were brothers, leading eventually to wars of succession, where they could use the provincial forces against each other.[5]

[1] II, 13–36.

[2] Hultzsch, *Corpus Inscriptionum Indicarum*, vol. i, p. xl.

[3] I, II, S.E.; Minor Rock Edict, Brahmagiri.

[4] I, 17.

[5] This happened with great frequency in later Indian history during the Mughal period.

This must certainly have happened among the sons of Bindusāra, when the struggle for the throne began. It is probable that Aśoka's successful viceroyalty further convinced him of his ability to succeed Bindusāra.

Governors administering smaller areas within the unit of the province were probably selected from among the local people. At Girnār, mention is made of Tuṣāspa, a local personality of foreign extraction who is referred to as the governor.[1] In the case of tribal peoples local kings were probably confirmed as heads of administration. This would tend to cause less disruption in organization when an area came under Mauryan control, apart from the fact that a foreign administrator might be resented more than a local ruler. In such cases local autonomy may have been retained at a lower level of administration.

In provincial administration the council of ministers had more power than their counterparts at the centre. They acted even in practice as a check on the prince and were, if occasion demanded, in direct contact with the king. This is apparent from two events before and during the reign of Aśoka. The revolt in Taxila during the reign of Bindusāra was against the local ministers and officers and not against the prince.[2] It would seem that the ministers had assumed more power than their situation demanded. The second indication was the story of the blinding of Kunāla at the orders of Aśoka.[3] This story suggests that direct orders from the king to the ministers, without the viceroy knowing about them, were a regular occurrence, since the ministers were not surprised at the prince being kept in ignorance of the king's order. The viceroy had the power to appoint some of his officials. For instance those *mahāmattas* who made tours of inspection every five years would be appointed, some by the king and others by the viceroy.

The precise designation of the *mahāmattas* in Mauryan administration remains uncertain. A great variety of officials are referred to as *mahāmattas* in various sources. The term appears to have been used for any senior official irrespective of the duties assigned to him. The *Arthaśāstra* uses it in the sense of a minister, a narrower interpretation than in Buddhist literature.[4] In his edicts Aśoka uses the term to include many types of officials, and there are references to the *mahāmattas* as a ministerial or

[1] Sircar, *Select Inscriptions* . . ., p. 169.

[2] See Ch. II.

[3] See Ch. II.

[4] In Buddhist literature the particular work of the *mahāmatta* is often specified in his title. Thus we have the judicial officer *vohārikamahāmatta*, the military officer *senānāyakamahāmatta*, the chief minister *sabbatthakammahāmatta* and the assessment officer *donamāpakamahāmatta* (*Mahāvagga*, I, 40; *Jātakas*, vol. ii, pp. 30, 70). Thomas has analysed the compound as *mahatī mātrā yasya*, denoting a person of high standing (*JRAS*, 1914, p. 386).

advisory council as well.[1] Among these categories, some were concerned with general administration such as those to whom the Minor Rock Edict is addressed.[2] Judicial officers of the city are referred to in the 1st Separate Edict.[3] The same term is used for officers who are to be sent on tours of inspection to inspect the work of magistrates and judicial officers. Obviously these officials would be senior to the latter. They were sent on tour both by the centre and the provincial viceroy. In the Queen's Edict the *mahāmattas* are expected to register whatever gift the Queen Kāruvāki should make.[4] The *ithījhakha-mahāmattas* controlled the harem and other departments involving women.[5] There are frequent references to a new type of *mahāmatta*, the *Dhamma-mahāmatta*, which was a service inaugurated by Aśoka in his fourteenth regnal year.[6]

The *mahāmattas* were thus a highly responsible cadre of officials and doubtless were greatly respected since they held senior positions and controlled various aspects of administration and justice. Megasthenes, when referring to his seventh caste of councillors and assessors, was probably referring to the *mahāmattas*. Diodorus quotes Megasthenes as saying that, 'the seventh class consists of the Councillors and Assessors, of those who deliberate on public affairs. It is the smallest class as regards number, but the most respected on account of the high character and wisdom of its members; for from their ranks the advisers of the king are taken, and the treasurers of the state, and the arbiters who settle disputes. The generals of the army also, and the chief magistrates usually belong to this class.'[7] Strabo quotes as follows, 'The seventh class consists of the Councillors and Assessors of the king. To them belong the highest posts of government, the tribunals of justice, and the general administration of public affairs.'[8] Arrian writes, 'The seventh caste consists of the Councillors of state, who advise the king, or the magistrates of self-governed cities in the management of public affairs. In point of numbers this is a small class, but it is distinguished by superior wisdom and justice, and hence enjoys the prerogative of choosing governors, chiefs of provinces, deputy governors, superintendents of the treasury, generals of the army, admirals of the navy, controllers and commissioners who superintend agriculture.'[9]

On an examination of these statements it is apparent that they tally closely with the description of the service of *mahāmattas* available from other sources. It would certainly be most advisable for the king to choose

[1] VI R.E., Girnār. Bloch, *Les Inscriptions d'Asoka*, p. 107.
[2] Ibid., p. 145.
[3] Ibid., p. 136.
[4] Ibid., p. 159.
[5] XII R.E., Girnār. Ibid., p. 121.
[6] V R.E.; XII R.E.; VII P.E.
[7] Diodorus, II, 41.
[8] Strabo, XV, 1, 48.
[9] *Indica*, XII.

his ministerial council from among the *mahāmattas*, since their experience of administration would be of great help. The arbiters who settle disputes were probably the judicial *mahāmattas* referred to in the edicts. Arrian's remark concerning the seventh caste working as magistrates of self-governed cities may be a somewhat confused account of the posting of *mahāmattas* as administrators amongst the tribal republics, which was certainly a possible action on the part of the Mauryas. Of the *mahāmattas* the only branch neglected by European sources was that of the *dhamma-mahāmattas*, but since this was not started until the reign of Aśoka, it would not be mentioned in the account of Megasthenes. It would seem that the *mahāmattas*, certainly those in senior posts, were an exclusive group. This naturally led to Megasthenes regarding them as a separate class.

Jurisdiction in the cities was carried out by *mahāmattas* specially appointed for this purpose, to whom the 1st Separate Edict is addressed.[1] The edict is devoted to emphasizing the importance of just behaviour and impartial judgments. Aśoka cautions against weaknesses such as anger, laziness, fatigue, want of patience, etc.; any of which may prejudice a judgment. As a further defence against injustice, the king has decided to send a *mahāmatta* every five years, to inspect the judiciary in the cities. In addition to the royal inspector, there was to be a provincial inspection every three years, by a locally appointed *mahāmatta*. These judicial *mahāmattas* were concerned with problems arising from the administration of the cities, connected with the artisans, merchants and other townspeople, many of which problems are discussed in the *Arthaśāstra*.[2] Civil cases dealing with marriage and inheritance must also have been brought before these officers.

Jurisdiction in the rural areas was conducted by the *rājūkas*. They acted as assessment officers as well, but here we shall consider only their judicial functions. An entire pillar edict is devoted to this aspect of the work of the *rājūkas*.[3] The edict is dated to the twenty-seventh regnal year which suggests that Aśoka's delegation of power to these officials took place late in his reign. It is possible that previous to this, jurisdiction in the rural areas was in the hands of the higher officials, who were not accessible to the entire population. The *rājūkas* had control over problems related to agriculture and land disputes.

In the same edict there occurs a sentence concerning procedure and punishment, which raises the question of whether Aśoka discontinued the usual Hindu practice of grading punishments according to caste, which

[1] Bloch, *Les Inscriptions d'Asoka*, p. 136.
[2] Book IV.
[3] IV P.E. Bloch, *Les Inscriptions d'Asoka*, p. 164.

would certainly have been a most daring step. The sentence reads as follows,

'. . . *icchitaviye hi esā kimti viyohālasamatā ca siya daṃḍa samatā cā* . . .'[1] 'But it is desirable that there should be uniformity in judicial procedure and punishment.'

The crucial word in the text is *samatā*. One authority translates it as 'impartiality', which suggests in the context more than a lack of prejudice on the part of the judge.[2] It suggests that punishments should not be given with a partial attitude towards the social position of the offender. Such a rule would contradict legal procedure as laid down in traditional sources, which was no doubt observed. The *Arthaśāstra* for instance is very clear on this point. It states, 'Taking into consideration the [social position of] persons, the nature of the offence, the cause whether grave or slight [that led to the perpetration of the offence,] the antecedent and present circumstances, the time and the place; and without failing to notice equitable distinctions among the offenders, whether belonging to the royal family or the common people, shall the commissioner determine the propriety of imposing the first, middlemost or highest amercements.'[3] Similarly penalties for leading a brahman astray are far more severe than those for the same offence against a member of a lower caste.[4]

For Aśoka to have abolished discriminations of caste and position in the ordering of punishments would certainly have been in keeping with the principles of *Dhamma*, but at the same time Aśoka must have realized that such a radical step would cause untold upheavals in society. Furthermore such a step would antagonize not only the brahmans but also the *kṣatriyas*, the combined strength of which would have been difficult to keep under control. Although Aśoka attacked the brahmanical position through indirect measures such as the abolition of animal sacrifices, he was shrewd enough not to openly antagonize this powerful factor in Indian society. In his edicts he was careful to placate the brahman element by insisting that the utmost respect must be shown to the brahmans. As suggested by a recent translation, the word 'uniformity' conveys more accurately the meaning of the word *samatā*.[5] According to this interpretation a uniform legal procedure was to be adopted in all areas under Mauryan administration, and similarly a uniform penal code was to be used. This would assist the *rājūkas* in their decisions and would make each case more compre-

[1] IV P. E. Bloch, *Les Inscriptions d'Asoka*, p. 164.

[2] Hultzsch, *Corpus Inscriptionum Indicarum*, vol. i, p. 125.

[3] IV, 10; Shamasastry (trans.), *Arthaśāstra*, p. 255.

[4] IV, 13.

[5] Bloch, *Les Inscriptions d'Asoka*, p. 165.

hensible to the higher authority not present during proceedings, since such a uniformity would lead to legal cases being treated in a system of regular categories.[1]

According to Megasthenes the amount of crime committed in Mauryan India was small, and he describes the Indians as an honest people.[2] This may well have been true in comparison with Greece or Asia Minor. Pāṭaliputra being the capital city, must certainly have been well policed, and its authorities merciless in putting down crime. The *Arthaśāstra* envisages the possibility of a variety of crimes. Three lengthy chapters are devoted to the detection and suppression of criminals.[3] Buddhist literature refers to groups of bandits operating in the country-side.[4]

Punishment was largely in the form of fines.[5] Those who could not pay were permitted to sell themselves into bondage in order to do so.[6] A punishment of mutilation could sometimes be changed to that of payment of a fine.[7] Capital punishment was known and practised. In spite of the fact that Aśoka was a Buddhist he did not abolish the death penalty. He did, however, make a concession whereby those condemned to die were granted a three-day respite.[8] During this period it was possible to make a final appeal to the judges. This could be in terms either of a retrial or the payment of a ransom. This system is not unknown to the *Arthaśāstra*.[9] If neither of these was possible, then relatives or friends could attend to the last needs of the condemned man.[10] It is clear from the passage in the edict that the idea of capital punishment was disliked by Aśoka. This may be regarded as an example of an occasion when prudent statecraft triumphed over his ideals.

Provinces were subdivided into districts for purposes of administration, and groups of officials worked in each district. The group consisted of three major officials, the *prādeśika*, the *rājūka*, and the *yukta*. These were in turn assisted by many others.[11] The functions of the *prādeśika* were similar to those of the *pradeṣṭṛ* in the *Arthaśāstra*. These officers were in charge of

[1] Bloch has suggested further, that by the addition of an *anusvāra* to *samatā*, it would read *sammatā* (Sanskrit, *samyaktā*), which would then mean 'correctness' instead of 'uniformity' (*Les Inscriptions d'Asoka*, p. 164 n. 10). This interpretation is feasible, though it is indeed surprising that the *anusvāra* did not occur in any other version.

[2] Strabo, XV, 1, 53-56.

[3] IV, 4, 5, 6.

[4] *Jātakas*, vol. iv, p. 430.

[5] *Arthaśāstra*, III, 11, 17-20; V, 1.

[6] III, 13.

[7] IV, 10.

[8] IV P.E.

[9] II, 36.

[10] Kern maintains that the fetters referred to here are spiritual ones and not those of physical imprisonment (*Asoka*, p. 64). This is a false interpretation, since the context of the edict makes it amply clear that it refers to legal and judicial proceedings and whatever punishments might ensue from them.

[11] III R.E., Girnār. Bloch, *Les Inscriptions d'Asoka*, p. 96.

the overall administration of a district of a particular province, each district being under one *pradeṣṭṛ*. Much of their work consisted of touring. They had to inspect the work of both the district officials and the village officials and had to make reports to the chief collector or *samāhartṛ*.[1] In their judicial capacity three *pradeṣṭṛs* could form a judicial bench for trying offenders against the law.[2] The text speaks of either three *pradeṣṭṛs* or three ministers fulfilling this function. This was presumably an administrative measure, since in some areas the former were more easily available than the latter, and vice versa. It is clear from this passage that the *pradeṣṭṛs* had a high status since they are included in ministerial rank. Apparently only the serious cases were brought before them, the milder ones being dealt with by the *rājūkas* or the city magistrates as the case might be. The *pradeṣṭṛ* is also expected to check the work of the superintendents and the subordinate officers.[3] This again points to the elevated position of the officer. The duty of the *prādeśika* may therefore be summed up as one of supervising the collection of revenue and of maintaining law and order both in the rural areas and in the towns within his district.

The status of the *rājūka* was subordinate to that of the *prādeśika*, although other writers have suggested the reverse.[4] The description of the officer as being in charge of many hundreds of thousands of people does not necessarily imply that he was a minister of the central government; it can refer to a responsible position in local administration. Among the duties of the *prādeśika* is included that of making a tour every five years to inspect the entire administration of areas under his control. He is accompanied by the *yukta* and the *rājūka*.[5] The officials are mentioned in the following order, *yukta*, *rājūka*, *prādeśika*. Normally the first or the last mentioned would be the seniormost. The *yukta* we know to have been a subordinate official. It is unlikely that the seniormost official would be mentioned in the middle of the list. If we also take into consideration the work of the *prādeśika*, it becomes clear that he was the seniormost of the three.

The 4th Pillar Edict states that the *rājūkas* are occupied with many hundreds of thousands of people. The edict continues with advice to the *rājūkas* on their relationship with the people over whom they are thus empowered. This is concerned largely with the giving of rewards or

[1] II, 35.
[2] IV, 1.
[3] IV, 9.
[4] Jayaswal has attempted to prove that they were ministers of the central government. In addition to the fact that they are in charge of many hundreds of people, he maintains that the word is derived from *rājū* meaning king or ruler (*Hindu Polity*, pp. 195, 287, 301–2). The latter argument is based on false etymology. The first syllable in *rājūka* is lengthened because double consonants could not be written in *Brāhmī* at that time.
[5] III R.E. Girnār. Bloch, *Les Inscriptions d'Asoka*, p. 96.

punishments. The *rājūkas* worked in a judicial capacity as well as being revenue administrators. The fact that their administrative work was of equal or greater importance is clear from the statement that they were occupied with many hundred thousand people, since in their judicial work alone they would be dealing with a far smaller number. Since they are referred to collectively in this edict the total number of people over whom they had administrative control would naturally run into many hundred thousands. Further in the edict they are commanded to obey the agents of the king who are acquainted with the wishes of the king. If they had been very senior officials, the king would not have stated so categorically, and in public, that they were to obey his agents.[1] The work of the *rājūkas* was restricted to the rural areas, since they were appointed to work for the welfare of country people, *janapada hitasukhāye*.[2] In the course of their work they were also expected to teach people to practise the *Dhamma*.

The fact that in his twenty-seventh regnal year, Aśoka ordered that judicial decisions were to be made by the *rājūkas* would suggest that in previous years these decisions were made by more senior officials. This new policy gave the *rājūkas* greater power. By not having to refer every judicial decision to a senior officer, the effectiveness and pace of administration was improved. With regard to the death sentence an appeal could be made to the *rājūkas*. Presumably in border-line cases they may have referred the entire matter to their superior officers, the *prādeśikas*. The judicial nature of the duties of the *rājūkas* becomes more clear, and their importance in provincial administration becomes more apparent when we consider their administrative work.

There is agreement among various sources that the *rājūka* belonged to the department of administration responsible for surveying and assessing land. An identification has been made between the Mauryan *rājūka* and the *rajjugāhaka* mentioned in the *Jātakas*.[3] The *rājūka* or *rajjugāhaka* was the rope-holding officer who measured the lands of the tax-paying cultivators. The land-tax was assessed according to the size and quality of the land. Assessment on the share of produce was made by another official. The *rājūka* is also known to the *Arthaśāstra*.[4] The *cora-rajjuka* is described as a rural officer who is concerned with the sources of revenue. The market officers, *agoranomoi*, mentioned by Megasthenes probably referred to the

[1] The use of the word *pulisāni* for agents suggests that they were not high-ranking inspectors or emissaries of the king, but possibly public relations officers who informed the king of public opinion, and received from him orders regarding policy on this subject.

[2] Bloch, *Les Inscriptions d'Asoka*, p. 164.

[3] Buhler, *ZDMG*, 1893, vol. xlvii, pp. 466 ff. *Jātakas*, vol. iv, p. 169.

[4] II, 6; IV, 13.

rājūkas.[1] Their work is described as follows, 'Some superintend the rivers, measure the land as is done in Egypt, and inspect the sluices, from which water is let out from the main canals into their branches so that everyone may have an equal supply of it. The same persons have charge also of the huntsmen, and are entrusted with the power of rewarding and punishing them according to their deserts. They collect the taxes and superintend the occupations connected with the land, as those of the wood-cutters, the carpenters, the black-smiths, and the miners. They construct roads, and, at every ten stadia, set up a pillar to show the by-roads and distances.'

It is evident why Aśoka devotes an entire edict to the work of the *rājūkas*. Clearly they were the backbone of the rural administration. The fact that they were given increased judicial powers in the settlement of disputes, during the reign of Aśoka was a logical step. The conflicts brought to them would be largely concerned with agricultural problems, assessment, remission of taxes, land disputes, water disputes, grazing disputes between cultivators and herdsmen, and quarrels amongst village artisans. If each of these disputes had to be taken to the *prādeśika* for judgment, it would have acted as a break on the pace of administration, especially as the *rājūka* himself would have to present the case since he was the officer directly responsible for the administrative measure concerning the particular issue. Thus a far more satisfactory step was to increase the power of the *rājūka*, even at the risk of the *rājūka* becoming high-handed in his dealings with the rural people, a risk which Aśoka appears to have been aware of. Another factor which may have influenced this decision was that in the later part of Aśoka's reign, when he was incapable of maintaining the same degree of personal control as in his early years, he may have decided on a policy of decentralization in some departments. The office of the *rājūka* was thus given more power.

The check on the *rājūka* abusing his power was already in existence in the form of the *prādeśikas* who were expected to lay great stress on inspection and surveillance. More specifically, in his thirteenth regnal year, Aśoka had ordered that a quinquennial inspection should be undertaken by the group of three officials, the *prādeśika*, *rājūka*, and *yukta*. The purpose of this tour was no doubt that each *rājūka* would present his work, both administrative and judicial, to the *prādeśika*, and the latter's report would be recorded by the *yukta*. The presence of the *rājūka* at the inspection, raised it to an altogether more valuable level. The purely judicial aspect of the *rājūka's* work may also have been inspected by the special *mahāmatta*

[1] Strabo, XV, 1, 50; *Age of the Nandas and Mauryas*, pp. 120 n. 1 and 224.

sent to inspect the urban judicial administration. The report was made available by the *yuktas* to the council of ministers.

The *yuktas* mentioned in the 3rd Rock Edict appear to have been subordinate officials. Early writers have attempted to translate the word in various ways.[1] The duties of the *yuktas* were largely secretarial work and accounting. They accompanied the *rājūkas* and the *prādeśikas* in order to register decisions taken by the senior officers and on the basis of these to draw up reports which were then submitted to the ministers and the ministerial council. The *yukta* as an accountant is referred to in the *Arthaśāstra*, where it is said that superintendents of all departments are to work with the *yuktas* and other officers, in order to prevent the embezzlement of funds.[2] The fact of their being accountants would be an added reason for them to accompany the *rājūkas* and the *prādeśikas* on their quinquennial tours.

There was an intermediate level of administration between the district level and that of the village. The unit here was formed by a group of five or ten villages. The two important officials concerned with the administration of this unit were the *gopa* and the *sthānika*.[3] The *gopa* worked as an accountant to the unit. His duties included the setting up of village boundaries, the registration of various kinds of land, of buildings, and of gifts and remission of agricultural taxes. He also kept a census of the population of each village according to their tax-paying capacity, their professions and their age. Income and expenditure of such persons was also recorded. The livestock of each village was noted. The tax was collected by the *sthānika* who worked directly under the *prādeśika*. Together with the *gopa*, he was subject to periodic inspections from senior officers. It would seem that the *sthānika* was the equivalent of the modern assistant collector, and the *prādeśika* was the district collector, both grades of officials working under the final authority of the *samāhartṛ* or the chief collector.

Individual villages must have had their own set of officials who were directly responsible to the *gopas*. The village headman was no doubt chosen from amongst the village elders. He may have supervised the tax collection of the village and other obvious matters such as discipline and defence. In the smaller villages it is likely that the headman was the sole functionary. In larger villages he may have been assisted by others, necessary to administration, such as an accountant and a scribe. These semi-official functionaries may have been paid by a remission in taxes. Some of the full-time officials employed by the king were paid with land grants.[4] However,

[1] *IA*, 1891, p. 246 n. 50; *ZDMG*, vol. xxxvii, p. 106; *JRAS*, 1914, pp. 387 ff.

[2] II, 9.

[3] Ibid., II, 35.

[4] *Arthaśāstra*, II, 1.

they did not own the land, as they had no right to sell or mortgage it, but were entitled only to its produce.

Other officials functioned at various levels of the organization. We have already mentioned the king's agents or *pulisāni*, who probably belonged to a subordinate rank similar to that of the *yuktas*.[1] They functioned in a similar way as modern Public Relations Officers. They were acquainted with public opinion which they reported to the king, and the king in turn used them to ensure that his policy was being made known even in the more remote parts of the kingdom. Owing to the nature of their work they were not all of the same grade. Aśoka mentions that they were appointed to three grades.[2] Those closest to the king who may have contributed to decisions on policy, must have belonged to the highest grade. Associated with the *pulisāni* were the *paṭivedakās* or special reporters, also mentioned in the edicts.[3] They had direct access to the king at any moment and it would seem that the king placed great reliance on their evaluation of public opinion. Both the *pulisāni* and the *paṭivedakās* must also have served as a link between the central administration and the provincial administration. The *paṭivedakās* may be compared with the institution of spies mentioned in the *Arthaśāstra* (*cāra* and *gūḍha-puruṣa*).[4] The Aśokan organization does not appear to be as complex as that envisaged by Kauṭalya. In the work of the latter the espionage system is of the utmost importance. Spies are sent all over the country disguised as ordinary citizens in every walk of life. Even ministers are watched by spies. Aśoka, on the other hand admits in the edicts that he employs both agents and reporters. These may have been travelling inspectors (those of a high grade), who were known to the population and the administration, who went from place to place examining the governmental organization and making reports to the king.

Such officials are not unknown to the administration of other empires. The Achaemenids sent an officer every year to make a careful inspection of each province. He was known as the king's eye or the king's ear or the king's messenger.[5] His work was an additional control on the part of the king over the administration. Charlemagne had evolved a similar but even more efficient system. Two officials known as the *Missi* were sent each year to tour the country.[6] One was the secular representative and the other was the representative of the church. They usually travelled in pairs thus acting as a check on each other's work. They had the power to dismiss

[1] IV P.E. Bloch, *Les Inscriptions d'Asoka*, p. 164.
[2] VII P.E. Ibid., p. 168.
[3] VI R.E. Ibid., p. 107.
[4] I, 12; IV, 9.
[5] Olmstead, *History of the Persian Empire*, p. 59; Ghirshman, *Iran*, p. 144.
[6] Winston, *Charlemagne*, p. 210.

lower officials if any were found to be inefficient. They insisted on the king's decrees being read out at public meetings, and wherever necessary these decrees were translated from Latin to the vernacular. It is quite probable that the *pulisāni* were also expected to read aloud the edicts of Aśoka whenever opportunity demanded. Of the two *Missi*, the clerical representative investigated the work of monks and nuns, and the secular official examined the judicial and financial records of the administration. In the case of Charlemagne, the *Missi* acted as a check on the growing feudal power of the local lords. In the case of Aśoka, the king's agents curbed the ambition of provincial rulers.

The frequency of inspections and the existence of spies must have carried with it the flavour of a totalitarian state. Since there was no elected representative body to assist the king in governing, he could have recourse only to such means of eliciting public opinion. When used with caution and in a responsible manner they may have served their purpose well. For Aśoka, these officers were of use as a vast propaganda machine in addition to their other functions. The policy of *Dhamma* for instance would be explained by them to the population, and the reaction of the latter ascertained. This reaction may well have been the basis for some of the edicts.

The sixth class mentioned by Megasthenes is that of the officers who supervise and inquire into various affairs and present reports to the king, or a superior officer such as the local magistrate. The extract quoted by Diodorus uses the term *episcopoi* for this class.[1] Strabo speaks of the same group and stresses the fact of their inspecting the army and the courtesans as well, and making secret reports to the king.[2] He uses the term *ephoroi* for them. Arrian in his account uses the same term and speaks of them reporting to the king, or to the magistrates in self-governing areas.[3] Most earlier writers argue that this was a class of spies.[4] In the light of the text, this is an exaggerated interpretation of the terms used by the Greek writers. The literal meaning of the two terms is more that of an overseer or a superintendent rather than a spy.[5] The fact that they were asked to make secret reports to the king does not imply that they belonged to the espionage service. The mention of these reports may be better interpreted as indicate ing that they had direct access to the king, and that their important reports could reach him without having to go through the many channels of

[1] Diodorus, II, 41.

[2] Strabo, XV, 1, 48.

[3] *Indica*, XII.

[4] e.g. Timmer, *Megasthenes en de Indische Maatschappij*, p. 170.

[5] *Episcopoi* is translated as 'the one who watches over: overseer; guardian'. *Ephoroi* is translated as 'overseer: guardian; ruler'. The term is used for officials in corporations and was the title of the magistrates at Heraclea (Liddell and Scott, *Greek-English Lexicon*, pp. 657, 747).

bureaucratic organization. Furthermore, it seems hardly feasible that spies could be distinguished as a class, apart from the rest of the population. The purpose of having spies is lost if their numbers and activities are widely known.

The sixth class was that of officials junior in rank to the councillors. They would thus be the same as the *adhyakṣas*, the superintendents of various departments mentioned in the *Arthaśāstra*.[1] These officials were responsible for the efficient working of a particular department under their charge. It would not be unusual that in the course of their work they would be expected to make reports either to the king or to the higher officials. The institution of spies as described in the *Arthaśāstra* is not similar to this sixth class. The use of spies in various disguises for gathering information is not only a known practice, but is suggested as a normal part of statecraft.[2] But spies are nowhere treated as a separate class. They are a group within the administrative system and are recruited from various strata of society, from orphaned children to brahman widows and *śūdra* women, including a variety of state employees.

Spies are not described working as inspectors or overseers. Their purpose is to merge themselves within the group that they are sent to spy upon, and identify themselves completely with members of the profession which will give them the closest access to the matter which concerns them. Thus it is suggested that spies should work in the guise of fraudulent disciples, recluses, householders, merchants, ascetics, students, mendicant women, and prostitutes. Such an array of spies could work in many sections of society. Secrecy is naturally emphasized in this work. Not only are the spies unknown to the general public, but they are unknown to each other as well. It is stated that the officers in the institute of espionage should not know the working spies, but should give written directions. The espionage system was used not only in the detection of crime and eliciting of public opinion in the home country, but spies were also sent to foreign countries, just as spies from foreign countries were known to be active in the home country.

Urban administration had its own hierarchy of officials. The maintenance of law and order in the city was the chief concern of the city superintendent or *nāgaraka*.[3] Every stranger to the city had therefore to be reported and registered. At night a strict curfew was enforced, forbidding movement to all but those who had special permission. The cleanliness of the city was

[1] Book II. The Sanskrit *adhyakṣa* is etymologically similar to the terms used by Diodorus and Arrian.

[2] II, 35; IV, 4; I, 11; I, 12.

[3] II, 36.

also the concern of the *nāgaraka*. Because of the prevalence of wooden buildings in some cities, the danger of fire was a constant fear. The *nāgaraka* in supervising fire precautions had to see to it that all blacksmiths and others who used fire in their trade, inhabited one particular section of the city. In times of famine the city superintendent was in charge of the distribution of grain from the granaries.[1] The *nāgaraka* was assisted by two subordinate officials, the *gopa* and the *sthānika*.[2] Their functions were similar to those of their namesakes in rural administration. The *gopa* kept the accounts of ten, twenty, and forty households. This was a detailed procedure since he was supposed to know the income and expenditure of each household. He also kept a register of each person recording the name, occupation, *gotra*, and caste. The *sthānika* kept the accounts of the various sections of the city and presumably collected general taxes when and where they were due. Matters of any importance were reported first to the *gopa* or *sthānika* and they in turn informed the *nāgaraka*.

The Aśokan inscriptions mention the *nagalaviyohālaka mahāmattas* and refer to them largely in their judicial capacity.[3] This is not a reference to the *nāgaraka* since these *mahāmattas* appear to conduct judicial proceedings whereas the *nāgaraka*, in terms of judicial administration, is only concerned with the release of prisoners on certain auspicious occasions, such as the birth of a prince. It would seem that the *nagalaviyohālaka mahāmattas* were judicial officers who worked under the general administration of the *nāgaraka*. The latter may have intervened in their work during the proceedings of special cases, and sometimes when determining which prisoners were to be released on certain occasions. The *nagalaviyohālaka mahāmattas* held positions similar to those of modern magistrates.[4]

In describing city administration, Megasthenes outlines a more elaborate system.[5] According to him the officials are divided into six committees each with a membership of five. The first committee was concerned with matters relating to industrial arts. The second occupied itself with the entertainment of foreigners. Its work consisted of providing lodgings, and keeping a watch on foreigners through people who were ostensibly assisting them. They were escorted part of the way when they left the country, or, if they died, their property was forwarded to their relatives. They were given medical attention when sick. The third committee kept a register of births

[1] Mahāsthān and Sohgaurā Inscriptions. Sircar, *Select Inscriptions . . .*, pp. 82, 85.

[2] *Arthaśāstra*, II, 36.

[3] I S.E. Bloch, *Les Inscriptions d'Asoka*, p. 136.

[4] The *nagalaviyohālaka mahāmattas* may have been similar to the *paura-vyavahārakas* briefly mentioned in the *Arthaśāstra* as among the more important officials in the city administration.

[5] Strabo, XV, 1, 50.

and deaths both by way of a census, and for purposes of taxation. The fourth committee was in charge of matters of trade and commerce such as inspecting weights and measures, organizing public sales, and ensuring that each merchant dealt with a single commodity, since more than one required a double tax. The fifth committee supervised the public sale of manufactured articles. The sixth committee collected the tax on the articles sold, this being one-tenth of the purchase price.

Indian sources do not mention the existence of these committees. Nevertheless each of the committees mentioned by Megasthenes has its equivalent official in the list given in the *Arthaśāstra*. It is possible that for certain sections of the administration of the city, or more particularly of Pāṭaliputra, committees were found to be more efficient than an individual official. A city as large as Pāṭaliputra must have been divided into a certain number of sectors, each with an identical administrative organization. It is quite likely that officials of one department met in a group and delivered their reports to the central organization and received their orders in the same way. That the *Arthaśāstra* does not mention such a procedure is possible, since it was not a detailed description of Mauryan administration, but rather a text-book on general administration. Without doubt the Mauryas must have modified parts of it in practice, or even deviated from it where necessary. Megasthenes' description may therefore apply to the administration of Pāṭaliputra alone.[1] Timmer has suggested that Megasthenes perhaps saw groups of officers of various ranks working in one department, and mistakenly believed them to be a committee of equals.[2] The committees mentioned by him correspond with the offices of various superintendents mentioned in the *Arthaśāstra*. These officials, the *adhyakṣas*, were assisted by subordinate officers. Possibly each office consisted of the superintendent and four assisting officers thus leading Megasthenes to believe that it was a committee. This is only one of many possible explanations.

The first committee supervised the industrial arts. This may have been the officers who were in charge of the artisans of the city. The second committee has no exact equivalent in the *Arthaśāstra*. Considering the close watch that was kept on foreigners, as is clear from the duties of the *nāgaraka*,

[1] The use of committees of five is completely foreign to Indian administration. Although in Indian sources there is generally one person at the head, nevertheless such committees based on the idea of the *panchāyat* are mentioned in the *Jātakas* (*Mahābodhi Jātaka*, vol. v, p. 228), and the *Mahābhārata* (II, 5). An even more interesting parallel to the description of Megasthenes can be observed in the administration of the village of Uttaramerur in the Cola period (N. Sastri, *The Colas*, pp. 283-4).

[2] *Megasthenes en de Indische Maatschappij*, p. 199.

it seems obvious that there would be a group of officials specially concerned with aliens. Such a body would naturally have more work in the capital, which was likely to be visited by foreigners. Foreigners did not mean only non-Indians. Visitors from the more distant parts of the empire would also be included in this category. If indeed such a detailed register was kept of all the inhabitants of the city as the *Arthaśāstra* suggests, then it is likely that any non-resident of the town was classified as a foreigner. Those that were escorted on their way when leaving the country would be the more important foreigners. The fact that they were watched by the assistants specially appointed to look after their welfare, agrees in spirit with the emphasis placed by the *Arthaśāstra* on the use of spies in various guises for obtaining information. The statement that the committee forwarded the property of those that died in Pāṭaliputra, seems somewhat idealistic. Presumably this only applied in cases where the relatives were in areas under Mauryan jurisdiction. The mention of the committee burying the bodies of those that die, points in this instance to non-Hindu foreigners, else cremation would be the accepted form of disposal of the body.

The third committee registering births and deaths and keeping census reports tallies very closely with the work of the *gopas*, mentioned earlier. The fourth committee appears to have had responsibilities similar to the various superintendents connected with trade and commerce mentioned in the *Arthaśāstra*. The fifth committee covers almost the same work as that done by the superintendent of commerce. The sixth committee, responsible for the collection of the tax of one-tenth, is probably a reference to the office of the *sthānika* who was responsible for the collection of various taxes.[1]

Other officers concerned with the administration of the city appear to have been overlooked or were forgotten by the time Megasthenes came to write his memoirs. Thus the *nāgaraka* or city superintendent must certainly have been an important official at Pāṭaliputra, but Megasthenes makes no mention of him. It is possible that parts of the original account of Megasthenes on city administration have been lost, and that the full account may have mentioned the *nāgaraka* and other officials. The *Arthaśāstra* constantly emphasizes the importance of central control and certainly Mauryan administration was in favour of this centralization. It is unlikely that Megasthenes, an otherwise intelligent observer, would have missed this emphasis. It is not outside the bounds of possibility that this was another instance of the author investing India with institutions based on his own political idealism.

[1] II, 19; II, 16; II, 36.

Among the other officials mentioned by Aśoka in the edicts are the *aṃta-mahāmattas*.[1] These were the officers who worked among the frontier peoples and the less civilized tribes. Because they are ranked as *mahāmattas* they may have been in charge of the administration of these areas. They were directly concerned with carrying out Aśoka's policy towards the frontier people. This policy was largely an effort to gain the confidence of the border tribes, so that with mutual trust, their loyalty might also be depended upon. He expects the *aṃta-mahāmattas* to work towards creating this confidence and asserts again that they, the border tribes, are like his children, and his relationship towards them is that of a father. This administrative policy is linked closely with the propagation of *Dhamma* amongst the borderers, which was included as one of the duties of the *aṃta-mahāmattas*.

Elsewhere in his edicts, Aśoka has mentioned the establishing of centres of medical treatment for men and animals in neighbouring countries, which he claims was done at his instigation; the same applied to the southern borderers as well.[2] It is possible that the *aṃta-mahāmattas* acted as liaison officers in matters of this kind where the bordering peoples were involved. The Greek kingdoms may have received envoys, since their relationship does not appear to have been quite as close to Aśoka as that of the southern borderers. Together with acquainting the borderers with the principles of the *Dhamma* the *aṃta-mahāmattas* were also responsible for preventing rebellions against Mauryan authority amongst the frontier peoples. These *mahāmattas* were aided in their work by special officers whom the king appointed for this purpose, and who were called *ayutike*.[3] The similarity of the designations *yukta* and *ayutika* suggests a similar category of officials. The *aṃta-mahāmattas* of the edicts may have been the equivalent of the *anta-pālas* of the *Arthaśāstra*.[4] These were the superintendents of tolls. No doubt each province had its own *anta-pālas*, and possibly in some provinces a toll had to be paid even in exchanging goods in the various districts, But toll-houses must have existed along the borders of the empire. It is quite likely that the duties of the *aṃta-mahāmattas* included the collection of revenue from the toll dues. They would thus supervise the work of the toll collectors and the superintendent of tolls would be responsible to them.

Owing to the suppressed condition of women in the society of his time, it is possible that Aśoka may have felt the need to appoint a

[1] II S.E.; I P.E. Bloch, *Les Inscriptions d'Asoka*, pp. 140, 161.

[2] II R.E., Girnār. Ibid., p. 93.

[3] II S.E. Ibid., p. 140.

[4] II, 21.

special group of *mahāmattas* who would be concerned mainly with the welfare of women. The term used for these officers was *ithījhakha-mahāmattas*, literally, the officers who were the superintendents of women.[1] A connection has been suggested between these officers and the *gaṇikādhyakṣas* or superintendents of prostitutes.[2] It seems hardly feasible that officers of the rank of *mahāmattas* would have been appointed merely to supervise the city's prostitutes. Certainly the work of these *mahāmattas* would include the supervision of the prostitutes, but it would also concern itself with other duties connected with women. Much of their time must have been given to the royal harems. That these harems were large enough to warrant a special class of officers, is clear from the inscriptions of Aśoka. The king mentions that the *dhamma-mahāmattas* are busy working in many places, including his own residence and those of his brothers and sisters, and whatever other relatives the king has, both in Pāṭaliputra and elsewhere.[3] The organization of the harems for instance, must have required this special body of officers. It has been suggested that Aśoka maintained harems outside Pāṭaliputra, and subsidiary to his main palace.[4] Here the women were of a lower caste. This is an exaggerated estimate of Aśoka's indulgence in harem life. As the edict indicates, the harems were not only those of Aśoka but also of his various relatives.

The 7th Pillar Edict speaks of the *dhamma-mahāmattas* and many other chief officers, whose duty it is to record charitable gifts made by the members of his family.[5] The chief officers were probably the *ithījhakha-mahāmattas*, and kept detailed records of donations, etc.; whereas the *dhamma-mahāmattas* were responsible for preaching the *Dhamma* and encouraging the members of the royal family to make donations, the *ithījhakha-mahāmattas* were concerned with the administrative matters in the harem On other occasions when women were in need of help, it is possible that they may have appealed to the office of these *mahāmattas*.[6] The more subordinate officers were concerned with the type of work envisaged in the *Arthaśāstra*, the employment of women in the craft of weaving, or the regulation of prostitutes.

Every official of the Mauryan administration had to propagate the *Dhamma* in the course of his work, whether it was the *prādeśika* going on tour, or the *rājūka* in his judicial capacity. In speaking of the *Dhamma*

[1] This is clear from the Shāhbāzgarhi version of the edict where the word used is *istridhiyakṣamahāmatta*. Bloch, *Les Inscriptions d'Asoka*, p. 124.

[2] Hultzsch, *Corpus Inscriptionum Indicarum*, vol. i, p. 22 n. 4. *Arthaśāstra*, II, 27.

[3] V R.E., Dhauli. Bloch, *Les Inscriptions d'Asoka*, p. 104.

[4] Bhandarkar, *Asoka*, p. 12.

[5] VII P.E. Bloch, *Les Inscriptions d'Asoka*, p. 168.

[6] Bhandarkar, *Asoka*, pp. 56–57.

stress was laid on general observances such as consideration towards slaves, servants, brahmans, *śramaṇas*, parents, aged people, animals, and even abstinence from the killing of animals, and the welfare of prisoners. But Aśoka did not rest at the general propagation of *Dhamma* by his officers. In his fourteenth regnal year he started a new service, that of the *dhamma-mahāmattas*, whose particular concern was the spreading of the *Dhamma* and explaining the policy wherever necessary. As a service this group of officers was new to Indian administration.[1] Originally their work was largely that of welfare, but gradually their power increased until they could interfere in the working of various religious sects and secular institutions. The king became increasingly dependent upon them. They appear to have become similar in their attitudes to a religious order.

Most matters of importance in the daily administration of the country were attended to by the general administrative officers. Irrigation for instance was handled by the office of *rājūkas*, or the *agoronomoi* of Megasthenes, who inspected the rivers and sluices and supervised the distribution of water among the cultivators. The Rudradāman Inscription states that a dam was built on the Sudarśan lake during the reign of Candragupta Maurya, to facilitate water supply to the neighbouring countryside.[2] The importance of forests was recognized during this period, and the *Artha-śāstra* mentions a superintendent of forest produce, who also supervised the care of the forests.[3] The ill-effects of the random cutting down of forests must have been felt during the Mauryan period. Forests were also preserved since they were a source of revenue, which was provided by the tax on timber and on hunters who maintained a livelihood from the animals in the forest. Moreover timber from the forests was essential for building purposes. Thus the clearance of forests had to be regulated. The *Artha-śāstra* suggests the employment of guards to prevent unnecessary damage. This was also to ensure that on each occasion that the land was cleared and brought under cultivation, the local administration would be informed, so that the land could then be registered and the cultivator would have to pay the required taxes. The wanton burning of forests is prohibited in one of the edicts.[4]

The administration of the armed forces is described in detail both by Kauṭalya and by Megasthenes. The former classifies troops in the main into three categories, hereditary troops, hired troops, and soldiers belonging to corporations.[5] The first were of primary importance. These con-

[1] We have discussed their role in detail in the following chapter.

[2] Sircar, *Select Inscriptions* . . . , p. 169.

[3] II, 17.

[4] V P.E. Bloch, *Les inscriptions d'Asoka*, p. 166.

[5] II, 33.

stituted the standing army of the king and were probably the troops referred to by Megasthenes in describing the fifth class, that of the soldiers.[1] Since they formed the core of the fighting force they were given special treatment. Megasthenes speaks of them being numerically the second largest group, smaller only than that of the peasants. The troops are described as being very well paid; during periods of peace they are said to be lazy and seem to spend their time enjoying themselves. The statement that they are so well paid that they support others on their salary is not an exaggeration. According to the *Arthaśāstra* the trained soldier was to be paid 500 *paṇas*, which in the range of salaries was listed as a very comfortable income.[2] The maintenance of the army was the concern of the commander-in-chief and the superintendent of the infantry. Other sections of the army, the cavalry, the elephant corps, and the armoury, were each under their respective officer.[3]

The extension of the empire under the first two Mauryas meant that the army had to be given priority in many matters, in order that it might be constantly ready for major campaigns. Hence it was regarded as constituting a special class. The hereditary troops were no doubt linked with the *kṣatriya* element in society which gave them added prestige. The armed strength of the Mauryas and of the Nandas before them is always described in colossal numbers in European sources. Plutarch writes that Candragupta conquered with an army of 600,000 foot soldiers, apart from cavalry, chariots and elephants. Pliny speaks of 80,000 infantry, 1000 horses and 700 elephants.[4] These figures would represent the regular and reserve forces. Plutarch was describing this force by way of explaining the armed opposition that Alexander would have met if he had continued his campaign beyond the river Beas. It is therefore possible that some of the figures are exaggerated.

When describing the administration of the armed forces Megasthenes speaks of there being six committees with five members on each, similar to those administering Pāṭaliputra.[5] This exact parallel in numbers is unusual and may be the result of a mistake in one of the two records. Again, Megasthenes may have had the superintendents of various sections in mind, as described in the *Arthaśāstra*. The first committee co-operates with the admiral of the fleet, and is therefore concerned with naval warfare. Ships and boats must have been used in battles where there was a possibility of river transport or a river attack, though this form of warfare does

[1] Diodorus, II, 41.

[2] V, 3. In later centuries, the sepoys in the armies of the East India Company are known to have employed personal servants.

[3] II, 33; II, 18; II, 33–36.

[4] *Historia Naturalis*, VI, 21, 22; *Life of Alexander*, lxii.

[5] Strabo, XV, 1, 50.

not seem to be highly developed. The second committee would be equivalent to the modern commissariat. It supervises the bullock-trains used for transporting equipment, food, and other necessities. Although the *Arthaśāstra* does not speak in detail of the commissariat it is assumed that every army is accompanied by such a section. It is mentioned for instance in the chapter on the encampment of the army.[1] The servants of the regular soldiers, grooms, and other attendants are included in this section.

The remaining four committees are concerned with the four branches of the army regularly listed in the Indian sources: infantry, cavalry, the chariots, and the elephants. Each of these is discussed in detail in the *Arthaśāstra*.[2] Megasthenes states that the soldier was expected to return his arms to the magazine. This was probably true, since the armoury as described by Kauṭalya is an extensive establishment periodically inspected, suggesting that all the arms were kept in one place.[3] Horses and elephants were the property of the king and private ownership of these was not permitted. Megasthenes, like most Greek writers in India, appears to have been very impressed with elephants, and his accounts of the catching and breeding of elephants are amazingly correct.[4] All this information confirms the fact that soldiers were paid their salaries in cash and not with land grants. It is curious that in describing military administration, Megasthenes once again omits mentioning the central authority, in this case the commander-in-chief. The *Arthaśāstra* stresses the fact that the man who holds this office must be skilled in handling the four branches of the army.

Another aspect of Mauryan administration is mentioned briefly in passing, in the European sources. Diodorus in his account refers to kingless states. He mentions that Dionysius established a kingdom in India and after many generations of his descendants had ruled, the kingdom was dissolved and democratic government was set up in the cities.[5] The same is stated regarding a kingdom built by Heracles.[6] In the latter case some of the cities retained kings, others adopted a democratic form of government. Elsewhere it is stated that the sixth class, that of the overseers, sent in their reports to the magistrates in cities where there was no king.[7] Arrian makes similar remarks, and in addition mentions that the peasants bring their taxes to the king and to the cities which are autonomous. The members of the sixth caste likewise bring reports to the magistrates in self-governing cities.[8] He mentions the same procedure with regard to the seventh class, that of councillors. Strabo refers to a system of government by councillors

[1] X, 1.
[2] II, 30, 31, 33; X, 1–6.
[3] II, 18.
[4] Strabo, XV, 1, 41–43.
[5] Diodorus, II, 35.
[6] Ibid., 39.
[7] Ibid., 41.
[8] *Indica*, IX.

in the country beyond the Hypanis. It is an aristocratic form of government consisting of 500 councillors, each of whom furnished the state with an elephant.[1]

An earlier writer on the subject is of the opinion that Megasthenes was aware of the system in which cities had a semi-independent status within an empire, as was the case in the Seleucid empire.[2] This independence was naturally limited to the control of internal affairs. Megasthenes states that these autonomous cities were a part of Candragupta's empire, yet Aśoka makes no mention of them. A further suggestion is that Megasthenes may have been thinking of the autonomous tribes known to have formed part of the empire, as for instance the Āṭavikas referred to in the *Arthaśāstra*, and he automatically ascribed to them the organization of other independent cities. Megasthenes' kingless states are called *polis*, a city, and not *ethnos*, people.[3] This implies a system of government and not a tribal people living on plunder.

Evidence from another source which may throw some light on the matter can be obtained from a series of inscribed coins. Among the coins found at Taxila, a number of oblong, copper coins contained the legend, *negama*.[4] The word has been variously interpreted as either referring to traders or a market merchant guild, or 'mercantile money token issued by traders', or 'coin of commerce'.[5] Although this suggests that there was some local autonomy in certain matters, these cities cannot be regarded as free cities, since the autonomy applies only to merchant guilds or large-scale business organizations, and that too mainly in the matter of commerce. It does not imply the political autonomy of the entire city. There may have been some arrangement with these guilds, whereby the cultivators of certain products used by the guilds in their manufacture or by the artisans, paid their taxes directly to the guilds.

This reference to independent cities could also have arisen from a misunderstanding of the original text, by Diodorus and Arrian, or from an inability on the part of Megasthenes to state clearly what the actual situation was. In the Buddhist period, tribes with an oligarchical system of government existed in the Ganges valley.[6] Some tribes of the Indus valley are described in European sources as being under a republican form of government.[7] Some of the tribes led an independent semi-civilized

[1] Strabo, XV, 1, 36.

[2] Timmer, *Megasthenes en de Indische Maatschappij*, pp. 233 ff.

[3] Ibid.

[4] Allan, *Catalogue of the Coins of Ancient India* (British Museum), pp. cxxv ff.

[5] Ibid.; Cunningham, *ASR*, XIV, p. 20; Buhler, *Indian Studies*, III, p. 49.

[6] *Sumaṅgala Vilāsani*, II, p. 519; *Majjhima Commentary*, I, p. 394.

[7] Arrian, *Anabasis*, VI, 6, 14; McCrindle, *Invasion of India by Alexander the Great*, pp. 350–1.

existence. With the conquest of this region by the Mauryas these tribes would be incorporated within the empire. It is possible that during the reign of Candragupta Maurya, since the conquest was recent, Mauryan administration may have dealt leniently with them, allowing them to continue many of their older institutions, although the overall administration would be controlled by the Mauryan authorities. This system may have created the illusion of these tribes or of their cities being semi-independent. As the administration was expanded and began to gain greater control over the outlying provinces, these cities would increasingly lose their remaining independence, until, in the reign of Aśoka, they were completely amalgamated within the empire.

The traditional memories of monarchical rule with intervening periods of republican government, may be explained by the fact that recollection of early periods, when kings were elected, was still present. The oligarchical system may have had its origin in the Vedic system of government with the help of the two assemblies, the *samiti* and the *sabhā*. The Greek authors were familiar with the idea of the Greek city states and for them the independent city was not an unusual political phenomenon. It is possible that Diodorus may have inserted the reference to the independent cities as a matter of course from his knowledge of Greek political institutions, without being consciously aware that a similar institution may not have existed in India during the Mauryan period.

A misunderstanding of the original text of Megasthenes may have resulted in references to independent cities. This is possible particularly in the passage where it is stated that the overseers sent reports to the magistrates in the cities where there were no kings. Megasthenes may have been referring to those cities where neither the king nor any important representative of the king was in residence. Thus, in Pāṭaliputra, or in any of the provincial capitals under the control of a viceroy, the superintendents would be in a position to send their reports directly to the king or the king's representative. In other cities where no such representative had been stationed, the reports would naturally be sent to the highest administrative body, that of the magistrates. Megasthenes may have meant that they were self-governing as opposed to the other cities which were governed by the king's representative. The description of such cities as self-governing may have been added by the later authors, by way of elucidation, although the term was incorrect. In writing his *Indica*, Arrian may have consulted the earlier work of Diodorus on the subject, particularly as Diodorus was in turn quoting from Megasthenes. Arrian's introduction of the self-governing cities into his description of the seventh class for example, may well have been his own addition, following, to his mind, quite logically from the statement of Diodorus.

It is clear from the administration of the period that the king had control over even the most remote part of the empire. An efficient bureaucracy was essential to this. The control extended to the very details of daily life. Even if the administrators did not supervise these details in practice, the mention of them as included in their responsibilities, suggests the degree of organization demanded from the officials. Efficient as this system may have been, it must also have produced at times too much interference or regulation in the lives of the people by the officials. Together with the latter worked the *dhamma-mahāmattas* and this must on occasion have been too oppressive a combination for the average citizen to accept without feeling restricted. The administration was partly imperial and partly local in its day-to-day functioning. Policy was dictated by the centre and the tendency of centralization in the administration was very strong, as is apparent from the edicts. For obvious reasons such a system works well where the ruler himself is efficient. But a weak central authority is bound to produce unfortunate results in the provinces. This inherent weakness in the administration of the early Mauryas was partially responsible for the decline of the dynasty under the later Mauryas.

The picture of the administrative machinery as given in the preceding pages, related to conditions within the Mauryan empire. The geographical extent of the empire during the reign of Aśoka can fortunately be indicated fairly precisely. The distribution of his rock and pillar edicts is unchallenged evidence of his authority. Places connected with his name by tradition may be taken into account, as also the peoples and areas mentioned by him in his edicts, as being within the empire. In the north-west his inscriptions extend as far as Mānsehrā, Shahbāzgarhi, and Laghman, with the westernmost extension reaching as far as Kandahar. He mentions the Gandhāras, the Kambojas, and the Yonas as his borderers. The domains of Antiochus II of Syria bordered the empire on the west. The references to the three peoples above as his borderers is rather ambiguous, since it is not certain whether this term meant that they were within the empire or just outside it along the frontier. Judging from the location of the inscriptions it would seem that the peoples mentioned were within the empire. The southern borderers, however, do not seem to have been included within the empire. These were the Colas, Pāṇḍyas, Sātiyaputras, and the Keralaputras. No Aśokan inscriptions have yet been found in these areas, the southernmost inscriptions being in the Raichur district. The relationship between these peoples and the empire appears to have been a closer one. The exact frontier in the south is not defined. It would seem that it ran from the west coast to the east, just south of the Chitaldroog district. The valley of the Pennar river may have been used as a natural frontier on the eastern side of the southern boundary. In the east, the empire extended as far as the Ganges delta. Tamluk was within the empire, and was a busy port.

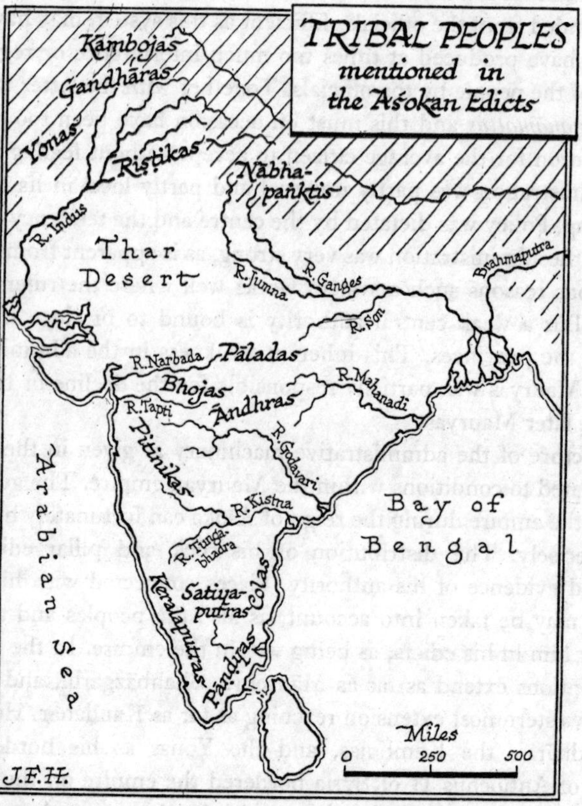

In determining the quality of governments or rulers, an evaluation of their foreign relations is essential. This would include relations based both on diplomacy and on geographical proximity. The century in which Aśoka lived was one of tremendous intercommunication between the eastern Mediterranean and South Asia. Aśoka was aware of the importance of foreign relations and contact with peoples outside his empire. Most of his contacts were to the south and the west. The east was as yet almost outside his sphere of interest. It would appear that this interest was not onesided. There must have been a fair number of foreigners in Pāṭaliputra to necessitate special committees under municipal management appointed to supervise the needs and welfare of the visitors. The term foreigner may have referred as well to people from the outlying parts of the empire, who would be almost as foreign to the citizens of Pāṭaliputra as the Greeks themselves.

The fact of Indians going in large numbers to foreign countries and travelling in distant places appears to have been a new development;[1] although Megasthenes states that Indians have never migrated from their own country.[2] This new spirit of adventure was no doubt due in part to familiarity with other peoples after the Greek campaign, and in part to the opening up of trade with foreign countries, particularly with the West. Aśoka's missions to various parts of the Hellenic world must also have assisted.[3] These missions were the main contact that Aśoka had with neighbouring countries. They can be described as embassies, though the word mission is more appropriate. Their main purpose was to acquaint the countries they visited with the policies of Aśoka, particularly that of *Dhamma*. They were not resident in any single country for a long period. They may be compared to modern goodwill missions, moving from area to area, addressing the local people, exchanging gifts and messages, and generally helping to create an interest in the ideas and peoples of the country from which they come.[4]

Had the missions been resident embassies, and if they had had some degree of permanent success, there would have been a reference to them in European sources. The fact that they are quite unheard of in contemporary literature or any later source would suggest that they made only a short-lived impression. They did, however, succeed in opening up a

[1] Although Indian troops are known to have fought under Xerxes. Herodotus, *Histories*, VII, 65.

[2] Strabo, XV, 1, 6–8.

[3] XIII R.E., Kālsi. Bloch, *Les Inscriptions d'Asoka*, p. 130.

[4] Aśoka claims that the rulers to whom he sent these missions had accepted his policy of cultivating medicinal herbs for their subjects and planting trees, etc. It is possible that in order to encourage this idea, Aśoka sent packets of seeds and cuttings of plants with the missions. In the botanical work of Theophrastus there is no direct reference to the knowledge of new plants from India, among Greek botanists of the time (Rostovtzeff, *Social and Economic History of the Hellenic World* vol. ii, pp. 1164–9, 1182). Pliny states that the Seleucids attempted to naturalize certain Indian plants such as amomum and nardum, which apparently were brought by sea from India. He also says that the *Asiae reges* and the Ptolemies made attempts to plant frankincense trees (*Historia Naturalis*, XVI, 135; XII, 56). The introduction of these plants may have been the direct result of Aśoka's missions or their cultivation may have been encouraged due to commercial reasons since there was already a demand in the West for spices and herbs from farther east.

channel as it were for the inflow of Indian ideas and goods. Indian life was not unknown in the Hellenic world. The missions familiarized it even further to the inhabitants of the neighbouring countries. It is unlikely that Aśoka expected all the kings who had received missions to put the policy of *Dhamma* into practice, completely and immediately, although he claims that this did happen. As long as these missions provoked some interest among the people they visited, Aśoka was convinced of their success.

It is curious that there should be no reference to these missions in the last important public declaration of Aśoka, the 7th Pillar Edict. In this edict, Aśoka mentions the success he has had with his welfare services and the widespread propagation of *Dhamma*, but all within the empire. The more obvious explanation is that the missions did not succeed to the extent that the king had hoped. Mention of them in the Major Rock Edicts was due to the fact that they had recently been sent and therefore the king in all enthusiasm was confident of their success. But by the twenty-eighth year of his reign he had had enough time and experience to realize that the missions might have increased the interest in things Indian, but had achieved nothing tangible in the way of establishing the practice of *Dhamma* in the countries which they had visited. Rather than admit failure, the king refrained from mentioning them. A more plausible reason as to why these missions were ignored in this edict, is that the king had restricted himself entirely to matters of domestic policy in this declaration. The missions appear to have been successful in Ceylon, where Tissa became a firm adherent of the *Dhamma* idea, and this would have deserved mention in the edict, even at the exclusion of mentioning the other countries to which they were sent.

The territory immediately adjoining the empire of Aśoka on the west, the Achaemenid empire in pre-Mauryan times and now held by Antiochus, had been a close neighbour both in thought and action. There is ample evidence of contacts between Iran and India. Some are of a superficial nature, such as the fact that Indian mercenaries from the north-west border fought in the Achaemenid army on various occasions, others of a more lasting kind, as was the inclusion of the Indian province of Sindhu and Gandhāra in the empire of Cyrus, mentioned in the Persepolis Inscription of Darius.[1] Some similarities of custom and culture have been described as due to the influence of Iran on India. This is a dangerous attitude in approaching the past, since it results largely from imposing twentieth-century national boundaries on culture systems of two thousand or more years ago. The study of cultures as carried out by modern archaeologists

[1] Sircar, *Select Inscriptions* .... pp. 6–8.

has made it necessary that present-day historians should consider the matter with a new and more correct perspective. On the question of Achaemenid 'influence' neither of the two previously held theories are acceptable. One maintains that everything Aśokan in art is derived from Achaemenid Iran, the other equally vehemently claims that it is all indigenous. Archaeology has shown that Achaemenid Iran and north-western India were very close cultural groups, and similarities were bound to exist. The then known world was a small but active one, with a considerable amount of intercommunication and trade. This enlarged the scope of cultural developments to more than local needs and the influence of religious movements to more than theological dogma.

Some of these customs similar to Iran and India were the result of practical necessity and are common to many cultures. For example the shaving of the head on certain occasions is described as an Iranian form of punishment.[1] Both the *Arthaśāstra* and the *Mahāvaṃsa* list it as a punishment as well.[2] But this punishment has been practised even in modern India, where the eyebrows of a criminal were shaved in order to make him more conspicuous. Doubtless it was for this reason that it was employed as a form of punishment in an older period. Many of the other customs were held in common ancestry. The Iranians and the Indo-Aryans, coming from the common stock of early Aryans, would naturally continue many of the earlier customs even when the two had settled in new areas. One such may have been the ceremonial hair-washing on the king's birthday.[3]

Further evidence of a common culture is the similarity between the edicts of Darius and those of Aśoka. There is no certainty as to whether Aśoka knew the edicts of the former. He may have known that the Achaemenids engraved inscriptions on rock surfaces and decided to do the same. The similarity of the form of address suggests that Aśoka may have read the text of an Iranian edict. Darius uses the phrase,

> '*thatiy Darayavush kshayathiya* . . .'[4]
> 'thus saith the king Darius . . .'

Aśoka uses the following phrase,

> '*devānaṃpiya Piyadassi rājāevam ahā* . . .'[5]
> 'the king, the beloved of the gods, Piyadassi, speaks thus . . .'

It is also possible that Aśoka knew only the formula for commencing

[1] Kingsmill, *Athenaeum*, 19 July 1902; Smith, *Early History of India*, p. 137 n. 2.

[2] *Arthaśāstra*, IV, 9; *Mahāvaṃsa*, VI, 42.

[3] Herodotus, *Histories*, IX, 110; Strabo, XV, 69.

[4] Senart, *IA*, vol. xx, pp. 255–6.

[5] III R.E., Girnār. Bloch, *Les Inscriptions d'Asoka*, p. 95.

edicts, which appears to have been, 'thus speaks the king . . . ', and which was probably used by many of the kings both Iranian and Indian.

The tone of the Aśokan edicts is certainly far more humble than of the inscriptions of Darius.[1] This difference is largely due to the difference in the contents of the inscriptions. Darius was concerned mainly with proclaiming his greatness and the value of his achievements. Aśoka, though he did not refrain from boasting about his achievements in some edicts, was nevertheless more concerned with preaching the *Dhamma*. This difference is markedly apparent in the titles taken by both kings. Darius writes of himself, 'I am Darius the Great King, King of Kings, King of countries containing all kinds of men, King in this great earth far and wide . . . '[2] Aśoka, an equally impressive figure with an equally large empire, refers to himself as, 'the king, the beloved of the gods, Piyadassi . . . '[3]

That this similarity in culture did not rest only with ideas is clear from the linguistic affinity between the inhabitants of the north-west part of the Mauryan empire and those in Achaemenid Iran. The use of *kharoṣṭhī* in the Shahbāzgarhi and Mānsehrā edicts in the north is evidence of strong contact with Iran. The fragmentary Aramaic inscription at Taxila and the Aramaic inscription from Kandahar, point to continued intercommunication between the two areas. The use of the Iranian words *dipi* and *nipiṣṭa* in the northern versions of the Major Rock Edicts, adds conviction to this idea.[4]

The Junāgadh inscription of Rudradāman mentions the area of Aparānta governed by the *yonarājā* Tuṣāspa, a governor of Aśoka.[5] The inscription describes him as a Greek, yet the name is clearly Iranian. Greek settlements in the north-west took place after the campaign of Alexander. The nucleus of the settlers were either deserters from the Greek army or were those who had deliberately stayed behind. Tuṣāspa could have been an Iranian or an Indian who had lived for some time in an area that had a predominance of Iranian culture. The Periplus mentions that relics of Alexander's invasion were to be found as far as Broach.[6] While Alexander's expedition never reached this region, it may be suggested that Greek contact with Gujarat existed in Mauryan times and a small Greek colony at Broach formed the basis for the false statement in the Periplus.[7] It is equally feasible that Iranian mercenaries whom no doubt Alexander must have employed for

[1] Cf. Kosambi, *Introduction to the Study of Indian History*, p. 189.

[2] Ghirshman, *Iran*, p. 153.

[3] For a further discussion of the titles adopted by Aśoka, see Appendix II.

[4] Hultzsch, *Corpus Inscriptionum Indicarum*, vol. i, p. xliii.

[5] Sircar, *Select Inscriptions...*, p. 169.

[6] *The Erythraean Sea*, 41, 47.

[7] For a further discussion on this matter see Narain, *The Indo-Greeks*, pp. 34, 89, 93–94.

Edicts from the Aśokan inscription at Shahbāzgarhi

his Indian campaign may have deserted at this point. Thus Tuṣāspa may have come from an important family of Greeks or Iranians of Indo-Greek or Indo-Iranian descent.

The architectural closeness of certain buildings in Achaemenid Iran and Mauryan India have raised much comment. The royal palace at Pāṭaliputra is the most striking example and has been compared with the palaces at Susa, Ecbatana, and Persepolis.[1] The ground plan is much the same as that of Persepolis. The central hall at Persepolis has an alignment of a hundred pillars and the one at Pāṭaliputra has eighty pillars. A mason's mark on one of the stones at Pāṭaliputra is remarkably similar to those found at Persepolis, suggesting a common source of the craftsmen. The Aśokan pillars with their animal capitals have been discussed in a similar light. If in fact they were made in Taxila as we have suggested, then the similarity is logical and not to be wondered at.

Farther west, the Mauryan period saw the development of trade and commerce with Babylon.[2] This was of great assistance to communication between India and the West, since it kept the maritime route open. Contact with the Greeks was again not a new development. The word used for the Greeks, *yona* or *yavana*, comes via Iran. The Iranians first came into contact with the Ionian Greeks and therefore employed the term *Yauna* when referring to the Greeks in general. In Sanskrit the word became *yavana* using what appears to be a 'back-formation', and in Prākrit it occurs as *yona*.[3] There is evidence of Greek settlement in the trans-Indus and Afghanistan areas during a period before the coming of Alexander. Xerxes, it was claimed, settled a colony of Ionian Greeks in the area between Balkh and Samarkand. They are referred to as the Branchidae and were later massacred by Alexander during the course of his campaign in that area.[4] The people of Nysa in the Swāt valley claimed Greek descent when questioned by Alexander.[5] There is a reference to *yavana-lipi* in the work of Pāṇini, and this text is believed to be pre-Mauryan.[6] The campaign of Alexander although it appears to have made little immediate impression on India at the time, must certainly have familiarized the local people with Greek ways.

Interest in India on the part of the various Greek kings is apparent from the fact that they sent ambassadors to the Indian court, particularly during the Mauryan period. Megasthenes, Deimachus, and Dionysius resided at

[1] Waddell, *Discovery of the Exact Site of Aśoka's Classic Capital at Pāṭaliputra.*

[2] Bevan, *House of Seleucus*, vol. i, p. 239.

[3] Rapson, *Indian Coins*, p. 86.

[4] Strabo, XI, 11, 4; XIV, 1, 5; Narain, *The Indo-Greeks*, p. 3.

[5] Arrian, *Indica*, I, 4–5.

[6] Pāṇini, 4, 1, 49; Kātyāyana, Varttika, 3 on Pāṇini, 4, 1, 49.

the court at Pāṭaliputra. There is no certainty as to whether Megasthenes came as an official ambassador or as a private visitor, since the sources are not in agreement on this point. In view of the early contacts it is likely that Indians visited Greek centres, even prior to the sending of Aśoka's missions, but no accounts of such visits have yet been found. There are references to the *yonas* in the rock edicts of Aśoka. On certain occasions the word refers to the Greek settlements in the north-west, and on others to the Hellenic kingdoms, depending on the context. Antiochus II Theos of Syria is more frequently mentioned. It is understandable that Antiochus would be better known to Aśoka than the other Greek kings because of earlier family connections and also because Antiochus was the nearest Greek ruler geographically. The other Hellenic kings to whom diplomatic missions were sent, were Ptolemy II Philadelphus of Egypt, Magas of Cyrene, Antigonus Gonatas of Macedonia, and Alexander of Epirus.

There was probably no rigid boundary line on the north-west frontier. The Greek settlements were probably dotted all along this frontier and their friendliness or hostility to the Mauryan state depended largely on their relations with the local viceroy at Taxila. No doubt the Mauryan state must have had a fairly direct control over them. Although mainly Greek in character, the proximity of India may have produced much Indian influence in these settlements. The *dhamma-mahāmattas* must have worked in the centres both within the empire and just outside. There would be no strong objections to this, even in areas outside, as it meant assistance in matters of welfare, such as the building of roads and the planting of medicinal herbs. Their geographical proximity would bring them into the Mauryan 'sphere of influence'.

In the north relations with Kashmir have been postulated by various authorities, but there is no actual evidence of the precise extent of Aśoka's control. Kalhaṇa states in the *Rājataraṅgiṇī* that Śrīnagara was built by Aśoka.[1] According to another tradition, Aśoka after quelling the revolt at Taxila, conquered the area of Khaśa, which is located in the south-west of modern Kashmir.[2] Hsüan Tsang relates an involved story concerning the officials who were responsible for the blinding of Kunāla and who were exiled to a region to the east of Khotan.[3] Here they came into conflict with an exiled Chinese prince who had settled, at almost the same time, in the

[1] I, 101–7; Cunningham has attempted to identify this town with Pandrethān, three miles north of modern Srinagar (*Ancient Geography of India*, p. 110).

[2] Tāranātha, *Geschichte des Buddhismus in Indien*, VI, p. 27; Stein, *JASB*, Extra No. 2, 1899, p. 69.

[3] Watters, *On Yuan Chwang's Travels in India*, vol. ii, p. 295.

region to the west of Khotan. It would seem from the literary evidence that there was considerable activity in the area of Kashmir, but unfortunately the region has not produced any remains which can be dated with certainty to the Aśokan period. Owing to its comparative inaccessibility it was obviously not as important as the north-western border. There is no reason to disbelieve that the empire included Khaśa. If Kashmir was not actually within the empire it must all the same have been within the sphere of influence, and the people of the region had the same status as the rest of the borderers.

Tibetan tradition maintains that Aśoka visited Khotan 250 years after the death of the Buddha, in 236 B.C.[1] It is also recorded that the kingdom of Khotan was founded by Indians and Chinese during the reign of Aśoka, the events being similar to those related by Hsüan Tsang, who probably first heard it when he visited Khotan. Aśoka's journey to Khotan does not sound very convincing. In his thirty-third regnal year he must have been at least sixty years old and for him to have made such a hazardous journey over the mountains is hardly probable. It is possible though that he sent *Dhamma* missions to Khotan.

Aśoka appears to have had close connections with the area of modern Nepal. Part of it at least was within the empire, since Aśoka's visit to Rummindei cannot be regarded as a visit to a foreign country. Tradition has it that he was accompanied on this visit by his daughter Cārumatī and that she was married to a *kṣatriya* of Nepal, Devapāla.[2] If his administration did not extend right into Nepal, despite the fact that he was supposed to have suppressed a rebellion there when he was still a prince, it must certainly have included the Tarai region. Nepalese tradition maintains that Aśoka actually visited Nepal. This may be a reference to the visit to Rummindei, or he may have journeyed farther into Nepal on the same occasion.[3] Some Nepalese temples are ascribed to Aśoka, among them the sanctuary built by Buddhist monks on the hill of Svayambunātha in western Nepal.[4] But this could well be a later story, invented to give prestige and antiquity to the shrine.

On the east the empire included the province of Vaṅga, since Tāmralipti, the principal port of the area, was one of the more important maritime centres during the Mauryan period. Indian missions to and from Ceylon are said to have travelled via Tāmralipti.[5] The conquest of Kaliṅga must have strengthened the Mauryan hold in eastern India. Recent excavations

[1] *JASB*, 1886, pp. 195–7.

[2] Oldfield, *Sketches from Nepal*, vol. ii, pp. 246–52; *IA*, vol. xiii, p. 412; Wright, *History of Nepal*, p. 110.

[3] Tāranātha, *Geschichte des Buddhismus in Indien*, p. 27.

[4] Lévi, *Le Népal*, pp. 10, 11.

[5] *Mahāvaṃsa*, XI, 38.

have produced, not surprisingly, evidence of extensive Mauryan settlements in the Ganges delta.[1]

The extent and influence of Aśoka's power in south India is better documented than in north India, though here again a fair amount is left to speculation. Evidence is available both in literary and epigraphical sources. A late Pallava charter mentions Aśokavarman as one of the rulers of Kāñci.[2] This may refer to the Mauryan emperor or to a south Indian ruler who assumed the same name. To some extent the south Indian sources may be regarded as more authentic than some of the Buddhist texts, since the southern tradition did not seek to obtain prestige by connecting events with the more important north Indian rulers. Furthermore, with regard to the reign of Aśoka, there were no Buddhist chroniclers to interfere with the original tradition. The epigraphical evidence consists of the edicts of Aśoka found at the following south Indian sites, Gāvimath, Pālkiguṇḍu, Brahmagiri, Maski, Yeṟṟaguḍi, Siddāpur, and Jaṭiṅga-Rameshwar. These sites provide some indication of the southern borders of the empire. There are references to the peoples of these areas in the edicts as well.

There is a tradition that Tamil poetry was first committed to writing in the third or second century B.C. by foreign immigrants who were inveterate makers of stone inscriptions.[3] The foreign immigrants were the Aryan tribes pushing south. The reference to stone inscriptions strongly suggests the Aśokan period. If the tradition can be accepted then we may say that there was no script in south India until the coming of *Brāhmī* from the north. Bindusāra was largely responsible for the conquest of the southern dominions of the empire.[4] Mamulanar and other Tamil poets refer to the Nandas and Mauryas in Tamil literature of the first three centuries A.D. The Nandas are described as accumulating treasure in Pāṭaliputra and then hiding it in the waters of the Ganges.[5] Tamil anthologies refer to the invasion of the Moriyar, who appear to be the Mauryas.[6] They are described as a splendid force coming from the area north of the Tamil region, Vaṭukar, but they have to retreat when they arrive at a narrow pass, which they cannot penetrate. On one occasion they do succeed, but their shining *cakra* is brought low by those defending the pass. They are said to have come from the broad kingdom which is described as the land of the sun. The commentary explains that the pass was situated in the Vĕḷḷimalai or the

[1] *AI*, 1953, vol. ix, p. 154. Excavations carried out by the Asutosh Museum of Calcutta University, in Candra Ketugarh (Lower Ganges delta), revealed considerable Mauryan material.

[2] *South Indian Inscriptions*, vol. ii, p. 342; *Epigraphia Indica*, vol. xx, p. 50.

[3] Aiyangar, *The History of the Tamils*, p. 215.

[4] See Ch. I.

[5] *Aham*, 265.

[6] *Puram*, 175, 6–9; *Aham*, 69, 10–12; *Aham*, 281, 8–12; *Aham*, 251, 10–14.

Silver Mountain and the reference to the Vaṭukar defending it would suggest that it may have referred to the Āndhras or the Kannada-Telegu people.[1] The land of the sun is explained as Ādityamaṇḍala in the commentary. It would seem that the Mauryan conquest of the southern kingdoms was by no means easy. It was perhaps the memory of this as well as other factors that kept Aśoka from a conquest of the extreme south. In the first century A.D. there is a reference to Varkadu in Tamil literature.[2] This was the boundary line of the northern empire. It corresponds very closely to the southern limits of Aśoka's empire.

Hsüan Tsang mentions two *stūpas* which he saw in southern India, one in the Cola kingdom and one in the Pāṇḍya kingdom, both said to have been built by Aśoka.[3] This would suggest that Buddhist missionaries may have reached those areas. The Chinese pilgrim refers to further *stūpas* built by Aśoka and by Mahinda in the kingdom south of the river Cauvery. We cannot be sure that his informants were not trying to impress him with the antiquity and importance of the places he visited by associating them with Aśoka. This may also be the result of the confusion of two traditions. Aśoka must have sent *Dhamma* missions to these south Indian kingdoms. These missions may have been resident missions. Buddhist missionaries may have arrived at much the same time, building monasteries and proclaiming Aśoka as an ardent Buddhist. Mahinda, if he did not go to Ceylon by sea, must have stopped at these places en route to Ceylon.

The degree of civilization of these south Indian kingdoms is an interesting question. That they were able to build up an important trade with the Roman empire three centuries later would suggest that they were already fairly advanced in the Aśokan period. It is possible that these kingdoms were not wholly antagonistic to Mauryan authority under Aśoka, and therefore there was no need for Aśoka to conquer any farther south. His Kaliṅga experience did not make him too eager to indulge in war for its own sake. From the descriptions of the Mauryan forces in Tāmil poetry it would seem that they made a great impression on the people of the south and no doubt the Mauryans were held in considerable awe, since the conquest had taken place hardly a generation earlier. The reports of the Kaliṅga War must have played an important part in their decision to submit to the Mauryan emperor. Those outside the boundary of the empire probably accepted Aśoka as the nominal suzerain, allowing as his other borderers had allowed the entry of the *dhamma-mahāmattas*, but not being in effect a part of the empire.

[1] *Age of the Nandas and Mauryas*, p. 255.

[2] Aiyangar, *The Beginnings of South Indian History*, p. 83.

[3] Watters, *On Yuan Chwang's Travels Travels in India*, vol. ii, pp. 224, 228.

Throughout the reign of Aśoka, Ceylon remained a friendly neighbour in the south. It is referred to in the edicts under the name of Tambapanni.[1] Information is available in the Ceylonese chronicles on contacts between India and Ceylon. Allowing for the interpolation of later centuries we may use this as evidence. The coming of Mahinda to Ceylon was not the first official contact between the two countries. It is clear from the 13th Rock Edict that *Dhamma*-missions had been sent to Ceylon prior to the journey of Mahinda. It seems fairly certain from the evidence that not only was Ceylon in contact with India before Aśoka, but also that Buddhism had already arrived in Ceylon before the coming of Mahinda. Mahinda's importance lay largely in the fact that he persuaded the king Devānmapiya Tissa to become a Buddhist, which in Ceylon gave the religion a more or less official status. Mahinda arrived in the north of Ceylon. It would seem that Buddhist temples of an earlier date existed in the south since the southern area has the ruins of very ancient *stūpas*.[2] Numerically too the north has fewer remains of such shrines.

The coming of Buddhism to Ceylon raises the problem of the language used by the preachers. It would appear that the early Buddhist missionaries had already started teaching in Prākrit. The inscribing of edicts in south India in Prākrit would suggest that the language was not completely unknown in the southern territories. The fact that the Ceylonese chronicles relate the story of the coming of Vijaya from India as the civilizing force, is of some importance.[3] Perhaps the story disguises a large-scale immigration of a maritime force from India, resulting in a cultural and political conquest of the island. The strange legend of the origin of Vijaya seems an obvious attempt at making him an extraordinary person, as also the fact that he landed in Ceylon on the day of the *Parinirvāṇa*. It is possible that the first Buddhists came with Vijaya as part of his entourage, and no doubt brought the language with them. Prākrit inscriptions in Ceylon, the earliest of which dates back to Uttiya the successor of Tissa, are not very different in language from Aśokan Prākrit and are inscribed in the *Brāhmī* script.[4] This would suggest that the language had a history prior to the coming of

[1] Some writers equate Tambapanni with the river Tāmraparṇi in the Tinnevelly district of south India. This view has now been generally discarded owing to the fact that many other sources use the name Tambapanni for Ceylon, e.g. *Dīpavaṃsa*, V, 80; IX, 20; XVII, 5; *Rāmayana*, IV, 41, 17). The context in which it occurs in the 13th Rock Edict, supports the latter view.

[2] It is related in the *Mahāvaṃsa* (XXII, 2–9), that Tissa's brother, the vice-regent fled to Rohana in southern Ceylon to a Buddhist monastery. The existence of this monastery so far south would point to its having been established before the coming of Mahinda.

[3] *Mahāvaṃsa*, VII.

[4] *Epigraphia Zeylanica*, vol. i, pp. 139 ff. Ritigala Inscriptions.

Mahinda, which would give it greater justification for being used in an official document.

The Ceylon chronicles describe Vijaya as coming from the kingdom of Vaṅga in eastern India, but there appears to be some confusion as regards his original home. He is described as landing first at Suppāraka during the journey to Ceylon.[1] This would suggest that he came from an area on the west coast of India, since Suppāraka is the modern Sopārā. This would confirm the strong tradition among the Sinhalese that their ancestors came from the west coast of India.[2] Although early Sinhalese was influenced by eastern Prākrit, the substitution of *ha* for *sa* suggests a western source. It is curious that when Ariṭṭha travels to Pāṭaliputra, he goes by sea and then crosses the Viñjha mountains, which would indicate that he travelled along the west coast and across the Vindhya range to Pāṭaliputra.[3] It would appear, therefore, that the Indian settlers in Ceylon came from both the east and the west and that the confusion in the texts is due to these two traditions. The *Mahāvaṃsa* suggests that people of all sects resided in Ceylon before the coming of Mahinda. The princess who became Vijaya's wife, came from the Paṇḍyan kingdom, so that there was considerable contact between Ceylon and south India during that period.[4] She is said to have been related to the Buddha and strangely enough she and her women friends arrive disguised as nuns, presumably as a means of protection on the journey. This in itself would suggest that Buddhism was known in Ceylon before Mahinda. This existing contact was no doubt strengthened by the arrival of Aśoka's *dhamma-mahāmattas* in the fourteenth regnal year of Aśoka. Mahinda arrived later, to convert the king Tissa, and to organize monastic orders in Ceylon.[5]

Aśoka's relationship with Ceylon was not purely political. He and Tissa were on very close terms. As a young man Tissa must have come into contact with the *dhamma-mahāmattas* sent to Ceylon five years before Tissa's coronation. Obviously the personality of Aśoka as it emerged from the work of these officers, impressed Tissa. He may perhaps have decided to model himself on the older king. His first coronation took place in Aśoka's seventeenth year, and some time later he had a second coronation to which he invited a representative of the Indian king. Aśoka returned the courtesy with gifts and a mission. Mahinda probably came with this mission as a personal representative of Aśoka, and, no doubt, was accompanied by other monks.[6] Tissa accepted the faith and appears to have made it the state

[1] *Mahāvaṃsa*, VI, 46; *Dīpavaṃsa*, IX, 26.

[2] *CHQ*, 1952, January, No. 2, vol. i, pp. 163 ff.

[3] *Dīpavaṃsa*, XV, 87.

[4] *Mahāvaṃsa*, VII, 48.

[5] Adhikaram, *Early History of Buddhism in Ceylon*, p. 48.

[6] See Ch. II.

religion. Tissa also adopted the title of Devānampiya, probably through his enthusiasm for Aśoka.[1] Tissa's enthusiasm does not imply that he was a vassal of the latter. It was a relationship based on the admiration of the one for the other, among other things. Though there must have been a considerable interchange of missions, Ceylon remained an independent kingdom. No doubt trading facilities existed between the two countries and strengthened the political ties.

[1] It can be argued that this was a royal title, but it is significant that he was the first among the Ceylonese kings to adopt it.

V
THE POLICY OF *DHAMMA*

'In vain does a sense of righteousness enter its protest (that of the concatenation of deeds and destiny to which ambitious men are drawn), in vain do millions of prayers of the oppressed rise to Nemesis; the great man, frequently unconsciously consummates higher desires and an epoch is expressed in his person, while he believes that he himself is ruling his age and determining its character.' This in essence expresses the verdict of Burckhardt on Constantine and his age.[1] Not that he suggests that Constantine or any man of similar ambitions is entirely the product of his age but that no man is outside or too early for his age. The single man who dominates his race, his society, his community, often in opposition to the larger body of his compatriots, is not an isolated prophet or an evil genius, or a man of supernatural vision born out of his time. The germinal matter which he may have used in order to found his position and power will, on analysis, be found to lie within the group from which he arose. It is largely the reactions to the particular conditions of a given society which are responsible for the attitudes of its individual members. These attitudes may be the result of a compromise with, or an acceptance or non-acceptance of these conditions.

It is sometimes said that personal idiosyncrasies are often responsible for the policy of a man in power and that these are unrelated to the larger society and age to which he belongs. But even this apparent autonomy of personality is only on the surface. Investigation reveals a social influence in the promptings of many personal actions, or at least the influence of a social force outside the isolated man. With the exception of authentic mystics who may have an inner isolated life which is not dependent on the doings of the men and women around them (though even this is a questionable point), the actions of other men are schooled by their experience of the thoughts and deeds of the people amongst whom they live.

Aśoka was thus not a visionary. Nor was he a prophet who had received special enlightenment, Buddhistic or otherwise. Nor do we agree with the view that his ideas were too advanced for his age and that their failure was due to a premature expression. If we consider Aśoka not as an isolated phenomenon but in the context of his historical background it will become

[1] *The Age of Constantine the Great*, p. 262.

apparent why he adopted the policy of *Dhamma* and what purpose it served. In order to be better acquainted with his age, we must further consider the immediate background of the Mauryas, the development of Buddhism at this period, and the relationship between Buddhism and the ideas of Aśoka.

That the Mauryas displayed an unusually lively interest in the ideas and intellectual trends of the age is apparent from their various connections with the social and intellectual life of the time. Candragupta is said to have accepted Jainism in his later years, and in fact to have abdicated the throne and become a wandering ascetic dying through slow starvation in the orthodox Jaina manner.[1] Considering the difficulties that he faced in making himself king and building an empire it is hardly likely that he would have abdicated at the end of his reign in order to become a wandering ascetic. It is possible though that he accepted the teachings of Mahāvīra and became a Jaina. This interest may be excused as originating in the fact that he was of low origin, a *vaiśya*, and by accepting Jainism he eluded the contempt of the higher caste nobility. Since the teachings of Mahāvīra were at this period regarded more as an offshoot of Hinduism, an extremist discipline, and the Jainas themselves as a sub-sect of the earlier religion, we can discountenance the above idea. The interest it would seem was largely intellectual. Accepting Jainism did not raise one's social prestige in the eyes of high-caste Hindus whose social ethics were already being determined by caste rules.

Jainism was established by Mahāvīra, a close contemporary of the Buddha. Consequently, Buddhism and Jainism have a certain amount in common. Mahāvīra started his career by joining a group of ascetics called the *Nirgranthas*. Later, the same term came to be used for Jaina monks. In Jaina belief, the universe functions in accordance with a natural law; this eliminates the necessity of any commitment regarding the existence of God. The universe moves in a series of waves, a regular movement of progress and decline. The human body is merely the dross covering the soul and release from rebirth can only be achieved when the soul is again in its original pure state. Jainism drew its major support, then as now, from the commercial classes.

Jainism was not, however, the only influence at the court of Candragupta. A foreign element which may have supported some degree of eclectic thinking, was that of the few Greeks who were undoubtedly present at the court. Some European sources have stated that Candragupta actually met Alexander, though this event has been doubted by at least one modern

[1] *Pariśiṣṭaparvan*, VIII, 435–45.

historian of the period.[1] We know that Megasthenes came as a friend of Seleucus and lived at the court of Pātaliputra for a while. He must certainly have been questioned at length about the thought and institutions of Greece and Asia Minor with which he was familiar. That he must have responded with enthusiasm seems obvious since it appears from his accounts of India that he was a man of lively observation and intelligence.

In the north-western part of the kingdom, the nucleus of this foreign element and of a cosmopolitan Indo-Greek intellectual life, was the city of Taxila. Bordering on the Greek settlements of the trans-Indus region and farther west, situated on an important highway, it acted as the crucible of the two streams of Indian and western ideas. Since it also had the official prestige of a provincial capital and was a commercial centre, the result was a happy situation where alien ideas, although they did not modify Indian orthodoxy, were at least allowed to co-exist. A fair amount of mutual understanding and respect must undoubtedly have ensued.

Once again we may speculate on the interesting possibilities of the marriage alliance between Candragupta and Seleucus. Whether it was an *epigammia* or a *kedos*, one or more Greek ladies of noble families must have been introduced into the Mauryan court circles. This would suggest that the rigidity of orthodox Hinduism could on occasion be stretched to include non-orthodox elements. It would appear that the atmosphere at the court was considerably freer then than it was during the rule of many succeeding dynasties. Aśoka as a young boy would have met these Greek ladies in the harem.

Bindusāra, Aśoka's father, seems to have been aware of contemporary trends. There is no evidence as to whether he too was a Jaina as his father Candragupta was said to have been. If his father was a partisan of Jainism, Bindusāra may well have been partial to the Jainas. Thus it would not have been unexpected of Aśoka to have interested himself in a non-orthodox sect such as the Buddhists or the Jainas. He may well have first met with this catholicity of religious taste at the court itself when he was a young man. The members of the various sects probably moved quite freely at the court.

We know that the Ājīvikas were acceptable at the court since it was an Ājīvika saint who at the conception and later the birth of Aśoka, predicted the future of the child.[2] We also know that Bindusāra was sufficiently interested in the debating of ideas to request that a sophist be sent to him as a present from Greece.[3] Thus the immediate surroundings in which

[1] See Ch. I.

[2] *Divyāvadāna*, XXVI, pp. 370 ff.

[3] *Athenaeus*, III, 444.

Aśoka lived and grew up did not exclude the possibility that he might adopt a non-conforming philosophy of life, not entirely in keeping with orthodox principles.

Even prior to the Mauryan period, Brahmanism had developed into a complicated religious system. The two tendencies apparent in most religions, those of philosophical speculation and ritualism, had assumed great complexity. Vedic ritual still persisted, though the outer forms had been adjusted to contemporary needs. The sacrifice remained an important part of the ritual, though its practice was restricted to the twice-born castes, the priests and aristocrats, and on occasion to the wealthier members of the commercial community. The other tendency, that of philosophical speculation, which had its roots in the *Ṛg Veda* itself, led gradually to the rise of a considerable number of sects each seeking an explanation of the universe by a different method or a combination of different methods. The most important among these sects were the Buddhists, the Ājīvikas, and the *Nirgranthas*.[1] The theories of these three sects were concerned not just with philosophical innovations, but with influencing the general mass of the people as well.

Of these three, Buddhism was certainly the most important. It began as a schismatic movement from the more orthodox outlook of Brahmanism. The motivating force was to escape from *sansāra*, from the supposed fetters of earthly life and the cycle of rebirth. The solution was found in the idea of the 'Middle Way', which was based on a high degree of rational thinking. The latter was a doctrine rooted in the earlier Hindu tradition, but which was nevertheless comprehensible even to the uneducated. To this extent Buddhism was a protest against the malpractices which had crept into Hindu ritual and thought. The latter was largely due to the power of the brahmans, who regarded themselves as God's elect, and began to enjoy the dominant position to which increasing temporal power had brought them. Thus, although Buddhism never reached the stage of becoming an independent state religion in India for any length of time, it was during its early period a strong counter-movement against the control which Brahmanism exerted in religious and social life. To this degree the ferment of the period may be compared to that of the Reformation in Europe when the Protestant element broke away from the Catholic church. However, the analogy is not exact, since Buddhism, unlike Protestantism in Europe, was not merely a dissident movement from Brahmanism. Because it included popular cults and practices in its ritual, it gradually began to be distinguished as a separate religion from Brahmanism. The fact that in India the

[1] VII P.E., Delhi-Topra. Bloch, *Les Inscriptions d'Asoka*, p. 170.

Buddha had to preach and constitute an entirely new order was largely due to the absence of such an order from earlier Hinduism. Had the latter been founded on the teachings of an historical personage and through the work of a regular religious order, Buddhism might well have begun and ended as merely the schism movement of a dissident element.

Doctrinal differences were largely the cause of the antagonism between the various sects. These were debated in theological circles and among the lay followers. The situation is again similar to the antagonism of the various Christian opinions during the Reformation and Counter-Reformation in Europe. With consistent opposition from the brahmans and increased understanding and support from other sections of society, Buddhism ceased to be a body of dissident opinion and began to develop as an independent religion.

In the earlier stages Buddhism was supported largely by the commercial classes. This can be explained by its attitude to the caste system. The Buddha himself was a *kṣatriya* and the movement was not averse to reducing the power of the brahmans. Little or no emphasis was given to the caste system in theory. The commercial classes rapidly gaining economic importance were socially still inferior, and this inferiority, stressed by the brahmans and *kṣatriyas*, was no doubt galling. The *vaiśyas* though theoretically included amongst the *dvija* or twice-born, were in practice generally treated contemptuously.[1] Thus the social equality preached by Buddhism would naturally have made a strong appeal to those that were considered socially inferior.

Buddhism certainly made its appeal to the lower orders of society. In its essentials it was easily understood by the unsophisticated mind. It offered a workable solution to the problems of life in the 'Middle Way', which demanded neither a subtle understanding of obscure metaphysics nor an impractical emphasis on abnegation and asceticism. Further, it made no expensive demands of ritual.

During the time of Aśoka the propagation of Buddhism through the order of monks and nuns was fairly widespread. The *bhikkhus* preached the law during the cold and the hot season, returning to their monasteries during the rainy season. Instead of the elaborate sacrifice, Buddhist ritual was centred round the cult of the *caityas* and the worship of the *stūpas*. The *caityas* were sacred enclosures associated previously with earth spirits and the fertility cult.[2] Thus Buddhism made a particular point of attracting

[1] *Aitareya Brahamana*, VII, 20.

[2] A clear indication of this can be seen in the sculpture on the gateways at Sanchi, where the relevance of the tree and woman motif can be explained by the above.

the simple folk and incorporating popular cults, without, however, over-emphasizing their magical and superstitious aspects. The *stūpas* were the tumuli within which were placed the ashes of the Buddha or a revered elder of the Buddhist Order. Very often the monastery or *vihāra* was built in association with the *caitya*, as at Sanchi. It has also been suggested that the column, possibly the survival of a phallic emblem or megalith, was another feature of the Buddhist cult.[1] Although no definite connection has yet been established, the idea is certainly feasible. The non-existence of large temples and shrines in the Aśokan period can be explained by the fact that the use of the image of the Buddha for purposes of worship, appears not to have been a common practice. Surviving examples of the Buddha image dating to the first century A.D. have been found at Gandhāra. It has been suggested, however, that the first images were made at Mathura and not at Gandhāra,[2] but whatever their origin all the surviving images are post-Mauryan.

The Mauryan period was the culminating epoch of a few centuries of rational inquiry and cultural advance. The change from the nomadic pastoral culture of the early Aryans to a more settled culture of an urban nature was due in no small part to the increased use of iron resulting in improved techniques. New lands were cleared and the population began to move towards the east. The fertile land of the Ganges valley was a good area for settlement and colonization. This change was taking place between *c.* 800–600 B.C.[3] By the sixth century the northern kingdoms had taken shape and Magadha was assuming importance. The Ganges itself was introduced to a new economic life, that of river trade. Campa was prized owing to its position along the Ganges, which enabled it to control this trade. With these tremendous changes in the economic life of the times changes in the social structure were inevitable. It was natural that the commercial classes would assert themselves and chafe under the indignity of being regarded socially as a lower order. They were denied social prestige, yet it was through their enterprise that many technical improvements were possible. This resentment was expressed in many of the current schools of thought. As opposed to the boast of the brahmans that they possessed revealed knowledge, these schools emphasized empirical knowledge. At the level of the laity a satisfactory working solution was sought, eliminating excessive indulgence in ritual or asceticism.

The implications of these new ideas in the existing system of social

[1] Basham, *The Wonder that was India*, p. 263.

[2] van Lohuizen de Leeuw, *The 'Scythian' Period . . .*, pp. 145 ff.

[3] *BSOAS*, Warder, 1956, pp. 43 ff.

ethics were vast, though very often subtle. The change to an urban culture meant a more closely defined social organization. Community life having become more complex it was necessary to revise previously held ideas on individual participation in communal living. The brahmanical solution to this problem was to increase the rigidity of the caste system. The Buddhists came nearest to understanding it, and developed a system of social ethics whereby the responsibility was placed in the hands of each individual member of society. The terrifying determinism of the brahmanical social code did not pursue the man born in the lower castes. The promise of an eternal heaven was held out to those who, within the confines of social life could rise above human temptations.

The connection between these new ideas and the political organization of the time also requires some analysis. With the transition from a pastoral to an urban culture the old political ties were bound to change. Whereas previously many of the early settlements in northern India had arbitrarily grouped themselves into confederacies and republics, based broadly on tribal affinities, there was now the need for a properly defined political organization. The emphasis shifted from tribal ties to that of social responsibility in urban units. With the complexities of urban living as against small pastoral settlements, and the emergence of commerce as a major occupation, a more closely knit organization was demanded. The primitive democracy of the *sabhā* and the *samiti* had to give way to the concentration of power in the hands of a small centralized body, which controlled and co-ordinated with greater success the workings of the new society. The social transition and the territorial expansion of this time gave it the character of a period of emergency, which made a strong controlling force all the more necessary. Thus the confederacies and republics gave way to kingdoms with a tendency towards the consolidation of smaller units into larger units, until the peak was reached in the Mauryan empire. This political change introduced the idea of a wider citizenship concerned with more than just local happenings. Buddhism was suited to this situation in so far as it emphasized a broader social consciousness, unlike Brahmanism in which social responsibility was significant largely within the confines of each caste.

Before we analyse the nature of the policy of *Dhamma* expounded by Aśoka, it is necessary to inquire into the reasons for this new policy. It is impossible for us at a distance of over two thousand years to state precisely what the personal prejudices of the king may have been. At best we can make a guess by using his edicts as our source. These we shall discuss at a later stage. We can, however, attempt to explain why the outside conditions, e.g. environmental, demanded this policy. During the latter years of the Nanda dynasty, the first attempt was made under Mahāpadma, at building a centralized empire on a large scale. The fact that it was not entirely a success was due largely to the failure of the individual rulers to understand the workings of an empire. Candragupta Maurya, on conquering the Nanda domains, completed the policy of centralization with great success. The empire, administered by an efficient bureaucracy, extensively covered by good communications, and under the control of a powerful ruler, was probably as centralized as was possible during that period. All these three characteristics, efficient bureaucracy, good communications, and a strong ruler, existed under the Mauryas, as is evident from the *Arthaśāstra*. The central control of the ruler had to be maintained at all costs and this could be achieved by the adoption of either of two policies. One was that of exercising a ruthless control through armed strength, self-deification, and various other means, such as those adopted by Aśoka's near contemporary Shi Huang Ti in China. The other was certainly more subtle. The king declared himself in favour of a new belief (or one of the less well-established ones), possibly even an eclectic collection of views from varying groups. Thus the dominance of the other groups could be undermined and the central authority could increase its power. The population under the direction of officials would pay at least lip-service to the ideas of the rulers. This was the policy selected by Aśoka, in essence the same, though different in form, to that adopted by Akbar eighteen centuries later.

We know that Aśoka was not an avowed Buddhist at the time of his accession and that his interest in Buddhism grew after some years.[1] As we have seen he had considerable trouble fighting his way to the throne. It may well be possible that in the early years of his reign, while he was consolidating his position, he did not have the enthusiastic support of the older and more orthodox elements at the court. By moving away from orthodox Brahmanism though not opposing it, and by giving open support to Buddhism and certain other sects such as the Ājīvikas, he was seeking the potential support of non-orthodox elements which may eventually have succeeded in weaning the people away from orthodoxy, and in the end making his own principles more acceptable to the populace. He was aided in this by the fact that these sects had the support of the newly risen commercial class and the mass of the population was not antagonistic to them. In addition to this, the new beliefs were not violently opposed to the old and it was therefore possible to bring about a compromise. Thus Aśoka saw the practical advantage of adopting the idea of the *Dhamma*.

[1] See Ch. II.

Another factor connected with the general scheme of centralization, is that of unifying small political units, of welding divergent groups into at least a basic cohesion. This is of particular importance where centralization extends over large areas including a diversity of racial and cultural types. It demands loyalty to a larger cross-frontier group than to its own immediate group. If racial variations were not so great, cultural differences were certainly tremendous in the Mauryan empire. We have only to think of the four provincial capitals Taxila, Tosalī, Ujjain, and Suvarṇagiri to appreciate the full cultural scope of the empire and the range of peoples within it. The adoption of a new faith and its active propagation would act as a cementing force, welding the smaller units. It could be used as a measure to consolidate conquered territory, provided that it was used wisely, and was not forced upon unwilling people. Aśoka certainly showed a considerable degree of understanding.

Examples of this policy can be seen in the histories of many civilizations. To quote an example, Charlemagne conquered the Saxons and then used Christianity as a cementing factor. The Saxons were converted to his own religion and were thus brought more directly into the general pattern of the Carolingian empire.[1] A new religion can be used as an emblem or a symbol of a new unity. It can be a most effective means of propaganda. Sometimes merely an idea used judiciously in the right circumstances can appear to be a new creed. The emperor Constantine, with whom Aśoka has been most frequently compared, used Christianity on occasion for political ends. A clear example was his adoption of the Greek monogram ☧ (deriving from the word χριστος, Christos), on his standard, while on his coins, he retained the old gods. Thus, though he himself favoured Christianity and adopted its symbols, the older belief continued and there was freedom of worship for all religions. Certain pre-Christian practices such as performing sacrifices at home were forbidden, but not for religious reasons. The ban was rather due to the fear that these gatherings might develop into politically subversive groups.[2] Far from being given over-riding privileges, the Christians were merely restored to a position where they could feel safe. They were no longer persecuted and were allowed to lead a normal human existence.

A similar background no doubt prevailed at the time of Aśoka. The Buddhists, who had previously been frowned upon and quite possibly had been persecuted as heretics, were now restored to a respectable position and were recognized as a religious sect.

[1] Winston, *Charlemagne*, p. 104.

[2] *The Age of Constantine the Great*, pp. 294 ff.

In analysing the political implications of Aśoka's new policy the question of the *cakravartin* ideal is of some importance. Buddhist literature gives us a description of the *cakravartin*.[1] He is described as a universal emperor whose dominions included the whole of Jambudvīpa. His rule was just and his reign prosperous. He was so virtuous a king that he came to be regarded as having the power of divinity. Since the emphasis on conquering the whole of Jambudvīpa is so great, it would appear that the idea is a late one, possibly post-Mauryan. We know that the Jainas were acquainted with the concept, and the epic heroes such as Yudhiṣṭhira, Rāma and others were referred to as *digvijayins*.[2] The latter term may have been used figuratively for the heroes, as is often the case in early literature. But more than likely the concept was known before the Mauryan period, though a concrete example could only be quoted after the reign of Aśoka.[3] However, it is unlikely that the *cakravartin* idea was a fully developed political concept in the pre-Mauryan period, or that most of Aśoka's ideas were inspired by his ambition to be a *cakravartin*. Had this been the case he would surely have mentioned it somewhere in his edicts, particularly as he does give expression to many of his ambitions in these sources. A verse in the *Dīpavaṃsa* relating to Aśoka concludes with the following words,

'. . . the wheel of his power rolled through the great empire of Jambudvīpa . . .'[4]

This may be an early attempt to connect the *cakravartin* idea with the reign of Aśoka, or it may be a later interpolation after Aśoka had been invested with the mark of a *cakravartin* in Buddhist tradition. The theorists when describing a *cakravartin* emphasized political and territorial power. The symbols accompanying the image of the *cakravartin* were known as the seven jewels and generally consisted of the wheel — signifying universal power — the goddess of fortune, the queen, the crown prince, the minister, the imperial elephant, and the horse.[5] Judging from the edicts, Aśoka's definition of universal power would have had a far greater degree of humility and humanism.

It is indeed no paradox to say that Aśoka's political use of Buddhism did

[1] *Dīgha Nikāya*, III. *Cakkavatti Sihanādasutta*, pp. 58 ff.

[2] Basham, *The Wonder that was India*, p. 83.

[3] Kern (*Asoka*, p. 34), is of the opinion that this concept was unknown during Aśoka's time or prior to it, and that it was created by the Buddhist monks who based it on his life in order to flatter him. But if this had been the case, they would have associated his name directly with the idea. There is no such indication in any of the texts.

[4] VI, 2.

[5] Basham, *The Wonder that was India*, p. 84. The list of the seven jewels varies in the different texts in which the story is related.

not exclude him from joining the ranks of the sincere believers. He did not ignore the practical usefulness of the religion to himself both as a man and a ruler. As in every religion, there was a discrepancy between theory and practice, the two being made to tally eventually by each individual believer according to his personal needs and his special environment. These little adjustments when accumulated in a society can often colour the original teachings of a religious leader. An example of this in the political sphere with reference to Aśoka can be cited in connection with the Buddhist idea of kingship. Early Buddhism preached the theory of *Mahāsammata*, the Great Elect, a contractual theory based on an agreement between the population and the person whom they elect as king. The king was regarded as serving the state, the collection of taxes being his due.[1]

A close study of the Aśokan edicts, however, reveals that Aśoka did not regard himself as the Great Elect in his relations with his subjects, but rather as a father-figure. He constantly stresses the father-child relationship between the king and the populace.

. . . *savve munisse pajā mamā. athā pajāye icchāmi hakaṃ kiṃti savvena hitasukhena hidalokikapālalokikena yūjjevū ti tathā . . . munissesu pi icchāmi hakaṃ* . . .[2]

'All men are my children, and just as I desire for my children that they should obtain welfare and happiness, both in this world and the next, so do I desire [the same] for all men.'

This paternal attitude is a new feature in the relationship between the king and the population. Possibly the *Mahāsammata* theory was now receding into the background. This was due to the fact that the opportunity for direct democracy was giving way to a trend towards centralized control, as we have explained earlier. A centralized monarchy demands far more dependence on the part of the population. The monarch is now to be regarded as the paternal benefactor and not as a servant of the state. Such a paternal approach introduces the possibilities of despotism, and it is not a far step from centralized authority to despotism.

Many views have been expressed on the exact nature of Aśoka's interpretation of Buddhism. Some historians are of the opinion that he actually

[1] *Dīgha Nikāya*, III. *Aggaññasutta*, pp. 92–93. This is the first reference in Indian political thought to what may be termed a theory of social contract. In order to preserve certain social institutions such as the family, property, justice, etc., the people elected a king to remain in office as long as he satisfied their needs. In return he was given a share of their produce.

[2] I S.E., Dhauli. Bloch, *Les Inscriptions d'Asoka*, p. 137.

became a Buddhist monk for a short period of his life.[1] Others believe that he was a *bhikkhugatika*, i.e. an intermediate position between an *upāsaka* (lay worshipper) and a *bhikkhu*.[2] The *bhikkhugatika* was a householder who for certain periods would live in a monastery, a system permitted by Buddhism.[3] This has in turn led to a controversy over the term *saṃgham upāgate* used by the king in his edicts. If he did become a monk for a short period then it would naturally refer to this period. If, however, he was never more than a lay-follower, then his approaching the *Saṃgha* might be for instruction or aid in religious matters and not necessarily as a temporary monk. It has also been suggested that Aśoka was the ecclesiastical head of the *Saṃgha*, but this suggestion remains unproven. Aśoka's political position was so strong that the *Saṃgha* would have welcomed his active interest especially as he was personally a believer. But it is clear that he did not regard himself as the ecclesiastical head, despite his ordinances to the *Saṃgha* from the fact that he was not responsible for summoning and directing the work of so important an institution to Buddhism as the Third Buddhist Council held at Pāṭaliputra.

Variations in the interpretation of the evidence for the religious convictions of Aśoka are many. Some have even maintained that Aśoka was not a Buddhist but a brahmanical Hindu.[4] In view of the fact that the majority of the sources of his reign being Buddhist and sympathetic to him, and the evidence from his own edicts, it is amply clear that he was not a brahmanical Hindu. In Tāranātha's confused and imaginative account Aśoka is associated with Tantric Buddhism. The Tibetan chronicler declares that the king was a devotee of the mother-goddess.[5] The cult of the mother-goddess was prevalent among the humbler folk in Aśoka's time, but Tantric Buddhism developed many centuries later.

It has been suggested that the *Dhamma* of Aśoka is in fact original Buddhism, as preached by the Buddha, and what we know today as Buddhism are theological encrustations added through the course of

[1] Smith (*Early History of India*, p. 168), believes that he was both monk and monarch at the same time, and accepts the remark of I Tsing as evidence of this (I Tsing, Takakusu trans., p. 73). I Tsing in a passage in which he discusses the robes worn by Buddhist monks, refers to an image of Aśoka which he saw and in which the king was dressed in monk's robes. The evidence of I Tsing is not of much value in this instance, since mere wishful thinking on the part of the Buddhist monks may have led them to depict Aśoka in a monk's habit. His Buddhist sympathies were well known, so a statue such as this would not be surprising, particularly as I Tsing does not state whether it was made in the king's lifetime.

[2] Mookerji, *Asoka*, p. 23; Bhandarkar, *Asoka*, pp. 79–81.

[3] The system of spending short periods at a monastery prevails to this day in Burma, Thailand, and other Buddhist areas of South-East Asia.

[4] Dikshitar, *Mauryan Polity*, p. 276.

[5] *Geschichte des Buddhismus in Indien*, VI p. 28.

centuries.[1] Unfortunately there is not enough cross-evidence to prove the validity of this view. An intensive analysis of the chronological sequence of Buddhist literature has yet to be undertaken, and even the results of such an analysis may leave us uncertain of the sequence. On the basis of the work that has been done so far, it is thought that Aśoka was familiar with much that is now found in the *Nikāyas*,[2] and that a major portion of the *Nikāyas* existed in the fourth century B.C.

We are of the opinion that *Dhamma* was Aśoka's own invention. It may have borrowed from Buddhist and Hindu thought, but it was in essence an attempt on the part of the king to suggest a way of life which was both practical and convenient, as well as being highly moral. It was intended as a happy compromise for those of his subjects who did not have the leisure to indulge in philosophic speculation, in fact the majority of his subjects. His edicts provide ample evidence of this. If his policy of *Dhamma* had been merely a recording of Buddhist principles, Aśoka would have stated so quite openly, since he never sought to hide his support for Buddhism.

In connection with the religious aspects of the edicts the mention in them that the attainment of heaven is the reward of a moral life, needs some elucidation. We may well ask whether it was merely the desire for heaven which prompted Aśoka to formulate *Dhamma*. If so, it is indeed a poor thought as compared with the nobility of the moral ideal of *Dhamma*. We are not suggesting that Aśoka did not have faith in an after-life but we believe that the reference to heaven was an insertion by Aśoka in an attempt to relate the degree of reward to a known and valued symbol in the mind of the average person reading the edict. According to the religious and philosophical systems of the time, the attainment of heaven was a worthwhile reward. Aśoka was suggesting that a life led according to the principles of his *Dhamma* would bring such a reward. If the attainment of heaven in itself was what Aśoka was aiming at, then surely he would also have mentioned another current belief and one that was regarded as a new and significant idea at the time, namely, the theory of the transmigration of souls.[3] The very fact that there is no reference to this proves that he was not concerned with the religious aspect of the attainment of heaven.

The nature and quality of Aśoka's religious inclinations are difficult to determine. There is no doubt that he was a religious man. But it would appear that until his later years he was not given to religious formalism. The question of whether he did or did not don the monk's robe for a short

[1] Senart, *Les Inscriptions de Piyadassi*, vol. ii, p. 322; Mrs. Rhys Davids, *Buddhism*, pp. 226 ff.; Bhandarkar, *Aśoka*, pp. 72 ff.

[2] Pande, *Studies in the Origin of Buddhism*, p. 15.

[3] Kern, *Asoka*, p. 32. The theory of the transmigration of souls was under discussion from the time of Yajñavalkya onwards.

period is, in the final analysis, of minor importance. His determination as a young prince to become king against all opposition, shows him to have been extraordinarily ambitious and far reaching. If, as is often believed, he was suddenly converted to Buddhism, we feel that this change would have swung him to the other extreme. He was not a man of half measures. If he had thought of becoming a monk he would have abdicated and retired to a monastery. Much has been made of the supposed conflict in his mind between the desire to be a monk and his responsibility as a ruler, of which conflict there is no clear evidence anywhere.[1]

If such a state did exist, it could not have arisen on a sudden stirring of his mind. He must have felt it even as a young prince when he was ambitious enough to fight for the throne. It would be nearer the truth to explain this conflict as a dilemma. He saw on the one side, the personal relationship between himself as a man and Buddhism as his religion. Equally distinct was the other side of the picture; as the ruler of the Mauryan state he could use certain aspects of Buddhism to further his own ideas, treating Buddhism not merely as the religious philosophy taught by the Buddha but also as a social and intellectual force upon society as indeed it was. The solution to this dilemma was expressed in the theory of *Dhamma.*

The edicts gave Aśoka the opportunity to expound his *Dhamma.* Therefore the best reconstruction of the latter is by an examination of the principles as expressed in the edicts. These can be divided into two categories; one group consisted of his public pronouncements, the second were personal epistles directed to the *Saṃgha.* For the moment, however, we propose to consider them in the chronological order in which they were issued, thereby attempting to reconstruct the sequence of ideas as well.

The earlier major rock edicts were issued from 256 B.C. onwards. The 1st Rock Edict contains the prohibition of animal sacrifice and festive gatherings. The relevant text runs thus,

. . . *idha na kiṃci jīvam ārabhitpā prajūhitavyaṃ na ca samājo kattavyo* . . .[2]
'. . . Here no living thing is to be killed and sacrificed, and no assembly is to be held . . .'

The interpretation of the first line is not absolutely certain. The word *idha* may refer to Pāṭaliputra or to the local site where the edict was inscribed. We feel that it can hardly refer to Pāṭaliputra alone or to the royal palace, as one authority suggests,[3] for in the same edict he confesses that two peacocks and a deer are still being killed daily in the royal kitchen. A

[1] Kern, *Asoka*, pp. 34–39.
[2] Bloch, *Les Inscriptions d'Asoka*, p. 91.
[3] Ibid., p. 91 n. 5.

possible explanation may be that this order applies only to state reserves of certain animals. We know from the *Arthaśāstra* that the killing of animals listed as inviolable was a punishable offence.[1] Possibly the Aśokan order was a continuation of the same policy.

There is however an alternative translation of the passage, '. . . here no animal having been killed is to be sacrificed . . .'[2] Here the emphasis is laid more on the sacrificing of animals rather than their killing. The prohibition is of the ritual sacrifice of animals. If there was a general ban on the killing of animals for food, then surely the king would be the first to discontinue the practice himself. The mention of the animals killed for the royal kitchen (even though the king adds later in the edict that he wishes to discontinue this practice at a future date), points to the order being no more than a desire on his part to make his own belief in non-violence widespread. The hints against useless practices in other edicts, and the prohibition of festive gatherings would suggest that he did not approve of the type of ritual that led finally to the sacrificing of animals. Possibly the idea was even more repugnant to him than the act, as he associated it with primitive cults.[3] Thus to him an animal sacrifice would be a symbol of backwardness. The prohibition of animal sacrifices could not have been a popular move with the brahmans, since it was a regular source of livelihood for them.

In this connection it has been stated, 'Animal or vedic sacrifices went out of fashion with the pastoral economy when independent petty kingdoms had been wiped out. The agrarian economy had won at last, the pastoral life and ritual were finally defeated.'[4] This interpretation gives too much significance to a comparatively straightforward action. The change from a pastoral economy to a village economy had by now been effected, else it would have been impossible to maintain such a large centralized empire as the Mauryan empire. Much of the pastoral ritualism would have died a natural death, and the number of sacrifices must have been reduced. It can therefore be said that Aśoka's prohibition gave sanction to an already existing trend.

The other prohibition, that of festive meetings or gatherings, is contrary to his otherwise sincere insistence on toleration. He adds that he sees much evil in festive assemblies. The term *samāja* which he uses may refer to secular gatherings of a non-religious nature as well. In another edict he speaks of festive meetings (most probably state sponsored), where celestial

[1] I, 26.

[2] This translation was suggested to me by Prof. A. L. Basham.

[3] An interesting comparison can be made with Charlemagne, who forbade sacrifices for a similar reason, that they were associated with pagan worship (Winston, *Charlemagne*, p. 168).

[4] Kosambi, *Introduction to the Study of Indian History*, p. 189.

apparitions may be seen.[1] The precise reasons for this measure are uncertain. It may have been a puritanical objection on the part of the king, the 'evil' being economic waste and immoral behaviour. He does go on to say that some festive meetings are considered meritorious by the king. These were no doubt the official gatherings referred to above. The use of the word *samāja* is interesting. Buddhist literature speaks of *samajja* or *samajo* as an assembly.[2] It is thought that the term has a cult significance although the term was also used for gatherings of a general bonhomie.[3] Thus the *samāja* and the sacrificing of animals may have been part of the same ritual based on primitive cults of which Aśoka disapproved.

The suppression of these popular meetings and assemblies is in conformity with the idea of strict centralization. Such gatherings may have been feared as occasions for attacks on the king's new ideas. The continuance of all the old traditional festivals would keep alive the older ideas and would periodically raise doubts in the minds of the participants regarding the new preaching. On the other hand organized festivals, if properly handled, would produce the required emotional effects and could therefore be used as propaganda machines. Once again we have a parallel example from the reign of Charlemagne.[4] He denied the Saxons freedom of assembly, and this included gatherings to celebrate the old festivals. Except for judicial assemblies, gatherings were permitted only by order of the royal commissioner or of the courts. Charlemagne feared opposition from the Saxons and this was one way of preventing them from gathering together.

The 2nd Rock Edict relates certain measures of social welfare which are included in the working of *Dhamma*.[5] Medical centres for men and animals, the construction of roads supplied with wells and lined with shady trees, and the planting of medicinal herbs are amongst these measures. It is worth noticing that Aśoka realized the importance of good communications. This was not only of assistance to trade and commerce but also enabled his ideas to infiltrate more widely.

The 3rd Rock Edict contains a vague reference to religion, in that it declares that liberality to brahmans and *śramaṇas* is a virtue.[6] The statement could have been made by any tolerant and broad-minded man of the time. It was as we shall see from further edicts, one of the principles of *Dhamma*.

[1] V R.E., Girnār. Bloch, *Les Inscriptions d'Asoka*, p. 98.

[2] *Pali Text Society Dictionary*, p. 425.

[3] Pande, *Studies in the Origin of Buddhism*, pp. 319–20.

[4] Winston, *Charlemagne*, p. 169.

[5] II R.E., Girnār. Bloch, *Les Inscriptions d'Asoka*, p. 93.

[6] III R.E., Girnār. Ibid., p. 95.

The 4th Rock Edict was an important document in the development of *Dhamma*.[1] The text commences by explaining that for a long while a lack of morality prevailed in the land. This was evident from the killing of animals and living beings, discourtesy to relatives and discourtesy to brahmans and *śramaṇas*. There is nothing specifically Buddhist in this description of immorality. It is proof of his tolerant attitude towards religious sects that, here and elsewhere, he mentions brahmans and *śramaṇas* together.

The edict continues with the statement.

. . . ta ajja devānaṃpriyassa priyadassino rāño dhaṃmacaraṇena bherīghoso aho dhaṃmaghoso vimānadarsaṇā ca hastidassaṇā ca aggikhaṃdhāni ca aññāni ca divyāni rūpāni dassayitpā janaṃ . . .[2]

'But today, thanks to the practice of *Dhamma* on the part of the Beloved of the Gods, Piyadassi the king, the sound of the drum has become the sound of *Dhamma*, showing the people displays of heavenly chariots, elephants, balls of fire, and other divine forms . . .'

The king begins by assuming with complete conviction that his policy of *Dhamma* has improved the general condition of the people, since the moral advance has been tremendous. The phrase, 'the sound of the drum has become the sound of *Dhamma*', has been the centre of much controversial interpretation by various scholars.[3] It seems fairly clear from the context, however, that the author wishes to say that the sound of the drum is now associated with edifying spectacles. The term *bheri* does not specifically mean a war-drum, as one authority has maintained, since it was a drum which was used either when leading forces into battle or for general announcements in towns and villages. To interpret it as a war-drum is to narrow its meaning arbitrarily.[4] The word *bheri* for drum is commonly used in the *Jātakas*.[5] It is usually mentioned together with the *vīna* and the *sankha* as a necessary part of the equipment of actors and musicians.

We are of the opinion that the view of Bhandarkar is closest to the idea that Aśoka may have had when he composed the phrase. He writes, 'The sound of a drum invariably precedes either a battle, a public announcement, or the exhibition of a scene to the people. But since Aśoka entered on his career of righteousness it has ceased to be a summons to fight but invites people to come and witness certain spectacles; and as those spectacles are of

[1] IV R.E., Girnār. Ibid., p. 98.

[2] IV R.E., Girnār. Ibid., p. 98.

[3] de la Vallée Poussin, *L'Inde aux temps des Mauryas*, p. 110; Senart, *Les Inscriptions de Piyadassi*, p. 113.

[4] Raychaudhury, *Political History of Ancient India*, p. 327.

[5] *Bheri Jātaka*, vol. i, pp. 283–4. The drummer is generally referred to as the *bherivādaka*.

such a character as to generate and develop righteousness, the drum has become the proclaimer of righteousness.'[1]

The representations of aerial chariots, elephants, and divine forms have often been wondered at. It would appear that these representations were shown during the few festival meetings of which Aśoka approved. They may have been officially sponsored performances woven around the symbols and mythology of popular belief, but containing *Dhamma* propaganda at the same time. For instance a story involving chariots, elephants, divine figures, and the whole repertoire of popular cult might be enacted at a festival and might also contain an emphatic and obvious moral based on the principles of *Dhamma*. A situation in effect not very different from the early Christian morality plays performed in England, except that the Aśokan spectacles would have been organized by the administration. The *Arthaśāstra* maintains that the staging of celestial apparitions can be used for propaganda.[2] No doubt they were used for this purpose by Aśoka.

In the same year of his reign, i.e. the thirteenth year, Aśoka donated two caves in the Barābar hills to the Ājīvikas.[3] We know that Aśoka's life was at various periods linked with the Ājīvikas. Piṅgalavatsa, an Ājīvika ascetic, prophesied Aśoka's greatness,[4] and Aśoka appears to have been on very friendly terms with them. If it is true that the household ascetic of the queen was an Ājīvika, then Aśoka must have had a fair amount to do with them as a child. He may even have had a sentimental partiality for them and have been concerned about their protection. In the 7th Pillar Edict he orders the *dhamma-mahāmattas* to busy themselves with the brahmans and the Ājīvikas.[5] Despite his supreme self-confidence in *Dhamma* he was nevertheless concerned with the well-being of the other sects. He was neither bigoted nor fanatic enough to demand the exclusion of all other beliefs. Both the Ājīvikas and the *Nirgranthas* were disapproved of by the Buddhists, as is apparent from the legends describing the events prior to the calling of the Third Buddhist Council.[6]

In the thirteenth regnal year, a Minor Rock Edict was issued, inscribed at places in central India, Bairāṭ, Rūpanāth, Sahasrām, and farther south at Brahmagiri, Gāvimath, Siddāpur, Yeṟṟaguḍi, and Maski. This edict as we have shown in a previous chapter was issued when Aśoka was on tour.[7] The phrase *saṃgham upāgate* or *upayate* which we have discussed earlier in this chapter occurs in this inscription, as also the reference to the 256 nights

[1] *IA*, 1913, pp. 25 ff.
[2] X, 3; XIII, 1.
[3] Bloch, *Les Inscriptions d'Asoka*, p. 156. The Banyan cave and the cave in the Khalatika mountain.
[4] *Divyāvadāna*, pp. 370 ff.
[5] Bloch, *Les Inscriptions d'Asoka*, p. 171.
[6] See Ch. II.
[7] Ibid.

which we have considered in a previous chapter.[1] A much debated sentence from this edict is the one which reads,

. . . *yā imāya kālāya jambudipassi amissā devā husu te dāṇi missā kaṭa* . . .[2]
' . . . the gods, who in India, up to this time, did not associate with men, now associate with them . . .'

This passage can be explained as a naive belief on the part of Aśoka that the heavenly gods had in fact come down to earth, or more specifically to Jambudvīpa, since his policy of *Dhamma* took effect. He describes it as the fruit of his zeal. Certainly such an idea was known at the time, though belief in it may have been metaphorical.[3]

The reading of the word *amissā* as 'not mingled' is based on the Sanskrit root *miśra* (mingled). The alternative translation traces the word to *mṛṣa* meaning 'false'. On the basis of the latter, it has been stated that Aśoka was referring in this sentence to the true and the false gods, and this in turn has been the cause of the controversy.[4] We prefer the first interpretation of the word *missā*, meaning mingled or associated with. The sense of the phrase is thus more clear, particularly in connection with the word *munisā*, 'with the people'. However, we believe that this statement was not meant literally in the sense that, because of Aśoka's zeal in propagating *Dhamma*, the very gods themselves had come down from heaven to mingle with the people in Jambudvipa, though he may well have believed that there had been divine indications of approval of his policy. It was meant to be taken in a metaphorical sense. Aśoka was confident that his policy of *Dhamma* had achieved so much good in the country that it was just as it had been in the righteous days of the *Kṛtayuga* when the gods in their pleasure visited the earth and associated with the people. Here again he was using a value judgment with which his average reader was familiar. The concept of an ideal state, a period of prosperity and righteousness when men lived as gods and when gods were not afraid to mingle with men, a concept which later became crystallized in the idea of *Rāma Rājya*, was no doubt constantly in the minds of people at this period. In this statement Aśoka is suggesting that such a golden age has been brought about by the efficacy of *Dhamma*.

At about the same time, the 5th Rock Edict was issued.[5] By this time the king's intention of what might be termed a welfare policy towards his subjects is evident, and there are no religious tones in his reference to it.

[1] Ibid.
[2] Bloch, *Les Inscriptions d'Asoka*, p. 146.
[3] *Āpastamba Dharmasūtra*, II, 7, 16; *Harivaṃsa*, III, 32, 1.
[4] *JRAS*, Hultzsch, 1910, p. 1310; *Corpus Inscriptionum Indicarum*, vol. i, p. 166; de la Vallée Poussin, *L'Inde aux temps des Mauryas*, p. 112.
[5] Bloch, *Les Inscriptions d'Asoka*, p. 101.

He is concerned about the relationship between servants and masters and the treatment of prisoners, both of which are subjects of general concern to any ruler, no matter what his religious convictions may be. The master-servant relationship is of great consequence in any society, and it is to Aśoka's credit that he appointed a special body of officers for this work.

The statement concerning officials who attend to the welfare of prisoners brings out a particularly humane aspect of Aśoka's policy. The text runs,

... *baṃdhanabaddhassa paṭividhānāye apalibodhāye mokkhāye cā iyaṃ anubaṃdh pajāvati vā kaṭābhikāle ti vā mahālake ti vā viyāpaṭā te* ...[1]
'... They are busy in promoting the welfare of prisoners, should they have behaved irresponsibly, or releasing those that have children, are afflicted or are aged ...'

Kern has a strange interpretation of this passage.[2] He believes that it refers to the fetters of the spirit and the freeing of the soul. But this is a forced interpretation. The edict is devoted to matters of social and administrative welfare and quite obviously the prisoners referred to are the state prisoners. It would appear that prison was not a place of torture or a house of doom. The edict hints at something more on the lines of a reformatory. In any case there was always the hope for the prisoner that his release was at hand. Looking after the prisoner's family is a modern concept in the penal system and speaks well for the foresight of the Mauryan administration.

It is in the 5th Rock Edict that Aśoka first introduces the institution of the *dhamma-mahāmattas*, the officers of *Dhamma*. This special cadre of officials was started by him in his fourteenth year. It is clear from the edicts that as a group of officers they were of great importance as they were directly responsible for the practical working of *Dhamma*. They were a privileged group who had the favour of the king and were in direct contact with him. In the early years their work was connected with the general welfare of the populace, with particular emphasis on the teaching and practice of *Dhamma*. They were permitted entry to the homes of people of all classes of society, and even to those of the royal family and their relatives. We shall see from our analysis of the edicts how the power of the *dhamma-mahāmattas* to interfere in the lives of the people increased gradually over the years. These officials were active not only in the heart of the empire at Pāṭaliputra but also in the distant frontier regions, and among neighbouring peoples.[3] Furthermore they worked both among religious communities and secular groups.

[1] V R.E., Kalsi. Bloch, *Les Inscriptions d'Asoka*, p. 104.
[2] *Asoka*, p. 64.
[3] V R.E. Bloch, *Les Inscriptions d'Asoka*, p. 101.

The institution of the *dhamma-mahāmattas* is one of the strongest arguments in support of the view that Aśoka's *Dhamma* did not conform to the religious policy of any one of the existing religions of his time, and further that it was not a purely religious policy but in fact covered a more extensive field, including broad aspects of economic, social, and political life. Had the *Dhamma* conformed to any of the religions, more particularly Buddhism, the institution of the *dhamma-mahāmattas* would have been superfluous. Each religion had either its group of devoted believers or its order of monks who could have been organized into active propagandists with greater efficiency as they would already have been ardent believers. Buddhist *śramaṇas* for example would not have had much difficulty in adjusting themselves to working for the welfare of Aśoka's subjects, by assisting the destitute and the aged, and attending to the needs of the unfortunate.

But this was not the case. In fact one of the responsibilities of the *dhamma-mahāmattas* was to attend to the welfare of such religious orders and sects. The *Dhamma* was above and apart from the various religious groups. In comparison with China, social ethics tended to lag behind in India after the formalism of the caste system had set in. Even the attempt of the Buddha was in the end unsuccessful. Monkish orders of this period were concerned largely with their personal salvation through retreat and asceticism.[1] Apart from conversions and alms-giving, the secular community was on the whole, left to its own devices. The low-born was always an outcaste, and the brahmans and *śramaṇas* were too confined by social pressure even to dare to regard him as a human being. The institution of the *dhamma-mahāmattas* was an attempt made by Aśoka to provide some system of social welfare for the lower castes and the less fortunate members of the community. It was a form of social welfare which in practice was eliminated by the rigidity of the caste system and which was neglected by the Buddhist *bhikkhus*.

Aśoka's inauguration of this system may well have been prompted by charitable and sympathetic feelings. But there was also a practical necessity for it. A centralized administration is always more efficient if social welfare at all levels is attended to. Aśoka's concept of centralization certainly included the welfare of his subjects. By giving the *dhamma-mahāmattas* this title he ensured against the accusation that they were mere officials who had been given too much power. Now they became a privileged body carrying out a special mission of the king. By giving them extensive control over the high and the low, the religious and the secular, he was assured of

[1] Kern, *Manual of Buddhism*, p. 73.

a constant proximity with all levels of society. This control also served the purpose of bringing about an intensive infiltration of the *Dhamma* policy into all sections of society.

The next Rock Edict, the 6th, makes this relationship between the king and his subjects via the *mahāmattas* even more clear,[1] and creates a new departure from the past procedures. The *mahāmattas* are told to make their reports to the king at any time, irrespective of what he may be occupied with at the moment; whether he be in the palace partaking of its various pleasures, or engaged in occupations of a private nature, or if he be outside in the park, the officials had access to him at any time. Even when approached on such occasions Aśoka would take a decision on the matter concerned. This emergency is particularly stressed in regard to any matter arising in the ministerial council where the action of the king was debated, or if the council took an *ad hoc* decision which had to be reported directly to the king.

The class of officers bringing news of the people to the king are referred to by Aśoka as the *paṭivedakās*,[2] whereas the views of the ministerial council are brought specifically by the *mahāmattas*. It would seem that the two groups were specific, but it is more than likely that the first group or 'reporters', were a sub-section of the general body of the *mahāmattas*. The constant availability of the king was regarded as an important characteristic of a good monarch and was stressed in all theoretical works. The *Arthaśāstra* even though it gives the king a very close schedule for each working day, insists that a king who makes himself inaccessible to his people not only causes public disaffection but endangers his own position as well.[3] That this was not regarded as merely a theoretical axiom by Candragupta, is clear from Megasthenes' statement, that the king, even when being massaged, did not hesitate from attending to matters of state and giving audiences to people who wished to see him.[4]

The second half of the edict reaffirms Aśoka's preoccupation with the welfare of his subjects. He regards the execution and dispatch of business as the root of the success of this welfare. Once again the stress is on the efficient organization of the system of administration. He describes the reason for such action as the wish to discharge the debt which he owes to living beings. This idea emerges from the personality of Aśoka, from his own sense of responsibility towards his subjects, rather than from any religious convictions. Emphasis on the welfare of the subjects is again not

[1] VI R.E., Kalsi. Bloch, *Les Inscriptions d'Asoka*, p. 106.
[2] Ibid.
[3] I, 19.
[4] Strabo, XV, 1, 55.

alien to the theoretical ideas of the time. The *Arthaśāstra* has a verse which might well have been the inspiration of portions of this edict. Speaking of a king's duties Kauṭalya writes, 'In the happiness of his subjects lies his happiness; in their welfare his welfare; whatever pleases himself he shall not consider as good but whatever pleases his subjects he shall consider as good.'[1] The edict conveys the impression that Aśoka exercised control over the state through a well-organized system of officers and couriers. He is in touch with all parts of the empire. His experience of kingship, his knowledge of it from the theoretical works of the period, and his own personality, have made him aware of the responsibilities of being king of such a vast territory.

The 7th Rock Edict is a short one, pleading for toleration amongst all sects.[2] It would seem that differences of opinion were expressed in direct and antagonistic ways amongst the various religious sects. The plea that every sect desires self-control and purity of mind is that of a man who generalizes thus for the sake of a broader principle. Aśoka must have realized the harm that these sectarian conflicts would produce. The influence of *Dhamma* would also have been undermined by these conflicts, since there was always the danger that people would regard his *Dhamma* as merely the dogmas of another sect, which would have been fatal to its future. Communities and sects are also asked to mingle in their places of habitation. This would serve the dual purpose of assisting religious toleration and preventing politico-religious sectarianism. This is not to suggest that Aśoka's sole purpose in asking for toleration was a political one. No doubt his wish would have remained the same in other circumstances as well. But the insistence was made more urgent because of *Dhamma*.

On the question of Aśoka's toleration of religious sects, it has been said that the necessity for toleration extended only to the other sects;[3] within Buddhism he is strict about conforming to the rule. Kern refers to the Schism Edict as being the one directed specifically to the Buddhist Order. This opinion arises out of a misunderstanding of the relationship between Aśoka and the *Saṃgha*. Speaking both as a lay supporter and a monarch, his tone has to be at once that of a warm enthusiast and a strict disciplinarian. Since he is addressing a single sect he naturally calls upon its members to be unified in their principles and in their policy. The attitude he adopts would have been the same had he been addressing a similar edict to any other distinct order. Nowhere does he say that the Buddhists should not tolerate the other sects, or that they should hinder the freedom of action

[1] I, 19.
[2] VII R.E. Bloch, *Les Inscriptions d'Asoka*, p. 110.
[3] Kern, *Asoka*, p. 82.

and speech of these sects. In his edicts toleration is treated as among the more purposeful goals of life. If anything it would be more correct to say that he was far more concerned about the discipline of his own *Dhamma* than of any of the other sects. Peace between the various groups was of the utmost importance to his policy.

In the tenth year of his reign Aśoka went on a visit to Bodh-Gaya, to see the Bodhi-tree. Following this event he started a system of *Dhamma-yātās* which he describes in the 8th Rock Edict.[1] *Dhamma-yātās* were occasions when he toured the country for the furtherance of *Dhamma*. Previous to Aśoka, besides the military expeditions, hunting excursions and pleasure trips were the only tours undertaken by the king. We are acquainted with the pleasurable side of such tours through the detailed account that Megasthenes has left to us of a hunt during the reign of Candragupta.[2] Such hunting expeditions were stopped by Aśoka, as might have been expected in view of his attack on the wanton killing of animals and the unnecessary expenditure and waste of energy involved in these *vihāra-yātās*. Aśoka went on tour and instead of hunting took it upon himself to further the principles of *Dhamma*. Travelling from place to place and preaching, as a method of spreading an idea, has been adopted by teachers throughout the world. Thus Aśoka's adaptation of the custom of royal tours to the spreading of *Dhamma*, was by no means whimsical.

As he himself states, the purpose of these tours was manifold, visiting *śramaṇas* and brahmans and making gifts, visiting the aged and supporting them with gold, visiting the people of the country and instructing them in high morals and questioning them about their morality. It is obvious from this list that the purpose was not specifically religious; visiting religious sects was just a small part of the whole. Nor were the *Dhamma-yātās* mere pilgrimages to places sacred to Buddhism, as has been suggested on the basis of his visit to the Bodhi-tree.[3] Aśoka has not described them as such in the text of the edict. The mention of brahmans together with *śramaṇas* makes it amply clear that in this case at least Aśoka was not favouring one sect more than the other. It is also certain that neither a journey to a particular place nor a religious tour is meant. We may interpret the *Dhamma-yātā* as a tour of an area where by various means such as through meeting the religious sects of that community, the peasants and the country people and the old people, Aśoka is trying to further his own contacts with his subjects, and to proclaim to a broader cross-section of his

[1] VII R.E. Bloch, *Les Inscriptions d'Asoka*, p. 111.

[2] Strabo, XV, 1, 55.

[3] Eggermont, *The Chronology of the Reign of Asoka Moriya*, p. 81.

people his policies of *Dhamma*. Thus he uses the term *Dhamma-yāta* to mean a tour undertaken primarily to further peoples' acquaintance with *Dhamma*.

The tours must have included the royal inspection of various places. Since Aśoka took a tremendous interest in the happenings in his kingdom it would not have been an unusual procedure for him to make extensive tours of the country. For an intelligent ruler such excursions would provide a satisfactory means of gauging public opinion in the broad sense. Aśoka must certainly have used them for this purpose as well. Furthermore they acted as a check on local officials, and with an empire as large as the Aśokan it must have become almost imperative for the ruler to visit the rural areas and the more outlying parts. The Minor Rock Edict as found at Brahmagiri and neighbouring areas, is evidence that Aśoka journeyed as far as the southernmost part of his empire, since this particular edict, as we have seen, was issued on tour.

It was probably during these early tours, that the idea of having *dhamma-mahāmattas* came to him. These officials would act as intermediaries between him and his people, in a capacity different from that of the usual functionaries of a bureaucracy. Thus the task of the implementation of *Dhamma* would be well distributed among a body of able and selected men. This would not in any way make him unaware of the results of their work, as he would be continually in contact with the *mahāmattas*. In the position of the co-ordinator and controller, he would then have the vast network at his command and, at the same time he would be in a position to devote himself to other matters of policy and state.

It is interesting to note that Aśoka is probably the first Indian king on record to appreciate the importance of the rural population. This was due primarily to his wish to be acquainted with the views of as large a cross-section of the people as possible.[1] The tours were instrumental in making this possible, as were some other measures he took. The contact between towns permitted the spread of news and ideas from one town to another. The easy accessibility of the towns and the good communications connecting them, provided this interflow. But the people living in the rural areas were still isolated. Aśoka naturally wanted contact with this section of his subjects. Further, it could hardly be claimed that *Dhamma* had succeeded if it left the country people untouched. There was no better way of

[1] Cf. Bloch, *Les Inscriptions d'Asoka*, p. 112. Bloch takes the word *darśanam* in its traditional sense, i.e. the king shows himself to the people. This may be so. Such ceremonial appearances acted as a focus of loyalty and were necessary particularly in a large and somewhat unwieldy state. In Aśoka's case, they also gave a window on public opinion.

achieving both ends than by making extensive tours and travelling amongst the people.

It may also be suggested that the significance of the peasantry was realized by Aśoka owing to the fact that the economy had changed from a pastoral to a predominantly agrarian one. Thus the village and the peasants through the organization of land revenue, became the main source of subsistence of the state. Increasing dependence on land revenue as the biggest single source of income of the state, placed the peasant in a new and important role in the administrative organization of the country.

The somewhat puritanical streak in Aśoka appears again in the 9th Rock Edict.[1] The first part of the inscription attacks the value of many of the most widely practised ceremonies, but in the second part Aśoka is a little less severe. Once again he maintains that the practice of morality is infinitely more valuable than the observance of these ceremonies. It can be argued that this edict was an indirect attack on the brahmans and members of other religious groups who lived entirely on the proceeds of performing various ceremonies for the people. Aśoka mentions specifically, ceremonies performed during illnesses, at the birth or marriage of a child, or when setting out on a journey. He particularly censures mothers and wives as practising vulgar and useless ceremonies.

No doubt he realized the excessive emphasis on ritual in the religious observances of his time. He was aware that much of it was meaningless and was merely a source of income to the officiating priest. His contention that these ceremonies bear little fruit, and as compared to them the practice of morality is truly valuable, is an attempt at regarding ritual from a rational point of view. He does not condemn the *śramaṇas* and the brahmans who encourage rituals, in fact he demands liberality towards them. He is merely asking for a reasonable attitude in these matters. The observances with which he wishes to replace these ceremonies are really quite straightforward and obviously of greater value from the point of view of developing human relationships in society. He asks for a proper courtesy towards slaves and servants, reverence to elders, and gentleness to animals.[2] By way of reward he holds out the attainment of the desired object in this world and endless merit in the next; in short it is a meritorious practice which can result only in the general good, and surely this is a better objective than expensive rituals and ceremonies of a personal nature.

[1] Bloch, *Les Inscriptions d'Asoka*, p. 113.

[2] This edict expresses a sentiment very similar to that in the *Sigalaovāda Sutta* (*Dīgha Nikāya*, vol. iii, pp. 180–93; *Apadāna*, II, 604). The uselessness of certain traditional practices and the benefits of certain practical actions in their place, are pointed out by the Buddha to a young householder.

Aśoka's objection to these practices was not entirely on religious grounds. He was concerned with the great expense demanded by each of these ceremonies, an expense which few were able to afford, and which, as far as its evaluation in terms of economics went, was money badly employed, since it tended to accumulate in the hands of a small section of society. It would then be expended largely in fulfilling unnecessary requirements. This condemnation of popular practices is connected with the request in the 3rd Rock Edict for a moderation in expenditure and a moderation in possessions.

In the 10th Rock Edict, Aśoka denounces fame and glory and reasserts that the only glory he desires is that his subjects should follow the principles of *Dhamma*.[1] He maintains that the reason for his efforts in this direction is twofold; obtaining merit in the next world, and the elimination of danger to men in this. The first is mentioned but not discussed. The second he explains as the danger of demerit. He adds that it is more difficult for a highly placed person to adhere to the principles of *Dhamma*, since it demands a greater sacrifice. Presumably it demands the forfeiture of the goods and services that come to be accepted by the highly placed. This in itself shows an understanding of human weakness in the light of daily routine. Instead of demanding the impossible from every person Aśoka realizes that the degree of difficulty in acting according to *Dhamma* can be extremely varied, and is willing to grant that problems may arise because of this. In this edict he assumes the tone of a preacher and at the same time is full of the confidence of a man who believes in the intrinsic goodness of his ideas.

The next Rock Edict, the 11th, contains a further explanation of *Dhamma*.[2] Here he refers to the gift of *Dhamma*, the distribution of *Dhamma*, and kinship through *Dhamma*. This edict follows closely the contents of the 9th Rock Edict. Here again no religion is referred to, but an attempt is made at explaining *Dhamma*. We can say with even greater assurance that if *Dhamma* was an attempt at preaching Buddhism it would have been inevitable for Aśoka to have added that the lay person should also pay special attention to the words of the Buddhist monks and preachers. But Aśoka's explanation of what he means by the *Dhamma* indicates that it was a secular teaching. Emphasis is given to respecting elders, both the religious elders in the community and the elders in the family. The plea to be liberal and charitable towards friends, acquaintances, and followers of religious orders, might be addressed to any community that prides itself on having a developed sense of social ethics. The request to abstain from killing animals

[1] Bloch, *Les Inscriptions d'Asoka*, p. 117. [2] Ibid., p. 119.

is again a humane plea which has been heard through the centuries in many cultures.

For Aśoka, *Dhamma* was a way of life, the essence of what he had culled from the moral teachings of the various thinkers known to him, and probably his own experience of life. It was based on a high degree of social ethics and civic responsibility. Not being a theorizing brahman he saw this in terms of practical everyday life, rather than in the idealized theory of caste structure. Conscious social behaviour based on a simple reasoned understanding of secular relationships, was for him essential to any society. Under the influence of brahmanical teaching this tendency was dying out in the society of his time. The twice-born were given privileges and priorities not because of individual merit, but because of the happy accident of their birth. This feature of brahmanical teaching was amongst the many that would thus be disputed by the teachings of Aśoka. Because he insisted on humane social behaviour, he sought to avoid social hypocrisy, commonly found in most societies. Thus by holding out the possibility of heavenly bliss and similar rewards, he tried to raise the idea of responsibility from mere etiquette to a genuinely felt responsibility, investing it with a certain spiritual significance which would be easily understood by a people already acquainted with the idea of spirituality in religion.

Throughout his edicts he stresses the importance of the family. No doubt he saw that the family would provide an ideal nucleus for the development and spread of *Dhamma*. The caste system with its overwhelming emphasis on kinship ties, accelerated the development of the family as an institution of primary importance in the sophisticated social system of the Mauryan period. Hereditary caste and ancestral professions meant that the relationship between the generations was a very closely knit one, and therefore the permeation of ideas would be equally direct. The household of one family, ranging from the patriarchal father or grandfather down to the paid servants and the slaves, was an important social unit. The rise of a money economy which was taking place at this time, and the emergence of new commercial occupations, assisted in establishing the family as an even stronger unit, since the accumulation of a large capital became a prime incentive amongst those families. Thus Aśoka frequently calls upon the father, the son, the brother, and the master, in addition to friends and neighbours to act according to *Dhamma*.

At Dhauli and Jaugada, the 11th, 12th, and 13th Rock Edicts have been omitted and two separate edicts have been added to the others. These two are not included at the remaining sites. It is of interest to examine the three edicts and to inquire as to why they were not included in the Kaliṅga region. The 11th Edict as we have just seen, is concerned with the practice of morality, and is similar in content to the 9th Rock Edict. The 12th Rock Edict is a direct and emphatic plea for toleration amongst the various sects.[1] It would appear that there were still considerable differences of opinion which were not conducive to happy relationships among the sects. These differences were obviously of some significance, otherwise Asoka would not have given the matter so much publicity as to devote an entire edict to it, and a fairly lengthy one at that. This edict may also have been the result of criticism of Aśoka's policy by leaders of the other sects, who imagined or realized, from the degree of support for *Dhamma* by the populace, that this new teaching might cut the ground from under their feet. Possibly groups such as the brahmans argued that the author of *Dhamma* was trying to oust every other sect and install his own ideas. Or there may have been complaints about the irreligiousness of the people as a result of following *Dhamma*, in so far as traditional practices may have been reduced, thereby affecting the influence of the local priests.

The king explains that he is still honouring all sects, both ascetics and householders. Nevertheless he adds that he considers the 'progress of the essential doctrines of all sects' as the highest honour. This progress lies in toleration, not a passive co-existence but an active frame of mind in which opinions are expressed in a manner that does not cause any offence. He asks for restraint when speaking of the various sects lest one's own be over-praised and the others insulted. In the honouring of other sects lies the welfare and honour of one's own. Once again the idea of social behaviour is foremost. The superior man though unruffled in his own belief, is supremely tolerant in both word and action of the views of his fellow men, and through such toleration he enhances his own position and that of the group to which he owes his loyalty. An almost Confucian concept of 'virtue' creeps into the edict. The author adds that concord is meritorious and that all sects should obey and hear each other's moral teaching. This approach led to an advancement of his *Dhamma*, since the latter was based on the essentials of various sects. Thus he vindicated his own position by showing that there was nothing in *Dhamma* which was contrary, in thought at least, to the essentials of the sects, and at the same time satisfied the leaders of these sects that his intention was not to supplant their teaching with *Dhamma*, but rather to insist on mutual toleration.

In order to promote these essentials his own contribution was to increase the power of the *mahāmattas*. He states once more that the *dhamma-mahāmattas* are occupied in the propagation of *Dhamma*. So also are the

[1] Bloch, *Les Inscriptions d'Asoka*, p. 121.

ithījakha mahāmattas, the officers in charge of the women. The precise work of these officers remains uncertain.[1] But clearly, the promotion of *Dhamma* was meant to reach every member of the society. The same applies to officials who are inspectors of animal farms or are occupied in other assignments. They have all been instructed in *Dhamma* and religious toleration, and it is expected of them that they will spread this instruction in the course of their daily work. The final sentence of this edict sums up the king's view of this approach. He says,

. . . ayaṃ ca etassa phala ya ātpapāsaṃḍavaḍḍhī ca hoti dhaṃmassa ca dīpanā . . .
'The result of this is the increased influence of one's own sect and glory to *Dhamma* . . .'

The point that Aśoka wishes to make is that the practice of *Dhamma* does not exclude loyalty to one's own sect, even if it may necessitate disassociation from certain rituals. This is a defence of *Dhamma* against those critics who held that to support *Dhamma* in word or action would mean excommunication from one's sect. Aśoka points out the expanse of *Dhamma* by his own actions and by his good relationship with members of all sects, a sincerely felt tolerance being the way in which this relationship can be achieved.

The 13th Rock Edict is among the most important documents of Aśokan history.[2] It appears to have been inscribed a few months after the earlier edicts, since it conveys a tone of recapitulation. It also expresses a new idea, that of conquest by *Dhamma* instead of by war and violence. This must have been a later thought of Aśoka's, else he would have mentioned it in one of his earlier edicts. It seems that Aśoka, when reviewing the early part of his reign in retrospect, was extremely upset at the unhappiness caused by the Kaliṅga War. It appears that his remorse over the war grew with the years but did not exist to a great extent immediately after the war. It is indeed strange that Aśoka did not announce his remorse in the first few edicts that he issued, as for example the Minor Rock Edict. Eventually, by way of repentance he devoted himself to a zealous study of *Dhamma*. He considers deplorable, the deaths and deportations that accompany war. Even more worrying to him is the fact that the venerated group of the brahmans and *śramaṇas* meet with such misfortune. The normal rules of social behaviour are upset.

Aśoka's use of the terms brahman and *śramaṇa* is of interest in the context

[1] For a detailed discussion of the work of these officers see Ch. IV.

[2] Bloch, *Les Inscriptions d'Asoka*, p. 125.

of what is meant by *Dhamma*. He states in the edict that there are no peoples amongst whom these two classes do not exist, except among the Greeks.[1] In view of the fact that the countries known to him were all bordering on Jambudvīpa, and were acquainted with Indian religions and in many cases had religions similar to those in his own kingdom, such a remark is obvious. The Greeks are excluded because they were known to have totally different beliefs and therefore their religious orders were not the same. The brahmans were known to the Greeks as one of the more important classes of Indian society, referred to by Megasthanes as the philosophers.[2] But there was some confusion in their minds as to the distinction between a brahman and a *śramaṇa*. A fragment of Megasthenes refers to the ascetics as the *hylobioi*, and adds that there are some philosophers who follow the precepts of 'Boutta'.[3] It is not clear from this passage whether the author means that the *hylobioi* were followers of the Buddha or whether they were a separate group. The latter appears to be a more probable interpretation. The *hylobioi* were probably the brahman ascetics, and the followers of Boutta were the *śramaṇas*. The author may have confused the two groups. It appears from these accounts that the brahmans and the *śramaṇas* were both highly respected groups.

The brahmans and the *śramaṇas* in the eyes of Aśoka were more or less equals, in so far as they were both highly respected groups, being the religious leaders in the community. Apart from the occasions when he specifically states his faith in Buddhism, he does not in any way differentiate between the two groups when referring to them in the edicts. Usually the terms occur together almost as a compound. The placing of one in precedence to the other is quite arbitrary.[4] Aśoka cannot be accused of partiality towards the Buddhists on this count.

The idea of conquest through *Dhamma* is a logical development of the theory of *Dhamma*. It is opposed to conquest by force and thus eliminates aggressive warfare. By conquest Aśoka does not mean the actual overrunning or control of foreign territory. The use of the term conquest implies the adoption of the principles of *Dhamma* by the country in question. Thus he includes the Greek kingdoms of Syria, Egypt, Cyrene, Macedonia, and Epirus as having been conquered by *Dhamma*, whereas in fact all that may have happened was a cordial exchange of embassies or

[1] Ibid., p. 128.

[2] Strabo, XV, 1, 59.

[3] Clement of Alexandria, *Strom.*, I, p. 305 A, B.

[4] We have counted the number of times the word brahman precedes *śramaṇa* in the edicts and vice versa, and we find them almost equally divided. Brahman, precedes in about twenty instances and *śramaṇa* in about sixteen, and the word brahman alone occurs in about five instances (III, IV, V, VIII, IX, XI, XIII R.E.).

missions or merely the sending of one of these by Aśoka to the Greek kings mentioned. It is of particular interest to note that although the conquest by *Dhamma* brings great satisfaction to Aśoka and he hopes that his descendants will not wish to make the more usual type of conquests, he nevertheless does not prohibit the latter altogether. He merely modifies older conventional views of international ethics, by saying that if a conquest is necessary it should be accompanied by mercy and light punishments.[1]

Kaliṅga was conquered in the ninth year of Aśoka's reign. After this conquest Aśoka ceased to indulge in wars of aggression. This, we believe, was not because he completely forsook the idea of war as a means to an end, though he claims to have done so, but because with the conquest of Kaliṅga the consolidation of the empire was complete. Furthermore there was now no opposing power within the empire. The people on the frontier were generally too weak to consider a war against him. The only possibility was a campaign against the Greek kingdoms of Asia Minor. But they were too distant and the acquisition of their territory was not of particular interest to the Aśokan empire.

It may be asked why Aśoka did not continue the Mauryan campaign in southern India and include the entire peninsula within the empire. Such a war would have been for him both unnecessary and against his principles. The kingdoms of southern India were on very friendly terms with the Mauryan empire, judging from the edicts. As long as these kingdoms received the *dhamma-mahāmattas* and made at least a show of respecting the policy of *Dhamma*, Aśoka would not be ill-disposed towards them. Passages from Tāmil literature which we have dealt with elsewhere suggest that the Mauryan power was held in awe by the southern peoples when the first Mauryan invasions took place.[2] This predisposition towards remaining in Aśoka's favour applied to Ceylon as well, particularly with the accession of Tissa. Hindu theorists have glorified war.[3] Wars could be interpreted as opportunities for the display of power and might. A king's greatness depended more than usually on his military prowess. This was an attitude that Aśoka could not accept. He did not believe in passive resistance, nevertheless war was an extreme measure not to be used unless absolutely necessary. Whereas a Samudragupta in his place would have marched right down to Kanyā Kumari and perhaps even have taken a fleet across to Ceylon, Aśoka was willing to pause at Mysore and leave the now friendly southern kingdoms alone, until such time as they should become provocative. The conquest of Kaliṅga was of importance both to the strategy and

[1] XIII R.E., Kalsi. Bloch, *Les Inscriptions d'Asoka*, p. 132.

[2] See Ch. III.

[3] Manu, *Dharmaśāstra*, VII, VIII.

the economy of the Mauryan empire. As we have suggested earlier, it stood in the way of the southern routes from the Ganges valley, and it was also a powerful maritime area, which if included within the empire would provide a convenient source of income.[1] After the conquest of Kaliṅga further territorial conquest was almost at an end for Aśoka, unless he were to be deliberately provoked by any country. Thus Aśoka could with assurance feel satisfied with the principle of conquest by *Dhamma*, as the empire now had few enemies to fear and the strongly centralized administration was rapidly crystallizing.

The last of the Major Rock Edicts is the 14th.[2] It is a short edict in which the author explains that he has had these edicts inscribed throughout the country in complete or abridged versions. It appears from this that the extant inscriptions were not the only ones to be published and that many more versions were either inscribed on rock and remain as yet undiscovered, or else were made public in other forms. With his enthusiasm for *Dhamma* Aśoka must have done his utmost towards having these edicts dispersed in every part of his domains, so that the word of *Dhamma* would penetrate all over the country. Where there were no suitable rocks, the edicts may well have been written on tablets of wood or on cloth banners and posted in the more important parts of each town, thereby giving them as much publicity as was possible. They also appear to have been read aloud at public gatherings and similar occasions.[3]

The insertion of the Separate Edicts at Dhauli and Jaugada in lieu of the 11th, 12th, and 13th Edicts, makes it apparent that the edicts could be varied according to the locality in which they were inscribed. The reason for omitting the 13th Rock Edict from the Kaliṅga area is obvious. The reference to the suffering caused by the Kaliṅga War was too close to the feeling of the people of Kaliṅga to make it pleasant or instructive for them to read the edict. Further, it was politically unwise to publicize the king's remorse over the war amongst the people against whom the war was fought.

The 1st Separate Rock Edict is addressed to the *mahāmattas* at Tosalī and Samāpa and deals largely with instructions to these officials in the proper administration of justice in the territory.[4] The term *mahāmatta* is

[1] See Ch. IV. Aśoka refers to the region as *Kaliṅgas*, which Kern takes to mean the *trikaliṅga* or 'three Kaliṅgas' of the medieval inscriptions (*Asoka*, p. 84). We have no good evidence of the extent of Kaliṅga before its conquest, or after Khāravela. The phrase *trikaliṅga* is a late one and refers to the times when the area was divided into three kingdoms. There is no evidence that *trikaliṅga* was ever used after the Gupta period. The context of the word in the edict shows that it is used in the plural because it refers to the people of Kaliṅga and not to the kingdom itself. Similar usages are frequent in the Aśokan inscriptions and are widely to be found in Pāli and Sanskrit literature.

[2] Bloch, *Les Inscriptions d'Asoka*, p. 133.

[3] Ibid., p. 139.

[4] Ibid., p. 136.

qualified by reference to *nagalaviyohalaka*, the city magistrates. The first demand made by the king on these officials is that their aim should be to gain the affection of the people; for he adds,

. . . *savve munisse pajā mamā* . . .[1]
'All men are my children.'

He desires the welfare of his subjects in the same way as he would that of his children. In the first part of the statement there can be a play on the word *pajā* since it can mean the children or the subjects of the king, and either meaning would apply in this case. The latter meaning would imply that since all men under the jurisdiction of these officials are his subjects, he wishes that the officials gain their affection. But the latter part of the statement makes it quite clear that he means 'children' in using the word *pajā*.

The king is aware that there are lapses in justice owing to a number of reasons, some of them connected with the personal character of the officials. He lays great emphasis on impartiality in judgment and on the efficient working of the judicial system. He speaks of the debt which the officers owe to the king and declares that their efficiency will win them not only his satisfaction and pleasure but enough merit to attain heaven. Here again heaven is held out as a reward beyond even the pleasure of the king.

The public reading of the edict is insisted upon on each day of the *Tisya* (a planet), and also on frequent occasions in between. This information bears out our suggestion that the edicts were read to the public at special gatherings, or even in the ordinary course of events in the towns. This no doubt had the double purpose of making the public aware both of the king's wishes with regard to it, and also of the relationship he envisaged between the officials and the public. As a further check on the officials a supervisory officer was to be sent every five years to tour and inspect the working of the judiciary and insist on the king's instructions being carried out. In the 2nd Separate Edict he states that even a single person can demand to have the edict read out to him.

The 2nd Separate Rock Edict is directed mainly to those officials at Tosalī and Samāpa who worked amongst the people on the frontier; perhaps the less civilized tribes of eastern India, who after the Kaliṅga War had either been incorporated within the empire or placed in much closer relations with the empire. Once again the king states that his subjects are to him like his children, and this time he includes the frontier people or the

[1] Bloch, *Les Inscriptions d'Asoka*, p. 137.

borderers. It is the duty of the officials to create confidence in the government amongst these peoples. They must feel that the king has a paternal love for them and will care for them. This idea of the king treating his subjects as his children, was to become fairly current in ancient Indian political thought. Passages occur in the *Arthaśāstra*, where the king is called upon to place the welfare of his subjects among his foremost duties, and is told that only if he regards them with the same concern as a father regards his children will the kingdom prosper.[1] Aśvaghoṣa repeats much the same sentiments.[2] The emphasis is largely on building up confidence, particularly among the borderers. The fact that Aśoka's approach to these people is distinctly different from that to his other subjects, shows not only the tremendous variety of the people he had to deal with, but also his own understanding of the type of appeal to be employed with each individual group. Obviously with the tribes on the eastern frontier the main thing was to gain their confidence. Then possibly they would be more amenable to *Dhamma*.

After the last of the Major Rock Edicts there is an interval of a few years, before another set of edicts, the Pillar Edicts, were issued. During this period of about twelve years, a number of minor Pillar Edicts were inscribed, some of which referred to a specific site or institution. Whether any major edicts were issued during this period remains open to doubt. Since there is as yet no evidence of such edicts we must perforce work on those that exist. The interval therefore afforded a convenient break in which the ideas of *Dhamma* might be assimilated by Aśoka's subjects. His own thinking on the subject was given time to develop and change, as it did, from the evidence of the Major Pillar Edicts.

The Minor Pillar Edicts belong to the second category of edicts, i.e. those that were associated with his purely Buddhist activities. These were either based on his relationship with the *Saṃgha*, or indicated a place of pilgrimage which he had visited. The idea of inscribing pillars with the public edicts probably came to him after the Minor Pillar Edicts had been completed, and the result was impressive. After seeing the Minor Pillar Edicts, he may have decided not to look for rock surfaces, but instead to erect finely polished pillars and inscribe these. However two Minor Rock Edicts were issued during this period. One of these found in abundance in south India certainly preceded the inscribing of pillars. The other, the Kandahar Inscription appears to have been somewhat later, judging by the contents.

The Minor Rock Edict inscribed largely in the south was issued at about

[1] I, 19.

[2] *Buddhacarita*, II, 35.

the same time as the Major Rock Edicts.[1] The Minor Edict has been referred to earlier in the chapter, when considering the relationship between Aśoka and Buddhism. Aśoka's status was at first that of a lay worshipper, but later he had a closer relationship with the *Saṃgha* and consequently be became more zealous in his belief. The result of this zeal is the considerable spread of righteousness in the country. He calls upon his subjects to be zealous as this will lead to progress, but he does not equate *Dhamma* with Buddhist teachings. Buddhism remains his personal belief. The Yeṟṟaguḍi version of the Minor Rock Edict makes it even more certain that he wishes *Dhamma* to permeate through all social levels, from the brahmans to the elephant drivers and the responsibility for this lies with the officials.[2] In speaking of his principles he lays deliberate stress on the importance of the family, and refers this to ancient custom and usage. Nowhere else in the edicts has the institution of the family been referred to in such a pointed way.

Since the versions of the Minor Rock Edict refer chiefly to a private matter, Aśoka's personal conviction in Buddhism, it may be said that they were therefore a token of respect for the southern peoples. The same edict occurs elsewhere but not in so many versions as in the south. Aśoka may have felt that since the people of the south were more distant and less familiar with the development of his ideas, it would make his position clearer if he first declared his personal belief and then followed it with an explanation of *Dhamma*. Thus the concluding half of the edict introduces the idea of *Dhamma*, and suggests practical ways in which it could be put into action. Compared to the Major Rock Edicts, this edict expresses a certain uneasiness as to whether the readers and listeners will fully understand what the author wants of them. This attitude is justifiable in that few north Indian rulers had penetrated so far south. For Aśoka, the land and the people of this region were still unfamiliar. Indeed if it be true that the *Brāhmī* script was their first acquaintance with the symbols of writing, then a certain amount of bewilderment on the part of Aśoka as to how best to explain himself is excusable.

During the interval of twelve years, events in the Buddhist world were moving fast. In 250 B.C. the Buddhist Council was held and later missionaries were sent to various parts of the sub-continent.[3] Aśoka as a Buddhist must certainly have been most interested in these developments. Yet his

[1] We have discussed the Major Rock Edict before the Minor Rock Edict, because we believe that the former are more revealing as far as his *Dhamma* policy is concerned, and taken as a series give us a better indication of the development of *Dhamma*.

[2] Bloch, *Les Inscriptions d'Asoka*, p. 151.

[3] See Ch. II.

lack of narrow sectarianism is proved by the fact that even at this stage when the Council was busy weeding out dissident elements and attacking other sects, Aśoka in his twentieth regnal year, donated a further cave to the Ājīvikas in the Barābar Hill.[1] It is clear that though Aśoka was a Buddhist he was not unconcerned with the welfare of other sects, even those in opposition to Buddhism. The legends relating the events leading up to the calling of the Council do not speak of the Ājīvikas in a friendly manner.[2] It is to his credit that Aśoka was conscious of his responsibilities as the head of the state to be impartial in his patronage.

The Kandahar Inscription heralds the assurance that is to be found in the Major Pillar Edicts.[3] Admittedly it was written as a piece of propaganda, to publicize the benefits of *Dhamma* amongst the Greek and Aramaic speaking settlements on the western frontier. As a document on *Dhamma* it does not provide any further knowledge than the other edicts. If anything the description of *Dhamma* is extremely vague, the greatest stress being laid on the prohibition of killing animals. We are told that not only has the king made men more pious, but also that all things now prosper throughout the whole world. Clearly this edict was meant to excite the curiosity not only of the local people but also of the traders who frequented the route passing through Kandahar, and who would then create an interest in *Dhamma* on reaching their own countries.

It is in the same tone of confident assertion that the first six Pillar Edicts were issued by Aśoka, in his twenty-seventh regnal year. The new set of edicts were again meant primarily for the public, and are therefore similar in spirit to the Major Rock Edicts. They were inscribed on pillars situated in places where people gathered so that ample publicity was given to them. The explanation of *Dhamma* is resumed in these edicts.

In the 1st Pillar Edict, Aśoka states that *Dhamma* has progressed through the years.[4] On viewing it in retrospect he is satisfied with the result. He mentions his agents of various ranks, who, in practising *Dhamma* have been able to stir the waverers. (Presumably this refers to the activities of the *dhamma-mahāmattas*.) The original text refers to those yet undecided about *Dhamma* as *capalam*, 'the waverers'.[5] But the point of interest is that the tone of the sentence and indeed of the edict suggests that the officers have made the propagation of *Dhamma*, wherever and whenever possible, their sole function. The king appears to be obsessed by the idea that everyone must practice *Dhamma*. Whereas previously the king spoke

[1] Bloch, *Les Inscriptions d'Asoka*, p. 156.
[2] See Ch. II.
[3] *JA*, 1958, vol. ccxlvi, pp. 2–3, 22.
[4] Bloch, *Les Inscriptions d'Asoka*, p. 161.
[5] Ibid.

of the virtues of *Dhamma* with enthusiasm and presented it as a new and possible solution to the ills of society, now a note of imperiousness creeps in. The constant repetition of the word *Dhamma* shows that his enthusiasm is no longer that of someone propagating a new idea, but has become part of his very being.

Previously, simple virtues and a high-minded social code were enough to secure merit. Now the latter depends on a great love for *Dhamma*, careful examination, great obedience, great fear, and great energy.[1] The clear thinking of a man determined to establish the superiority of social behaviour has been obscured by the erroneous belief that his own understanding of the problem is responsible for whatever clarity there exists. For he adds that it is through his instruction that *Dhamma* has progressed. The picture of the *mahāmattas* persuading the waverers is not entirely a happy one. The degree of self-responsibility that was apparent in the early pronunciations of *Dhamma* seems to have given way to an ordered approach which leaves little choice with the individual. *Dhamma* seems to have acquired a far more organized set of rules which the *dhamma-mahāmattas* enforce, not entirely according to the will of the individual. *Dhamma* seems to be turning into a magical formula to solve all problems, and *Dhamma* workers begin to assume the form of a religious body. The closing sentence of the edict runs thus,

. . . *esā hi vidhi yā iyaṃ dhaṃmena pālanā dhaṃmena vidhāne dhaṃmena sukhiyanā dhaṃmena gotti ti* . . .
'For this is my principle: to protect through *Dhamma*, to administer affairs according to *Dhamma*, to please the people with *Dhamma*, to guard the empire with *Dhamma*.'

The germ of fanaticism and megalomania begins to show itself in this edict.

The 2nd Pillar Edict continues in much the same strain.[2] Aśoka describes *Dhamma* as a minimum of sins, many virtues, compassion, liberality, truthfulness, and purity. He adds that he has bestowed the gift of *cakhudāne*, 'the gift of the eye', in many ways.[3] The idea that he attempts to convey is that through the practice of *Dhamma* social and personal relationships become clarified within themselves, and this leads to a better understanding of social life and the real merit of the virtuous deeds which may ensue. Thus 'the gift of the eye' may well have been just a turn of phrase suggesting that Aśoka was providing insight or stating, 'I have shown the way'.

[1] I P.E. Bloch, *Les Inscriptions d'Asoka*, p. 161.
[2] II P.E. Ibid., p. 162.
[3] Cf. Hultzsch, *Corpus Inscriptionum Indicarum*, vol. i, p. 120; Bloch, *Les Inscriptions d'Asoka*, p. 162.

His remark in the same edict, that he has conferred many boons on men and animals and has performed innumerable righteous deeds is another manifestation of his growing self-adulation. This was a most unfortunate tendency since it must have led at times to a complacent satisfaction which no doubt prevented him from maintaining his earlier contact with the opinion of his subjects. Even at this stage when his obsession with *Dhamma* increases, he still sees it as an ethical concept and not a religious idea. The means he adopted for its publicity may have rivalled those of religious systems but the teaching itself did not assume a religious garb.

The 3rd Pillar Edict attempts to differentiate between virtuous deeds and evil doings.[1] The sinful passions are listed as fierceness, cruelty, anger, pride, and envy. An indulgence in these is said to be ruinous. There is on occasion an indirect reference to greed as a sinful passion. Strangely enough Aśoka never mentions lust among these, particularly as the passionate enjoyment or desire for something would be regarded as sinful according to the principles of *Dhamma*. Nowhere is the actual practice of *Dhamma* indicated in detail. At best even Aśoka's pronouncements in the edicts are of a general nature. It is significant that in the elucidation of social bearings the relationship between men and women is not included. It would seem from this that the role of women was by now so completely regulated, that any remark in relation to it was considered unnecessary.

The edict closes with the sentence,

. . . *iyaṃ me hidattikāye, iyaṃ mana me pālattikāye.*

'This is important to my happiness in this world; that, on the other hand, for the next.'

This brings us to a fundamental concept in ethics, that of relative morality. It is indeed unfortunate that the edict closes at this point, and that no explanation of the concluding sentence is given. It would appear from the sentence as it stands that Aśoka was beginning to think in terms of a double standard of virtuous action, one that was conducive to earthly happiness and the other to heavenly bliss. This would imply a serious deviation from his original ethical concept of virtue being meritorious here and in the life to follow. However, if we regard this sentence as a continuation of the earlier debate on sin and virtue, its interpretation is somewhat different. The happiness on earth refers to the brief pleasure which the satisfaction of a passion brings, whereas the avoidance of passion leads to eternal happiness in heaven.

Another change from the earlier ideas of *Dhamma* is the continual

[1] Ibid., p. 163.

stress laid on sin and actions that are sinful. Possibly his increasing association with Buddhism brought with it a fear of sin, and a fear of involvement in actions which may be called sinful. There is a strong hint in these later edicts that he was becoming involved in a puritanical fantasy of sin and virtue, and that the pristine force which had moved him to his earlier social ethics was beginning to die away.

There is a return to the tone of the Major Rock Edicts in the 4th Pillar Edict.[1] To some extent this edict is connected with the two Separate Edicts at Dhauli and Jaugaḍa. There the officers are called upon to be responsible and efficient. By now it would seem that both qualities are recognized in them, for the power to reward or punish is delegated to the local officers. After the tendency to centralize as seen in the quinquennial inspections and the institution of the *dhamma-mahāmattas*, this may appear to be a step in the reverse direction. Elsewhere in this work, this has been explained in the light of administrative expediency.[2] In order that these officials may perform their duties fearlessly and confidently, and yet remain undisturbed, the king has given them the power of reward and punishment. This was indeed a very advanced step and demanded considerable confidence on the part of the king in the officials. It would seem that the bureaucracy and the administration of the country were functioning well otherwise this authority would not have been delegated. However, we must not overlook the fact that with increasing years, any king in the position of Aśoka would have had to delegate some powers, since old age does not permit the energetic interest of early years to continue.

Another move of great importance was that of insisting on a uniformity of judicial proceedings and of punishments. This was not meant merely as a pious thought. If there was no intention of its being carried out it need not have been mentioned. The statement can be interpreted in two ways. Either as the equality of all subjects in the eyes of the law, or as the equality of law throughout the country.[3] In either case it was an unprecedented step, and shows the emphasis that Aśoka wished to place on social justice. Continuing his efforts to secure greater welfare for his subjects, he orders a respite of three days before a death sentence is carried out. This is an act of grace, since he recognizes that this time may, in certain cases, be utilized to prove the innocence of the condemned person or to secure his repentance. It is curious that, despite his firm belief in Buddhism, he did not abolish capital punishment. Doubtlessly he regarded capital punishment as essential to the maintenance of law and order, and, despite his

[1] IV P.E. Bloch, *Les Inscriptions d'Asoka*, p. 163.

[2] See Ch. IV.

[3] Ibid.

personal convictions to the contrary, felt that justice in the state must be based on recognized painful punishments or pleasurable rewards.[1]

Much the same idea is expressed in the 5th Pillar Edict, where he orders that certain animals are not to be killed on certain days, and others are not to be killed at all.[2] The list given is most perplexing. Some are obviously beasts of burden such as bulls, others are edible, as for example some of the fish. But many are declared inviolable without any apparent reason.[3] The curious feature is that he does not, as a pious Buddhist, order non-violence throughout the empire, he merely specifies the particular animals which are not to be killed. He was probably aware that complete abstention from killing animals would be an impossible law, in that it could never be enforced.

In the 6th Pillar Edict, Aśoka briefly explains the purpose of the edicts in general.[4] The primary reason was a concern for the welfare and happiness of his subjects, who, if they ordered their lives according to the principles of *Dhamma* would attain happiness. He claims that in this effort of bringing *Dhamma* to his people, he has been impartial to all classes and all sects; and this, because he considers visiting the people personally to be his duty. *Dhamma* combined a system of welfare with his own humanitarian approach. He genuinely wished *Dhamma* to be the means of communication between him and his subjects. This alone apart from any other reason, made it imperative that *Dhamma* and consequently Aśoka himself in his capacity as the ruler should be impartial to all sects and beliefs.

The 7th Pillar Edict was inscribed in the twenty-eighth regnal year.[5] It occurs on only one of the pillars, the Delhi-Topra. It is difficult to explain why it was omitted from the other pillars, unless so ordered by Aśoka as an afterthought.[6] The edict may have been revoked after it had already been inscribed on the one pillar. Aśoka may have thought that, as it was largely a summary of his work in connection with *Dhamma*, and contained no further elucidation of *Dhamma* it served no particular purpose and therefore it was better to withdraw it. It was however allowed to remain on the Delhi-Topra pillar.

The edict states that many improvements in the well-being of the people have been carried out. For instance, roads have been built and many shady banyan trees and mango groves planted along their length. At

[1] There is an interesting passage in the *Mahābhārata* (*Śānti parvan*, 259), which expresses an attitude very similar to Aśoka's attitude in this matter. According to the Chinese travellers, capital punishment was abolished in later centuries.

[2] V P.E. Bloch, *Les Inscriptions d'Asoka*, p. 165.

[3] We have discussed this matter at length in Ch. III.

[4] Bloch, *Les Inscriptions d'Asoka*, p. 167.

[5] Ibid., p. 168.

[6] Cf. Sen, *Asoka*, pp. 142–3.

intervals of eight *kos*, wells were dug and water was made available for man and beast. But all these schemes are of little value as compared with the one ambition of Aśoka's rule, the practice and spread of *Dhamma*. This gives him real satisfaction, much more so than any amount of welfare work. The king states that in the past, although progress in *Dhamma* was desired, it did not come about. So Aśoka adopted a double policy; one was to issue edicts explaining *Dhamma*, and the second was to appoint officials who were responsible for publicizing *Dhamma* and encouraging people to accept it.

The activities of the *dhamma-mahāmattas* are not restricted to any one group in the community. They range through the entire scale of society from one extreme to the other, or as Aśoka expresses it, from the householder to the ascetic. This remark is of some significance in so far as it exposes the workings of the king's mind. He does not classify his subjects as brahman theoreticians were wont to do, ranging them from brahmans to *śūdras*.[1] He does not measure the range of society on the basis of social prestige but on that of social responsibility. The householder being the head of the family represents a fundamental unit of society and should have of necessity the greatest amount of social responsibility. The ascetic who deliberately lives outside the confines of society has therefore the least amount of such responsibility. The *dhamma-mahāmattas* are expected to work impartially amongst the various sects. Some, however, are specially assigned to particular sects. Among the latter, mention is made of the *Saṃgha*, brahmans, Ājīvikas, and *Nirgranthas*.

Another group of officers are concerned solely with the charitable donations made by the king and the various members of the royal family. These donations are made with the purpose of furthering *Dhamma*. Possibly the idea was much the same as among certain royal families to this day, wherein each member adopts a particular institution or sect and makes regular donations towards its maintenance. In this case no doubt the donations would be brought by a *dhamma-mahāmatta* who would in addition, preach to the institution on the value of *Dhamma*. This system appears to be linked with the inscribing of the Queen's Edict in which Aśoka orders the officials to record the donations of the Queen Kāruvākī.[2]

Further in the edict Aśoka explains that *Dhamma* has been taught in

[1] He does on occasion refer to brahmans and *ibhyas*, the latter being taken usually to mean *vaiśyas* since the literal meaning is wealthy men. But this would appear to be a general term referring more to the various castes rather than to the general range of society.

[2] See Ch. II and Bloch, *Les Inscriptions d'Asoka*, p. 159.

two ways, by regulations and by persuasion. Aśoka admits that much more has been achieved by persuasion and that the regulations have been of little consequence. By way of an example he explains that he has declared certain animals inviolable and has therefore placed a restriction on their killing. However, through an understanding of *Dhamma* there would automatically be no killing of animals, thereby making the restrictions unnecessary. Even at this stage Aśoka appreciated the value of persuasion as a stronger force than restriction, and although by now the institution of the *dhamma-mahāmattas* had acquired tremendous powers of interference in the lives of the people, nevertheless Aśoka still theoretically stressed the importance of persuasion.

There are four edicts which belong to the second general category of edicts: the ones in which Aśoka expresses his belief in Buddhist teachings and which are addressed specifically to fellow-Buddhists and to the *Saṃgha*. These are the Rummindei Inscription, the Nigalisāgar Inscription, the Schism Edict, and the Bhabra Edict. Here Aśoka is expressing himself, not as a Mauryan emperor, but entirely as a private individual. We see him here as the practising Buddhist, making the required pilgrimages and accepting the conventions of a pious believer.

The inscription on the pillar at Rummindei, commemorates, the pilgrimage made by the king to the Lumbinī grove, which was regarded as a sacred site, since it was the place where the Buddha was born.[1] The pilgrimage to Lumbinī was one of the four recognized pilgrimages that a good Buddhist was expected to make. The Nigalisāgar Inscription records the fact of the king having visited the Konākamana *stūpa* in his fifteenth regnal year, and at a later date had it enlarged.[2] The second date cannot be read in the inscription owing to its damaged condition. This visit was probably made during his pilgrimage to various Buddhist sites. The visit to Lumbinī we are told was made in his twenty-first regnal year. The second visit to the Konākamana *stūpa* must have been made at about the same time. It is apparent from the Nigalisāgar inscription that his personal attachment to Buddhism has grown stronger with the years.

The Schism Edict, with three known versions, at Sanchi, Sārnāth, and Kosam, was issued in the later part of his reign, in *c.* 240 B.C.[3] It threatens monks and nuns with expulsion should they attempt to cause disunity in the *Saṃgha*. As a Buddhist, Aśoka is concerned with the unified function-

[1] Ibid., p. 157. Rummindei is the modern name for Lumbinī. A reduction was made in the land tax and revenue assessment of the village. The latter section of the edict may be regarded as part of the royal archives. We have discussed this edict in Chs. II and III.

[2] Bloch, *Les Inscriptions d'Asoka*, p. 158.

[3] Ibid., p. 152. We have given reasons for this date in Ch. II.

ing of the *Saṃgha*, and by issuing this edict he wishes it to be known that he will not tolerate dissident elements in the *Saṃgha*. He orders that one copy of the edict should remain in the office of the *Saṃgha*, and another copy be made public, so that lay-worshippers and the officials concerned, may know his wishes on the subject. The edict is addressed to the special *mahāmattas* who work for the *Saṃgha*. The edict must have been sent to all the Buddhist centres and the local *mahāmattas* must have received these instructions.

The last remaining edict, the Bhabra Edict, is undated, but we believe it to have been issued towards the end of Aśoka's reign.[1] The hill on which it was found contains the ruins of two Buddhist monasteries.[2] This agrees entirely with the inscription which is addressed to the *Saṃgha* and is an avowal of the king's faith in Buddhism, and an enumeration of the many Buddhist scriptures with which all Buddhist monks or lay worshippers should necessarily be acquainted. This edict is of importance since it states in no uncertain terms the fact of Aśoka being a Buddhist. It speaks of his faith in the Buddha, the *Dhamma*, and the *Saṃgha*.[3] There is no ambiguity in the statement. Nevertheless this is a personal edict addressed by the king directly and solely to the *Saṃgha*, and not to the public at large. It is more than likely that it was addressed to the monks at the two monasteries near the present-day site of Bhabra. The edict is issued by Aśoka as a Buddhist. This explains why he refers to himself not with his usual title of *Devānampiya Piyadassi rājā*, but with the far more humble title of *piyadassi lājā magadhe*, 'Piyadassi, the king of Magadha'.

The *Dhamma* of Aśoka emerges as a way of life incorporating a number of ideals and practices. Abstinence from killing was an important principle, as also was the insistence of considerate family relationships and social relationships, whether these were between parents and children, elders and young people, friends, or various ideological sects. What would be regarded as a programme of social welfare, in twentieth-century parlance, such as providing medical facilities, good communications, and prohibiting useless expenditure on superstitions, was included. Moderation was the key-note of thought and action. Yet to begin with there was no attempt at coercion of any kind. Principles were suggested and it was left to the conscience of each individual to make a choice. In the later edicts we have noticed a marked change. In the Major Pillar Edicts, the advice becomes more abstract and is far less valuable than that given in the Major Rock Edicts.

[1] Bloch, *Les Inscriptions d'Asoka*, p. 154. Also known as the Calcutta-Bairāṭ rock inscription.

[2] *Archaeological Reports*, II, p. 248.

[3] This belief constitutes the Buddhist creed.

The author is so obsessed with the idea of the success of *Dhamma*, that the reality of the situation does not appear to register.

In interpreting the term *Dhamma* we must beware of equating it with the Buddhist *Dhamma*, or any other accepted system which was called by this generic term. The true interpretation of *Dhamma* can only come about after a detailed analysis of who used the term and in what context. To suggest that all the *Dharmas* or *Dhammas* expressed in the literature and thought of ancient India are identical or nearly so, would be as foolhardy as to maintain that the meaning of the term Socialism used in any context in the past two hundred years has been identical or nearly so. Fortunately there is no need to seek equations for the *Dhamma* of Aśoka as has been frequently done in the past. There is a large enough and reliable enough body of literature in his own edicts, which provides the answer to the question, 'What was the *Dhamma* of Aśoka?'

The concept of *Dharma* used in the sense of Law and Social Order was by no means new to Mauryan India. Aśoka, with the propagation of his *Dhamma*, made an attempt to humanize it and show that in fact what mattered most was virtuous behaviour. The ability to distinguish between virtuous and unvirtuous behaviour is what distinguishes man from the rest of creation, and the practice of virtue can be made common to all men. The *Dhamma* embodying such behaviour transcends all barriers of sectarian belief. As we have said before, *Dhamma* was largely an ethical concept related to the individual in the context of his society. In the propagation of his *Dhamma* Aśoka was attempting to reform the narrow attitude of religious teaching, to protect the weak against the strong, and to promote throughout the empire a consciousness of social behaviour so broad in its scope, that no cultural group could object to it.

VI
THE LATER MAURYAS

THE years after the death of Aśoka saw the end of the Mauryan dynasty as a political force in India. Mauryan rulers continued to rule for another half-century until, in the earlier part of the second century B.C., the dynasty collapsed completely and gave way to the Śuṅgas. Within this half-century there was a disintegration of the Mauryan empire, and the vast territory held by Aśoka dwindled to the nucleus of the kingdom with which Candragupta had started his career, more or less confined to the province of Magadha. In contrast with the fullness of evidence available on the reign of Aśoka, there is a mere glimmer of evidence on the later Mauryas. This too is of such a confused and uncertain nature, that the reconstruction of the last fifty years of the Mauryan dynasty varies from historian to historian, each of whom can at best suggest only hypothetical reconstructions. Such a reconstruction of the later Mauryas is suggested in this chapter.

Dynastic lists of the later Mauryas are available from many sources. A comparison of these lists with whatever evidence is available on individual rulers, may provide the best starting point. Purāṇic sources give extensive king lists of the later Mauryas, but these lists are much at variance, as will be apparent from the following.

Vāyu and Brahmāṇḍa Purāṇas[1]		Regnal years
Aśoka	was followed by	
Kunāla	,, ,, ,,	
Bandhupālita	,, ,, ,,	8
Indrapālita	,, ,, ,,	10
Devavarma	,, ,, ,,	7
Śatadhanus	,, ,, ,,	8
Bṛhadratha		7

The dynasty ended with Bṛhadratha, as he was assassinated by Puṣyamitra, the founder of the Śuṅga dynasty. Since this event is mentioned by all the *Purāṇas* we shall not refer to it on every occasion.

Matsya Purāṇa[2]		Regnal years
Aśoka	was followed by	
Daśaratha	,, ,, ,,	8

[1] Pargiter, *Dynasties of the Kali Age*, p. 29. [2] Ibid., p. 28.

Samprati	was followed by	9
Śatadhanvan	,, ,, ,,	8
Bṛhadratha		7

Viṣṇu Purāṇa[1]

Aśoka	was followed by
Suyaśas	,, ,, ,,
Daśaratha	,, ,, ,,
Saṃgata	,, ,, ,,
Śāliśuka	,, ,, ,,
Somavarman	,, ,, ,,
Śatadhanvan	,, ,, ,,
Bṛhadratha	

Pargiter suggests another king list based on what he calls the *eVāyu Purāṇa*, which differs from the lists already given.[2]

		Regnal years
Aśoka	was followed by	
Kulāla (Kunāla?)	,, ,, ,,	
Bandhupālita	,, ,, ,,	8
Daśona	,, ,, ,,	7
Daśaratha	,, ,, ,,	8
Samprati	,, ,, ,,	9
Śāliśuka	,, ,, ,,	13
Devadharman	,, ,, ,,	7
Śatadhanvan	,, ,, ,,	8
Bṛhadratha		7

If all these king lists were to be collected into one, we should obtain the following result.

		Regnal years
Aśoka	was followed by	
Kunāla	,, ,, ,,	8
Bandhupālita	,, ,, ,,	8
Indrapālita	,, ,, ,,	10
Daśona	,, ,, ,,	7
Daśaratha	,, ,, ,,	8
Samprati	,, ,, ,,	9
Śāliśuka	,, ,, ,,	13
Devavarman	,, ,, ,,	7
Śatadhanvan	,, ,, ,,	8
Bṛhadratha		7

[1] Ch. XXIV.

[2] Pargiter, *Dynasties of the Kali Age*, p. 29.

This list however is not acceptable. The one statement on which all the *Purāṇas* are in agreement is that the dynasty lasted 137 years. The first three Mauryas account for the first 85 years of the dynasty,[1] which leaves 52 years to be distributed amongst the later Mauryas. The above list is invalidated since it adds up to a total of 85 years, and so in fact are all the other Purāṇic lists, since each of them totals either more or less than 52 years. Thus we see that there are many variations and omissions in the Purāṇic lists and no single one can be accepted as completely authentic.

Other sources have also given lists of the later Mauryas. Among them, the *Aśokāvadāna* states the following .[2]

Aśoka	was followed by
Sampadi	,, ,, ,,
Vṛhaspati	,, ,, ,,
Vṛṣasena	,, ,, ,,
Puṣyadharman	,, ,, ,,
Puṣyamitra	

Jaina tradition has left us two names.[3] We are told that Aśoka was followed by his grandson Samprati, the son of Kunāla.

Tāranātha, the Tibetan historian, basing himself on Buddhist sources, gives the following lists,[4]

Aśoka,	was followed by,
Vigatāśoka,	,, ,, ,,
Vīrasena	

The *Rājataraṅginī* of Kalhaṇa introduces a completely new name as the successor of Aśoka in Jalauka, the king of Kashmir.[5] He was followed by Dāmodara.

The only evidence we have from European classical sources is that of Polybius, who writes that in 206 B.C., Antiochus the Great of Syria renewed his friendship with Sophagasenos who is described as the 'Indian King'.[6] Polybius then adds the following remarks, 'Here he procured more elephants so that his total force of them now amounted to 150, and after a further distribution of corn to his troops, set out himself with his army, leaving Androsthenes of Cyzicus to collect the treasure which the king had agreed to pay.' Sophagasenos is clearly the Greek version of the Indian name Subhagasena. We shall discuss the identification of this king a little later.

[1] Pargiter, *Dynasties of the Kali Age*, pp. 26, 27.

[2] Przyluski, *La Legende de l'Empereur Açoka*, p. 301 n. 3.

[3] *Pariśiṣṭaparvan*, IX, 34–54.

[4] *Geschichte des Buddhismus in Indien*, VIII, p. 50.

[5] I, 108–53.

[6] *Histories*, XI, 39.

The story of the assassination of Bṛhadratha by Puṣymitra is repeated by Bāṇa in the *Harṣacarita*.[1] He writes that the wicked general Puṣpamitra killed his master the Mauryan Bṛhadratha, who had little sense, and to whom the general had pretended to show the whole army in a review.

Another possible successor to Aśoka whose existence is attested by historical evidence was his son Tīvara, who is referred to together with his mother Kāruvākī, in the Queen's Edict.[2] But this is the sole reference to the prince, since he is not mentioned in literary sources unless under another name. If our earlier hypothesis is correct that the queen Kāruvākī was the same as Tissarakkhā of Buddhist legend (both being described as Aśoka's second queens), the former being her personal name and the latter her official name adopted after she became chief queen,[3] then the disappearance of Tīvara is understandable. The sources suggest that she was an ambitious woman who had considerable control over the actions of the ageing Aśoka.[4] Tīvara may have been born to Aśoka in his old age, and may therefore have been a spoilt and favourite child.

If Tissarakkhā was resentful of Aśoka's interest in Buddhism and regarded it as a rival to his interest in her (as the legend of her injuring the Bodhi-tree suggests), then it would not be beyond the bounds of possibility that she nagged at the king to make Tīvara his heir.[5] As an over-ambitious mother she may have had the young prince in her power. He would therefore be resented by the other princes, his step-brothers, some of whom such as Kunāla were considerably older than him, and owing to his youth may well have ignored him after their father's death. If it is true that Kunāla succeeded Aśoka, and if there be any truth in the legend that Tissarakkhā had Kunāla blinded, then it is not to be wondered at that both Tissarakkhā and her son disappear from the scene after the death of Aśoka.

Kunāla is frequently mentioned as the successor of Aśoka. Buddhist legend mentions a story of his being sent to suppress a revolt at Taxila, which we believe to be historically untrue.[6] Kunāla also plays a significant role in another Buddhist legend, where Tissarakkhā is responsible for having him blinded, the authenticity of which legend is also doubtful.[7] Nevertheless it would seem that Kunāla was the son of Aśoka, viceroy at Taxila and a possible if not probable successor to Aśoka.

The *Matsya Purāṇa* states that Aśoka was followed on the throne by his grandson Daśaratha. The *Viṣṇu Purāṇa* speaks of Suyaśas succeeding Aśoka, and Daśaratha coming after Suyaśas. This is the only occasion on

[1] VI.
[2] Bloch, *Les Inscriptions d'Asoka*, p. 159.
[3] See Ch. II.
[4] Przyluski, *La Legende de l'Empereur Açoka*, pp. 283 ff.
[5] *Mahāvaṃsa*, XX, 1–6.
[6] See Ch. II.
[7] Ibid.

which Suyaśas is mentioned in any of the sources. It has been suggested that Suyaśas was another name for Kunāla.[1] This may well be so. Kunāla is said to have been named after the bird with the beautiful eyes owing to the beauty of his own eyes.[2] It is possible that he took the official name Suyaśas 'of great glory', on becoming king, a custom prevalent in many dynasties. There may be a connection between the name Suyaśas and that given him in the *Divyāvadāna*, Dharmavivardhana. But the identification is very tentative.

If the story about his having been blinded is true, then this would be added reason for his wishing to change his name. However, if he was blinded, then the fact of his coming to the throne would be in doubt. Law books declared, and customary usage maintained, that a person having lost any vital faculty should be automatically excluded from kingship. It is unlikely that the Mauryan court would have permitted the blind prince to rule. Whether the Buddhist legends are historically true or not, the fact that Kunāla among all the princes was the central figure in both the stories proves that he was an important prince and may well have been the heir-apparent. The story of his being blinded can of course have a metaphorical meaning, i.e. his being blind to Buddhism. To Buddhist monks anyone turning away from Buddhism would be shutting his eyes to the right path. For a son of Aśoka to turn away would amount to his being blinded.

Daśaratha, apart from being mentioned in the *Matsya Purāṇa*, is also known to us from the caves in the Nāgārjunī Hills, which he dedicated to the Ājīvikas. Three inscriptions ordered by Daśaratha Devānaṃpiya state that the caves were dedicated immediately on his accession.[3] That they were inscribed soon after the reign of Aśoka is clear from the script, which is Aśokan *Brāhmī* and the general tone of the inscriptions, which are similar to Aśokan inscriptions. The wish that the abode may exist as long as the sun and the moon endure is reminiscent of the 7th Pillar Edict, where Aśoka wishes men and women to conform to the principles of *Dhamma* for as long as the sun and the moon endure.

The dedication of the caves, the inscriptions and the use of the title *Devānaṃpiya*, all suggest that Daśaratha was close in spirit to his grandfather Aśoka. It has been argued that the phrase *dasalathena devānaṃpiyena anantaliyaṃ abhisitena* contains a reference to Aśoka in the *devānaṃpiyena*. This argument is based on the fact that Aśoka always used the title

[1] de la Vallée Poussin, *L'Inde aux Temps des Mauryas . . .*, p. 164.
[2] Przyluski, *La Legende de l'Empereur Açoka*, p. 281.
[3] Sircar, *Select Inscriptions . . .*, p. 79.

devānampiya before his name Piyadassi and not after the latter as in this case. On the basis of this, de la Vallée Poussin translates the phrase as, 'the cave was given by Daśaratha soon after he was crowned by Aśoka'.[1] We do not accept this interpretation. It is quite possible that Daśaratha adopted the general title for a king *devānampiya*. The title can be placed either before the name or after it. Thus a monarch can be given his name and dynastic number, and then his titles may follow. *Devānampiya* is grammatically correct in the inscription as the title of Daśaratha, since it must qualify and agree with the king's name, which it does.

Daśaratha's expression of sympathy with a sect antagonistic to Buddhism, has been commented upon.[2] It has also been said that the anti-Buddhist spirit of Daśaratha may be inferred from his gifts to the Ājīvikas and the silence of the Buddhist texts on his reign.[3] If we did not have the precedent of Aśoka in these matters, this might have been a very plausible theory. But since Aśoka himself dedicated caves to the Ājīvikas, remaining at the same time an ardent Buddhist, the fact of Daśaratha having done so does not necessarily make him antagonistic to the other sects. At most it can be said that he held the Ājīvikas in special favour (not to the exclusion of other sects), since the caves were donated immediately on his accession.

That Daśaratha succeeded Aśoka directly is certainly possible, as he was not too young to do so in 232 B.C. Aśoka must have been over thirty years of age when he came to the throne. His reign lasting thirty-seven years, he must have been at least sixty-seven at his death. This allows for a possibility of a twenty-year-old grandson when the king died. If the boy was influenced by his grandfather, Aśoka may have decided to overlook the claims of his son, in favour of his grandson. If this did happen it must have caused much indignation among the sons of Aśoka.

Samprati, also mentioned in the *Matsya Purāṇa*, is referred to in both Buddhist and Jaina literature as the son of Kunāla. Here there is some confusion since the *Purāṇa* describes him as the son of Daśaratha. According to Jaina tradition he was a grandson of Aśoka and a patron of Jainism.[4] He is said to have been converted to Jainism by Suhastin, after which he gave the religion both his active support as a ruler, and encouragement in other ways. He is mentioned as ruling both from Pāṭaliputra and from Ujjain. Unfortunately we have no inscriptional or other evidence to support these accounts.

Buddhist literature has connected Samprati with a curious legend

[1] *L'Inde aux Temps des Mauryas . . .*, p. 165.
[2] Ibid., p. 166.
[3] Dutt, *Early Monastic Buddhism*, vol. ii, p. 255.
[4] *Pariśiṣṭaparvan*, IX, 54.

concerning the last days of Aśoka.[1] The king Aśoka decided to outdo the bounty of the king Sudatta and donated 100 crores of gold pieces to the Buddhist *Saṃgha*. This amount was taken from the treasury. When only 4 crores remained to be paid, Samprati, the heir-apparent, objected on the advice of the minister Rādhagupta. Aśoka therefore began to donate his personal possessions until such a time as he was left with only half a mango. Finally when the king died, the 4 crores were paid by the ministers and the kingdom which was held in forfeit was thus retrieved and Samprati was placed on the throne. Fa-hsien states in his account that near Rājagṛha there was an Aśokan column bearing an inscription to commemorate the fact of Aśoka having bestowed the inhabited part of the world on the priesthood, and then bought it back from them with money, on three occasions.[2] No trace of such a pillar has yet been found. It is probable that the story was related to Fa-hsien by local Buddhists and it may have been confused with the inscription on the pillar in his mind at a later date.

The Kashmir chronicle, Kalhaṇa's *Rājataraṅgiṇī*, mentions Aśoka's successor as Jalauka. We are told that Aśoka wished to exterminate the *mlecchas* (foreigners) and therefore he prayed for a son.[3] Jalauka was born as a result. The prince was an ardent Saivite, a worshipper of Vijayeśvara and Bhūteśa. His tutor is described as 'the vanquisher of crowds of Bauddha controversialists who at that time were powerful and flushed [with success]'. This would suggest a period fairly close to the reign of Aśoka. Jalauka expelled the *mlecchas* who oppressed the land and he conquered the earth up to the encircling oceans. In administrative matters he increased the number of state officials from seven to eighteen. The seven listed are the *dharmādhyakṣa*, *dhanādhyakṣa*, *kośādhyakṣa*, *sammulipati*, *dūta*, *purohita*, and *daivākṣa*. A legend is also related concerning Jalauka and his relations with Buddhism. He was met one day by a hungry sorceress who wished to eat his flesh. He immediately offered himself, as a result of which she showered praises upon him and revealed that he was in fact a *Mahāśākya*, and requested him to build the *vihāra* of Kīrti-āśrama, which request Jalauka complied with.[4] Jalauka then began to worship the divine sorceress though he continued at the same time to be a Śaivite. Jalauka was succeeded by Dāmodara II, who is said to have either descended from Aśoka's race or else belonged to some other family.

The neglect of Jalauka in Buddhist sources may be explained by the fact that he was pro-Hindu and anti-Buddhist, if his tutor had had any influence

[1] *Divyāvadāna*, XXIX, pp. 432 ff.
[2] Giles, *Travels of Fa-hsien*, p. 48.
[3] I, 107–53.
[4] Stein has identified the *vihāra* of Kīrti-āśrama with that of Ki-tche mentioned by Ou-kong (*JA*, 1895, VI, p. 354). The site of this ancient *vihāra* is traditionally associated with the son of Aśoka.

on him. Nevertheless this is an unsatisfactory explanation, since the story of the divine sorceress would certainly have been elaborated upon by Buddhist monks. The identity of Jalauka remains uncertain. His kingdom comprised Kashmir and Gandhāra, and later in his reign, considerable parts of northern India.

Owing to the confused account of early kings in the *Rājataraṅgiṇī* it is possible that he was not a son of Aśoka, and may have been a Kuśāṇa king whose name has been misread. But we are of the opinion that he was a Mauryan, and that the name Jalauka may possibly be a confused rendering of the name Kunāla. Jalauka is certainly foreign to any of the king lists of the Mauryas, and since it occurs only in the Kashmir chronicle, it can only be a local variant. Phonetically the two names are dissimilar, but the confusion may have occurred in the writing of the names where possibly the syllables became interchanged. In the *Brāhmī* script of the Aśokan period, the name Kunāla would be written thus, 𑀓𑀼𑀦𑀸𑀮 and the name Jalauka thus, 𑀚𑀮𑁅𑀓. It is possible that after the invasion of the Bactrian Greeks and the Kuśāṇas with their foreign names, a name such as Jalauka became accepted without much questioning.[1]

It is curious that among the seven important state officials mentioned, the first on the list is the *dharmādhyakṣa*. Generally in Indian theoretical sources on administration, priority is given to revenue officials and treasury officials. To list a 'superintendent of justice' first, is certainly unusual procedure. The author may have meant a judicial officer by this term. It may also be suggested that the mention of a *dharmādhyakṣa* was based on a tradition recalling the *dhamma-mahāmattas*. The special mention of administrative improvements could tally closely with administrative policy in Mauryan times.

The emphasis on Jalauka expelling the *mlecchas* is significant. It would seem that the *mlecchas* referred to the Bactrian Greeks and other foreigners on the north-west. The later Yavana invasion which threatened Śuṅga power, may have started as sporadic attacks during the time of Kunāla, i.e. in the years following Aśoka's death. It is of interest that in the 7th Pillar Edict, when summing up as it were the achievements of *Dhamma*, Aśoka speaks with great satisfaction about the results within his empire. However, on this occasion not a single reference is made to relations with the neighbouring countries, whereas the early edicts proclaim in no uncertain terms that converts to the *Dhamma* include the neighbouring countries of the north-west.[2] It is possible that ten years after the issuing

[1] Furthermore Jalauka means 'a fish' in Sanskrit, so that the word was not altogether foreign, although its use as a name may have been rare.

[2] XII R.E., Kalsi. Bloch, *Les Inscriptions d'Asoka*, p. 130.

of the edict, the hostility of the Greeks along the north-west border was beginning to be felt.

By 206 B.C. twenty-five years after the death of Aśoka, there was a closer contact between the Indians of the north-west and the neighbouring Greeks. Whether this contact was the result of a friendly relationship or a hostile one, is a debatable point. Antiochus is said to have renewed his alliance with Sophagasenos the Indian king. Tarn has suggested that in referring to this alliance Polybius was thinking of the treaty between Candragupta Maurya and Seleucus Nicator in 303 B.C.[1] But this renewal of friendship may have referred in general terms to the friendly relations between Aśoka and Antiochus II of Syria. Polybius nowhere suggests that Sophagasenos was a Mauryan king. He would hardly have taken the trouble to verify the dynasty to which the latter belonged. To state that he was an Indian was sufficient for his purpose.

The treaty between Sophagasenos or Subhāgasena and Antiochus does not appear to have been an alliance between equals. Subhāgasena was certainly in an inferior position. Had Antiochus merely acquired more elephants and supplies for his troops, it may have been a case of Subhāgasena helping Antiochus with reinforcements after the latter's war against the Bactrian Greeks under Euthydemos. But since the account states clearly that Antiochus left Androsthenes of Cyzicus with Subhāgasena, in order that he might collect the treasure that Subhāgasena had agreed to give, it is evident that the elephants, the supplies, and the treasure were all part of a tribute which Subhāgasena had to pay. If we compare this treaty with the treaty of 303 B.C. it is obvious that Subhāgasena was in some way subordinate to Antiochus. It would seem that the Indian king was unfortunate enough to be caught up in the strife between Antiochus and Euthydemos. With the rise and expansion of Bactria, it was only natural that the politically unstable kingdoms of north-west India would be crushed.

As we have seen there is no reference to Subhāgasena or to a closely similar name in any of the king lists. The nearest possibility is Vīrasena mentioned by Tāranātha as ruling in Gandhāra.[2] The *sena* ending in both names may suggest a relationship, but at the same time the name Vīrasena is also absent from the Mauryan king lists. We are told that Aśoka was succeeded by his grandson, Vigatāśoka, the son of the blinded Kunāla. The name Vigatāśoka has obviously come to Tāranātha via the *Divyāvadāna* where he is mentioned as the younger brother of Aśoka.[3] The succession

[1] *The Greeks in Bactria and India*, pp. 130, 154.

[2] *Geschichte des Buddhismus in Indien*, IX, p. 50.

[3] XXV, p. 370.

continues with Vīrasena the son of Vigatāśoka who is an honoured Buddhist. Vīrasena is followed by his son, Nanda, who reigned for twenty-nine years, and who is in turn followed by his son Mahāpadma who reigned at Kusumapura. Candanapāla followed Mahāpadma. The author then appears to concentrate on dynasties known to have ruled in Bengal, which area he describes as being ruled by Haricandra followed by seven other Candras, all supporters of Buddhism. The last of these, Nemacandra, was deprived of his throne by Puṣymitra. At this point the *mleccha* invasion took place and Puṣymitra died five years later. Very much later in his chronology there appears a Candragupta who is succeeded by Bindusāra. Bindusāra is said to have reigned for thirty-five years and was then succeeded by his heir Śrīcandra who was in turn followed by Dharmacandra, ruling only in the east.[1]

It is indeed difficult to obtain historical facts from this account, which is undoubtedly very confused. With regard to the Mauryan dynasty alone we can obtain two king lists. First we are told that Aśoka was followed by Vigatāśoka. Later we are told that Bindusāra's successor was Śrīcandra, who was in turn succeeded by Dharmacandra. We know that neither of the two latter names were connected with the Mauryas. It is therefore possible that Vīrasena was not connected either. It is more than likely that Tāranātha was basing this information regarding Vīrasena on the fact that Puṣyamitra's wife's brother was a Vīrasena, who was appointed by Puṣyamitra as commander of a frontier fortress in the Narmada region.[2] We may thus dismiss the possibility of Vīrasena being a Mauryan king.

There are, however, two points of considerable interest mentioned in Tāranātha's account. He states that Aśoka was succeeded by his grandson, and here he appears to be following the *Divyāvadāna* accounts. Secondly, whereas Bindusāra is described as being the king of the land between the eastern and the western seas, his grandson was king only in the east, suggesting thereby that there was a rapid dwindling of the empire.

Of the other names of the Mauryan kings mentioned in various sources, there is confirmation of Śāliśuka, listed as the fourth successor to Aśoka in the *Viṣṇu Purāṇa*. The *Gārgīsaṃhitā*, an astrological work, speaks of him as an unjust and wicked king, an oppressor of his people.[3] But the most important point is that it is prophesied that after his reign the Greeks will invade India and reach Pāṭaliputra. However, as has been pointed out this does not necessarily imply that the invasion took place immediately after the reign of Śāliśuka.[4] Since the authors of the *Purāṇa* were concerned

[1] *Geschichte des Buddhismus in Indien*, VIII–XVIII, pp. 48–90.

[2] Kālidāsa, *Mālvikāgnimitraṃ*.

[3] *Yuga Purāṇa*, 89–100 (Mankad edition).

[4] Narain, *The Indo-Greeks*, pp. 84–85.

only with narrating the major events, the invasion referred to may well have been the one that occurred half a century later, during the Śuṅga period.

The *Aśokāvadāna* king list is also confused. Vṛhaspati, Vṛṣasena, Puṣyadharman, and Puṣyamitra are said to succeed Samprati in turn. Clearly Puṣyamitra, the founder of the Śuṅga dynasty, has no place in a Mauryan dynastic list. The names of the other three do not correspond to any given in the other lists. At most it might be said that Vṛhaspati is an incorrect version of Bṛhadratha, but even this is unnecessarily stretching the point. It is more than likely that the Buddhist monks lost interest in the dynasty when its kings ceased to be patrons of Buddhism, and consequently their dynastic lists became confused.

There are three main legends in Buddhist literature connected with the last years of Aśoka, all of which occur in the *Aśokāvadāna*. The first concerns the revolt of the people of Taxila which Kunāla was sent to suppress.[1] The second involves Kunāla as well. It is the story of his being blinded at the instigation of his step-mother, the queen Tissarakkhā.[2] The third legend is that of Aśoka being left with only half an āmalā to bestow on the *Saṃgha* at the end of his reign.[3] We cannot prove whether the events described in the two latter legends actually took place or not, since there is no evidence to emphatically confirm or disprove them. But some indication of the state of affairs during the last years of Aśoka's reign is available from the situation described in these legends. They do suggest that towards the end of his reign Aśoka did not have the same control over affairs as he had had earlier. We must keep in mind the fact that he was at least sixty-five to seventy years of age when he died, and, with a strongly centralized government as the Mauryan government was, it is not to be wondered at that he began to lose control. But what is to be deplored is the tendency towards court intrigues which is evident from these legends.

Apart from the *Aśokāvadāna* there is another source containing versions of these legends, which throws a different light on the same events. This source has been generally ignored by historians, but we feel that it is very significant, particularly with regard to events after the death of Aśoka. Przyluski has translated relevant portions of the Chinese version of the story in the *Tripiṭaka* of Tokyo and he refers to this account as the *Kunālasūtra*.[4] He maintains that it was composed originally in the region of Gandhāra and Kashmir, and has been neglected presumably because it has been thought to be too localized a version. It is for this very reason that we

[1] Przyluski, *La Legende de l'Empereur Açoka*, pp. 281 ff.
[2] Ibid.
[3] Ibid., p. 296.
[4] Ibid., pp. 106 ff.

consider it significant. It relates the legends from a local perspective without the necessity of having to fit a tradition used by other Buddhist chroniclers. The authors of the *Kunālasūtra* did not write because they felt that Aśoka's character had to be sketched in a particular way, but because they wished to record the legends as they existed in local tradition.

According to this text the arrival of Kunāla in Taxila is not due to a revolt in the city. We are told that the king of Gandhāra died and that the people wished to place themselves under the protection of Aśoka. Kunāla was sent to govern them, and was so successful that Aśoka decided to divide the empire, placing the region from the Indus as far as the Chinese frontier under Kunāla. This area would include Khotan, Kashmir, and Gandhāra. It is possible that the people on the borders of Gandhāra asked for stronger Mauryan protection when the Bactrian Greeks began to harass them. The Bactrian revolt against the Seleucids had taken place during Aśoka's lifetime under Diodotus I and Diodotus II. The later Mauryas saw the rise of Euthydemus I in Bactria, who successfully opposed Antiochus III and no doubt saw that it was an opportune moment to invade the northern part of the now fast disintegrating Mauryan empire.[1] In the interests of political strategy and military strength, Aśoka had to safeguard the north-west frontier. This appears to be confirmed by the *Rājataraṅgiṇī* which speaks of Jalauka expelling the *mleccha* from Gandhāra. The success of Kunāla's administration of the north-west area may have suggested to Aśoka the possibility of dividing the empire on his death. The fear of such an event may have led to Tissarakkhā attempting to harm Kunāla in some way.

The *Kunālasūtra* repeats the legend of the blinding of Kunāla and further relates another legend of how his eyesight was restored to him by a *bhikkhu* called Sumanas. Needless to say Kunāla, on receiving back his eyesight, is converted to Buddhism, although the same text earlier describes him as a great supporter of Buddhism. Such inconsistencies tend to suggest a considerable fabrication with regard to this legend.

A point of some interest is the mention of Yaśas as the unpleasant minister of Aśoka. In the *Aśokāvadāna*, Yaśas is among the more pious Buddhist elders, but in the *Kunālasūtra* he becomes a secular Buddhist personage, to whom are attributed many disagreeable actions, and who is opposed to the saintly Buddhist elder Sumanas. In the *Aśokāvadāna* we are told that it was the minister of perverse views who advised the heir-apparent to curtail, and finally to stop altogether, the gifts which Aśoka gave as charity to the *bhikkhus* from the royal treasury.[2] It would appear

[1] Narain, *The Indo-Greeks*, pp. 13–20.
[2] Przyluski, *La Legende de l'Empereur Açoka*, p. 301.

that Yaśas was one of these ministers. The fact that he managed to persuade the heir, Samprati, to withhold funds from Aśoka, suggests that he had considerable influence over him. The only other occasion when a name recalling that of Yaśas appears in connection with the successors to Aśoka is in the *Viṣṇu Purāṇa*, where Suyaśas is mentioned as a successor to Aśoka, followed by his son Daśaratha.[1] There is no reference anywhere else to Suyaśas being the son of Aśoka. It is possible that Suyaśas was in fact an important minister of Aśoka, who was responsible for bringing Daśaratha to the throne when Aśoka died, and through some confusion in Purāṇic recording came to be described as the son of Aśoka.

On the basis of a *Divyāvadāna* legend it is argued that Aśoka abdicated and became a monk.[2] It is related that Rādhagupta, the minister of Bindusāra, who had supported Aśoka's attempts at becoming king, forced Aśoka to abdicate when he had become unpopular with his subjects at the end of his reign. This legend is highly suspect since it is unlikely that Rādhagupta could remain such a powerful minister through two long reigns, those of Bindusāra and Aśoka, totalling over sixty years. It is unlikely that an event of such great importance would have been overlooked by Buddhist chroniclers in other sources, since, apart from its being good material for moralizing on, it would also have provided welcome opportunities for imaginative legends.

In the *Aśokāvadāna* legend of the half-āmalā, the heir-apparent is referred to as Samprati the son of Kunāla. Yet the *Matsya* and *Viṣṇu Purāṇas* speak of Daśaratha as the successor to Aśoka and the inscriptions of the former in the Nāgārjunī Hills, are, as we have noticed earlier, suggestive of a period close to that of Aśoka. We are of the opinion that the empire of Aśoka was partitioned either just prior to his death or at his death. The western part including the north-western province, Gandhāra, and Kashmir was governed by Kunāla, the eastern part was left to Aśoka's grandson Daśaratha.[3] It is possible that Kunāla gradually extended his portion to include the western province of the empire.

The fact that the *Divyāvadāna* speaks of Samprati being heir to the throne after Aśoka can be explained on the basis of his coming to the throne at Pāṭaliputra, after Daśaratha, and since he was also the grandson of Aśoka the mistake is not impossible. Furthermore if Samprati happened to be more sympathetic to Buddhism than Daśaratha, it would be all the more reason for him to be recorded as the successor to Aśoka.

[1] Ch. XXIV.
[2] XXIX, pp. 432 ff.
[3] V. Smith put forward a similar view but according to him the empire was divided between Daśaratha and Samprati (*Early History of India*, p. 203).

The identity of Daśaratha remains hidden. He was a young man of about twenty years when he came to the throne, supported by the ministers. Samprati is mentioned in the *Matsya Purāṇa* as the son of Daśaratha.[1] This is probably a mistake since according to other accounts Samprati and Daśaratha were first cousins. If, however, it can be proved that Suyaśas was in fact another name for Kunāla and not the name of a minister, then it would seem that Daśaratha was the brother of Samprati. According to the *Purāṇas*, Daśaratha reigned for eight years. This would suggest that he died without an heir old enough to come to the throne without necessitating a regency of some sort. The same sources speak of Kunāla ruling for eight years. He must have died at about the same time as Daśaratha, so that Samprati now ruling in the west may have successfully regained the throne at Pāṭaliputra, thus uniting the empire again. This event occurred in *c.* 223 B.C.

However the empire had probably already begun to disintegrate. Jaina sources mention that Samprati ruled from Ujjain and Pāṭaliputra.[2] This would suggest that the capital of the western part of the empire was moved from the north to Ujjain. The decade following was to see the conflict between Antiochus III of Syria and Euthydemus of Bactria, with Bactria emerging as a strong power, ready to threaten north-western India. It is quite likely that a number of principalities in the trans-Indus region broke away from the empire while Samprati was occupied in establishing himself at Pāṭaliputra. Gradually the concentration of attention moved to Magadha and the main line of the Mauryan dynasty lived out its years at Pāṭaliputra, unable to prevent or control the breaking up of the empire in the more distant regions. After a reign of nine years Samprati was followed by Śāliśuka who ruled for thirteen years. If the *Gārgīsaṃhitā* is to be credited, his reign further reduced the power of the Mauryas.

Meanwhile the *Vāyu* and *Brahmāṇḍa Purāṇas* mention three names which are again isolated, in so far as they are not mentioned in any other source.[3] These are Bandhupālita, Indrapālita, and Daśona. The identification of these three is extremely difficult, since no other names even vaguely resembling them are to be found in the Mauryan king lists. Even the *Purāṇas* are not certain as to the relationship of one to the other. Indrapālita for instance is referred to as the *dāyāda* of Bandhupālita, a word which has been translated both as 'heir' and as 'brother'. A recent student of the subject, has explained that Bandhupālita should not be taken as a

[1] Pargiter, *Dynasties of the Kali Age*, p. 28.

[2] *Pariśiṣṭaparvan*, X, XI.

[3] Pargiter, *Dynasties of the Kali Age*, p. 29.

name, but as a phrase meaning 'protected by the kinsman', suggesting thereby something along the lines of a regency during the reign of one of these kings.[1] We can only suggest that these were members of the royal family who set themselves up as kings in a part of the Mauryan empire, other than Pāṭaliputra, possibly at Ujjain, perhaps as a subordinate line to the main Mauryas. The successor of Śāliśuka is mentioned as Somavarman in the *Viṣṇu Purāṇa*. This tallies fairly closely with the Devavarman of the *Vāyu Purāṇa*, who is said to have followed Daśona and ruled for seven years. It is possible that at this point the *Vāyu Purāṇa* breaks off from local tradition and resumes the lists with the kings at Pāṭaliputra. There is agreement amongst all three *Purāṇas—Vāyu*, *Matsya*, and *Viṣṇu*—over the last two kings of the Mauryan dynasty. These were Śatadhanvan or Śatadhanus, who is said to have ruled for eight years, and finally Bṛhadratha, who ruled for seven years and was assassinated by Puṣymitra.

Our reconstruction of the history of the later Mauryas is thus as follows: on the death of Aśoka in 233–232 B.C., the empire was divided into the western and eastern halves. The former was ruled by Kunāla and then for a short while by Samprati. Its southern portion may perhaps have been governed later by Bandhupālita, Indrapālita, and Daśona. This part of the empire was threatened by the Bactrian Greeks in the north-west and by the ambitions of groups within the area such as the Andhras in the northern Deccan.[2]

The succession of the main line of the Mauryas in the eastern half of the empire, ruling from Pāṭaliputra, took the following course on the death of Aśoka,

Daśaratha	ruled for	8	years
Samprati	,, ,,	9	,,
Śāliśuka	,, ,,	13	,,
Devavarman	,, ,,	7	,,
Śatadhanvan	,, ,,	8	,,
Bṛhadratha	,, ,,	7	,,

Thus we have a total of 52 years, which, combined with the 85 of the first three Mauryas, gives us 137 years for the Mauryan dynasty. Since the years given are not exact, we may allow a discrepancy of a year or two. The *Purāṇas* do not state any interregnums since they are only concerned with the actual regnal years of each king. Assuming that Aśoka died in 233–232 B.C., we may state that the Mauryan dynasty came to an end in 181–180 B.C.

[1] R. Smith, *JAOS*, October-December 1957, vol. 77, No. 4, pp. 276 ff.

[2] Smith, *Early History of India*, pp. 217 ff.; pp. 233 ff.

VII

THE DECLINE OF THE MAURYAS

An examination of the history of the Mauryan dynasty, leads inevitably to the further examination of the reasons why it declined. There is something almost dramatic in the way in which the dynasty petered out after the death of Aśoka. In most other examples of imperial decline, the downward movement sets in well before the political decline. Not so with the Mauryas, where, as we have seen in the previous chapter, the descent was completed within half a century.

One of the more obvious reasons for the decline was the succession of weak kings after Aśoka. A further and immediate cause was the partition of the empire into two, the eastern part under Daśaratha and the western part under Kunāla. Had the partition not taken place, the Greek invasions of the north-west could have been held back for a while, giving the Mauryas a chance to re-establish some degree of their previous power. The partition of the empire disrupted the various services as well. The political and administrative organization had been planned by the first three Mauryas in such a way that it necessitated a strict supervision from the centre, radiating in a network throughout the empire. After the partition, the eastern half was at an advantage, since Pāṭaliputra and the organization at Pāṭaliputra continued much as before although on a smaller scale. The western half had to rapidly expand the provincial government of Taxila and the north-west province into a near-imperial organization. In this process of change it was unable to give full attention to the Greek attacks.

The quality of the kings who followed Aśoka was strikingly in contrast to his own. The pattern of Aśoka's policy was not a conventional one. This was in part due to the new imperialism of the Mauryas and in part to Aśoka's ideology, which dominated his government. It naturally created a problem for his successors as to whether they should continue the existing policy or change to the conventional pattern. Had the empire remained united and had the successors continued the policy of Aśoka, there might have been some interesting results on the future politics of India. As it was it would have been impossible for the successors of Aśoka to have continued his policy, if they were not conscious of the reasons why *Dhamma* was so important to the third century B.C. in India. It is a debatable point whether any of the later Mauryas had this fundamental understanding of Indian conditions. It appears from his inscriptions that Daśaratha may have been aware of Aśokan policy and supported it, but probably his youth prevented him developing it.

From the considerable variation of names in the Mauryan king lists in the sources, it would seem that there was a general tendency for male relatives and members of the royal family either to claim the throne or else to proclaim themselves independent rulers in the provinces. Attempts have been made to explain this variation in names as being secondary names or *birudas* of the same king.[1] But this is not a convincing explanation. Most of the *birudas* do not have any connection semantically or phonetically with the best known name of the person. In fact the many short reigns within the fifty years suggests that some of the kings were deposed.

Much has been written on Aśokan policy being directly responsible for the decline of the Mauryan empire. This accusation is based on two main arguments. The first maintains that the revolt of Puṣyamitra was a result of the brahmanical reaction against the pro-Buddhist policy of Aśoka and the pro-Jaina policy of his successors. The second argument holds Aśoka's pacifist policies responsible for undermining the strength of the empire. The first opinion has been expressed by Haraprasad Sastri in no uncertain terms. The question has been examined in some detail by Raychaudhuri. We shall summarize the arguments of both scholars, adding our own comments where necessary.

Haraprasad Sastri maintains that the ban on animal sacrifices was a direct attack on the brahmans since much of their power and prestige lay in the fact that they alone could perform sacrifices, and thus act as intermediaries between the people and the gods.[2] Raychaudhuri states that this ban did not necessarily imply hostility towards the brahmans, since Brahmanical literature itself stresses *ahiṃsā*, and mentions the futility of laying great store on sacrifices alone.[3] In one edict Aśoka specifically states that no animals are to be sacrificed in the particular place, where the edict has been inscribed.[4] In the other edicts the ban is on the killing of certain animals even those regarded as edible, and not only on those used in sacrifices.

A second point on the same subject is the statement that this action was particularly resented by the brahmans since it was promulgated by a *śūdra* king. The *śūdra* origin of the Mauryas is based on a statement in the *Purāṇas* when, in speaking of the Nanda dynasty, it is said that all kings

[1] de la Vallée Poussin, *L'Inde aux Temps des Mauryas*, pp. 164–5.

[2] The arguments of Haraprasad Sastri are contained in *JASB*, 1910, pp. 259–62.

[3] For Raychaudhuri's arguments see, *Political History of Ancient India*, pp. 354–5.

[4] I R.E., Girnār. Bloch, *Les Inscriptions d'Asoka*, p. 90.

succeeding Mahāpadma will be of *śūdra* origin. Raychaudhuri points out that this can only refer to the Nanda kings who succeeded Mahāpadma, because if it referred to succeeding dynasties, then even the Śuṅgas and Kaṇvas would have to be included as *śūdras*, and we know that the Śuṅgas were of brahman origin. The *kṣatriya* origin of the Mauryas is stated in other sources.[1]

A further argument of Sastri's is based on the phrase from the Minor Rock Edict at Brahmagiri, referring to the gods in Jambudvīpa. He interprets it as meaning that the brahmans who were regarded as *bhūdevas* or gods on earth had been exposed by Aśoka as being false gods. As we have already stated, this argument is based on an alternative root for *amissā*.[2] It is generally accepted that the phrase refers to the gods mixing on earth with the people, and does not refer to false gods.

According to Sastri the *dhamma-mahāmattas* destroyed the prestige of the brahmans. As Raychaudhuri points out, this could hardly have been so, since some of them were concerned specifically with safeguarding the rights and welfare of the brahmans. Furthermore the *dhamma-mahāmattas* were concerned with social welfare generally, and covered a much wider field of work than the brahmans. It is probable, however, that the *dhamma-mahāmattas* may have become unpopular with the people in the later years of Aśoka's reign, and this prevented if anything, Aśoka's being in contact with public opinion. With the gradual increase in their powers of interference, these officers tended to form an order of their own, with official sanction and the right of entry everywhere. Since they had the special favour of the king, they were no doubt feared by the populace, and by way of appeasement were granted many privileges. Their powers of supervision extended over both the ordinary householder and the royal family. The stirring up of hesitant people suggests more than mere persuasion and propagation of *Dhamma*. It is possible that those citizens who proclaimed themselves followers of *Dhamma* in loud voices received preferential treatment compared to those who practised it in a quiet way. Officials, even those with the best of intentions, cannot be expected to act as superhumans, not even the *dhamma-mahāmattas*. It is likely that in the course of their routine duties, they assumed greater powers than Aśoka had intended or knew of. The creed of these *mahāmattas* was *Dhamma*, and in the more distant areas they were the interpreters of *Dhamma*. This is a situation not unknown to other cultures, for the church has known it in its priests and political systems have known it in their commissioners.

[1] *Divyāvadāna*, pp. 370–409; Rice, *Mysore and Coorg from the Inscriptions*, p. 10.

[2] See Ch. V.

The question of *vyavahārasamatā* and *daṇḍasamatā*, the uniformity of legal procedure and punishment, is raised by Haraprasad Sastri in support of his argument that privileges usually given to brahmans regarding penalties were stopped as a result of these two measures adopted by Aśoka. Raychaudhuri refutes this argument on the basis of the terms meaning, 'a uniformity of law and punishment'. We are in support of the latter view and have already examined the matter in detail.[1] Quotations from brahmanical literature can prove that the privileges of the brahmans in the matter of immunity in capital punishment were not so evident as Sastri would have us believe.[2] Aśoka's frequent requests in his edicts for due respect towards brahmans and *śramaṇas* hardly points to his being anti-brahmanical in outlook.

Sastri's final argument is even weaker than his previous ones. He maintains that Aśoka was strong enough to hold his own against the brahmans, but on his death a conflict arose between his successors and the brahmans which lasted until the assumption of power by Puṣyamitra, and the latter was the expression of a great brahman revolution. Neither of these statements are borne out by existing evidence, as Raychaudhuri has shown. We know from the *Rājataraṅgiṇī* that one at least of Aśoka's descendants was quite anti-Buddhist and very pro-brahman. Jalauka is described as an ardent *Śaiva*.[3] The idea of Puṣyamitra being violently anti-Buddhist has often been stated, but archaeological evidence suggests the contrary. Buddhist literature relates that Puṣyamitra wishing to gain notoriety decided that even a wicked action could be excused provided it made him well known. When questioning people as to why Aśoka gained fame, he was told that it was due to Aśoka having built 84,000 *stūpas* for Buddhism. Whereupon Puṣyamitra decided that he would gain fame by destroying these 84,000 *stūpas*.[4] Yet, an archaeological study of the *stūpa* at Sanchi proves that it was enlarged and encased in its present covering during the Śuṅga period.[5] The Aśokan pillar near it appears to have been wilfully destroyed, but this event may have occurred at a much later date.[6] It is more than likely that the *Aśokāvadāna* legend is a Buddhist version of Puṣyamitra's attack on the Mauryas, and reflects the fact that, with the declining influence of Buddhism at the imperial court, Buddhist monuments and institutions would naturally receive less royal attention. Moreover the source itself in this instance being Buddhist, it would naturally exaggerate the wickedness of anti-Buddhists.

[1] See Ch. IV.
[2] *Bṛhadāranyaka Upaniṣad*, III, 9, 26; *Mahābhārata*, *Ādi Parvan*, 107.
[3] I, 148.
[4] Przyluski, *La Legende de l'Empereur Açoka*, pp. 301–2.
[5] *AI*, ix, p. 160.
[6] Marshall, *Guide to Sanchi*, p. 90.

Since the Mauryan empire had shrunk considerably and the kings of the later period were hardly in a position to defend themselves, it did not need a revolution to depose Bṛhadratha. We are told that he was assassinated by Puṣyamitra whilst reviewing the army. This does not suggest a great revolution. In fact it points very strongly to a palace *coup d'état*. The organization of the state was by now at such a low ebb that subordinate officials were willing to accept anyone who could promise them a more efficient organization. If it had been a great brahmanical revolution, Puṣyamitra would have had the assistance of other neighbouring kings, as for example the descendants of Subhāgasena from the north-west.

It has been claimed that the propagation of Buddhism during the Mauryan period disturbed the brahmanical social and religious order[1] Nor was this confined only to Buddhism. Some aspects of Aśokan policy such as the discouragement of *maṅgalas* and similar ceremonies must have had the same effect. But this disturbance was not of a magnitude sufficient to weaken the Mauryan state. It may have started new trends of thought, but social behaviour continued much as before.

Raychaudhuri has attacked Aśoka on the basis of his having pursued a policy of non-violence with such vigour and determination that it resulted in a completely effete nation from a military point of view, and one that was not therefore able to withstand the Greek invasion.[2] He maintains that Aśokan policy was directly responsible for the rapid disintegration of the empire after the death of Aśoka. This policy of non-violence not only caused the military decline of the empire, but also led to a lack of control on the part of the king. This lack of control led to the officials becoming oppressive in the provinces, leading to the revolts referred to in Buddhist literature. In short, the pacifist policy of Aśoka tended to disorganize the administration of the empire. But this judgment on Aśokan policy is not acceptable in the light of the edicts.

The unconventional nature of the government of Aśoka did not lie in his taking to heart the doctrine of *ahiṃsā*. It lay in the fact that he was personally convinced that a greater degree of non-violence and mutual respect would be to the benefit of society, and furthermore that his personal conviction was so great that even as a king he did not refrain from preaching and requesting people to observe such behaviour. As far as possible he determined his administrative policy in accordance with such principles. Too much has been made of Aśoka's pacifism without a detailed examination of what this policy really meant. He disliked the killing of animals

[1] Ghoshal, *Studies in Indian History and Culture*, p. 258.

[2] *Political History of Ancient India*, p. 365.

whether for purposes of sacrifice or food, and he continually states in his edicts that animals should not be killed and where this is not possible, at least kindness to animals should be observed.[1] However, animals were still killed for food in the palace, although the number was considerably reduced.[2] We have no evidence of his having abstained from this practice altogether, though he states that he wishes to do so. The list of animals that are declared inviolable does not include the chief edible animals. It would seem that wherever possible, abstention from eating meat was observed, but on the whole the practice still continued.

Had he indeed been so complete a pacifist as Raychaudhuri would have us believe, he would surely have abolished the death penalty. But capital punishment continued throughout his reign. The only form of alleviation was introduced in his twenty-seventh regnal year, when a three-day respite was granted to those who were condemned to death.[3] Raychaudhuri maintains that the successors of Aśoka were brought up on a pacifist diet to such an extent that they were incapable of standing up to any armed force. They 'had heard more of *dhamma-ghosa* than of *bheri-ghosa*' (they had heard more of *Dhamma* than of war).[4]

It would appear from the above argument that Aśoka issued an order for the demobilization of all armies and settled down to a rule of non-violence in its literal sense. There is no hint of this in the edicts. The evidence suggests a stern monarch even though his reign saw only a single campaign. He states his attitude towards the frontier people for example, quite clearly. The king is willing to forgive those who have done wrong, but only that which can be forgiven is forgiven.[5] Even more precise is his message to the forest tribes. They are warned of the power which he possesses, in spite of his repentance, so that they may cease committing faults and therefore not be killed. The same edict contains further evidence which entirely contradicts Raychaudhuri's contention, that Aśoka wished his successors to forswear conquests of territory. Aśoka states that he believes that no further conquest is necessary, which is logical enough considering the fact that the Mauryan empire covered practically the entire sub-continent, but that, if his successors should have to make a conquest in the future, it was to be hoped that they would be merciful where possible and deliver light punishments.

Aśoka was in a position to maintain pacific policies because his frontiers were secure and so was the territory within the empire. The only area that

[1] III R.E., Girnār. Bloch, *Les Inscriptions d'Asoka*, p. 95.

[2] I R.E., Girnār. Ibid., p. 90.

[3] IV P.E., Delhi-Toprā. Ibid., p. 163.

[4] See Ch. V.

[5] XIII R.E., Kalsī. Bloch, *Les Inscriptions d'Asoka*, p. 125.

might have been troublesome, Kaliṅga, he conquered in the early part of his reign. The conquest of south India would not have been too difficult a task for the Mauryan armies, but there was no need for it.[1] The empire of Antiochus of Syria was the only serious rival to the Mauryan empire. To have attempted the conquest of the lands beyond the Hindu-kush would have been a foolhardy act on Aśoka's part, placing his forces in unnecessary danger, campaigning in the deserts and mountains. In any case the friendly relationship between him and Antiochus was on all counts a better relationship than any number of conquests. The only people from whom he could expect trouble were the frontier tribes already referred to. They may well have harassed his administrators and with them he used great firmness.

The absence of innumerable conquests does not in any way suggest that Aśoka merely wished to retain what his father and grandfather had conquered before him. That he himself was filled with the grandiose ideas of a conqueror cannot be doubted. As has been pointed out, it is strange that his pacifism did not lead him to reinstating Kaliṅga as an independent state.[2] But being a practical ruler, he accepted the conquest of Kaliṅga as a fact and did not raise any moral doubts on the question. Moreover he did not publicize his confession of remorse over the conquest, in Kaliṅga itself. No doubt he thought it was politically inexpedient to do so. He appears to have been quite convinced that he had the submission of the Greek states of the eastern Mediterranean, merely by sending them *Dhamma* missions, and what is more, he is proud of this supposed submission.[3] The difference between Aśoka and Samudragupta of the Gupta dynasty in this matter, is that Aśoka glories in the *Dhamma Vijaya* and the latter glories in the *Yuddha Vijaya*. Similarly the power of Aśoka over Devānaṃapiya Tissa of Ceylon was considerable, even though Ceylon was never actually conquered.[4] The military conquest of Ceylon, for instance, would have altered the relations between the two countries for the worse, in addition to creating untold other problems of an administrative nature.

Military conquests are not the only ones of any value, and the greatness of a king does not lie in the number and quality of such conquests. It is clear that Aśoka was not the naive and extreme pacifist that some historians have attempted to make of him. Even an entire generation of complete pacifism cannot weaken an empire and lead it to fast disintegration. Battles and territorial acquisitions are not alone responsible for the creation and destruction of empires. The causes must be sought in other directions as well.

[1] See Ch. IV.

[2] de la Vallée Poussin, *L'Inde aux Temps des Mauryas*, p. 119.

[3] XIII R.E., Kalsi. Bloch, *Les Inscriptions d'Asoka*, p. 130.

[4] *Mahāvaṃsa*, XI, 17–24; XIII; XIV.

It has been stated that the provincial governments were oppressive and this is given as a further cause of the decline of the Mauryas.[1] This statement is based on two stories in the *Divyāvadāna* regarding the revolt of the people of Taxila against the ministers. As we have maintained previously one of these two stories is a fabrication, namely that of the revolt at the end of Aśoka's reign, when Kunāla was sent to suppress it.[2] The revolt quelled by Aśoka during the reign of Bindusāra is supported by circumstantial evidence. Thus there is in fact no clear evidence of there having been ministerial oppression during the reign of Aśoka. It has been suggested that the advice to the *mahāmattas* in the 1st Separate Edict is to ensure against such oppression, since the king demands that the officers treat all persons under their charge in a just and humane manner. But the real significance of this edict lies in the fact that it is addressed only to the *mahāmattas* at Dhauli and Jaugada, both cities in Kaliṅga, and not to other officers in other parts of the empire. It is natural that Aśoka would pay particular attention to the welfare of the people recently conquered so as to secure their loyalty. In addressing these *mahāmattas* his tone is imperious. There is not the least hint of an emperor who is not in control of the administration.

Another writer has expressed the opinion that there was a considerable pressure on Mauryan economy under the later Mauryas.[3] This argument is based on two factors. Primarily, unnecessary measures were employed to increase the tax, as for example, the tax on actors and prostitutes mentioned in the *Arthaśāstra*. Secondly, the Mauryan punch-marked coins of this period show evidence of debasement. This view is largely the result of an analysis based on selected economic evidence, without taking into consideration the political factors of the time. It was during the Mauryan period that for the first time, the importance of taxation as the primary source of national income was fully appreciated. This resulted in a tendency to tax everything that could possibly be taxed. It is clear from the *Arthaśāstra* itself that the tax on actors, prostitutes, and the members of other such professions, was not an emergency measure, since this tax is considered a legitimate tax, and one as normal as that received from the cultivators. In fact the *Arthaśāstra* does mention certain measures that might be introduced in an emergency when the king's treasury began to empty, such as the system of double-cropping.[4] The tax on actors, etc., is not mentioned among these measures.

[1] Raychaudhuri, *Political History of Ancient India*, p. 363

[2] See Chs. I and II.

[3] Kosambi, *Introduction to the Study of Indian History*, p. 211.

[4] V, 2.

Debasement of coinage during the Mauryan period did not necessarily mean a pressure on the general economy. Owing to the laxity and dwindling of control during the period of the later Mauryas, it is possible that debased money began to circulate, particularly in the areas which were gradually ceding from the empire. Since the coins have been found largely in hoards, their provenance is often not known. In areas such as the above mentioned, the coins may have been punched by the authorities and put into circulation without properly ascertaining their quality. Furthermore such debasement may also indicate that there was an increased demand for silver in relation to other goods, and therefore the silver content in coins was dropped. Moreover Kosambi's argument is based on his own identification of the coins of the later Mauryas, and this is by no means certain.

Evidence from other material remains does not suggest a pressure on the economy. If anything, the picture is that of an expanding economy. From archaeological evidence at Hastināpura and Śiśupālagarh, it would appear that there was a considerable material improvement in the culture of the time, both from the point of view of technical advance and the use of a better quality of material.[1] This improvement appears to have been more equitably distributed than during the earlier Mauryan period. For instance, at the earlier level most of the pottery was a coarse grey ware, together with some deposits of the northern black polished ware. At the later level of the post-Aśokan Mauryas and the early Śuṅgas there is evidence of a widely distributed pottery, wheel-thrown and of a fine clay. A comparatively new element, that of town-planning and house-planning, becomes a more regular feature. There is a distinct improvement in the workmanship of objects such as beads, rings, terracottas, etc. The reign of Aśoka was of great advantage to the economy. The unification of the country under a single efficient administration, the organization and increase in communications, and peace, meant the development of trade as well as an opening up of many new commercial interests.

It is possible that during the period of extreme political confusion, particularly in the Ganges valley, there may have been some hoarding of money by the merchants and commercial classes. This hoarding may well have led to a debasement of coinage, but there is no doubt of the economic prosperity that prevailed with the political decline of the Mauryan empire. Surplus wealth was used by the rising commercial classes to decorate religious buildings. For a brief period, they were now the donors. The sculpture at Bharhut and Sanchi and the Deccan caves was the expression of this new bourgeoisie.

[1] *AI*, vol. ix, pp. 140, 168.

It has been said by one writer at least that the *coup d'état* of Puṣyamitra was a people's revolt against Mauryan oppression and a rejection of the Mauryan adoption of foreign ideas, as for instance in Mauryan art.[1] This argument is based on the idea that Śuṅga art, largely the sculpture at Bharhut and Sanchi, is more earthy and in the folk tradition than Mauryan art. Clearly Mauryan art expressed the imperialism of its emperors quite unashamedly as can be seen in the Aśokan capitals. Whether derived from foreign sources or not, this unmistakable character of Mauryan art would have remained nevertheless. The character of Śuṅga art changes because it serves a different purpose and its donors come from a different social class. The Aśokan columns are not so intimately connected with Buddhism as a religion, as are the railings and gateways at Bharhut and Sanchi. Śuṅga art conforms more to the folk traditions because Buddhism itself had incorporated large elements of popular cults, and because the donors of this art, many of whom may have been artisans, were culturally more in the main stream of folk tradition.

The idea of a popular revolt is further elaborated on the basis of Aśoka having banned the *samājas*, etc. It is possible that Aśoka's ban on festive meetings, and his discouragement of the eating of meat, may have antagonized the population, though it is still open to question whether these prohibitions were strictly enforced. In his later years, we have noticed a growing tendency towards authoritarianism, which may have resulted in measures that were irksome to the populace. This argument for a popular revolt also assumes that Aśokan policy in all its details was continued by the later Mauryas. Nevertheless, it is unlikely that there was a sufficient national consciousness among the varied peoples of the Mauryan empire to rise up in support of Puṣyamitra against Mauryan oppression, even if this existed.

Another argument that has been used on occasion in favour of the idea of a revolt against the Mauryas, is that the land tax under the Mauryas is described as being one-quarter (according to Greek sources), and this high taxation is too heavy a burden on the cultivator. If the tax was indeed uniformly one-quarter, there might be some truth in its causing rural discontent. But, as we have shown in an earlier chapter, the tax varied from region to region according to the fertility of the soil and the availability of water.[2] The figure of one-quarter stated by Megasthenes probably referred only to the extremely fertile and well-watered regions around Pāṭaliputra with which the Greek visitor would have been most familiar. That one-quarter of the produce was not the usual amount collected from

[1] Ray, *Maurya and Śuṅga Art*, p. 64. [2] See Ch. IV.

the cultivator seems fairly clear from the *Arthaśāstra*, where it is suggested that in periods of emergency the king may increase his demand to one-third or one-quarter.[1] Obviously therefore one-quarter was regarded as a high tax. It is unlikely that the Mauryas would have insisted on such high taxation in normal conditions. If that were so, then Aśoka's injunctions to the *rājūkas* to be just and fair in their judgments would be sheer hypocrisy.

The decline of the Mauryan empire cannot be satisfactorily explained by quoting military inactivity, brahman resentment, popular uprisings, or economic pressure. The causes were far more fundamental and included a much wider perspective of Mauryan life than any of those mentioned above. Furthermore, the decline of other empires and periods of political expansion, may also be explained in part by these same reasons. The organization of administration, and the conception of the state or the nation, were of great significance in the causes of the decline of the Mauryas.

Mauryan bureaucracy, had it been of a different nature, might still have saved the situation and prevented such a complete disintegration of the empire. The administration as we have seen, was of an extremely centralized character, with the higher functions as far as possible under the direct control of the ruler. This in itself necessitated a king of considerable personal ability. In such a situation the weakening of the central control leads automatically to a weakening of the administration. With the death of Aśoka and the uneven quality of his successors, there was a weakening at the centre, particularly after the division of the empire. The breaking away of the provinces was at this point almost inevitable.

Since the officials of the administration owed their loyalty to the king and not to the state, they became the personal employees of the king, particularly as the king had such overwhelming powers of personal selection.[2] This meant that a change of king could result in a change of officials, at least of the more senior and responsible ones.[3] This would be specially detrimental to a country during a period when there was a rapid succession of kings, as was the case in Mauryan India soon after the death of Aśoka. If the administration of contemporary France, since World War II had owed its loyalty to the government in power, France as a political unit might well have been on the way to disintegration by now.

Even with this fact of changing loyalties, the Mauryas could have employed a system to ensure the contribution of a well-trained bureau-

[1] V, 2.

[2] See Ch. IV.

[3] Cases of the continuity of officials are recorded in later times, largely through the hereditary tendency of appointments. Clearly this was not so strong in the Mauryan period.

cracy, which would maintain the pace of administration through many political upheavals. This was the competitive system of examinations which was used to such effect in later centuries by British administrators in India. It is curious that although the *Arthaśāstra* goes into such considerable detail regarding the administration of the kingdom, yet nowhere is there an indication of how the subordinate administrators were recruited. There is certainly no evidence whatsoever of any competitive system. We are told that the high officials were selected on the personal choice of the king. It is to be presumed that this system of personal selection continued down the scale. This strengthened the force of social kinship, since there would be a natural tendency for officers to select subordinates from members of their own social group or friends. This would in turn create either group loyalties or group antagonisms towards the new king. Should one official have to be dismissed for disloyalty to the new king, possibly an entire section of the administration would have to be changed. No doubt the later Mauryan kings must have frequently faced this situation. With a weak king at the centre, it was not difficult for a local ruler or prince to direct loyalty towards himself instead of the king.

The examination system had two obvious advantages. It eliminated social groups, since theoretically, applicants could be recruited from any social stratum. Secondly because it was an imperial service controlled from the centre, the officers could be posted to any part of the empire. This prevented local cliques from gaining too much power and threatening the position of the ruler at the centre. Such a system would have been contrary to the conception of social order in that period, since the maintenance of the social order depended on each member of the society knowing his position in society and remaining there. Kings of *śūdra* origin may have been accepted if they were powerful enough to hold their own, but administrators from the same class of society would have disrupted the entire social order.

It is not to be wondered at that Megasthenes describes administrators as forming two of the seven classes of society. They must certainly have been a privileged group. The senior officers gained tremendous social prestige owing to the fact of their being personally selected by the king, and the juniors would form a closed community with the other members of the bureaucracy. Together with social prestige, it is apparent from the scale of pay listed in the *Arthaśāstra* that they were economically well provided for.[1]

Because of the overwhelming powers of the king, and a complete absence of any advisory institution representative of public opinion, it was natural

[1] V, 3.

that he would have to maintain his contact with public opinion through various dubious means, methods which were not always ideal and which could at times react unfavourably against the king. Mauryan polity used, with the sanction of Kauṭalya, a system of espionage for this purpose. Not only were the subordinate officials such as the *gopas* actively employed in ferreting out information of every kind, in addition to their other duties, but at the same time an extremely complex system of spies was also employed. The use of reporters and agents is admitted by Aśoka in his edicts where he states that they have considerable priority of access to him.[1]

Apart from the lack of a representative institution, there was in addition no distinction between the executive and the judiciary in the function of the government. The only check which the king could impose consisted either of the *mahāmattas* in their role of royal inspectors, or else the spies and reporters. The efficiency of this system again depended very much on the personal ability of the ruler. A wise king could use these officers with great dexterity both to gauge public opinion and if need be to turn it in his favour. But equally, an incapable king could use these officers either for purposes of oppression or else be used by them to no good purpose. Efficient as the administration of Aśoka was during his lifetime, it was suited only to a strong and vigilant king and could not stand up to the corruption which inevitably sets in under weak and indifferent rulers. The machinery of the Mauryan administrative policy was so centralized that an able ruler could use it both to his own advantage and that of his people; to the same degree it could become harmful to both under a weak ruler who would lose its central control and allow forces of decay to disintegrate and wreck it.

In any political system, the type of administration and the conception of the state, if such a notion exists at all, are interrelated factors. The chief necessity for insisting upon the conception of a state lies in the fact that it becomes an idea above the king, the government, and the social order. It is an entity to which every citizen owes his loyalty irrespective of other barriers and differences between him and his fellow citizens. The state is then the supreme body and demands complete loyalty. Once the idea of the state becomes natural and clear to the thinking of a people, then national consciousness emerges.

Although in the pre-Mauryan period republics existed where the conception of a state was hinted at, and even on occasion defined in a general way, nevertheless, the conception of a nation was not in existence in Mauryan India. Many of the requisites for building up the idea of a nation

[1] See Ch. IV.

were not present. Common customs, a common language, and a common historical tradition did not exist throughout the area covered by the Mauryan empire. Nor can it be said that there was a common level of material culture in the Mauryan domains. If the idea of nationhood did not exist on this vast scale, there was equally no conception of it amongst the smaller units that constituted the empire.

For the purposes of this inquiry we shall for the moment restrict ourselves to the province of Magadha. Here, in a small area the requisites of a common language, common customs, and a common historical tradition were present. But despite this, the idea of the state was not known. If it had been a familiar idea it would have found expression in current thinking on political systems as it appears in political treatises and practice. Fortunately there is a treatise which is the direct expression of this people and this age, the Kauṭalya *Arthaśāstra*. Historians of this period have insisted that this demonstrates Mauryan ideas on the state. Nevertheless, the work fails on this count, when tested on the basis of two fundamental prerequisites. In the text, the loyalty of the subject is to the individual king and not to the state. Thus the state as an entity above the government, symbolized in the king, does not exist. Secondly, the work does not consider the possibility of various political systems in the light of attempting to discover which is best suited to that particular state, for instance, monarchy, oligarchy, republicanism, etc., but rather is concerned only with describing how best the king, as the motive power of the government, can function. To say that the *Arthaśāstra* embodies the Indian conception of the state, is to say in another context that Machiavelli's *Il Principe*, embodied the European conception of the state. Machiavelli at least, saw the limitations of *Il Principe* and regarded it as a detail from his larger study *I Discorsi*, where the conception of the state is examined at considerable length. Kauṭalya did not go beyond analysing the function of the king in a complex administration, and methods by which the king can govern. Later Indian theorists, following Kauṭalya, continued discussing the methods of government and recording changes in social usage. It is significant that the emphasis was always on the right and the wrong of social order.

With the development of political ideas in India, the loyalty which in most other cultures is given to the state was given to the social order. As long as the social structure remained intact, the idea of the overall state failed to draw either recognition or support. This was one of the reasons why an imperial structure could not hope to survive for long in India. The Indian social order changed by slow degrees. Since the change was never sudden it was hardly noticed and the loyalty continued unabated. The resentment of the brahmans against the Buddhists was possibly not religious resentment, since as a religion Buddhism was not acutely at variance with brahmanical thought, but rather a social one, since Buddhism may have upset the social order leading in turn to a new distribution of loyalties.

Ideally the three principles which mould the life of a Hindu are *Dharma*, *Artha*, and *Kāma* (the Law, well-being, and pleasure). *Dharma* is interpreted as obeying the sacred law and furthering the dictates of this law, the law being not the legislation which governs the citizens of a particular state, but social usage and the maintenance of social order. Hindu society has always stressed the fact that it gained its sanction from religious sources. The caste system had invariably a supernatural origin when described by Hindu theorists throughout the centuries before the impact of western thought. Similarly, Manu the law-giver is invested with godly powers. This position is strikingly in contrast to that of China for instance, where a distinction was made between social ethics and religion, and where Confucius has remained a mortal even among the most orthodox of his followers.

The absence of national unity in Mauryan India can be observed from other factors as well. Politically the idea of an Indian unity was non-existent. This is clear from the fact that even the resistance against the Greeks, the hated *mlecchas* was not an organized one. It was resistance offered by local rulers who were afraid of losing their newly acquired territory. It is significant that when Porus was fighting Alexander, or when Subhāgasena was paying tribute to Antiochus, they were doing so as isolated rulers in the north-west of India. They had no support from Pāṭaliputra, nor are they even mentioned in any Indian source as offering resistance to the hated Yavanas. Even the heroic Porus, who, enemy though he was, won the admiration of the Greeks, is left unrecorded in Indian sources. Since there was no fundamental political unity amongst the peoples of the Mauryan empire, political disintegration was almost inevitable.

Other factors of importance contributing to this disintegration and the lack of national unity were the ownership of land and the inequality of economic levels. Since the land was the *de facto* possession of the king it could change hands more easily. The partitioning and parcelling out of land did not require any sanction. Had it been regarded as state land it might have escaped too frequent a change of ownership. Within the large Mauryan empire there were smaller areas each developing its own resources, but the range of economic levels of production and income was obviously considerable. Owing to its fertility, the region of the Ganges basin was economically far more prosperous than the less developed region of the northern Deccan. The economies of the two areas varied considerably. The first was an agricultural economy with increasing possibilities for commercial interests. The second was a nomadic pastoral economy with occasional trade and agriculture.

Mauryan administration was just beginning to understand the economic advantages of these various economies, as is evident from the *Arthaśāstra*. Administrators were better acquainted with the northern economy since more attention had been paid to that system by the theorists. Had the economy of the southern regions particularly been developed to greater advantage, then economic homogeneity in the empire may have been possible.

It is apparent that the population of the sub-continent was not at a uniform level of cultural development either. The more sophisticated cities and the trade centres were a great contrast to the isolated village communities. Traditions varied from area to area, and social customs without as yet the sanction of many hundreds of years, still remained localized. Even in twentieth-century India where the equalizing process has been at work for many decades, cultural inequalities are a striking feature. Mauryan India must have been infinitely worse. Not only were economic and political structures distinct in each region, but even the languages spoken were varied and although Aśoka did attempt to support the potential emergence of national unity by the use of Prākrit all over the empire, nevertheless the range of the Greek and Aramaic speakers in the north-west to Tamil speakers in the south, must have remained a serious hindrance to this unity.

The study of Indian history has suffered in the past from some historians who have assumed that the pattern of Magadha through the centuries, has been valid for the entire sub-continent. This approach has resulted in analyses which on occasion have failed to evaluate the particular conditions in areas far removed. The history of India must now be treated as the history of a sub-continent, and the causal relationships, so essential to a proper study of history must be sought in every part of India. The causes of the decline of the Mauryas must in large part be attributed to a top-heavy administration where authority was entirely in the hands of a few persons, and an absence of any national consciousness. These and other factors may not be immediately apparent in Magadha itself, but are clearly in evidence when the perspective is broadened to include the entire Mauryan empire.

CONCLUSION

'THE prominent civilized nations — the Babylonians and Egyptians, the Hebrews and Hindus, the Persians, the Greeks and Romans as well as the Teutons and others — all began at an early stage to glorify their national heroes — mythical princes and kings, founders of religions, dynasties, empires or cities — in a number of poetic tales and legends.'[1] The cult of these heroes continues to the present day in all societies. It is not the concern of the historian to attempt their eradication, but rather to sift the true history of the cult-heroes from legendary material. It may almost be said that, it is the moral responsibility of the historian to keep a watchful eye on the growth of such cults, especially those relating to the past, and to interpose with critical data when the myth assumes unhealthy proportions or becomes distorted. The historian in claiming objectivity, should refrain from participating in the cult because of his particular significance as the interpreter of the historical patterns of his culture. This he can best do by a continual self-criticism of his motives: by analysing the prejudices of his society, which are generally responsible for his own prejudices and from which many of the popular myths emerge.

We have attempted in this work to place Aśoka in historical perspective, against the background of the third century B.C. in India, and also to distinguish, in so far as it is possible at this great distance in time, between Aśoka the man and Aśoka the monarch. The context of an historical event is as important as the event itself, since the latter emerges from the former. We have used this approach in our study of Aśoka and the Mauryan period. We believe this approach to be of significance because unfortunately, the institutions of the past have on occasion, been invested with qualities, which are required by the institutions of the present alone, thereby undermining the validity of historical research. A popular misconception about the Mauryan period describes it as one which was politically decentralized and individually democratic; whereas in fact, as we have seen, it was the beginning of political centralization and it also saw the triumph of a social order which did not permit of much individual liberty. Democracy and individualism were not the ideals which inspired the Mauryan period, and to find these we must search elsewhere in Indian history.

Indo-European scholarship has felt the impact for many decades of what has been described as the 'Greek miracle'. The superiority of Greek civilization has been so over-emphasized, as to produce an unfortunate inferiority

[1] Rank, *The Myth of the Birth of the Hero*, p. 3.

complex among members of certain other civilizations. This has quite naturally resulted in an effort to prove that non-Greek cultures had identical values as those of the Greek-dominated ones. But progressive research shows that every culture and every civilization has its own 'miracle', and it is the purpose of historical investigation to reveal it. This cannot be achieved by seeking to discover identical values in every civilization, but rather by pointing out the significant values of each culture within its own context. This demands considerable honesty, as shortcomings have to be admitted in the same way as achievements are proclaimed.

In contemporary India, the image of Aśoka has gathered about it, its own cult in the popular mind. Concepts such as *ahiṃsā* and the *panca-śīla* policy are associated with his ideas. It is felt that a long political tradition beginning with Aśoka, of conscious non-violence and a toleration of all beliefs political and religious, continued unbroken through the centuries culminating in the political philosophy of Gandhi. The fact that the work of Aśoka as a monarch, was almost erased from Indian history and thought, cannot be overlooked. The political value of Aśoka's ideas was successfully buried in the oblivion of the past. In the Indian secular sources Aśoka remained largely a name in the dynastic king lists, as obscure during the later centuries as the script in which he had had his edicts engraved. A few medieval inscriptions of no great importance do refer to Aśoka. But the association of Aśoka with *Dhamma*, which was an unconventional policy in terms of politics was not recorded. No later king of any standing, tried consciously to adopt these principles as the basis of his policy. Had a systematic study of Aśokan *Brāhmī* been maintained through the centuries, a record of Aśokan policy might have been preserved.

In Buddhist literature he appears as a fanatic, changing suddenly from extreme wickedness to extreme piety and eventually suffering at the hands of non-believers, a not unfamiliar treatment of the life and works of saints and pious men in any religion. Even the popular mind despite the existence of his inscriptions and pillars, failed to retain any legends or traditions regarding Aśoka. The contemporary cult is of recent origin. Curiously enough, some of the Aśokan pillars have reverted to their function of the pre-historic period, and are revered as *liṅgas*. One wonders what Aśoka's reactions would have been had he seen thus far into the future.

It is clear from his edicts that in his role as king, Aśoka was not the naive convert to Buddhism that Buddhist sources would have us believe. Certainly in the first half of his reign, he emphasized a tolerance and humanism which was by no means inconsistent with Buddhism, but which was a more personal expression of Aśoka, relating to general non-partisan attitudes which he wished his subjects to cultivate. We have shown in the chapter on the policy of *Dhamma*, how his humanitarianism gradually was overshadowed by his belief in his own achievement in having changed men's natures, until, at the end of his reign he appears to have become over-confident of this achievement, and succumbed to his own ego.

The social and economic conditions in India during the third century B.C. were such as to make the attempted policy on the part of Aśoka quite feasible. The transition from a pastoral to an agrarian village economy necessitated an adjustment to the new conditions. *Dhamma* underlined the more important aspects of this adjustment, such as the need for an increase in social responsibility. It is greatly to the credit of Aśoka that this change took place during an era of peace. A period of thirty years free from war, in itself no mean achievement, must have permitted a comparatively clear realization of these new social and economic values.

The form adopted by Aśoka for the communication of his ideas was a socio-religious one as is apparent from a study of *Dhamma*. His association of Buddhism with the new ideas was no doubt in part due to the fact that he was personally a Buddhist and because the religion was not averse to these ideas; but also due to the obvious advantage of adapting a comparatively new religion to contemporary ideas during a period of political and economic change. This last method has been employed to great effect by many other emperors, as for instance, Ikhnaton in Egypt, or the adoption of Zoroastrianism by Darius, Manichaeism by Shahpur I, and the Dīn-i-Ilāhī by Akbar. This idea is associated with a similar one of rulers who insist on a complete breaking away from the past, sometimes as extreme as in the case of Shi Huang Ti in China. It is, however, significant that Aśoka did not demand the mass conversion of all his subjects to Buddhism, but rather stressed the conscious application of humanitarianism in social behaviour, thus appealing not to the narrower religious instincts, but to a far wider and immediate feeling of social responsibility.

The development of *Dhamma* must also be considered in the context of the political system of the time. India in the third century B.C. was not a national unit, yet politically it was governed by a centralized monarchy and the administrative system hinged on centralized control. If the political system was to succeed it was inevitable that there would have to be some national factor in the multi-cultural society of the time. *Dhamma* was certainly a way of life acceptable at any level of cultural development and its adoption might well have acted as a cementing force throughout the country. In this the efforts of Akbar, eighteen centuries later, may well be compared with those of Aśoka.

This period was of immense advantage to the development of commerce in the form of free bargaining and speculative business. An efficient administration meant the establishment of good communications which were a vital necessity to the improvement of trade. The development of commerce during the thirty years of peace bore rich results in the succeeding centuries. It is important to keep in mind the fact that, though a political decline took place in the post-Aśokan period, there was an improvement in economic development as is demonstrated largely by archaeological finds. The stability of the reign of Aśoka was to a fair extent responsible for this.

Whatever may have been the personal weaknesses of Aśoka which were made manifest during his later years, our admiration for him is great when we consider the courage with which he attempted to expound and impose *Dhamma*, particularly in the complex cultural milieu of the third century B.C. Religious texts of the time stressed man's responsibility to his religion and to his ancestors. To these Aśoka added yet another responsibility, perhaps the most important, that of responsibility to one's fellow human beings as he expresses it in the 6th Rock Edict. Aśoka's humanism lay not in his insistence on non-violence whenever and wherever possible, but more important, it lay in his insistence on responsible social behaviour, and in his understanding of human limitations, when in his earlier edicts he preached moderation in action. It is apparent on reading the edicts that he constantly stressed the dignity of man. The divine certainly appears and the gods come down to earth and mix with man, but on a human level.

Yet the experiment of *Dhamma* disappeared soon after his death, with little trace in the Indian tradition. It lay neglected for over two thousand years until the deciphering of the edicts produced a discovery of the idea and a revival of interest in its author. Even in Cambodia when the Khmer king Jayavarman VII attempted, at the close of the twelfth century A.D., to enforce ideas similar to those once expounded by Aśoka, he had no knowledge of his predecessor. The precise reasons for the failure of *Dhamma* cannot be known with certainty after this gap in time. We can only suggest that, on the level of personalities involved, the excessive enthusiasm of its founder, as it would appear from Aśoka's later edicts produced a reaction against *Dhamma*. These edicts and the powers of the *dhamma-mahāmattas* suggest a tendency both of a regimentation of ideas and a somewhat overbearing intellectual authority. This not only reduced the force of *Dhamma*, but also acted as a barrier to any advancement of ideas. It is equally possible that the over-enthusiasm on the part of Aśoka led his successors to misinterpret *Dhamma* as a personal belief alone, and prevented them from realizing its social and humanitarian significance, such as it had originally possessed.

After examining the background which was largely responsible for the personality of Aśoka, we would reassert our earlier hypothesis that Aśoka's greatness lay in the fact that he was equipped both by his own endeavour and by circumstances, to understand the culture to which he belonged and its then rapidly changing requirements; this characteristic was coupled with an extraördinary degree of idealism. Both of these gave him the courage which he needed to experiment with the contemporary situation and strike out towards an uncommon solution.

APPENDIX I

THE DATE OF THE *ARTHAŚASTRA*

A CONSIDERABLE amount of literature has already accumulated on the question of the date of the *Arthaśāstra*. The range of suggested dates lie between the Mauryan and the Gupta periods of Hindu history. In this appendix we propose to briefly treat of the arguments already used in dating the text and to give our own suggestions on the subject.

Fleet in his introductory note to the English translation of Shamasastry states that he believes the text to be of an early date because of its archaic style, its contents, and the fact that early Indian writers are known to quote from it.[1] As a manual on kingship and government it may well have served as the first practical guide of its kind. As Fleet further states, it endorses passages from the account of Megasthenes and early inscriptions. Shamasastry supports this claim for an early date by various arguments. Among them, that a verse in the concluding chapter of the text refers to Kauṭilya overthrowing the Nandas, and to his other name, Viṣṇugupta.[2] Furthermore that Yājñyavalkya followed Kauṭalya and borrowed from the latter. This theory he bases on the idea that Kauṭalya appears to be unacquainted with the grammatical forms emphasized by Pāṇini, that the style of Kauṭalya is close to that of the *Upaniṣads* and the *Brāhmaṇas*, and furthermore that the type of society as described by Kauṭalya is certainly Mauryan if not pre-Mauryan.

Krishna Rao has also discussed this question and is of the opinion that the *Arthaśāstra* belongs to the Mauryan period.[3] However, his main argument which attempts to connect Aśokan policy with that advocated by Kauṭalya, is not very convincing. A further argument used by Krishna Rao is that Aśvaghoṣa mentions Kauṭalya, thereby suggesting that the *Arthaśāstra* was known to him. This is a weak argument since the text is not referred to, merely Kauṭalya. Aśvaghoṣa is generally placed not later than the second century A.D.

The two main contestants who have devoted much time and labour to

[1] *Arthaśāstra* (trans. Shamasastry), Preface. Fifth Edn.

[2] Ibid., pp. vii–xxxiii. There has been much discussion on the name Kauṭalya and its grammatical derivation (Jolly, *Arthaśāstra of Kauṭalya*, pp. 1–47; Kane, *JBORS*, vol. vii, 1926). We are of the opinion that the name was Kauṭalya and not Kauṭilya, and was derived from its owner's *gotra* which was Kuṭala.

[3] *Studies in Kauṭalya*, pp. xi, 6, 10.

this discussion are Jolly and Jayaswal. Jolly maintained that the text belonged to the third century A.D. or even later.[1] Since most of his arguments have been very ably countered by Jayaswal, we shall not consider them at length here. He maintains that Kauṭalya was the author of the *Arthaśāstra* and that the text dates to the fourth century B.C.[2] The one point on which Jayaswal was not able to provide convincing evidence is the fact that the term *cīnapaṭṭa* is used in the text. This is generally interpreted as silk (from China). Since Chinese silk via eastern India began to be imported into India at a later date, this reference to *cīnapaṭṭa* is frequently quoted as an indication of the late date of the text itself. However, there is evidence to prove that silk was used in Bactria, which was imported from India in the second century B.C., if not earlier.[3] Chang K'ien in about 129 B.C. found the Bactrians using Chinese silk, which according to the inhabitants came from India. The interesting point is that it is referred to as silk coming from the province of Szechuan. This province has always been known as the area where the silk worm flourished. The implications of this are that there was no silk manufactured in Gilgit. Thus it would appear that silk was available in India at an early period and that it came from Szechuan. The problem of the name remains unsettled. The *cīna* of the term *cīnapaṭṭa* is generally believed to refer to the Ch'in empire, which came into existence later than the Mauryan empire. It has been suggested that this may be a reference to the feudal state of Chin (during the Chou period), before the period of Shih Huang Ti.[4] It is possible that silk was referred to by another name in the early period, and that the term *cīnapaṭṭa* is a later interpolation introduced when the text was being revised.

Raghavan in his study of Kauṭalya and Kālidāsa, states that Kālidāsa has borrowed from the *Arthaśāstra* in certain passages of the *Raghuvaṃśa* (XVII, 49, 76; XVIII, 50).[5] This borrowing consists largely in the use of technical terms relating to a political context. Some of these terms were no doubt current at that time and were based on earlier texts such as the *Arthaśāstra*. Men of learning such as Kālidāsa would be familiar with these terms.

D. R. Bhandarkar has suggested that the *Arthaśāstra* was originally written in verse, as reference is made to *ślokas* in the body of the text.[6] The question arises as to when it was reduced to *sūtras*, if we accept this view. Bhandarkar quotes Daṇḍin, who refers to the text as written in metrical

[1] *Kauṭilyaṃ Arthaśāstraṃ*, Panjab S.K. Series, No. IV, Introduction.

[2] *Hindu Polity*, p. 364, Appendix C.

[3] Ssi-ma-Ts'ien, *Shi-ki* 123; trans. by Hirth. *JAOS*, vol. xxxvii, 1917, pp. 89 ff.

[4] Kosambi, *Introduction to the Study of Indian History*, p. 202.

[5] *Kalidasa and Kautilya*, *AIOC*, XIII Session, 1946, Nagpur.

[6] *ABORI*, vol. vii, 1926, pp. 82 ff.

form, and Bhavabhūti, who quotes it in the form of *sūtras*. Therefore, Bhandarkar is of the opinion that it was reduced to *sūtra* form in *c.* A.D. 400 when it started becoming popular. The original text must have been composed in verse. It is not possible to state categorically which form the earliest version of the *Arthaśāstra* took, since early texts are known to exist both in verse form and in *sūtras*. It would require an extremely detailed study of the present verse and prose passages of the *Arthaśāstra* to determine which are earlier.

Certain sections of the *Arthaśāstra* suggest that it was composed at the same period as some of the *Jātakas*. This is particularly noticeable in some features of economic life described in both sources, as for example the establishment of the guilds. Bhandarkar has drawn attention to a particular verse which is almost identical in both sources.[1] The verse concerns the acquisition of wealth. Bhandarkar adds rightly that it is more appropriate in the *Arthaśāstra* since it occurs at the conclusion of a chapter concerning the loss of men, wealth, and profits. The author of the *Jātaka* may have been familiar with the *Arthaśāstra* text and may have quoted from it. However, we cannot ignore the possibility that both authors were quoting from a common source, particularly as both these texts quote numerous popular gnomic verses.

Winternitz agrees on the whole with Jolly and doubts the authorship of Kauṭalya,[2] largely on the question of the seven-fold classification of the sovereignty of the state, which he regards as too pedantic for a practising politician to formulate. His criticism has been countered at length by Law who bases his views mainly on the argument that this classification was necessary to the theory of *maṇḍala*, otherwise it would not have been possible for a king to determine the relative power of his neighbour.[3] There has been much debate as to whether the work was written for a small kingdom or a large one. We would suggest that the work originated in the early years of Candragupta when the Mauryan empire had not been fully consolidated. The Nanda empire was known and was probably used by Kauṭalya as an example, and this was certainly not nearly as large as the Mauryan empire was to become. This early period may have given cause for the writing of the section on inter-state relationships. Later when the empire was established the section on administration may have been written or at any rate expanded. Since the concept of an empire on a scale as large as that of the Mauryas was quite new to Indian polity, it is not to

[1] *Arthaśāstra*, IV, 9; *Jātaka*, I, p. 258.
[2] *CR*, April, 1924.
[3] *CR*, September 1924, pp. 512 ff.; November 1924, pp. 228 ff.; December 1924, pp. 466 ff.

be wondered at that even a theoretician such as Kauṭalya wrote from the point of view of a smaller state. It is possible that he thought of the Mauryan dominion in terms of its nucleus, the province of Magadha. As such, even the section on inter-state relations would represent the logical expression of a political idea.

Raychaudhuri does not accept the Mauryan period as the date of the *Arthaśāstra* and maintains that it is a later work.[1] He states that none of the authors used for cross-dating can be definitely placed before A.D. 300. The language of the *Arthaśāstra* is Sanskrit, but the Mauryans used Prākrit. This argument is based on the fact that Aśoka used Prākrit for his inscriptions. However, since the inscriptions were meant to be read by the populace it is but natural that they should be written in the popular language. There was nothing to prevent the use of Sanskrit in court circles and among the better educated sections of society even during the Mauryan period. We know from the plays of Kālidāsa that even in the Gupta period when Sanskrit was widely employed there was a distinction between the classes of society who were expected to speak Sanskrit and those who spoke only Prākrit. Had any of the Gupta rulers wished to issue inscriptions for the same purposes as Aśoka they might well have used Prākrit. It is also possible that Aśoka encouraged Prākrit since it was a more widely used language, but for purposes of erudition Sanskrit was used.

A further point raised by Raychaudhuri is that Kauṭalya was against the use of wood for buildings and preferred the use of bricks, but Arrian on the authority of Megasthenes states that the cities near rivers or the sea were built of wood.[2] We see nothing contradictory in this. Kauṭalya saw the danger of building cities in wood, a more perishable material than brick. Since it was economically cheaper to build in wood, owing to the clearing of large forests at this time, Kauṭalya's advice on this matter tended to be disregarded. However, Arrian does add that cities other than the above-mentioned ones were built of brick, and that wood was only used in areas where brick would not be able to withstand the destruction of rain and flood. Although Kauṭalya advises against the use of wood for buildings, he is not unaware of the prevalence of construction in wood, as is evident from the elaborate precautions he lays down for the extinguishing of fire.[3] Judging from the fear expressed at the possibility of conflagration, it would seem that he lived at a time when there was a constant danger of wooden buildings catching fire.

[1] *History and Culture of the Indian People*, vol. ii (*The Age of Imperial Unity*), pp. 285–7.

[2] *Indica*, X.

[3] II, 36.

Raychaudhuri's next argument is that there is no reference in the *Arthaśāstra* to the royal titles used by the Mauryas. This is so because there was no set formula for royal titles at this time. *Devānaṃpiya* may have been a Mauryan title since it was used by two of the kings, but this may equally well have been a matter of personal choice in both cases. Since Kauṭalya does not mention any of the Mauryan kings by name, there is naturally no cause for mentioning any of the titles that may have been borne by them.

Certain official names in the *Arthaśāstra*, such as the *samāhartṛ* and the *sannidhātṛ* were current in a later period than that of the Mauryas, according to Raychaudhuri. It is possible that these titles were introduced in a later edition of the text. At the same time there is no proof that they were not used during the Mauryan period, from the fact that they do not occur in definitely contemporary sources. It is possible for instance that if Aśoka had had to refer to either of these officials in his inscriptions he may have used these titles. The official designation of *mahāmātra* occurs in rare instances in the *Arthaśāstra*.[1] This was most definitely a Mauryan designation and appears to have been discarded or altered in the early centuries A.D. This would indicate that at some stage in the history of the text the term was used quite extensively, probably during the Mauryan period when it was used as a title in practical administration. Gradually as it ceased to be used, it gave way even in the text to more contemporary terms. That it still occurs is probably due to the fact that it was overlooked in certain places during the later transcription or editing of the text.

As his final argument Raychaudhuri raises the question of geographical knowledge. The inclusion of the terms Pārasamudra, Cīnabhūmi and Kambu would suggest a later date. We have already seen that a knowledge of China was in existence at a fairly early period. We feel that this argument based on geographical knowledge is not sufficient evidence for giving the work a late date. As we have already accepted the fact of interpolations at various stages, it seems more than likely that the inclusion of new place names can be regarded as evidence of such interpolations. In bringing the text up to date it would be natural for the editor to extend the geographical horizon of the original work.

Ojha has suggested that the name Viṣṇugupta for Kauṭalya was a later fabrication, which came into use after the sixth or seventh century A.D.[2] Most of the earlier texts such as the *Purāṇas* and the *Mahāvaṃsa* refer to him as Kauṭalya or Cānakya. The present version of the *Mahāvaṃsa* is dated to the fifth century A.D. though it is based on an earlier original.

[1] I, 10; II, 5.

[2] *IHQ*, vol. xxviii, No. 3, September 1952, pp. 265 ff.

Furthermore since it is based largely on the material brought in by the Buddhists from Ceylon, there is no special reason why this tradition regarding Cānakya should be a fabrication. On the question of Viṣṇugupta we are of the opinion that the concluding passage at the end of the text is significant.[1] There is the usual concluding formula for the chapter, explaining that it is the first chapter of the fifteenth book and that it brings to a close the *Arthaśāstra* of Kauṭalya. Then there follows another sentence which has been translated thus,[2]

'Having seen discrepancies in many ways on the part of the writers of commentaries on *śāstras*, Viṣṇugupta himself has made this *sūtra* and commentary.'

We are of the opinion that this indicates that Viṣṇugupta was not the original author of the text but was responsible for putting it into its present form. The reference to converting it into *sūtras* would suggest that the earlier form was in verse. Quite possibly Viṣṇugupta's version was completed in the sixth or seventh century, as Ojha has suggested, or perhaps a couple of centuries earlier. Having been edited by Viṣṇugupta the latter's name would naturally tend to be linked very closely with the text, even to the extent of his being regarded on occasion as the author, a situation not altogether unknown in the literary world.

We believe that the *Arthaśāstra* as compiled by Viṣṇugupta was a much larger one than the original, incorporating other works on the same subject. The manuscripts which have come down to us are probably those in which the Kauṭalya *Arthaśāstra* has been extracted from a larger work. It is indeed strange that an entirely new section should be started at the end of the book containing only one chapter, which is a summary of the book, but which is so brief and so general that it could as well have been added to the previous section. In the original and complete work of Viṣṇugupta there may have been more sections dealing either with the earlier commentaries on the Kauṭalya text or with other smaller works on the same subject.

Because of the change of form that the work underwent at the hands of Viṣṇugupta, it is impossible to treat it in its present state as the work of entirely one period. Thus the analysis of Kalyanov based on philosophical attitudes cannot be used with certainty. Kalyanov states that the *Arthaśāstra* shows evidence of differentiation between philosophy and the natural and social sciences.[3] He explains further that this stage is usually

[1] XV, I.

[2] Shamasastry translation.

[3] XXIII Orientalists' Congress. Cambridge, August 1954.

associated with the downfall of slave society and the birth of feudalism, which in India he dates from the first to third centuries A.D. We are of the opinion that this argument tends to oversimplify changes in society. Terms such as slave society and feudal society may be applied as broad generalizations, but in every society the peculiarities and degrees of change vary, so that the validity of these generalizations demand a detailed study. Kalyanov is of the opinion that the *Arthaśāstra* as we have it today is a work of the third century A.D. because the means of production which it discusses, the social system and the economic and political institutions are all more advanced than those described by Megasthenes. Yet earlier in his paper Kalyanov states that Megasthenes' account cannot be relied upon entirely. The main part of the work, however, could well have come from Kauṭalya's school, since the period of Candragupta was one of stabilizing the country, and a philosophy advocating the use of any means of doing so would be very welcome. Kalyanov believes that the *Arthaśāstra* was based on a long tradition of political thinking and that it was revised and edited in later years. He points out that both the *Arthaśāstra* and the *Daśakumāracarita* emphasize the importance of philosophy. The central part of the *Arthaśāstra* is concerned with the description of the functioning of the economic, political, and social institutions. If these are described as being post-Mauryan when compared to similar institutions as described by Megasthenes then it is difficult to say as Kalyanov does that the main body of the work dates to the Mauryan period. We are of the opinion that the institutions are in the main Mauryan.

In connection with social institutions, it would seem that some of the ideas in the text suggest an early stage in the development of society. As for example the attitude towards actors and performers of all kinds in the *Arthaśāstra*.[1] They were regarded with great suspicion and were considered socially outcaste. It is unlikely that such a severe attitude would have existed during the Gupta period, when the theatre rose in esteem and people connected with it became socially much more acceptable. The strict attitude towards actors in the *Arthaśāstra* seems to agree with the puritanical mood of some of Aśoka's inscriptions, particularly the one which appears to forbid non-religious entertainment.

The attitude of mind of the author of the *Arthaśāstra* cannot be described as being uniform throughout the book. In the latter part of the book there is an increasing tendency to suggest magical and mystical means of achieving one's end. The strictly practical approach of the earlier part of the book appears to have been modified. For instance in the section discuss-

[1] II, 27.

ing methods of ridding the country of plagues and pestilences. both natural and animal, in every case the first suggestion is a rational' and practical one, after which the author resorts to some magic ritual.[1] It may be suggested that the author being a brahman felt that he had to make some concessions to the brahmans who alone could perform these rites and ceremonies. We prefer to believe that the first suggestion in each case was probably in the original text of Kauṭalya and that the latter suggestions incorporating magical means were put forward by later editors, when such practices were on the increase.

We have already in the course of this book indicated various occasions when certain measures adopted by Aśoka agree closely with those suggested by Kauṭalya. For instance the propaganda measures of informing the population of the king's nearness to the gods.[2] The curious ban on the killing of certain animals is also common to both sources.[3] In addition there are many technical terms which are similar.[4] A few of them are as follows:

Aśokan Inscriptions	*Arthaśāstra*
Yuta, R.E. III	Yukta, II, 5, 9
Prādeśika, R.E. III	Pradeṣṭṛ, IV, 1
Parisa, R.E. I, VII	Pariṣad, IV, 1
Pulisā, P.E. IV	Puruṣa, II, 5
Gananāyam, R.E. III	Gananayam, II, 6
Vraca, R.E. II, VI	Vraja, II, 1
Palikilesu, S.E. I	Parikleṣa, IV, 9

To conclude, we are of the opinion that the *Arthaśāstra* was originally written by Kauṭalya, the minister of Candragupta, and who was also known as Cāṇakya. It was edited and commented upon by various later writers, until in about the third or fourth century A.D. Viṣṇugupta worked over the entire text, with whatever interpolations had occurred by then. The text as it is known to us today is in this later form of Viṣṇugupta's. Borrowings and similarities in other works throughout the centuries can be explained by the fact that only the original text was written at the end of the fourth century B.C.

[1] IV, 3.
[2] See Ch. V.
[3] See Ch. III.
[4] Dikshitar, *Mauryan Polity*, p. 47.

APPENDIX II

THE TITLES OF AŚOKA

THE titles used by Aśoka are in themselves of some interest. The complete royal title read, *Devānaṃpiya Piyadassi rājā Aśoka*. This was a far more humble title than was used by later kings in India. Sometimes the full title is not used, but just *Devānampiya*, or as in the Barābar Hill cave inscriptions, only *Piyadassi rājā*. As Hultzsch explains, the etymological meaning of the term *Devānaṃpiya* is 'dear to the gods'.[1] Patañjali in the *Mahābhāṣya* states that this term was used as an honorific similar to *bhavān*, *dirghāyu*, and *āyuṣmān*.[2] Kaiyata's commentary on Patañjali refers to another meaning of this term, 'fool', which was known to Patañjali.[3] This may have been due to a hostile recollection among brahmans of the unorthodox Mauryan dynasty. However, in Jaina literature it occurs as an honorific.[4]

In Ceylonese literature *Devānaṃpiya* is used not for Aśoka but for his Ceylonese contemporary Tissa.[5] We have no evidence of this title having been used by Aśoka's predecessors or for that matter by any of the kings previous to him. But in the 8th Rock Edict he refers to previous *devānaṃpiyas*, implying thereby that the term was well known to his readers and audience in the sense of a royal title.[6] The fact that it was adopted as a title by his grandson Daśaratha,[7] and by various Ceylonese kings after Tissa[8] would suggest that it was a royal title.

The other name that occurs frequently with that of Aśoka is Piyadassi, meaning 'he who regards amiably', or 'of gracious mien'. This appears to have been a personal name of Aśoka, probably a throne name. He used this name alone in the Kandahar inscription. In the *Dīpavaṃsa* he is referred to largely as Piyadassi.[9] In later years it appears to have been adopted as a title of royalty. Anantadeva in the *Rājadharma Kauṣṭubha* quotes from the *Viṣṇudharmottara* in which Priyadarśana is mentioned as a title of royalty.[10] Vālmīki uses it in the *Rāmāyana* as a title for Rāma.[11] Smith suggests that

[1] *Corpus Inscriptionum Indicarum*, vol. i, p. xxix.

[2] Mahābhāṣya on Pāṇinī, II, 4, 56.

[3] Ibid.

[4] *JRAS*, Keilhorn, 1908, p. 505; Hemacandra, *Abhidānacintāmaṇi*, III, 17.

[5] *Dīpavaṃsa*, XI, 25–29; Fleet, *JRAS*, 1908, p. 485.

[6] Bloch, *Les Inscriptions d'Asoka*, p. 111.

[7] Sircar, *Select Inscriptions*, p. 79.

[8] Ibid., p. 231.

[9] VI, 1, 2, 14, 24.

[10] Kamal Krishna Smrithirtha edition, p. 43.

[11] I, 1, 3.

Aśokavardhana was the king's personal name and Piyadassi his title, which he used in the edicts because it meant 'the humane'.[1] We are of the opinion that Aśoka was his personal name, and Piyadassi was as it were, an official name, which he probably began to use after his coronation. *Devānaṃpiya* was a generally known royal title of the time.

[1] *Asoka*, p. 41.

APPENDIX III

THE GEOGRAPHICAL LOCATIONS OF THE EDICTS

THE locations of the edicts are of geographical importance, as the selection of their sites was not arbitrary. They were deliberately placed either near habitations, or on important travel routes, or at places of religious interest, thereby ensuring that they would be available to as many people as possible. The reasons for the choice of a particular site will be given in this appendix. Such an analysis demands considerable archaeological evidence to substantiate literary and epigraphical indications. Unfortunately not all the sites have as yet been excavated. Therefore, in some cases the reasons can only be regarded as suggestions. Concerning the importance of the sites in south India we must keep in mind that the area within which most of the edicts have been found tallies closely with the gold-mining area of the south. The *Arthaśāstra* mentions this activity in the south, and speaks of gold as a special commodity of trade with the south.[1] Thus this region was of tremendous economic importance and this may have been the prime reason for the selection of some of the southern sites. The inscriptions were probably situated in the well-inhabited mining areas or along the main routes to this area.

The list of sites is given in alphabetical order.

ALLAHABAD-KOSAM (Pillar Edicts I–VI, the Queen's Edict, and the Kauśāmbī Edict or Schism Edict). The importance of Allahabad, the old Prayāga was largely due to its being a pilgrim centre. It lay on what was then a great sandy plain between the two rivers, the Ganges and the Yamuna.[2] Hsüan Tsang describes it as a place sacred to Hindus and relates many legends regarding its temples.[3] Since the Kauśāmbī Edict is directed to the *mahāmattas* of Kauśāmbī, this pillar was originally situated at the latter site.[4] The site is the same as modern Kosam on the left bank of the Yamuna, twenty-eight miles south-west of Allahabad. Kauśāmbī having been a place of religious importance in Buddhist times may well have attracted pilgrims from various parts of the country and would therefore have been

[1] VII, 12.

[2] Cunningham, *Ancient Geography of India*, p. 445.

[3] Watters, *On Yuan Chwang's Travels in India*, vol. i, pp. 361 ff.

[4] Cunningham, *Inscriptions of Asoka*, p. 39.

an excellent site for the edicts. The Aśokan pillar was inscribed on, at later periods by various rulers including Samudragupta and Jahangīr. It would appear from Samudragupta's inscription that the pillar was still at Kauśāmbī during the Gupta period.[1] Probably Jahangīr was responsible for its removal to the fort at Allahabad, which he did in imitation of Firoz Shah, who had brought similar pillars from Toprā and Meerut to Delhi. Both Allahabad and Kauśāmbī being on the river Yamuna, the transportation of the pillar would not have been too difficult.

BAIRĀṬ (Minor Rock Edict and the Bhabra Edict). Bairāṭ is located in Rajasthan, forty-two miles north-east of Jaipur. It has been identified with Virāṭa the capital of the Matsya state.[2] The presence of the Bhabra Edict addressed specifically to the *Saṃgha* is explained by the fact that the remains of two monasteries have been discovered on a hill about a mile south-west of Bairāṭ.[3] More recently, excavations in the region revealed a brick chamber resembling a *stūpa*.[4] It may have been an early Buddhist shrine of a period prior to the emergence of the *stūpa* as a regular Buddhist feature.[5] This points to Bairāṭ being an old and established centre of Buddhism. It was thus both a centre of religious activity and an important city of the region, with a large population.

BARĀBAR HILL CAVES (Donatory inscriptions to the Ājīvika sect). The inscriptions in these caves are donatory, and therefore their significance does not rest in the particular importance of their site. The caves were in a group of hills girdling the city of Rājagṛha.[6]

BROACH is not mentioned in the edicts nor is it the site of any Aśokan inscription, but from other evidence it was clearly the most important commercial centre for trade with the West and as such must have held a prominent position during the Mauryan period.[7] It is mentioned with great frequency in the Periplus.[8] Since the ports of Saurāṣṭra had communication with the cities in the Ganges basin they became important in the course of this trade. Furthermore the Aparānta area to the west of the Mauryan empire, had considerable Greek and Persian contacts, which no doubt the people of this area wished to maintain.

BRAHMAGIRI (Minor Rock Inscription). Excavations at the site have

[1] Hultzsch, *Corpus Inscriptionum Indicarum*, vol. i, p. xx.
[2] Cunningham, *Ancient Geography of India*, p. 390.
[3] *Archaeological Reports*, 2, pp. 247–8.
[4] *AI*, ix, p. 150.
[5] Cf. Piggott, *Antiquity*, vol. xvii, 1943, pp. 2 ff.
[6] Cunningham, *Ancient Geography of India*, p. 530.
[7] Ptolemy, *Ancient India*, I, 62. Quoted McCrindle, pp. 38, 152. *Jātakas*, iii, p. 188; iv, p. 137; *Divyāvadāna*, xxvii, p. 576.
[8] *The Erythraen Sea*, 14, 21, 27, 32, 43.

revealed considerable archaeological evidence pointing to Brahmagiri having been an important centre in south India even well before the Mauryan period.[1] Continual habitation for many hundreds of years resulted in its emerging as an influential town, particularly after it had become one of the southern outposts of the Mauryan empire. It may also have been the starting point of pilgrimages to the sources of the two rivers, Godāvarī and Kāverī.

DELHI-MEERUT and DELHI-TOPRĀ (Pillar Edicts I–VI and I–VII respectively). The Delhi-Meerut and the Delhi-Toprā pillars are so called because they were transported to Delhi by Firoz Shah from their original sites at Meerut and Toprā.[2] Both these places lie to the north-west of Delhi. Neither of these two sites has been excavated as yet so that the reason for their being selected as the location for the Pillar Edicts remains uncertain. It would appear that both sites were important stopping places on the road from Pāṭaliputra to the north-west. If there were caravanserais at these two points no doubt a fairly large habitation must have grown up around them.

DHAULI (Major Rock Edicts). The Dhauli inscription has been cut high on a rock in a group of hills which rise abruptly from the surrounding plain. The site has been identified with Tosalī[3] which is mentioned by Ptolemy as a metropolis.[4] It was situated near the sacred pool of Kosala-Ganga and thus developed into a religious centre as well. The identification of Dhauli with Tosalī is most convincing and is borne out by the text of the 1st Separate Edict which is addressed to the *mahāmattas* of Tosalī.[5] It seems reasonable that the edicts would be as near the city as possible if not actually within it.

GĀVIMATH (Minor Rock Edict). Gāvimath is situated in modern Mysore and is one among the group of places in the neighbourhood of Siddāpur where this edict is found with great frequency.[6] Its importance may have been largely due to its being a mining area or on an important route.

GIRNĀR (Major Rock Edicts). The importance of Girnār is not difficult to account for. It is situated one mile to the east of Junāgadh in Kathiawar. That it was a site of immense importance is amply proved by the number of major inscriptions to be found there, including apart from those of Aśoka, those of Rudradāman and Skandagupta. It is mentioned as Girinagar in

[1] Wheeler, *Early India and Pakistan*, pp. 80, 84, 90, 154–6, 164.

[2] Hultzsch, *Corpus Inscriptionum Indicarum*, vol. i, p. xv.

[3] McCrindle (ed.). Ptolemy, *Ancient India*, pp. 230–1.

[4] Ibid., p. 225.

[5] Bloch, *Les Inscriptions d'Asoka*, p. 136.

[6] Ibid., p. 145.

the *Bṛhat Saṃhitā*.[1] By tradition the mountain is regarded as sacred both to brahmans and Jainas.[2] Its importance was increased by the fact that during the reign of Candragupta a dam was constructed on the Sudarśana lake in the neighbourhood of Girnār. The Rudradāman inscription informs us that the lake was originally built by Puṣyagupta the provincial governor of Candragupta.[3] Subsequently conduits were worked from it by Tuṣāspa in the reign of Aśoka. It refers to the town of Girinagar in the vicinity. It appears from the inscription of Skandagupta that the lake continued to supply water to the surrounding area until well into the Gupta period, eight hundred years later. Since it was the source of water for irrigation it must have been the focal point in the area. It is possible that in the Aśokan period the city of Girnār was closer to the lake than is the present site of Junāgadh, since it would have been more practical to build the city as near the water supply as possible. Thus the hill on which the inscription was engraved was the centre of considerable activity.

GUJARRA (Minor Rock Edict). Gujarra is located near Jhansi in the Datia district. It appears to have been on one of the more important routes from the Ganges valley to the west coast, possibly via Ujjain to Broach.

JAṬIṄGA-RĀMESHWAR (Minor Rock Edict). This site lies about three miles from Brahmagiri and the inscription belongs to the Mysore group. It might originally have been a place of religious interest since the inscription is within the precincts of the present Jaṭiṅga-Rāmeshwar temple.

JAUGAḌA (Major Rock Edicts, similar to the Dhauli version). The inclusion of the two Separate Edicts among the Jaugaḍa series would point to its being within Kaliṅga. It is now a ruined fort in the Behrampur *tāluka* of the Ganjam district. It is situated on the northern bank of the Rishikulya river. The two Separate Edicts are addressed to the *mahāmattas* of Samāpa, which was probably the name of the town in the Mauryan period. The area covered by the ruins would suggest that the town must have been a fairly large one, and the presence of the fort might point to its having been a military centre. Its proximity to the sea may have given it the added advantage of trade and maritime activities.

KĀLSI (Major Rock Edicts). The town of Kālsi lies at the junction of the Tons and Yamuna rivers, which in itself would give it religious significance. Recent excavations at the site have revealed a brick altar inscribed with Sanskrit verses placed almost opposite the rock inscription.[4] The altar

[1] XIV, 11.
[2] *Skanda Purāṇa*. Bastrapatha-mahāmatya, I, XI; Burgess, *Antiquities of Kathiawad and Kacch*, p. 175.
[3] Sircar, *Select Inscriptions* . . ., p. 169.
[4] *AI*, ix, p. 146.

marked the site of the fourth *aśvamedha* of King Śīlavarman during the third century A.D., indicating thereby that the site was of some significance during that period. The section of the Ganges plain lying between the foot-hills of the Himalayas and Delhi has always been a strategic area. It controls the entrance to the plain extending farther east. The main artery from north-west India to the east also runs through this region, a road system which was constantly maintained by Indian rulers and which until recent years was called the Grand Trunk Road. Kālsi being in the lower hills of the Himalayas was possibly the controlling centre of this area. It may also have bordered on the region inhabited by the Nābhaka tribes.

KANDAHAR (Bilingual Greek-Aramaic Inscription). The site of the inscription is Shar-i-Quna, the old city of Kandahar in southern Afghanistan. It grew to importance with the establishment of trade between the Hellenic world and north-west India after the campaigns of Alexander had established contact. Kandahar dominated the southern route from India to areas farther west.[1] The presence of a sizeable Greek-speaking population is attested to by the fact that the edict is in Greek as well as Aramaic.

LAMPAKA (Aramaic Inscription attributed to Aśoka). The Lampaka Aramaic Inscription now in the Kabul museum was found at the site of Lampaka or Lambaka in the neighbourhood of modern Laghman on the northern bank of the Kabul river near Jalalabad.[2] The inscription has been connected with the Aśokan period on the basis of the text referring to the setting up of a pillar inscription by *Devānampiya*.[3]

LAURIYĀ-ARĀRĀJ (Pillar Edicts I–VI). The pillar is situated at this site in northern Bihar. Its importance was probably due to the fact that the area was associated with Buddhism and consequently had a religious significance. It has also been suggested that the pillars in this region marked the course of the royal road from Pāṭaliputra to Nepal.[4]

LAURIYĀ-NANDANGARH (Pillar Edicts I–VI). This site is also in northern Bihar close to the village of Nandangarh and to the above site. Some funerary mounds have been discovered near the pillar which are believed to be of a pre-Buddhist period, and it has been suggested that these may have been the ancient *caityas* of the Vṛjjis referred to by the Buddha.[5] Recent excavations at one of these mounds produced a mixture of contents,

[1] See Ch. III.

[2] Cunningham, *Ancient Geography of India*, p. 49.

[3] Henning, *BSOAS*, vol. xiii, 1949, Part I, p. 80. Altheim, *Weltgeschichte Asiens in Griechischen Zeitalter*, I, pp. 25–43.

[4] Smith, *Asoka*, p. 120.

[5] Cunningham, *Ancient Geography of India*, p. 514; Udāna Commentary, pp. 233 ff.

including punch-marked coins, cast copper coins and terracotta figurines and clay sealings of the first century B.C.[1]

MAHĀSTHĀN (Pre-Aśokan Mauryan Inscription). The inscription was found at Mahāsthāngarh in the Bogra district of Bengal. The site was probably the headquarters of the local administrator (of the eastern section of the empire), its name during that period having been Puṇḍranagara, as is mentioned in the inscription. The *mahāmatta* of Puṇḍranagara is described as being in charge of measures for famine relief. So far, excavations at the site have revealed terracottas of the Śuṅga period.

MĀNSEHRĀ (Major Rock Edicts inscribed in Kharoṣṭhī). The site is that of a village in the Hazara district of the north-west province of Pakistan. The site lay on an important pilgrim route[2] and was on the main road running from the north-west frontier to Pāṭaliputra and beyond. It was probably also chosen because of its proximity to the northern border.

MASKI (Minor Rock Edict). Maski is located in the Raichur district of Hyderabad. An identification of Maski with Suvarṇagiri has been suggested but it is unacceptable as will be clear in the consideration of the location of Suvarṇagiri.[3]

NIGALI-SĀGAR (Pillar Inscription). The purpose of erecting a pillar at Nigali-Sāgar is clear from the inscription. It was originally situated near the *stūpa* of Buddha Konākamana to record first the enlargement of the *stūpa* and later Aśoka's visit to the site.[4] Hsüan Tsang writes that he saw the pillar at the site of the Konākamana *stūpa*, six miles from Kapilāvastu, and that the pillar was surmounted by a carved lion.[5] Neither the *stūpa* nor the lion have so far been found, since the pillar has been removed from its original site. It is now near Rummindei, within Nepalese territory.

PĀLKĪGUṆḌU (Minor Rock Edict). Pālkīguṇḍu lies at a distance of four miles from Gāvimath. This site again belongs to the group around Brahmagiri.

PĀṬALIPUTRA (it is mentioned in one of the edicts, but surprisingly no version of any of the edicts has been found in the neighbourhood). The identification of Pāṭaliputra is certain and its geographical importance is well known. It was the capital of the Mauryan empire and at the time of Aśoka had a long history going back three centuries to the rise of Magadha. It is referred to in literary sources both European and Indian and in the

[1] *AI*, ix, p. 148.
[2] McPhail, *Asoka*, p. 76.
[3] See p. 236.
[4] Bloch, *Les Inscriptions d'Asoka*, p. 158.
[5] Watters, *On Yuan Chwang's Travels in India*, vol. ii, pp. 6–7.

edicts of Aśoka.[1] Extensive excavations have shown that the city existed in certain sites in and around modern Patna, probably by the river, the course of which has changed somewhat through the centuries. These excavations have unearthed the wooden palisade which surrounded the city of Pāṭaliputra and which was mentioned by Megasthenes.[2] The pillared hall of the palace, similar in many ways to that of Persepolis and the *ārogya vihāra* (sanatorium) have also been found, including various smaller objects such as beads, terracottas, coins, and pottery of a type usually associated with the Mauryan period.

RAJULA-MAṆḌAGIRI (Minor Rock Edict). This site is included in the southern group of inscriptions not far from Yeṟṟaguḍi.

RĀMPŪRVĀ (Pillar Edicts I–VI). Rāmpūrvā is located thirty-two miles north of Bettiah in northern Bihar. This area between the Ganges and the Himalayas, being extremely fertile, was no doubt heavily populated and would thus be a good region for edicts. In addition many of the places sacred to Buddhism were in this area, and probably attracted pilgrims from all over the country.

RUMMINDEI (Pillar Inscription). The Rummindei Pillar stands near the shrine of Rummindei just within the border of Nepal. The pillar was erected by Aśoka to commemorate the birth-place of the Buddha, the Lumbinī grove. It is thought that the pillar locates the actual place, Rummindei being the modern name for Lumbinī.[3] According to Hsüan Tsang the pillar had a horse capital which had been struck by lightning, and the pillar itself had broken in the middle.[4] Today the lower shaft of the pillar still stands, the upper part having been split into two. There is no trace of the capital.

RŪPANĀTH (Minor Rock Edict). The location of Rūpanāth is on the Kaimur hills near Saleemabad in Madhya Pradesh. The existence of a *liṅga* now makes it a sacred place to Śaivites. It may have been of religious importance even in the Aśokan period visited by Hindu pilgrims. It was probably also along an important route. The route from Allahabad (Prayāga) to Broach must certainly have passed via Rūpanāth. From Allahabad there is a rise over the Kaimur hills. Thence to Jabulpur would be a fairly easy stretch along the top of the plateau. Jabulpur lies close to the Narmada

[1] Strabo, XV, 1, 36; Arrian, *Indica*, X; Bloch, *Les Inscriptions d'Asoka*, p. 104.

[2] Waddell, *Discovery of the Exact Site of Aśoka's Classic Capital at Pātaliputra*, p. 63; *AI*. vol. ix, p. 146; Strabo, XV, 1, 35, 36.

[3] Cunningham, *Ancient Geography of India*, p. 711.

[4] Watters, *On Yuan Chwang's Travels in India*, vol. ii, p. 14.

and from here the route has merely to follow the valley of the Narmada, arriving directly at Broach. An alternative route to Jabulpur may have been from Pāṭaliputra following the hills. This would explain in part the importance of Sahasrām.

SĀHASRĀM (Minor Rock Edict). It is located in the Shahabad district of Bihar not far from the river Son, and ninety miles south-west of Patna. The site of the inscription is not far from the modern town of Sahasrām. The edge of the Kaimur hills extends as far as this point. The existence of a town here would confirm our view that there was a route from Patna, up the Son valley, across the plateau to Jubbalpur and then down the Narmada valley to Broach. Sahasrām would then be an important town on the northern edge of the plateau, the outpost of Magadha before the rather uncertain journey across the plateau.

SANCHI (Schism Edict). The modern name of Sanchi was given to the site at a comparatively late period, since it was known as Kākanāḍaboṭa, from the Buddhist period until that of the Guptas.[1] The fragmentary surviving inscription addressed to the *dhamma-mahāmattas* and undoubtedly the *Saṃgha*, would point to Sanchi being an important Buddhist centre even in the Aśokan period. It is apparent from archaeological evidence that the *stūpa* was enlarged and encased in its present covering during the Śuṅga period.[2] No doubt the nearness of Sanchi to Ujjain gave it added importance. It is located near Bhopal, a few miles from Bhilsa, believed to be the ancient Vidiśā.

SĀRNĀTH (Pillar Inscription, Schism Edict addressed to the *mahāmattas*). The location of Sārnāth is three and a half miles from Banares. This pillar is situated in a place of immense importance to the Buddhists, since it was at Sārnāth that Buddha preached his first sermon. There appears to have been an important monastery at Sārnāth to the monks of which this edict was also directed. Hsüan Tsang writes that he saw the pillar carrying the inscription in front of a *stūpa* said to have been built by Aśoka.[3] Apart from its religious importance, Sārnāth was an important centre of trade.[4] Being on the banks of the Ganges it had a fair control over river traffic, which in those days of small boats, and not many roads must have been of a considerable magnitude, despite the fact that the town lay so far up the

[1] Cunningham, *Bhilsa Topes*, pp. 183, 241, 347; Fleet, *Corpus Inscriptionum Indicarum*, vol. iii, p. 31.

[2] *History and Culture of the Indian People*, vol. ii, p. 488.

[3] Watters, *On Yuan Chwang's Travels in India*, vol. ii, pp. 46 ff.

[4] *Aṅguttara Nikāya*, i, p. 213; *Jātakas*, iv, p. 342.

river. Its position midway between Prayāga (Allahabad) and Pāṭaliputra (Patna), meant that it must have acted as a point of exchange for goods coming from either place. It appears to have been included among the towns reached by the main road running from the north-west to Pāṭaliputra.

SHAHBĀZGARHI (Major Rock Edicts, inscribed in *Kharoṣṭhi*). The position of this site is near Mardan in the Yusufzai area of Peshawar. An attempt has been made to identify it with Arrian's description of Bazaria or Bazira.[1] According to Hsüan Tsang who calls it Po-lu-sha, the town was constructed on the ruins of an ancient stone-built city, which would confirm Arrian's description.[2] The area around Shahbāzgarhi has not yet been excavated, therefore there is no confirmation from archaeological sources. If there was a town at this site during the Aśokan period, as seems very probable, it was regarded as a frontier town, although not actually on the frontier, with an importance similar to modern frontier towns such as Peshawar. It would also have been linked to the main highway.

SIDDĀPUR (Minor Rock Edict). Siddāpur lies one mile to the west of Brahmagiri, and three miles south of the location of the Jaṭiṅga-Rāmeshwar inscription. This group of inscriptions may have marked the southern boundary of the empire, in addition to their importance from other points of view which we have already considered.

SOHGAURĀ (Copper-plate Inscription of the Mauryan period). Sohgaurā is located in the Gorakhpur district of Uttar Pradesh.

SOPĀRĀ (Major Rock Edict. Fragment of the 8th Edict). Sopārā situated in the Thāna district of Bombay is the site of an ancient sea-port and town, which no doubt was of importance during the reign of Aśoka. It has been identified with the Soupara of Ptolemy, described as a commercial centre.[3] Its ancient name was Suppāraka.[4] Sopārā was an advantageous position for an inscription since being a sea-port, the edicts would be read by a constant stream of people coming and going. Furthermore, foreigners visiting the port would thus be made acquainted with the *Dhamma* of Aśoka.

SUVARṆAGIRI (Minor Rock Edict). Suvarṇagiri is the modern town of Kanakagiri south of Maski in Hyderabad. The word means 'golden mountain' and this has been connected with the ancient gold-mining area

[1] *Anabasis*, IV, 27, 28.

[2] Watters, *On Yuan Chwang's Travels in India*, vol. i, p. 217.

[3] *Ancient India*, I, 6; quoted McCrindle, pp. 39, 40.

[4] *Brahma Purāṇa*, XXVII, 58.

in Raichur which to this day shows traces of ancient gold workings. Suvarṇagiri was the capital of the southern province of the empire.

TĀMRALIPTI. This Mauryan sea-port is generally identified with the modern Tamluk in the Midnapur district of Bengal. It was the principal port on the mouth of the Ganges. The chronicles from Ceylon refer to it as Tāmalitti.[1] Fa-hsien writes that he embarked from Tāmralipti for Ceylon.[2] Hsüan Tsang records having seen some *stūpas* built by Aśoka at the same site.[3] Apart from the sea traffic it controlled the river traffic going up the Ganges. Evidence of Mauryan occupation of Tāmluk is available from archaeological remains as well.[4]

TAXILA. Taxila is mentioned frequently in the literary sources on the Aśokan period. It was the capital of the northern province and one of the main cities of the empire. Archaeological remains indicate a high degree of craft and culture. The importance of Taxila can be accounted for by various reasons. Its long history of contact with regions to the west resulted in its becoming a cosmopolitan centre. It was noted as a place of learning and was the residence of well-known teachers.[5] It was the meeting point of three major trade routes, the royal highway from Pāṭaliputra, the north-western route through Bactria, Kāpiśa, and Puṣkalāvatī (Peshawar), and the route from Kashmir and Central Asia, via Śrinagar, Mānsehrā, and the Haripur valley.[6] When the sea traffic with the West increased, the land route through Bactria and Peshawar became less important and this was one of the factors which led later to the decline of Taxila.

UJJAIN. Ujjain was the capital of the western province of the empire. Apart from its political importance, it was, similar to Taxila, the meeting point of many routes. It was connected with the ports on the western coast, particularly Broach and Sopārā and controlled much of the trade that passed through these ports. Some of the southern routes terminated at Ujjain, which was in turn linked with Pāṭaliputra. Ptolemy refers to it as Ozene.[7] It was a Buddhist centre during the Mauryan period and judging by the importance of its monasteries, had a long history as such.[8] An excavation of a mound at Kumhar Tekri four miles north-east of Ujjain, reveals that it was a burial-cum-cremation ground dating back to before the

[1] *Mahāvaṃsa*, XI, 38; *Dīpavaṃsa*, III, 33.

[2] Giles, *The Travels of Fa-hsien*, p. 65.

[3] Watters, *On Yuan Chwang's Travels in India*, vol. ii, p. 189.

[4] *AI*, ix, p. 155.

[5] Fick, *The Social Organization in North-East India in Buddha's Time*, p. 200.

[6] Marshall, *Taxila*, i, vol. p. 1.

[7] Ptolemy, *Ancient India*, 63; quoted McCrindle, pp. 154–5.

[8] *Mahāvaṃsa*, XIII, 5; XXIX, 35.

third century B.C.[1] Hsüan Tsang writes that not far from Ujjain was a *stūpa* constructed on the site where Aśoka had built a 'Hell'.[2]

YER̲R̲AGUḌI (Major Rock Edicts and Minor Rock Edict). Yer̲r̲aguḍi is situated eight miles from Gooty on the southern border of the Kurnool district, and is eighty miles north-east of Siddāpur. Clearly it was a site of some significance since both the Major and the Minor Edicts are to be found here. No remains of a town have yet been discovered in the area, but it is possible that a frontier town may have existed at the site, with a route leading through it to the south Indian kingdoms.

[1] *AI*, ix, p. 160.
[2] Watters, *On Yuan Chwang's Travels in India*, vol. ii, p. 250; see Ch. II.

APPENDIX IV

POTTERY AND COINS OF THE MAURYAN PERIOD

Pottery

One of the methods of determining the date of a level at an excavation is by an analysis of the pottery found on the site. Thus, levels of habitation dating to the Mauryan period are revealed in excavations by the presence of common objects such as pottery, associated with that period. A study of pottery for purposes of dating is made on the basis both of material used and the form of the pot. The remains can either occur as complete vessels or as potsherds.

The pottery associated with the Mauryan period consists of many types of ware. The most highly developed technique is seen in the Northern Black Polished ware (to which we shall refer from now on as N.B.P.). Various types of coarse red and grey ware also occur. The N.B.P. ware is made of finely levigated clay, which when seen in section is usually of a grey and sometimes of a red hue.[1] It has a brilliantly burnished dressing of the quality of a glaze which ranges in colour from a jet black to a deep grey or a metallic steel blue. Occasionally small red-brown patches are apparent on the surface. It can be distinguished from other polished or graphite-coated red wares by its peculiar lustre and brilliance. This ware was used largely for dishes and small bowls.

In the Ganges valley where it is found in great abundance, it is sometimes difficult to use it in determining the date of the levels, since some of the sherds are rain washed. The original place of manufacture of this ware has not as yet been ascertained, though more recent opinion tends to place it in the central Ganges basin in the neighbourhoods of Kauśāmbī and Patna.[2] This hypothesis is based on the thick distribution and abundant occurrence of the ware in this area. It has been suggested that eastern Rajasthan, western, central and eastern India all imported this ware in some quantity either through traders or pilgrims.[3] The mass production and export of pottery is referred to in a literary source, which may well relate to the Mauryan period.[4] The Kauśāmbī area would certainly be a

[1] *AI*, i, p. 55. Wheeler and Krishna Deva.
[2] Ibid., ix, p. 142.
[3] Ibid., p. 119.
[4] A Jaina work, the *Uvāsaga Dasāo,* VI, pp. 163 ff.

suitable place from which to export the ware. Although N.B.P. was not so rare, it was obviously a more expensive ware than the other varieties, since potsherds of N.B.P. ware are occasionally found riveted with copper pins indicating that even a cracked vessel in N.B.P. ware had its value.

The ceramic technique of producing this ware has not yet been fully analysed. Nor is it certain how the process came to be used in India, whether it was a technique learnt from the Greeks or whether it was known in India before the coming of the Greeks. The Greek black ware which Marshall claims to have found in Taxila has a lustrous quality not entirely dissimilar to the N.B.P. ware. Evidence of N.B.P. ware in the form of sherds at Bhir Mound in Taxila, dating to *c.* 300 B.C., suggests that it may have been in use prior to the coming of the Greeks. During more recent excavations at Bhir Mound, a coin of Alexander was found at the Greek level. But N.B.P. sherds were found lower down.[1] This would suggest that N.B.P. ware was used before the invasion of Alexander. It is, however, just possible that these sherds may be strays from an upper level. The matter can be decided only by further and more extensive excavations in the area. Even more important is the fact that this ware does not occur in Taxila, even at later levels, with the same abundance as in the Ganges valley.

At Rājgīr, N.B.P. ware was found together with a plain black ware, throughout the Mauryan level.[2] The shapes of both wares were similar, the only difference between the two wares being that the black ware was not treated with the coating that was responsible for the gloss in N.B.P. ware. Here the N.B.P. ware consisted largely of dishes and of bowls with limited rim forms.

Most of the other ware found at Mauryan levels tends to be grey or red. At Śiśupālgarh during a recent excavation, Period I, which is dated to 300–200 B.C., revealed a plain ware dull grey or red, occasionally polished.[3] It showed evidence of a well developed technique of firing. Fragments of N.B.P. ware were also found. A later level of Period II A, dated to 200 B.C.–A.D. 100, showed a more developed type of pottery with applied and incised decoration, and a greater amount of N.B.P. ware.

Excavations at Ahicchatra produced a tremendous variety of pottery at Mauryan level.[4] In Stratum VIII, dated to 300–200 B.C., both plain and decorated grey and red ware were found. The plain ware of this period can be distinguished from earlier ware in that it is more heavy and lighter in colour. Occasional pieces show the use of a slip. The red ware is largely in the form of jar-like vessels with thin walls and a light body, evidence of a

[1] *AI*, x, p. 23.
[2] Ibid., vii, p. 71.
[3] Ibid., v, p. 79.
[4] Ibid., i, p. 43.

developed technique. In shape though, these jars do not have a well defined neck. More characteristic vessels of this period were also found fired to a dark buff colour. These consisted of two varieties. One was a jar with the neck rising from the shoulder and ending in a flat horizontal rim. The other type, shaped rather like a modern *hāṇḍi* with a very low rim or no rim at all, was apparently a cooking vessel. The more unusual pottery found at this stratum at Ahicchatrā was the decorated ware. Of this the most important type for our purposes, is one that has a stamped taurine design, a design which becomes more common during the next period. This consists of four conjoined taurines with a central prong, a design very similar to that found on the punch-marked coins of that period. The same design was found in the same stratum on grey terracotta figurines. We shall consider it in detail further in this appendix when the design of the punch-marked coins is discussed.

It is significant that from the excavations carried out so far there is no evidence of N.B.P. ware in southern India. It would seem that the ware was used not only largely within the confines of the Mauryan empire but more commonly in the Ganges valley than elsewhere. At the conclusion of this appendix we have listed the names of sites which we believe were inhabited during the Mauryan period. We have used as our evidence, the archaeological discovery of N.B.P. ware and punch-marked coins. We are aware that this is not precise evidence. The use of N.B.P. ware was not limited to the Mauryan period. It was used possibly earlier and certainly at a later date. All that we can say at this stage is that the frequent use of this ware appears to have been a Mauryan feature. Furthermore it is usually found in greater abundance in the Mauryan levels.

Punch-marked Coins

The term punch-marked coins generally refers to early Indian coins, largely silver, with a few copper coins as well, which are in fact pieces of metal in various shapes, sizes, and weights and which have one or more symbols punched on them. Uninscribed cast copper coins with similar symbols have also been found on occasion together with silver punch-marked coins.[1] The most common symbols on these coins are the elephant, the tree-in-railing symbol, and the mountain.

Before examining the punch-marked coins in India, we may briefly mention a few of the varieties of coins of foreign provenance discovered at Indian sites. It has been suggested that some early Persian coins, largely

[1] Allan, *Catalogue of the Coins of Ancient India*, p. lxxiv.

sigloi of Darius were in circulation in the Panjab, from *c.* 500–331 B.C.[1] Some of the silver *sigloi* bear counter-marks similar to Indian punch marks and some bear characters in *Brāhmī* and *Kharoṣṭhī*. This would suggest that there was a period when the *sigloi* and the punch-marked coins were in circulation together. The first coin of those issued by Alexander and found in India, was a copper coin roughly square in shape, bearing the legend *ΑΛΕΞΑΝΔΡΟΥ*.[2] Marshall discovered two silver *tetradrachms* of Alexander in Bhir Mound at Taxila.[3] One of them bears the legend *ΒΑΣΙΛΕΩΣ ΑΛΕΞΑΝΔΡΟΥ*. They were both found at the level dated to the third or fourth century B.C. From the same stratum a silver coin of Philip Aridaeus was also found. This has been dated to *c.* 317 B.C. These three coins were found in a hoard containing silver punch-marked coins, bent-bar Indian coins and a Persian *siglos*.

Another type of Greek coin which influenced the coinage of north-western India in the fourth century B.C., was the Athenian 'owl'. The originals were silver coins of a varied range, though usually *tetradrachms*. The owl was sacred to Pallas Athene the deity of the city. This symbol was also used on the handles of wine jars to indicate Athenian wine. These coins were of immense importance in the commerce of the Mediterranean region and farther east, and it is believed that the reasons for the imitations minted in north-western India, was largely that of facilitating trade.[4] Of the Indian imitations some were exact reproductions and in other cases the owl was replaced by an eagle.

A further group of silver coins influenced by Greek coins though thought to be minted in India, are the coins of Sophytes. He is generally identified with the Sopheithes mentioned by Arrian and Strabo,[5] and who is said to have ruled the region of the Salt Range in the Panjab during the period of Alexander's campaign. The identification of Sophytes is not certain. The coins bear the legend, *ΣΩΦΥΤΟΥ*. Unfortunately none have yet been found at Indian sites. Their close affinity to the imitation Athenian owls tends to strengthen the probability of their being an issue of Sophytes, the Indian king, who perhaps intended them largely for purposes of trade. The coins of Sophytes are also linked with certain Seleucid coins, suggesting the influence of the one upon the other. The elephant has been found as the symbol on some Seleucid coins. This may have been in commemoration of the Maurya-Seleucid alliance, when the Seleucids received five hundred elephants from the Mauryas.[6]

[1] Rapson, *Indian Coins*, p. 3. [2] Ibid., p. 4.

[3] *Archaeological Survey Report*, 1924–25, pp. 47, 48, pl. ix.

[4] Rapson, *Indian Coins*, p. 3.

[5] N. Sastri, *The Age of the Nandas and Mauryas*, p. 126; VI 2, 2; Strabo, XV, 699.

[6] Rapson, *Indian Coins*, p. 4; Babelon. *Rois de Syrie . . .*, pl. 1, 15.

It was against this background of foreign and foreign inspired coins that the punch-marked coins came into circulation. The technique of producing such coins was generally that the metal was cut first and then the device was punched. Amongst some of these coins however the symbol is half off the metal, suggesting that the coins were cut after the metal had been punched, or that the punching was done carelessly. Curiously in one group, the reverse symbol  is regular and complete, only the obverse is incomplete.[1] This would point to the regular symbol being that of a central authority. It was probably punched on to an entire sheet of metal which was then cut into coin shapes. The other symbol, sometimes not complete, may have been that of a subsidiary body, through whose hands the coins went into circulation.

Discussing the punch-marked coins, Allan believes that the tradition about the wealth of the Nandas may have arisen because they were the first dynasty to have issued coins on a large scale.[2] Since many of the earliest finds were located at Paila, Set Mahet and Gorakhpur, it is possible that this area was the region of their origin. Allan suggests that punch-marked coins were not long in existence, because in the second century B.C. they rapidly gave way to struck coins. Perhaps the idea of such a coinage was based on the Persian *sigloi* and was used in India in the late fifth or early fourth century B.C. Allan is convinced that they were issued by a government, because they appear to have been minted in a regular series. For instance the sun and the six-armed symbol are quite regular, and may have been symbols of a king and a high official. The variation of the symbol on the reverse is explained by its being the symbol of a district or local ruler. He makes the ingenious suggestion that the five symbols on the obverse represent five controlling organizations, possibly similar to the committees mentioned by Megasthenes. On the question of some coins bearing counter-marks or what have been called shroff marks, he suggests that these may have been earlier coins which were reissued.

Walsh who has also made a detailed study of this coinage suggests that the symbols are continuations of the seal designs from Mohenjo-daro.[3] This continuation appears to exist more in the idea than in the actual design. At the moment there is little or no evidence to suggest that the unbroken continuation of the tradition of this design from Mohenjo-daro to the Mauryan period, a continuation which would be necessary for the designs on the seals to be regarded as the prototypes of the devices of the

[1] Allan, *Catalogue of Indian Coins*, Class I, Group 1.

[2] Ibid., p. lxxxi.

[3] *Archaeological Survey of India, Memoirs*, No. 59, p. 20.

punch-marked coins. A number of views have been expressed on dating these coins to a period considerably earlier than the fourth century B.C., but again the evidence is not sufficient.[1]

Durga Prasad dates the coins to the Mauryan period on the basis of the following arguments.[2] The coins with the  symbol, when tested chemically, appear to have the same alloy content as the amount suggested in the *Arthaśāstra.* Furthermore, a similar symbol occurs in the Sohgaurā copper plate, and this inscription is generally accepted as being of the Mauryan period. That these symbols were not shroff marks is suggested by the *Arthaśāstra.* A passage in the text reads that coins were minted for the state for two purposes, for hoarding in the treasury and for use in commercial transactions. Thus they would be punched by the state and there would be no necessity for shroff marks.

The Taxila hoard of silver punch-marked coins, and other punch-marked coins from excavations at Taxila have been discussed by Marshall.[3] He is in general agreement with Walsh that the symbols and marks may be connected with the Harappā culture seals. Of the copper coinage he states that it was the coinage of Taxila, because of its abundance at Sirkap levels and its comparative rarity at Bhir Mound. This local coinage continued to be struck for some time after the Greek invasion and possibly after the Śaka conquest too. In interpreting the symbols he states for example, that  represents the Dharmarājika *stūpa.* The shape ∪ symbolizes 'the horns of divinity', an idea which occurs on prehistoric seals as well. This is too imaginative an interpretation. The symbol of the *stūpa,* if that was in fact what was intended would have been indicated in a more conventional design. As regards the date of this coinage, Marshall writes that more than half of the 'long-bar' variety and the 'round concave' type were found in Strata III and IV, which would suggest the fourth or fifth centuries B.C. Thus punch-marked coins must have been first issued in about 400 B.C. These coins were also found in small numbers at the Sirkap levels, therefore the circulation continued, even though the minting of the coins may have stopped with the break up of the Mauryan empire. The Bhir Mound produced two large hoards, mainly of silver punch-marked coins. Thus it would seem that there was a greater circulation of silver coins during the Mauryan period, but in the post-Mauryan period copper coinage was more extensively used at Taxila.

More recently Kosambi has worked on punch-marked coins. He has

[1] Decourdemanche, *JA,* xix, 1912, pp. 17 ff.; Kennedy, *JRAS,* 1898, pp. 279 ff.; Smith, *IG,* ii, p. 183; Rapson, *Indian Coins,* p. 2.

[2] *JASB,* xxx, Num. Sup., pp. 40–45.

[3] *Taxila,* ii, pp. 846, 756 ff.

examined a series of coins and has made a metallurgical analysis.[1] His analysis is based on the idea that handling a coin causes an erosion of the metal. This results in a loss of weight. If, therefore, the amount of weight lost in circulation can be measured, it may be possible to calculate the date of the coin. This method can be regarded as valid if the original weight of the coin is known. In the case of the punch-marked coins there is no certainty as to their original weight. Furthermore since the hoarding of coins was a common practice in those times, calculations of the date on the basis of erosion may not always be reliable. Although this method may indicate the number of years during which the coin was in circulation, the date of the coin would still have to be determined by the consideration of other factors as well. Nevertheless such a metallurgical analysis is of great interest, and in any attempt to date these coins one must consider a combination of various possible methods.

On the interpretation of the symbols, Kosambi has suggested that the sun symbol ✲ is the symbol of sovereignty, as also is the *ṣaḍaracakra* ✵. The crescent on arches ♎ is a Mauryan symbol and is often associated with the *ṣaḍaracakra*. According to him each symbol is associated with a ruler. The fourth mark in the cluster of symbols is the personal signet of the king, because there are about nine such variations. The fifth mark is that of the issuing minister. The symbols with human figures and without the *cakra* indicate coins of the tribal oligarchies. He does not accept any of the marks as the symbol of the mint. He believes that the later Mauryan coins suffered debasement as compared with the earlier coins from the Taxila hoard. This is explained by suggesting that possibly the new areas that were included in the empire had a debased currency which was allowed to circulate by the Mauryas. The symbol θθθ, three ovals and a tangent he maintains is an Aśokan symbol since it occurs most often, suggesting a long reign, and it also sometimes occurs on the coins which Kosambi believes were issued by Bindusāra. The peacock on arches he believes to be a symbol of Bindusāra, and states that it originates from the totem of the peacock associated with the Mauryas.

Further research was carried out on the subject by Dani, who has refuted many of Marshall's suggestions on the two hoards found at Taxila.[2] The larger hoard at Bhir Mound is dated by two gold coins of Alexander and one coin of Philip Aridaeus, as we have already seen, to *c.* 317 B.C. The smaller hoard is dated by a coin of Diodotus to *c.* 248 B.C. The presence of Hellenistic objects at what Dani calls 'phase B' at Bhir Mound, suggests the

[1] *JBBRAS*, xxiv-xxv, Num. Sup., 1948–49.

[2] *JNSI*, xvii, Part II, 1955, pp. 27 ff.

influence of the Indo-Bactrians over Taxila, towards the end of the Mauryan period. It is at about this time that local Taxilan coins begin to appear in large numbers. Dani continues to explain that the bar coins are not found elsewhere on the site, and suggests that they come from the Ganges-Yamunā area. Furthermore a necklace from the larger hoard tallies with beads from Sirkap. Therefore he suggests that the hoard is not pre-Mauryan. Although it is not earlier than 317 B.C. it can in fact be much later, since the Greek coins may have been hoarded. Nor is the larger hoard earlier in burial than the smaller, as Marshall asserts. Both hoards of coins occur in 'phase B' of Bhir Mound and the associated objects show that there was no great difference in the time of the burial of the two hoards. Thus the hoards would appear to be post-Mauryan, and consequently the evidence from Taxila should not be held to prove the pre-Mauryan existence of punch-marked coins. Dani adds that the local currency in Taxila was bar coins, which occur in what he terms 'phase A' in Bhir Mound. This analysis would suggest that the punch-marked coins were first minted by the Mauryas. Possibly bar coins were in circulation before the Mauryan period.

Apart from the silver punch-marked coins, there are examples of the bent-bar silver coins. These according to Allan were struck on a Persian standard and probably represented the double *sigloi* or staters.[1] They appear to have been earlier than the punch-marked coins, since there were none in the smaller hoard at Taxila, generally believed to be of the time of the later Mauryas, owing to the presence of the Diodotus coin dated to 248 B.C. Omphis is said to have made a present of 200 talents of silver to Alexander, which Allan believes was probably made in this form of coinage. He suggests that this coinage came to an end soon after the event mentioned above. Punch-marked copper coins are much rarer than the silver variety. Most of these coins have five symbols on the obverse and four on the reverse.[2] The silver variety generally have one symbol on the obverse and about five on the reverse.

Because of the close connection between the Mauryas and Buddhism, it was to be expected that the marks on the coins would at some stage be described as Buddhist symbols. Foucher is of this opinion.[3] The elephant and the bull which appear as symbols on the coins, represent according to him the traditional symbols of the Buddha's conception and the zodiacal sign of his birth, Taurus. This is a doubtful interpretation, since there is no very good evidence that the twelve constellation zodiac was used in

[1] *Catalogue of Indian Coins*, pp. 2, 3.
[2] Ibid., p. lxxviii.
[3] *Beginnings of Buddhist Art*, pp. 20 ff.

India at this time. Coins with the horse and the lion, the other two traditional symbols, have not been found so far. Foucher describes the *ṣaḍara-cakra* symbol as a variant on the lotus symbol of the birth, when the child took seven steps and at each step a lotus sprang up. The tree-in-railing symbol represents the *saṃbodhi*. The arches he takes as variants on the *stūpa* or tumulus symbol. There are , , , signifying the *stūpa*, crossed by the *yaṣṭi* or staff, with a *chatra* or parasol on top.

Owing to the absence of a legend on these coins our estimate of their date must rest largely on the significance of their symbols and whatever knowledge a scientific analysis can provide. We believe that coins were in circulation in the pre-Mauryan period. Probably the earlier coins were the bent-bar variety, the punch-marked coins coming into use later under the Mauryas. Coins were used extensively as a medium of exchange and as legal tender. This fact is corroborated by the *Arthaśāstra* which lists the above as the purpose of money.[1] The same text mentions two main types of coins. One is the silver coin or *paṇa* which has a range of 1, $\frac{1}{2}$, $\frac{1}{4}$ and $\frac{1}{8}$. The other is the copper coin called *māṣika*, which again has a similar range, the quarter piece being called *kākiṇī*. Gold coins are also mentioned, but these appear to have been very special issues which were hardly in circulation, since most transactions are paid for and salaries are given in the silver currency of the *paṇa*.[2] Even the extremely high salaries of senior officials are stated in *paṇas* and not in the gold coins. Punch-marked coins exist only in silver and copper, and the latter are rare. This is but natural since the silver coins are available to us largely through hoards. The copper coins being smaller in value were no doubt used very widely, whereas the silver coins, being of greater value, tended to be hoarded. If copper coins in some quantity should be found in the future lying scattered in a site under excavation, then Kosambi's metallurgical analysis would no doubt produce interesting results when applied to them.

It appears from the *Arthaśāstra* that there was a well organized mint, the officers of which carefully supervised the contents of the coins (which are stated in detail), and guarded against the possibilities of counterfeiting.[3] Judging by the descriptions and remarks concerning commercial transactions, fines, revenue, etc., it is apparent that money was handled with experience at this period, and a money economy was a familiar idea. This would suggest that punch-marked coinage was not the first type of coinage used in the area. We agree with Allan's view that the bent-bar silver coins preceded punch-marked coins and were therefore in use in the pre-

[1] II, 12.
[2] II, 5.
[3] Ibid.

Mauryan period. This fact is also borne out by the two Taxila hoards. The one containing the Philip Aridaeus coin dating to *c.* 317 B.C. also contained bent-bar coins. The smaller hoard containing the Diodotus coin of 248 B.C., even though it may have been buried at the end of the Mauryan period, does not contain any bent-bar coins, indicating thereby that they were out of circulation by then. The punch-marked coins, being easier to handle, probably replaced the bent-bar coins early in the Mauryan period.

The coins were issued by a central authority, probably the imperial mints situated perhaps in the five major cities of the empire. We do not accept the idea that these coins were traders' tokens which gradually acquired the status of a national coinage. The symbols possibly had some connection with local commerce, or local administration, but there again the symbol was probably passed on to the mint and became incorporated with other marks of royal authority. It is possible that, since commerce was at a comparatively nascent stage, local traders preferred a local symbol amongst others in order that they could differentiate between money minted in their own area and that of other areas. Thus though the issuing authority would be solely the royal mint, the symbols on the coins would represent, apart from the royal and dynastic symbols, various institutes such as the guilds, or administrative units such as the provinces.

The complicated problem connected with the punch-marked coins is to unravel the meaning of the symbols. The peacock on arches seems most certainly to be a symbol of the Mauryan dynasty. The connection has already been made in the past between the symbol of the crescent on arches and the name Candragupta, 'protected by the moon'. This is depicted by representing the moon against a background of hills. Bindusāra we believe may be represented by this symbol . Again the idea is linked with the meaning of his name, the stretching out or extension of a dot or particle. Similarly the sun symbol  and the *ṣaḍaracakra* may both be variants of this symbol. The Aśoka symbol seems most obviously the tree-in-railing, representing the Aśoka tree. The symbol of  which Kosambi believes to be Aśokan can only be attributed to Aśoka on the basis of its occurring more frequently than any other. On some coins it occurs with the *ṣaḍaracakra* which, if we accept it as the mark of Bindusāra, implies the restamping of Bindusāra's coins, during the reign of Aśoka, or possibly the issuing of coins from Ujjain when Aśoka was viceroy during the reign of Bindusāra.

We shall conclude this appendix by giving a list of places where N.B.P. ware or punch-marked coins were found during excavations, suggesting thereby that these places were inhabited during the Mauryan period.

These sites include the following, Amarāvati, Ahicchatrā, Atranji Kheda, Bahal, Bairāṭ, Bāngarh, Basarh, Bhīṭa, Buxar, Giriak, Hastināpur, Jhūsi, Kasrawādh, Kauśāmbī, Maheshwar, Mathurā, Masaon, Nāsik, Piprāwa, Patna, Rājghāṭa, Rājgīr, Rairh, Rupar, Sambhar, Sanchi, Sārnāth, Taxila, and Tripuri.

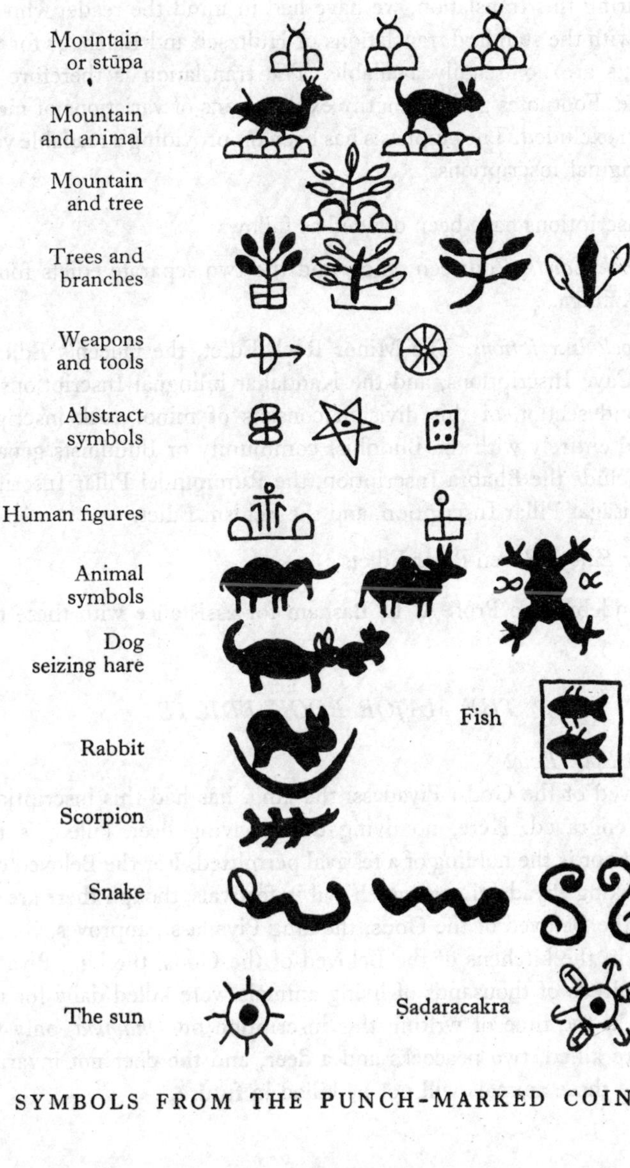

SYMBOLS FROM THE PUNCH-MARKED COINS

APPENDIX V

A TRANSLATION OF THE EDICTS OF AŚOKA

In preparing this translation, we have had in mind the reader who is not familiar with the standard translations of Hultzsch and Bloch, or for whom these texts are not readily available. The translation is therefore not a literal one. Footnotes giving lengthy explanations of variations of meaning have been excluded. The emphasis has been on providing a readable version of the original inscriptions.

The inscriptions have been divided as follows:

Major Rock Edicts. Fourteen edicts and the two separate edicts found at sites in Kaliṅga.

Minor Rock Inscriptions. The Minor Rock Edict, the Queen's Edict, the Barābar Cave Inscriptions, and the Kandahar bilingual Inscriptions.
A second section of this division consists of minor rock inscriptions concerned entirely with the Buddhist community or Buddhists generally. These include the Bhabra Inscription, the Rummindei Pillar Inscription, the Nigalisāgar Pillar Inscription, and the Schism Edict.

The Pillar Edicts. Seven Pillar Edicts.

I am indebted to Prof. A. L. Basham for assistance with these translations.

THE MAJOR ROCK EDICTS

1st Major Rock Edict

The Beloved of the Gods, Piyadassi the king, has had this inscription on *Dhamma* engraved. Here, no living thing having been killed, is to be sacrificed; nor is the holding of a festival permitted. For the Beloved of the Gods, the king Piyadassi, sees much evil in festivals, though there are some of which the Beloved of the Gods, the king Piyadassi, approves.
Formerly in the kitchens of the Beloved of the Gods, the king Piyadassi, many hundreds of thousands of living animals were killed daily for meat. But now, at the time of writing this inscription on *Dhamma*, only three animals are killed, two peacocks and a deer, and the deer not invariably. Even these three animals will not be killed in future.

2nd Major Rock Edict

Everywhere in the empire of the Beloved of the Gods, the king Piyadassi, and even in the lands on its frontiers, those of the Coḷas, Pāṇḍyas, Satyāputras, Keralaputras, and as far as Ceylon, and of the Greek king named Antiochus and of those kings who are neighbours of that Antiochus, everywhere the two medical services of the Beloved of the Gods, the king Piyadassi, have been provided. These consist of the medical care of man and the care of animals. Medicinal herbs whether useful to man or to beast, have been brought and planted wherever they did not grow; similarly, roots and fruit have been brought and planted wherever they did not grow. Along the roads wells have been dug and trees planted for the use of men and beasts.

3rd Major Rock Edict

Thus speaks the Beloved of the Gods, the king Piyadassi: When I had been consecrated twelve years I commanded as follows: Everywhere in my empire, the *yuktas* [subordinate officers] with the *rājūkas* [rural administrators] and the *prādeśikas* [heads of the districts], shall go on tour every five years, in order to instruct people in the *Dhamma* as well as for other purposes. It is good to be obedient to one's mother and father, friends and relatives, to be generous to brahmans and *śramaṇas*, it is good not to kill living beings, it is good not only to spend little, but to own the minimum of property. The council will instruct the officials to record the above, making it both manifest to the public and explaining why.

4th Major Rock Edict

In the past, the killing and injuring of living beings, lack of respect towards relatives, brahmans and *śramaṇas* had increased. But today, thanks to the practice of *Dhamma* on the part of the Beloved of the Gods, the king Piyadassi, the sound of the drum has become the sound of *Dhamma*, showing the people displays of heavenly chariots, elephants, balls of fire, and other divine forms. Through his instruction in *Dhamma* abstention from killing and non-injury to living beings, deference to relatives, brahmans and *śramaṇas*, obedience to mother and father, and obedience to elders have all increased as never before for many centuries. These and many other forms of the practice of *Dhamma* have increased and will increase.

The Beloved of the Gods, the king Piyadassi, his sons, his grandsons and his great grandsons will advance the practice of *Dhamma*, until the end of the world and will instruct in the law, standing firm in *Dhamma*. For this, the instruction in the law, is the most valuable activity. But there is no practice of *Dhamma* without goodness, and in these matters it is good to progress and not to fall back. For this purpose, the inscription has been engraved – that men should make progress in this matter, and not be satisfied with their shortcomings. This was engraved here when the Beloved of the Gods, the king Piyadassi, had been consecrated twelve years.

5th Major Rock Edict

Thus speaks the Beloved of the Gods, the king Piyadassi: It is hard to do good and he who does good, does a difficult thing. And I have done much good. And my sons, my grandsons and my descendants after them until the end of the world if they will follow my example, they too will do good. But he who neglects my reforms even in part will do wrong, for sin is easy to commit.

In the past there were no officers of *Dhamma*. It was I who first appointed them, when I had been consecrated for thirteen years. They are busy in all sects, establishing *Dhamma*, increasing the interest in *Dhamma*, and attending to the welfare and happiness of those who are devoted to *Dhamma*, among the Greeks, the Kambojas, the Gandhāras, the Riṣthikas, the Pitinikas, and the other peoples of the west. Among servants and nobles, brahmans and wealthy householders, among the poor and the aged, they [the officers of *Dhamma*], are working for the welfare and happiness of those devoted to *Dhamma* and for the removal of their troubles. They are busy in promoting the welfare of prisoners should they have behaved irresponsibly, or releasing those that have children, are afflicted, or are aged. They are busy everywhere, here [at Pāṭaliputra] and in all the women's residences, whether my own, those of my brothers and sisters, or those of other relatives. Everywhere throughout my empire the officers of *Dhamma* are busy in everything relating to *Dhamma*, in the establishment of *Dhamma* and in the administration of charities among those devoted to *Dhamma*. For this purpose has this inscription of *Dhamma* been engraved. May it endure long and may my descendants conform to it.

6th Major Rock Edict

Thus speaks the Beloved of the Gods, the king Piyadassi: In the past the quick dispatch of business and the receipt of reports did not take place at all times. But I have now arranged it thus. At all times, whether I am eating, or am in the women's apartments, or in my inner apartments, or at the cattle-shed, or in my carriage, or in my gardens – wherever I may be, my informants should keep me in touch with public business. Thus everywhere I transact public business. And whatever I may order by word of mouth, whether it concerns a donation or a proclamation, or whatever urgent matter is entrusted to my officers, if there is any dispute or deliberation about it in the Council, it is to be reported to me immediately, at all places and at all times.

This I have commanded. In hard work and the dispatch of business alone, I find no satisfaction. For I consider that I must promote the welfare of the whole world, and hard work and the dispatch of business are the means of doing so. Indeed there is no better work than promoting the welfare of the whole world. And whatever may be my great deeds, I have done them in order to discharge my debt to all beings. I work for their happiness in this life, that in the next they may gain heaven. For this purpose has this inscription of *Dhamma* been engraved. May it endure long. May my sons, grandsons, and great grandsons strive for the welfare of the whole world. But this is difficult without great effort.

7th Major Rock Edict

The Beloved of the Gods, the king Piyadassi, wishes that all sects may dwell in all places, for all seek self-control and purity of mind. But men have varying desires and varying passions. They will either practise all that is required or else only a part. But even he who is generous, yet has no self control, purity of mind, gratitude, and firm faith, is regarded as mean.

8th Major Rock Edict

In the past, kings went on pleasure tours, which consisted of hunts and other similar amusements. The Beloved of the Gods, the king Piyadassi, when he had been consecrated ten years, went to the tree of Enlightenment. From that time arose the practice of tours connected with *Dhamma*, during which meetings are held with ascetics and brahmans, gifts are bestowed, meetings are arranged with aged folk, gold is distributed, meetings with the people of the countryside are held, instruction in *Dhamma* is given, and questions on *Dhamma* are answered. The Beloved of the Gods, the king Piyadassi, derives more pleasure from this, than from any other enjoyments.

9th Major Rock Edict

Thus speaks the Beloved of the Gods, the king Piyadassi: People practise various ceremonies. In illness, at the marriage of sons and daughters, at the birth of children, when going on a journey — on these and on other similar occasions people perform many ceremonies. Women especially perform a variety of ceremonies, which are trivial and useless. If such ceremonies must be performed they have but small results. But the one ceremony which has great value is that of *Dhamma*. This ceremony includes, regard for slaves and servants, respect for teachers, restrained behaviour towards living beings, and donations to *śramaṇas* and brahmans — these and similar practices are called the ceremony of *Dhamma*. So father, son, brother, master, friend, acquaintance, and neighbour should think, 'This is virtuous, this is the ceremony I should practice, until my object is achieved.'

[Kālsi version]. Or else they should say to themselves: Other ceremonies are doubtful in their effectiveness. They may achieve their objects or they may not, and they are only effective in temporal matters. But the ceremony of *Dhamma* is effective for all time, for even if its object is not attained in this life, endless merit is produced for the life to come. But if the object is attained in this life, there is a gain in both respects. For in this life the object is attained, and in the next life, endless merit is produced through that ceremony of *Dhamma*.

[Girnār version]. Moreover, they say: 'Giving is good.' But there is no gift or favour comparable to the gift of *Dhamma* or the favour of *Dhamma*. So it is essential that a friend, companion, relative, or colleague should advise on all occasions, saying, 'This should be done. Through this one can gain heaven' — and what can be more important than to gain heaven?

10th Major Rock Edict

The Beloved of the Gods, the king Piyadassi, sets no great store by fame or glory, except in, that he desires fame and glory both now and in the future, in order that his people may obey *Dhamma* with obedience and follow the way of *Dhamma*. To this extent the Beloved of the Gods desires fame and glory. Whatever efforts the Beloved of the Gods, the king Piyadassi, makes, it is all done with a view to the after-life, that all men may escape from evil inclinations, for there can be no merit in evil inclinations. But this is difficult for men, whether humble or highly placed, without extreme effort and without renouncing everything else, and it is particularly difficult for the highly placed.

11th Major Rock Edict

Thus speaks the Beloved of the Gods, the king Piyadassi: There is no gift comparable to the gift of *Dhamma*, the praise of *Dhamma*, the sharing of *Dhamma*, fellowship in *Dhamma*. And this is — good behaviour towards slaves and servants, obedience to mother and father, generosity towards friends, acquaintances, and relatives and towards *śramaṇas* and brahmans, and abstention from killing living beings. Father, son, brother, master, friend, acquaintance, relative, and neighbour should say, 'this is good, this we should do'. By doing so, there is gain in this world, and in the next there is infinite merit, through the gift of *Dhamma*.

12th Major Rock Edict

The Beloved of the Gods, the king Piyadassi, honours all sects and both ascetics and laymen, with gifts and various forms of recognition. But the Beloved of the Gods does not consider gifts or honour to be as important as the advancement of the essential doctrine of all sects. This progress of the essential doctrine takes many forms, but its basis is the control of one's speech, so as not to extoll one's own sect or disparage another's on unsuitable occasions, or at least to do so only mildly on certain occasions. On each occasion one should honour another man's sect, for by doing so one increases the influence of one's own sect and benefits that of the other man; while by doing otherwise one diminishes the influence of one's own sect and harms the other man's. Again, whosoever honours his own sect or disparages that of another man, wholly out of devotion to his own, with a view to showing it in a favourable light, harms his own sect even more seriously. Therefore, concord is to be commended, so that men may hear one another's principles and obey them. This is the desire of the Beloved of the Gods, that all sects should be well-informed, and should teach that which is good, and that everywhere their adherents should be told, 'The Beloved of the Gods does not consider gifts or honour to be as important as the progress of the essential doctrine of all sects.' Many are concerned with this matter—the officers of *Dhamma*, the women's officers, the managers of the state farms, and other classes of officers. The result of this is the increased influence of one's own sect and glory to *Dhamma*.

13th Major Rock Edict

When he had been consecrated eight years the Beloved of the Gods, the king Piyadassi, conquered Kaliṅga. A hundred and fifty thousand people were deported, a hundred thousand were killed and many times that number perished. Afterwards, now that Kaliṅga was annexed, the Beloved of the Gods very earnestly practised *Dhamma*, desired *Dhamma*, and taught *Dhamma*. On conquering Kaliṅga the Beloved of the Gods felt remorse, for, when an independent country is conquered the slaughter, death, and deportation of the people is extremely grievous to the Beloved of the Gods, and weighs heavily on his mind. What is even more deplorable to the

Beloved of the Gods, is that those who dwell there, whether brahmans, *śramaṇas*, or those of other sects, or householders who show obedience to their superiors, obedience to mother and father, obedience to their teachers and behave well and devotedly towards their friends, acquaintances, colleagues, relatives, slaves, and servants — all suffer violence, murder, and separation from their loved ones. Even those who are fortunate to have escaped, and whose love is undiminished [by the brutalizing effect of war], suffer from the misfortunes of their friends, acquaintances, colleagues, and relatives. This participation of all men in suffering, weighs heavily on the mind of the Beloved of the Gods. Except among the Greeks, there is no land where the religious orders of brahmans and *śramaṇas* are not to be found, and there is no land anywhere where men do not support one sect or another. Today if a hundredth or a thousandth part of those people who were killed or died or were deported when Kaliṅga was annexed were to suffer similarly, it would weigh heavily on the mind of the Beloved of the Gods.

The Beloved of the Gods believes that one who does wrong should be forgiven as far as it is possible to forgive him. And the Beloved of the Gods conciliates the forest tribes of his empire, but he warns them that he has power even in his remorse, and he asks them to repent, lest they be killed. For the Beloved of the Gods wishes that all beings should be unharmed, self-controlled, calm in mind, and gentle.

The Beloved of the Gods considers victory by *Dhamma* to be the foremost victory. And moreover the Beloved of the Gods has gained this victory on all his frontiers to a distance of six hundred *yojanas* [i.e. about 1500 miles], where reigns the Greek king named Antiochus, and beyond the realm of that Antiochus in the lands of the four kings named Ptolemy, Antigonus, Magas, and Alexander; and in the south over the Çoḷas and Pāṇḍyas as far as Ceylon. Likewise here in the imperial territories among the Greeks and the Kambojas, Nābhakas and Nābhapanktis, Bhojas and Pitinikas, Andhras and Pārindas, everywhere the people follow the Beloved of the Gods' instructions in *Dhamma*. Even where the envoys of the Beloved of the Gods have not gone, people hear of his conduct according to *Dhamma*, his precepts and his instruction in *Dhamma*, and they follow *Dhamma* and will continue to follow it.

What is obtained by this is victory everywhere, and everywhere victory is pleasant. This pleasure has been obtained through victory by *Dhamma* — yet it is but a slight pleasure, for the Beloved of the Gods only looks upon that as important in its results which pertains to the next world.

This inscription of *Dhamma* has been engraved so that any sons or great grandsons that I may have should not think of gaining new conquests, and in whatever victories they may gain should be satisfied with patience and light punishment. They should only consider conquest by *Dhamma* to be a true conquest, and delight in *Dhamma* should be their whole delight, for this is of value in both this world and the next.

14th Major Rock Edict

This inscription of *Dhamma* was engraved at the command of the Beloved of the Gods, the king Piyadassi. It exists in abridged, medium-length, and extended versions, for each clause has not been engraved everywhere. Since the empire is large, much has been engraved and much has yet to be engraved. There is considerable repetition because of the beauty of certain topics, and in order that the people may conform to them. In some places it may be inaccurately engraved, whether by the omission of a passage or by lack of attention, or by the error of the engraver.

1st Separate Edict (Dhauli and Jaugaḍa).

By order of the Beloved of the Gods: the officers and city magistrates at Tosalī/Samāpa are to be instructed thus:

Whatever I approve of, that I desire either to achieve by taking action or to obtain by effective means. This is what I consider the chief method in this matter, and these are my instructions to you. You are in charge of many thousands of living beings. You should gain the affection of men. All men are my children, and just as I desire for my children that they should obtain welfare and happiness both in this world and the next, the same do I desire for all men. But you do not realize how far this principle goes — possibly one man among you may realize it, but even he only in part and not entirely. Reflect on it well even those of you who are well-placed. Often a man suffers imprisonment or torture and then is released from prison, without reason, and many other people suffer further. You should strive to practise impartiality. But it cannot be practised by one possessing any of these faults — jealousy, shortness of temper, harshness, rashness, obstinacy, idleness, or slackness. You should wish to avoid such faults. The root of all this is to be even-tempered and not rash in your work. He who is slack will not act, and in your official functions you must strive, act, and work. So he who approves this should say to you, 'Think of clearing the debt — thus and thus, does the Beloved of the Gods instruct.' There is great advantage in conforming to this instruction and great loss in not conforming to it. For by disregarding it you will gain neither heaven nor the favour of the king. Why do I devote my mind to this matter so extensively? Because by conforming you will reach heaven and will discharge your debt to me.

This edict is to be proclaimed on the eighth day of the star Tiṣya, and at intervals between the Tiṣya-days it is to be read aloud, even to a single person. By doing this you may be able to conform to my instructions. This inscription has been engraved here in order that the city magistrates should at all times see to it that men are never imprisoned or tortured without good reason. And for this purpose, I shall send out on tour every five years, an officer who is not severe or harsh; who, having investigated this matter . . . , shall see that they carry out my instructions. The prince at Ujjain shall send out a similar group of officers, but at intervals not exceeding three years. Similarly at Taxila when the officers go out on tour they shall investigate this, without neglecting their normal duties and shall carry out the king's instructions.

2nd Separate Edict

By order of the Beloved of the Gods. At Tosali the prince and the officers/ at Samāpa the officers charged with announcing the royal decrees, are to be ordered thus: Whatever I approve of, that I desire either to achieve by taking action or to obtain by some effective means. This is what I consider the chief method in this matter, and these are my instructions to you. All men are my children and just as I desire for my children that they should obtain welfare and happiness both in this world and the next, the same do I desire for all men. If the unconquered peoples on my borders ask what is my will, they should be made to understand that this is my will with regard to them — 'the king desires that they should have no trouble on his account, should trust in him, and should have in their dealings with him only happiness and no sorrow. They should understand that the king will forgive them as far as they can be forgiven, and that through him they should follow *Dhamma* and gain this world and the next.'

For this purpose I instruct you, that having done so I may discharge my debt to them, by making known to you my will, my resolve and my firm promise. By these actions, my work will advance, and they will be reassured and will realize that the king is like a father, and that he feels for them as for himself, for they are like his own children to him. My couriers and special officers will be in contact with you, instructing you and making known to you my will, my resolve, and my firm promise. For you are able to give the frontier people confidence, welfare, and happiness in this world and the next. Doing this you will reach heaven and help me discharge my debt to my people.

This inscription has been engraved here for this purpose – that the officers shall at all times attend to the conciliation of the people of the frontiers and to promoting *Dhamma* among them. This edict is to be proclaimed every four months on the day of the star Tiṣya; it may optionally be proclaimed from time to time in the interval between Tiṣya-days, and on occasions may be proclaimed even to a single person. By doing this you will be able to conform to my instructions.

THE MINOR ROCK INSCRIPTIONS

Minor Rock Edict (a conflation of the various versions)

From Suvarṇagiri, on the order of His Highness the Prince, and the officers: good health to the officers of Isila who are to be instructed thus: Thus speaks the Beloved of the Gods, Asoka: I have been a Buddhist layman for more than two and a half years, but for a year I did not make much progress. Now for more than a year I have drawn closer to the Order and have become more ardent. The gods, who in India up to this time did not associate with men, now mingle with them, and this is the result of my efforts. Moreover this is not something to be obtained only by the great, but it is also open to the humble, if they are earnest and they can even reach heaven easily. This is the reason for this announcement – that both humble and great should make progress and that the neighbouring peoples also should know that the progress is lasting. And this investment will increase and increase abundantly, and increase to half as much again. This matter must be inscribed here and elsewhere on the hills, and wherever there is a stone pillar it is to be engraved on that pillar. You must go out with this document throughout the length and breadth of your district. This announcement has been proclaimed while on tour; 256 nights have been spent on tour.

Thus says the Beloved of the Gods. Whatever the Beloved of the Gods orders must be carried out in every respect. The *rājūka* [rural officer] is to be instructed and he will instruct the people of the countryside, assembling them with the sound of the drum; likewise the local chiefs. 'Obey mother and father, obey the teachers; have mercy on living beings; speak the truth. These virtues of *Dhamma* should be followed.'

Thus you will instruct them on the orders of the Beloved of the Gods, and also you will ensure that elephant trainers, clerks, fortune-tellers, and brahmans instruct their apprentices according to ancient tradition, that they should honour their masters . . . righteous masters. In a family relatives must treat each other with respect.

This is the ancient custom, conducive to long life, and thus it must be carried out. Carved by the engraver Capaḍa.

The Queen's Edict

On the order of the Beloved of the Gods, the officers everywhere are to be instructed that whatever may be the gift of the second queen, whether a mango-grove, a monastery, an institution for dispensing charity or any other donation, it is to be counted to the credit of that queen . . . the second queen, the mother of Tīvala, Kāruvākī.

Barābar Cave Inscriptions

I.

The king Piyadassi, when he had been consecrated twelve years, gave the Banyan Cave to the *Ājīvikas*.

II.

The king Piyadassi, when he had been consecrated twelve years, gave this cave on the Khalatika mountain to the *Ājīvikas*.

III.

The king Piyadassi, consecrated since nineteen years . . .

Kandahar Bilingual Rock Inscription

[Greek Version][1] Ten years being completed king Piyadassi showed piety [i.e. Dhamma] to men. And from that time [onwards] he made men more pious. And all things prosper throughout the whole world. And the king refrains from [eating] living beings, and indeed other men and whosoever [were] the king's huntsmen and fishermen have ceased from hunting, and those who were without control [over themselves] have ceased as far as possible from their lack of [self-] control, and [have become] obedient to father and mother and to elders, such as was not the case before. And in future, doing all these things, they will live more agreeably and better than before.

[Aramaic Version][2] Ten years having passed, our Lord the king Piyadassi, decided to instruct men in *Dhamma*. Since then, evil among men has diminished in the world. Among those who have suffered it has disappeared, and there is joy and peace in the whole world. And even in another matter, that which concerns eating, our Lord the king kills very few animals.

[1] Translated by Prof. Basham, based on the text recorded in *JA*, ccxlvi, 1958, pp. 2–3.

[2] We have based this translation on that of André Dupont-Sommer, in *JA*, ccxlvi, 1958, p. 22.

Kandahar bilingual inscription in Greek and Aramaic

Seeing this the rest of the people have also ceased from killing animals. Even those who catch fish, their activity has been prohibited. Similarly those that were without restraint have now learnt restraint. Obedience to mother and father, and elders, and conformity with the obligations implied in this, is now in practice. There are no more trials for men of piety. Thus the practise of *Dhamma* is of value to all men, and it will continue to be so.

MINOR ROCK INSCRIPTIONS

(Concerned specifically with Aśoka's interest in Buddhism.)

Bhabra Inscription

The king of Magadha, Piyadassi, greets the Order and wishes it prosperity and freedom from care. You know Sirs, how deep is my respect for and faith in the Buddha, the *Dhamma* and the *Saṃgha* [i.e. the Buddhist creed]. Sirs, whatever was spoken by the Lord Buddha was well spoken. And Sirs, allow me to tell you what I believe contributes to the long survival of the Buddhist *Dhamma*. These sermons on *Dhamma*, Sirs – the Excellence of the Discipline, the Lineage of the Noble One, the Future Fears, the Verses of the Sage, the *Sūtra* of Silence, the Questions of Upatissa, and the Admonition spoken by the Lord Buddha to Rāhula on the subject of false speech – these sermons on the *Dhamma*, Sirs, I desire that many monks and nuns should hear frequently and meditate upon, and likewise laymen and laywomen. I am having this engraved Sirs, so that you may know what I desire.

Rummindei Pillar Inscription

The Beloved of the Gods, the king Piyadassi, when he had been consecrated twenty years, came in person and reverenced the place where Buddha Śakyamuni was born. He caused a stone enclosure to be made and a stone pillar to be erected. As the Lord was born here in the village of Lumbinī, he has exempted it from tax, and fixed its contribution [i.e. of grain] at one-eighth.

Nigalisāgar Pillar Inscription

The Beloved of the Gods, the king Piyadassi, when he had been consecrated fourteen years, increased the *stūpa* of Buddha Konākamana to double [its former size] . . . And when he had been consecrated . . . years he came in person, worshipped . . . brought . . .

Schism Edict (a conflation of the various versions)

The Beloved of the Gods orders the officers of Kauśāmbī/Pāṭa[liputra] thus:

No one is to cause dissention in the Order. The Order of monks and nuns has been united, and this unity should last for as long as my sons and great grandsons, and the moon and the sun. Whoever creates a schism in the Order, whether monk or nun, is to be dressed in white garments, and to be put in a place not inhabited by monks or nuns. For it is my wish that the Order should remain united and endure for long. This is to be made known to the Order of monks and the Order of nuns. Thus says the Beloved of the Gods: You must keep one copy of this document and place it in your meeting hall, and give one copy to the laity. The laymen must come on every *uposatha* day [day of confession and penance] to endorse this order. The same applies to special officers who must also regularly attend the *uposatha*, and endorse this order, and make it known. Throughout your district you must circulate it exactly according to this text. You must also have this precise text circulated in all the fortress districts [under military control].

THE PILLAR EDICTS

1st Pillar Edict

Thus speaks the Beloved of the Gods, the king Piyadassi: When I had been consecrated for twenty-six years, I had this inscription of *Dhamma* engraved. It is hard to obtain happiness in this world and the next without extreme love of *Dhamma*, much vigilance, much obedience, much fear of sin, and extreme energy. But, through my instructions, care for *Dhamma* and love of *Dhamma* have grown from day to day, and will continue to grow. My subordinates too, whether high or low or of middle station, endorse it and practise it sufficiently to win over the wavering, and likewise do the frontier officials. For this is my principle: to protect through *Dhamma*, to administer affairs according to *Dhamma*, to please the people with *Dhamma*, to guard the empire with *Dhamma*.

2nd Pillar Edict

Thus speaks the Beloved of the Gods, the king Piyadassi: *Dhamma* is good. And what is *Dhamma*? It is having few faults and many good deeds, mercy, charity, truthfulness, and purity.

I have given the gift of insight in various forms. I have conferred many benefits on man, animals, birds, and fish, even to saving their lives, and I have done many other commendable deeds. I have had this inscription of *Dhamma* engraved that men may conform to it and that it may endure. He who conforms will do well.

3rd Pillar Edict

Thus speaks the Beloved of the Gods, the king Piyadassi: One only notices one's good deeds, thinking, 'I have done good', but on the other hand one does not notice one's wicked deeds, thinking, 'I have done evil', or 'this is indeed a sin'. Now, to be aware of this is something really difficult. But nevertheless one should notice this and think, 'Cruelty, harshness, anger, pride, and envy, these are indeed productive of sin.' Let them not be the cause of my fall. And this one should especially notice, thinking, 'This is important to my happiness in this world; that, on the other hand, for the next.'

4th Pillar Edict

Thus speaks the Beloved of the Gods, the king Piyadassi: When I had been consecrated twenty-six years I had this inscription on *Dhamma* engraved. My *rājūkas* [rural officers] are appointed over many hundred thousands of people. In judgment and punishment I have given them independent authority, so that the *rājūkas* may fulfil their functions calmly and fearlessly and may promote the welfare and happiness of the country people and benefit them. They will learn what makes for happiness and unhappiness and together with those devoted to *Dhamma*, they will admonish the country people that they may obtain happiness in this world and the next. The *rājūkas* are eager to obey me and they will likewise obey my envoys who know my wishes. These likewise will admonish [the erring *rājūkas*] so that they will be able to give me satisfaction.

Just as one entrusts his child to an experienced nurse, and is confident that the experienced nurse is able to care for the child satisfactorily, so my *rājūkas* have been appointed for the welfare and happiness of the country people. In order that they may fulfil their functions fearlessly, confidently, and cheerfully, I have given them independent authority in judgment and punishment. But it is desirable that there should be uniformity in judicial procedure and punishment.

This is my instruction from now on: Men who are imprisoned or sentenced to death are to be given three days respite. Thus their relations may plead for their lives, or, if there is no one to plead for them, they may make donations or undertake a fast for a better rebirth in the next life. For it is my wish that they should gain the next world. And among the people various practices of *Dhamma* are increasing, such as self-control and the distribution of charity.

5th Pillar Edict

Thus speaks the Beloved of the Gods, the king Piyadassi: When I had been consecrated for twenty-six years I forbade the killing of the following species of animals, namely: parrots, *mainās*, red-headed ducks [?], *cakravāka*-geese, swans, *nandī-mukhas* [birds encountered in rice fields?], pigeons, bats, ants, tortoises, boneless fish, *vedaveyakas*, *pupuṭas* of the Ganges [fish?], skate, porcupines, squirrels, deer, lizards, domesticated animals, rhinoceroses, white pigeons, domestic pigeons, and all quadrupeds which are of no utility and are not eaten. She goats, ewes, and sows which are with young or are giving suck are not to be killed, neither are their young up to the age of six months. Capons must not be made. Chaff which contains living things must not be set on fire. Forests must not be burned in order to kill living things or without any good reason. An animal must not be fed with another animal.

On the first full moon days of the three four-monthly seasons, and for three days when the full moon falls on the star Tiṣya, and the fourteenth and fifteenth of the bright fortnight, and the first of the dark, and regularly on fast days, fish are not to be caught or sold. And on these same days in the elephant-park and fisheries, other classes of animals likewise must not be killed. On the eighth, fourteenth, and fifteenth days of the fortnight, on the days of the star Tiṣya and Punarvasu, on the three first full moons of the four-monthly seasons, and on festival days, bulls, goats, rams, boars, and other animals which it is customary to castrate are not to be castrated. On the days of the stars Tiṣya and Punarvasu, on the first full moon days of the four-monthly seasons, and on the fortnights following them, cattle and horses are not to be branded.

In the period [from my consecration] to [the anniversary on which] I had been consecrated twenty-six years, twenty-five releases of prisoners have been made.

6th Pillar Edict

Thus speaks the Beloved of the Gods, the king Piyadassi: When I had been consecrated for twelve years I had an inscription of *Dhamma* engraved for the welfare and happiness of the world. Whoever follows it should obtain progress in *Dhamma* in various ways. Thus do I provide for the welfare and happiness of the world — in the same way as I bring happiness to my relatives, both close and distant and work for it, so do I provide for all classes. I honour all sects with various kinds of reverence, and I consider visiting them in person to be most important. When I had been consecrated for twenty-six years I had this inscription of *Dhamma* engraved.

7th Pillar Edict

Thus speaks the Beloved of the Gods, the king Piyadassi: In the past, kings searched for means whereby people's interest in *Dhamma* would increase, but the people did not respond accordingly with a greater devotion to *Dhamma*. Hence the Beloved of the Gods, the king Piyadassi says: This idea occurred to me. In the past kings sought to make the people progress . . . but they did not . . . How then could people be made to conform to *Dhamma* and increase their interest in it? . . . How could I elevate them through devotion to *Dhamma*? . . . I shall make them hear proclamations of *Dhamma*, and instruct them with the knowledge of *Dhamma*. When they have heard this, the people will endorse it and will be elevated, and will progress greatly in *Dhamma* . . . For this reason there have been proclamations of *Dhamma* and many instructions of *Dhamma* were ordered, and my administrators were appointed over many people; they will admonish them and explain *Dhamma* to them.

The *rājūkas* [rural officers] are appointed over many hundreds of thousands of people; I have instructed them duly to encourage those people devoted to *Dhamma*.

Thus speaks the Beloved of the Gods, the king Piyadassi: With this same idea in mind I have made pillars of *Dhamma*, appointed officers of *Dhamma*, and made proclamations of *Dhamma*.

Thus speaks the Beloved of the Gods, the king Piyadassi: On the roads I have had banyan trees planted, which will give shade to beasts and men, I have had mango-groves planted and I have had wells dug and rest houses built at every eight *kos*. And I have had many watering places made everywhere for the use of beasts and men. But this benefit is important, and indeed the world has enjoyed attention in many ways from former kings as well as from me. But I have done these things in order that my people might conform to *Dhamma*.

Thus speaks the Beloved of the Gods, the king Piyadassi: My officers of *Dhamma* are busy in many matters of public benefit, they are busy among members of all sects, both ascetics and householders. I have appointed some to concern themselves with the Buddhist Order, with brahmans and *Ājīvikas* . . . , with the Jainas . . . , and with various sects. There are many categories of officers with a variety of duties, but my officers of *Dhamma* are busy with the affairs of these and other sects.

Thus speaks the Beloved of the Gods, the king Piyadassi: These and many other chief officers are busy with the distribution of charity both on my behalf and on that of my queens; and in all my harem, in various forms, they . . . assist in the recognition of virtuous deeds, here and in all regions. And I have ordered them to be concerned with the distribution of charity on behalf of my sons, and of the other princes, that they may glory in *Dhamma* and conform to it. Thus the glory of *Dhamma* will increase throughout the world, and it will be endorsed in the form of mercy, charity, truthfulness, purity, gentleness, and virtue.

Thus speaks the Beloved of the Gods, the king Piyadassi: Whatever good deeds I have done, the world has consented to them and followed them. Thus obedience to mother and father, obedience to teachers, deference to those advanced in age, and regard for brahmans and *śramaṇas*, the poor and wretched, slaves and servants, have increased and will increase.

Thus speaks the Beloved of the Gods, the king Piyadassi: The advancement of *Dhamma* amongst men has been achieved through two means, legislation and persuasion. But of these two, legislation has been less effective, and persuasion more so. I have proclaimed through legislation for instance that certain species of animals are not to be killed, and other such ideas. But men have increased their adherence to *Dhamma* by being persuaded not to injure living beings and not to take life.

I have done all this so that among my sons and great grandsons and as long as the sun and moon endure, men may follow *Dhamma*. For by following it one gains this world and the next. When I had been consecrated twenty-seven years I had this inscription of *Dhamma* engraved. The Beloved of the Gods speaks thus: This inscription of *Dhamma* is to be engraved wherever there are stone pillars or stone slabs, that it may last long.

APPENDIX VI

MAURYAN ART

THE art remains of the Mauryan period have been so overshadowed by their closeness in style to those of the Achaemenid period of Persian history, that they tend to be regarded more as ammunition in the battle between those art-historians who treat them as products of Persian craftsmen, and the opposing school which regards them as purely indigenous. It is not our intention in this appendix to enter into the debate which centres largely round the problem of artistic impulses, and which requires a detailed consideration of both Greek and Achaemenid art. We merely wish to point out the more relevant aspects of Mauryan art in relation to Mauryan society.

Art remains of the Aśokan period, are found in association with the inscriptions. The inscriptions were placed either in sacred enclosures or else in the vicinity of towns. The most commonly found remains are the animal capitals of the pillars. The significance of the pillars is not difficult to determine.[1] The origin of the pillar as a structure goes back to the monolith of the prehistoric period. These were generally cut from a single block of stone and stood in an enclosure which was regarded as sacred. Sometimes they were worshipped as a phallic emblem or *liṅga*. The advantage of inscribing a text on such a pillar was that of associating the text with a place of importance. Moreover, as Smith points out,[2] the Sahasrām inscription states that edicts are to be inscribed on rocks and pillars, and of the latter, wherever a stone pillar is standing.[3] This suggests that some of the pillars antedate Aśoka's reign. Uninscribed pillars of this kind may have served a ritualistic purpose.

Coomaraswamy distinguishes between court art and a more popular art during the Mauryan period.[4] Court art is represented by the pillars and their capitals. In these the stone is polished and cut with great technical skill. He describes this art as being advanced and of a late type with realistic modelling and movement.

Undoubtedly a tradition in wood or some other perishable medium existed previous to the stone work of the Mauryas. Since wood was used

[1] We are not here considering pillars as a part of architecture, but free-standing pillars.

[2] *History of Fine Art in India and Ceylon*, p. 20.

[3] Bloch, *Les Inscriptions d'Asoka*, p. 149.

[4] *History of Indian and Indonesian Art*, p. 16.

extensively for the building of cities,[1] its use in sculpture and for decorative purposes generally would be normal. Excavations at the Mauryan level at Śiśupālgarh have revealed wooden remains. On examination the wood was found to be of the same species of trees as now found in Orissa.[2] The decline in the use of wood may have been in part due to the influence of contact with Achaemenid Persia, but the more practical reason was probably the denudation of the forests in the Ganges plain.[3]

The pillars are of two types of stone. Some are of the spotted red and white sandstone from the region of Mathura, and others of buff-coloured fine grained hard sandstone usually with small black spots quarried in Chunar near Banaras. The north-western province was no doubt familiar with the use of stone for ornamental purposes owing to its having been in close association with Achaemenid centres. Taxila must have had its share of stone carvers, as a number of stone objects of a decorative nature were found at Bhir Mound. With the establishment of the Mauryan empire and improvement in communications, it became possible to transport large blocks of stone from one region to another and also to send craftsmen to carve the stone. The uniformity of style in the pillar capitals suggests that they were all sculpted by craftsmen from the same region. The stone is similarly, only of the two above-mentioned types. It would seem, therefore, that stone was transported from Mathura and Chunar to the various sites where the pillars have been found and here the stone was cut and carved by craftsmen. The latter probably came from Taxila, and had had experience in handling stone. Remains of chippings from Taxila suggest that the sculpture was fashioned by local craftsmen.[4]

The stone elephant at Dhauli does not appear to belong to the same tradition as the animal capitals. It was probably carved by local craftsmen and not by the special craftsmen who were responsible for the animal capitals. The image of the elephant emerging from the rock is a most impressive one, and its purpose was probably to draw attention to the inscription near by.

The work of local sculptors illustrates the popular art of the Mauryan period. This consisted of sculpture which may not and probably was not, commissioned by the emperor. The patrons of popular art were the local governors and the more-well-to-do citizens. It is represented by figures such as the *yakṣī* of Besnagar, the *yakṣī* of Parkham and the *chaurī*-bearer from Didarganj. Whether or not these particular pieces are of a pre-

[1] *Arthaśāstra*, II, 36.

[2] Chowdhury and Ghosh, *AI*, vol. viii, p. 28.

[3] Basham, *The Wonder that was India*, p. 348.

[4] Marshall, *Taxila*, vol. i, p. 103.

Dhauli. Elephant carved from the rock at the site of the Aśokan inscriptions

Mauryan period, they appear to belong, artistically, to the same group as the Dhauli elephant. Technically, they are fashioned with less skill than the pillar capitals. They express a considerable earthiness and physical vitality.[1]

Wheeler has suggested that the Mauryan craftsmen employed by the state may have been unemployed Persians who had settled in India.[2] This is feasible in view of the fact that Persians, or Indians of Persian origin, were employed by the Mauryans in the western and north-western provinces, as for example, the governor Tuṣāspa. It is surprising, however, that if there was a large number of Persian craftsmen settled in these areas, objects of Achaemenid origin have not been found in great quantity. In examining the court art of the Mauryan period, it is as well to keep in mind that the artistic expression of an imperial structure is seldom national. An empire is in its very nature more cosmopolitan than a small state, largely because it comprises areas which were foreign to one another previous to the establishment of the empire.

Smith has suggested that the Sārnāth lion-capital may have been the work of foreign artists, because a century later when the same type of sculpture was attempted on the south gateway at Sanchi, it failed.[3] The argument here is that Indian craftsmen when left to themselves could not produce the same piece. In this connection it is important to remember, that the purpose of sculpture has much to do with its estimated success or failure. The sculpture on the south gateway if considered in isolation from the monument and compared with the lion-capital, may not be sculpturally as noble and imposing as the latter. Yet, if the gateway had been adorned with sculpture in the precise style of the lion-capital, the result would have been artistically a far greater failure. The purpose of the Sārnāth capital is to emphasize a finely proportioned pillar containing an imperial message, and therefore suits a mood of isolation and majesty. The sculpture at Sanchi represents a completely different idea and is consequently of a very different genre. It is the expression of a community wishing to revere a monument which it regards as sacred.

Terracotta objects of various sizes have been found at Mauryan sites. A continuation of the tradition of making mother-goddesses in clay, which goes back to the prehistoric period, is revealed by the discovery of these objects at Mauryan levels at Ahicchatrā.[4] They are found more commonly at sites extending from Pāṭaliputra to Taxila. Many have stylized forms and

[1] Coomaraswamy, *History of Indian and Indonesian Art*, p. 17.
[2] *AI*, vol. iv, p. 94.
[3] *History of Fine Art in India and Ceylon*, p. 16.
[4] Ghosh, *AI*, vol. iv, p. 106; Coomaraswamy, *History of Indian and Indonesian Art*, p. 20.

technically are most accomplished, in that they have a well-defined shape and clear ornamentation. Some appear to have been made from moulds, yet there is little duplication. Terracottas from Taxila consist of primitive idols, votive réliefs with deities, toys, dice, ornaments, and beads.[1] Toys were mostly wheeled animals, the elephant being a particular favourite. Amongst the ornaments were round medallions, similar to the *bullae* worn by Roman boys, which were meant to act as a protection against the 'evil eye'.

[1] Marshall, *Taxila*, vol. ii, pp. 440, 454, 460.

AFTERWORD

In the period since this book was first published in 1961 there have been, not unexpectedly, fresh interpretations of the Mauryan period and of the activities of Aśoka in particular; new data is available as well. My own ideas on the subject have also undergone some change. I thought it appropriate to add an Afterword to this new edition of the book, rather than to attempt redrafting the book and incorporating the data and interpretations since 1961. There are therefore few changes in the earlier text except for some small corrections. In this Afterword I have surveyed the epigraphic and archaeological evidence, discovered and discussed in the last thirty-five years, some of which constitutes the more important fresh data. I have also referred to studies concerning this evidence and the treatment of other sources, such as the texts. I have concluded with a brief discussion of some recent views on Aśoka and Buddhism and on the Mauryan period generally.

Inscriptions

In the listing of sources, the epigraphic data in the form of statements made by Aśoka has priority. Minor Rock Edicts (Minor REs) were discovered at Bahapur (New Delhi), Panguraria (Sehore Dt), Nittur (Bellary Dt), and Udegolam (Bellary Dt). These have been published and discussed both individually and in collated studies.[1] There is also a useful listing and locating of Aśokan inscriptions found upto the mid-80s.[2] Major Rock Edicts (MREs) were found at Sannati (Gulbarga Dt) and at Kandahar (Afghanistan). Another edition of the Separate Edicts (SEs) also occurs at Sannati. A fragmentary inscription apparently in the style of the Pillar Edicts (PEs) series has been located at Amarāvatī and another is said to have come from Buner (near Peshawar). Aramaic inscriptions occur at Laghman. A claim was made that an Aśokan inscription was found at Ghuggus in the Chandrapur District of Maharashtra, but it remains untraceable.[3] An attempt was made to read what were referred

[1] D.C. Sircar, *Asokan Studies*, Calcutta, 1979. P.K. Andersen, *Studies in the Minor Rock Edicts of Aśoka*, I, Critical Edition, Freiburg, 1990. M.A. Mehendale, 'North-western and Western Influence on the Versions of Aśoka's Minor Rock Edict', *BDCRI*, 17, pp. 81–97. K.R. Norman, *Collected Papers*, vols I–IV, London, 1990–93, analyse many edicts.

[2] F.R. Allchin and K.R. Norman, 'Guide to the Aśokan Inscriptions', *South Asian Studies*, 1985, 1, 43–50.

[3] A.M. Sastri, 'Fifty Years of Epigraphical Studies in India: A Brief Survey', *Puratattva*, 1994–95, 25, p. 27. Incidentally, mention is also made of a second post-Aśokan reference to Aśoka in a fifth century inscription in Sanskrit at a rock shelter at Narasinghagarh in the Rajgarh District of Madhya Pradesh. Ibid., p. 28.

to as inter-linear inscriptions of medieval times in Sri Lanka, pertaining to the Mauryas, but these readings have been rejected.[4]

The length of the text of the Minor REs varies. In addition to the standard text there is, at some places concentrated in three districts of Karnataka, a longer text. It is also at sites in this area, as noticed earlier, that a *kharoṣṭhī* knowing scribe declares his presence. The sites in these three districts of Karnataka are close to earlier settlements, and to the Hutti and Kolar gold mines, gold reefs and areas known for semi-precious stones. The coinciding of areas geologically known to be gold-bearing and the distribution of Aśokan inscriptions is striking.[5] The mines could have been under the control of the state, necessitating a nucleus of administration in the area to supervise the workings. Hence the references to the *mahāmattas* and the *kumāras*. In addition, local élites may have been the suppliers of resources and this would have required an administration largely limited to the senior levels. Reference is also made to the edict being dispatched throughout the king's domain — *sava-paṭhaviyaṁ*.[6]

The reference to 256 nights occurs in most but not all the versions, the inference being that the standard text was issued for engraving at one point in time; nevertheless some changes were introduced in each version in the ordering of the text and the language. Sircar's reading of the Bahapur version is that the 256 nights/days refer to the number of days since the relics were installed by the king.[7] Narain's alternative reading of the figure 256 as referring to the years after the death of the Buddha, in the Ahraura inscription, has not met with general acceptance.[8]

The additional part has some orders from the king. The *rājūka* was to be instructed by the *mahāmattas* and would in turn instruct the people. This included the *raṭṭhikāni*, possibly those with authority over a *rāṣṭra*, or local chiefs. The reference to instructing the elephant riders may have been to those associated with such chiefs. The Mauryan official would then have been the

[4] S. Paranavitana, *The Greeks and the Mauryas*, Colombo, 1971.

[5] R. Nanda, *The Early History of Gold in India*, Delhi, 1992, has a map of the gold bearing sites, Map. 1, p. 2. F.R. Allchin, 'Upon the Antiquity and Methods of Gold Mining in Ancient India', in *JESHO*, 1962, 5, pp. 195–211.

[6] D.C. Sircar, *Aśokan Studies*, pp. 123ff. The Udegolam inscription does not carry this phrase. Ibid., pp. 129ff.

[7] D.C. Sircar, 'New Delhi Inscription of Aśoka', *Ep. Ind.*, 1970, 38, 1, pp. 1–4. M.C. Joshi and B.M. Pande, 'A Newly Discovered Inscription of Aśoka at Bahapur', *JRAS*, 1967, pp. 96–8. K.R. Norman, 'Notes on the Bahapur Version of Aśoka's Minor Rock Edict', *JRAS*, 1971, pp. 41–3.

[8] A.K. Narain, 'A New Version of the Minor Rock Edict I of Aśoka', *Bharati*, 1961–2, 5, 1, pp. 1–5; D.C. Sircar, 'The Ahraura Inscription of Aśoka', *Ep. Ind.*, 1965, 36, 5, pp. 239–48. K.R. Norman, 'Notes on the Ahraura Version of Aśoka First Minor Rock Edict', *IIJ*, 1983, 26, pp. 277–92. S. Sankaranarayanam, 'Ahraura Inscription of Aśoka', *IHQ*, 1961, 37, 4, pp. 217–24. J. Filliozat, 'Studies in Aśokan Inscriptions', Calcutta 1967.

intermediary between the imperial authority and the local. The imperial attempt is not to change local society and bring it in line with mainstream Mauryan society, but rather to communicate with local society. The qualifier of *putta* in Pāli, added to the name of a people, has been taken to mean that they belong to a tribe. Thus MRE II mentions the Kelalaputto and the Satiyaputto, and although the suffix *putta* is not used for the Coḍa and Pāṃḍya, they are included in the general reference. (Interestingly Aśoka uses the Prākrit forms of the names and not the contemporary Tamil forms such as Cera-man and Adiya-man). In contrast, the Hellenistic kings are referred to as the *yonarāja*. The instruction consisted of the rudiments of *dhamma*: obedience to mother, father and teachers, mercy towards living creatures, speaking the truth and following the *dhamma*. Mention is made of the *brāhmaṇas* but not of the *śramanas*, who were presumably still rare in Karnataka.

The Panguraria inscription was located at a monastic site.[9] A short inscription has been read as addressed to the *kumāra* Saṃva as a preface to the Minor RE but this reading has been questioned. Mention is made of the king named Piyadassi, which indicates a personal name. In the Nittur inscription he is called *rājā asoka* whereas in the Udegolam version he is *rājā asoka devānampiya*. The Panguraria inscription repeats the statement that this edict was to be inscribed wherever there are rocks and stone pillars.

Both the MREs at Sannati and Kandahar are significant but for different reasons. The stone slab of the Sannati inscription, was being used as a *pīṭha*/ pedestal for an image in a temple and was damaged by the cutting out of a section in the middle to hold the tenon at the base of the image. Both surfaces of the slab are inscribed.[10] One surface has the partial texts of the MREs XII and XIV (Face A). The other surface has fragments of the SE I and the SE II (Face B), previously known only at the sites in Kaliṅga, and presumably replacing MRE XIII. The two groups of edicts may have came from different sources, since in the MREs *la* is used in place of *ra* whereas in the SEs *ra* is retained in *rājā*. According to Norman the positioning of the two SEs reinforces the theory that SE I was engraved after SE II. That they have similarities and dissimilarities with the Dhauli and Jaugada versions would suggest that there was a master copy from which these versions derived.[11] It had been

[9] D.C. Sircar, 'Panguraria Inscription of Aśoka', *Ep. Ind.*, 1981, 39, 1, 1–8.

[10] K.R. Norman, 'Aśokan Inscriptions from Sannati', *South Asian Studies*, 1991, 7, pp. 101–10. K.V. Ramesh, 'The Aśokan Inscriptions at Sannati', *Indian Historical Review*, 1987–8, xiv, 1–2, pp. 36–42. J. Howell, 'Note on the Society's Excavations at Sannati, Gulbarga District, Karnataka', *South Asian Studies*, 1989, 5, pp. 59–62. I.K. Sharma and J. Varaprasada Rao, *Early Brāhmī Inscriptions from Sannati*, Delhi, 1993.

[11] M.A. Mehendale in, 'What was the Place of Issue of the Dhauli and Jaugada Separate Edicts', BDCRI, 1953, 17 and in JOIB, 1, pp. 240–4 had suggested that linguistic forms in these edicts, 'show affinity with the north-

assumed that since the SEs had so far occurred only at Kaliṅga they were a substitute for the MRE XIII in which the king expresses his remorse at the suffering caused by the campaign in Kaliṅga. But the occurrence at Sannati raises the question of why they should have been included at this site. Was there another campaign associated with this area which has not been mentioned in the sources? Was it an administrative error which led to its inclusion? Or were these edicts intended for administration in other parts of India as well, as Norman maintains, although they may have been for reading out and not for engraving. However if they were replacing any MRE then they must have been intended for engraving.

At Kandahar, apart from the Greek and Aramaic bilingual reported earlier (Kandahar I), a Greek version of part of the MRE XII and the opening section of MRE XIII, have also been found (Kandahar III). This is a fragment from a larger set of stone slabs. These are not translations but renderings in a condensed form, with some omissions.[12]

Fragments of what could be PEs have been recorded at Amarāvatī and Kandahar. The Amarāvatī inscription is on a stone which is not from Chunar (from where transportation would have been extraordinarily difficult), but from the closer Nallamalai range. The stone has traces of the characteristic Mauryan polish. The text, only partially preserved, does not conform to any of the known edicts although the palaeography and the language are akin to Aśokan *brāhmī* and Prākrit.[13] Possibly it was intended as a new series or even another version of the existing edicts, meant for the peninsula, since this is the only one in that area. The site is close to the port of Dharanikoṭa which was doubtless in contact with other ports along the east coast and which also gave access to the Krishna valley and the Kolar goldfields. If the inscription was Aśokan then possibly the foundations of the *stūpa* could be dated to the Mauryan period, a date which is endorsed by excavations. However, it could also have been an edict of a successor of Aśoka, although Sircar's attempted reading suggests sentiments similar to those of other edicts of Aśoka.[14]

At Kandahar, an inscription has been read as an Aramaic rendering of a

---

western language of the Aśokan inscriptions, thus pointing towards that area as the most probable source of the issue of these two separate edicts'.

[12] D. Schlumberger, et al., 'Une Bilingue Gréco-Araméene d'Asoka', *JA*, 1958, 1–48. E. Benveniste, 'Edits d'Asoka en traduction grecque', *Journal Asiatique*, 1964, pp. 137–57. K.R. Norman, 'Notes on the Greek Version of Aśoka's Twelfth and Thirteenth Rock Edicts', *JRAS*, 1972, 2, pp. 111–18. D. Schlumberger and E. Benveniste, 'A New Greek Inscription of Aśoka at Kandahar', *Ep. Ind.*, 1967, 37, 5, pp. 193–200.

[13] D.C. Sircar, *Aśokan Studies*, p. 121.

[14] D.C. Sircar, 'Fragmentary Pillar Inscription from Amaravati', *Ep. Ind.*, 1963, xxxv, part 1, pp. 40–4. I.K. Sarma, *Studies in Early Buddhist Monuments and Brāhmī Inscriptions in Andhra Pradesh*, Nagpur, 1988.

part of PE VII (Kandahar II).[15] The inscription is in Aramaic but with glosses to explain the terms used in Prākrit. An earlier reading of an Aramaic inscription from Lampaka, introduced the possibility of glosses.[16] It would seem that *kharoṣṭhī* was not familiar in this area. The readings of these inscriptions have suggested parallels with a number of terms occurring in the MREs and PEs, which would in turn suggest that the Greek and Aramaic inscriptions were of a later date than the ones in Prākrit. Two Aramaic inscriptions from Laghman (Laghman I and II) refer to the name Priyadarśin as does the one from Taxila.[17] The Aramaic inscriptions are concentrated along the Khyber and in Kandahar, whereas the Greek inscriptions remain in the vicinity of Kandahar. The Greek-speaking population seems to have preferred living in the cities whereas the Aramaic-speaking people were to be found both in the cities and along the routes. The Greek presence in Kandahar is further confirmed by a Greek inscription on the base of a Hellenistic statue of this period.[18] The earlier bilingual Graeco-Aramaic edict has also been examined in some detail and is said to be contemporary with the MREs.[19]

Recently a puzzling fragment of PE VI in *brāhmī* was said to have come from Buner near Takht-i-Bahi in the north-west — puzzling as it would be the sole inscription in *brāhmī* in this area.[20] Its language agrees with other such edicts from the Ganges plain. Its genuineness is however not above doubt, especially as it was not found *in situ*. Taddei's explanation is that there was a *brāhmī*-knowing scribe travelling with Aśoka in the north-west and he was asked to engrave the edicts. The inscription is on schist and not on Chunar sandstone. It would seem therefore that the main distribution of the PEs is still largely confined to the Ganges plain. However some attempts

15 E. Benveniste et al., 'Une inscription indo-araméenne d'Asoka provenant de Kandahar (Afghanistan)', *Journal Asiatique*, 1966, 254, Fas 3–4, pp. 437–70. See also Allchin and Norman, op. cit. S. Shaked, 'Notes on the New Aśoka Inscription from Kandahar, *JRAS*, 1969, 118–22.

16 W.B. Henning, 'The Aramaic Inscription of Aśoka Found at Lampaka', *BSOAS*, 1949, 13.1, pp. 80–8.

17 A. Dupont Sommer, 'Une nouvelle inscription araméene d'Asoka trouve dans la vallée du Laghman (Afghanistan)', in *Academie des Inscriptions et Belles-Lettres*, 1970, pp. 158–73; Ito, op. cit., 1979. G. Ito, 'Asokan Inscriptions, Laghman I and II', *Studia Iranica*, 1979, 8, pp. 175–84. B.N. Mukherjee, *Studies in Aramaic Edicts of Aśoka*, Calcutta, 1980.

18 P.M. Fraser, 'The Son of Aristonax at Kandahar', *Afghan Studies*, 1979 (1980), 2, pp. 9–21.

19 G. Pugliese-Carratelli and G. Garbini, *A Bilingual Graeco-Aramaic Edict by Aśoka*, Rome, 1964. See also J. Filliozat, 'Graeco-Aramaic Inscription of Aśoka near Kandahar', *Ep. Ind.*, 1961–2, 34, 1–8.

20 K.R. Norman, 'A Newly Found Fragment of an Aśokan Inscription', *South Asian Studies*, 1988, 4, pp. 99–102. M. Taddei, 'Nuovo Iscrizione di Asoka del Nordvest', in G. Gnoli and L. Lanciotti (eds), *Orientalia Iosephi Tucci Memoriae Dicata*, Rome, 1988. B.N. Mukherjee, 'A *Brāhmī* Inscription of Aśoka from the North-west', *IHR*, 1989–90, 16, 1–2, 130–1.

were being made to convey their ideas to the north-west. The locations were connected not only to the north-western routes but perhaps with central Asia as well, judging by the recently discovered Kuṣāṇa presence in Gilgit and Chitral.

The discovery of Greek and Aramaic inscriptions points not only to Mauryan control over parts of Afghanistan and the presence of Greek and Aramaic-Iranian speakers in the area, but also to Aśoka's emphasis on maintaining a dialogue with people whom he regarded as important. It has been suggested that these were the areas described as *yonakamboja*, where *yona* clearly referred to Hellenized Greeks and *kamboja* to the Iranians. The latter may have been a local community associated with Mazdaism.[21] The significance of these inscriptions increases because they provide translations of various terms which have been controversial in the Prākrit versions. Humbach argues that contemporary Zoroastrian terms as well as ideas from Greek philosophy were used to render Buddhist concepts.[22] It could also be said that the intention may have been to show the universality of some concepts. The word *dhamma* is translated as *eusebeia* meaning 'piety, loyalty, reverence for the gods and for parents'. It has also been explained as that sentiment which the group or the individual entertained towards certain specified obligations such as respect for ancestors and parents and participation in civic sacrifices and offerings. Interestingly there is no reference to the Buddha, which might have been expected if the edicts were centrally concerned with propagating Buddhism among those unfamiliar with it. If the *dhamma* of Aśoka was to be translated as 'law' then as asserted by Schlumberger the Greek should have been *nomos*.[23] The intention was to introduce *dhamma* to the local people and describe what was meant by it, while using their own idiom. The style is literary and the phraseology echoes Pythagorean and Platonic thought. The term *eusebeia* is used in a context very similar to the Aśokan in an inscription of Antiochus of the first century BC where he states that he considers *eusebeia* the safest and most pleasurable possession for all men and that he regards saintliness as his most faithful guardian. It would seem that he was familiar with the Greek inscriptions of Aśoka at Kandahar.[24]

The Greek translation of *pāsaṃḍa* is *diatribe* which at this time carried the meaning of a sect, but not necessarily a heretical sect, as was also the case in Prākrit. It refers more to philosophical schools than to doctrinaire religious

[21] F. Scialpi, 'The Ethics of Aśoka and the Religious Inspiration of the Achaemenids', *East and West*, 1984, 34, 1–3, pp. 55–74.

[22] H. Humbach, 'The Aramaic Aśokan Inscription from Taxila', *Journal of Central Asia*, 1978, I, 2, pp. 87–98.

[23] D. Schlumberger, op. cit.

[24] F.R. Adrados, 'Aśoka's Inscriptions and Persian, Greek and Latin Epigraphy', in S.D. Joshi (ed.), *Amṛtadhārā*, Delhi, 1984, pp. 1–15.

groups. The meaning of *pāsaṃḍa* was also to change in the latter direction in the post-Mauryan period. The absence of the conjoint *bramaṇaśramaṇa* reflects the king's awareness that these two categories were absent in the land of the Yonas, to which he draws attention in MRE XIII. It is significant that the terms used for *dhamma* in Greek and Aramaic which are *eusebeia* and *qsyr*, have no doctrinal or sectarian meaning.[25]

Humbach prefers to call the Aramaic of these inscriptions, Armaeo-Iranian, as the Aramaic has an admixture of Iranian. Since these inscriptions generally belong to the period subsequent to Aśoka's support for Buddhism, the earlier reading of the Taxila inscription should more correctly be, 'Our lord Priyadarśin, the king', which occurs as a formula. *Dhamma* in the Aramaic inscription, has been translated as 'the conduct of the good', or as Truth. Reference is also made to pious men being above judgement. This has been interpreted in the context of MRE IV, which these inscriptions seem to parallel, as referring to the officers of the law who have the power to judge.[26] Again an alternative reading could be that it refers to the Zoroastrian notion of judgement after death. Since this idea was less familiar to the Greeks, it is not introduced in the Greek translation. Was Aśoka stating that those who observe the *dhamma* or the conduct of the good, would be regarded as pious and therefore exempt from judgement after death? This would show a degree of interest in and sensitivity to, the belief of those who were his subjects in this part of the empire, which is remarkable. (The same sensitivity is not however evident in his dialogue with his southern subjects, who were also at this time unfamiliar with Buddhism and with Prākrit. He may have been hampered in the use of a south Indian language because of the absence of a script specific to the language). That he was concerned with the after-life is evident from various versions of the Minor RE where he speaks of *svarga*, and interestingly not of *nirvāṇa*, as the goal of human existence. There is little reference in the Greek and Aramaic inscriptions to officials or administration. This could be because the area was only recently and loosely under Mauryan control. Given this and the obvious presence of Greek speakers, the *epigamia* in the treaty between Seleucus and Candragupta would more likely have been a *jus conubii*, the freedom for Greeks and Indians to intermarry, rather than being restricted to a marriage alliance within the royal families.[27] The discovery of the Aramaic inscriptions, suggesting Iranian connections, makes the governorship of Tuṣāspa in Saurashtra more plausible. It does raise the question however of how an

[25] A.L. Basham, 'The Rise of Buddhism in its Historical Context', *Asian Studies*, 1966, 4, p. 405.

[26] A. Dupont-Sommer, op. cit.

[27] U. Scerrato, 'A Bi-lingual Greco-Aramaic Edict by Aśoka', *Series orientale Roma*, 1964, XXIX, pp. 1–27.

Iranian would have fared in governing a non-Iranian population, unless one argues that Iranian settlements along the borderlands would already have had an admixture of Indian ways of life with which Iranians were familiar. Tuṣāspa may have been from a family sent by the Achaemenids to administer the deltaic area of their Indian territory.

An epigraphic confirmation of the existence of the Satiyaputtas comes from a Tamil-brāhmī inscription of the period just after Aśoka, at the site of Jambai in the South Arcot District. It records the donation of a cave shelter for monks and the donor refers to himself as Adiyan Neduman Anci, the Satiyaputta.[28] He was also referred to as Adiya-man in the texts. It is significant that although the inscription is in Tamil, the equivalent name in Prākrit is also used. The poems of the *Cankam* collection would have been approximately contemporary with the edicts.

Attention has been drawn to the contemporary histories of the reign of Firuz Shah Tughluq and mention of his shifting and setting up Aśokan pillars from their original provenance to buildings which he had had built. The ones from Topra and Meerut at Delhi are well-recorded. The one said to have been brought from Kauśāmbi to Allahabad is again under discussion. But the histories mention two others: at Hissar (Punjab) and at Hissar (Haryana), whose identity as Aśokan pillars is close but not conclusive. They are now located in mosques in the two towns. It has been suggested that the inscribed surface may have flaked off.[29]

The origin of the *brāhmī* script remains subject to periodic discussion. A detailed and careful study of Mauryan *brāhmī* supports the sub-continental use of the script although with some variations which are not consistent with regional characteristics.[30] C.S. Upasaka maintains that the script is neither borrowed nor entirely indigenous but evolved from both the functionality of the phonetic form of the language as developed by Sanskrit grammarians and contact with traders using a script. The innovation would have been pre-Mauryan as it was well-developed by the time of Aśoka. A survey of early Indian palaeography also supports the idea that the script was partially evolved from the structure of the language but also partially borrowed, probably from the Semitic.[31] The semi-syllabic character of *brāhmī* was suited to the structure of the language, although there are problems in the placing of conjuncts. Another view is that the *brāhmī* script was invented in the early third century BC

[28] I. Mahadevan, 'Recent Discoveries of Jaina Cave Inscriptions in Tamil Nadu', in *Rishabha-saurabha*, Delhi, 1994, pp. 123–7.

[29] W.H. Siddiqi, 'A Study of Aśokan Pillars: Re-erected by Firuz Shah Tughluq' (mimeographed), 1976. B.Ch. Chhabra, 'Aśokan Pillar at Hissar, Punjab', *Vishveshvarananda Indological Journal*, 1964, p. 3.

[30] C.S. Upasak, *The History and Palaeography of Mauryan Brahmi Script*, Nalanda, 1960.

[31] A.H. Dani, *Indian Palaeography*, Oxford, 1963, pp. 29–30.

to facilitate Aśokan administration and that the idea and technique of writing came from the west with a borrowing from the Achaemenid model.[32] If this was the case it is likely that the inscriptions would have been uniformly in Prākrit and *brāhmī* irrespective of local usage in language and script. The relationship between *kharoṣṭhī* and *brāhmī* has also to be considered. If *kharoṣṭhī* was also an invention to facilitate administration, then it could have been widely used elsewhere in the Mauryan empire for Prākrit edicts. This would have eliminated the need to evolve yet another script for administrative functions. Given the wide use of Aramaic in the Achaemenian empire and the fact that Gandhāra and much of the trans-Indus region were claimed as part of this empire, it is unlikely that a script was not known earlier, at least in the north-west. That Aśokan *brāhmī* was well-developed would suggest a start in pre-Aśokan times, although its widespread use was Aśokan. A recent study of early Indian palaeography rejects Semitic links and revives an earlier theory of possible Greek influence on the earliest forms of *brāhmī* the invention of which suggests that the script dates to the first Mauryan ruler.[33] Opinion remains divided on the origin of *brāhmī*.

Pre-Mauryan royal inscriptions may not be discovered since pre-Mauryan politics may not have required these, but graffiti on potsherds, especially in conjunction with Northern Black Polished Ware, is a likely archaeological context for a script. Such graffiti at Amarāvatī has been dated to the early Mauryan period.[34] Graffiti in *brāhmī* on local potsherds are also reported from Anuradhapura dating to levels of *c.* 450–350 BC, thus earlier than at other archaeological sites. The reading suggests Prākrit names. Interestingly there are also sherds with graffiti symbols similar to those on megalithic B-and-R ware from peninsular India.[35] These very early dates are so far restricted to this site but possibly other graffiti may provide evidence of a pre-Mauryan *brāhmī*. Similarly, Sircar dates the Piprahwa Relic Casket inscription to the third century BC,[36] although such an early reading has been doubted. An inscriptional label on a casket would point to an established script. Inscribed potsherds suggest uses other than administration for it.

Nevertheless the late development of a script with a long lacunae from the

[32] S.R. Goyal, *Brahmi — an Invention of the Early Mauryan Period*, pp. 16–18.

[33] H. Falk, *Schrift in Alten Indien: Ein Forschungsbericht mit Anmerkungen*, Tubingen, 1993. See also, R. Salomon, *JAOS*, 1995, 115, 271–80.

[34] *Indian Archaeology — A Review*, 1973–4, p. 4.

[35] S.U. Deraniyagala, 'Radio-carbon Dating of Early *Brāhmī* Script in Sri Lanka', *Ancient Ceylon*, 1990, 11, pp. 149–68. *The Prehistory of Sri Lanka*, II, Colombo, 1992, p. 739 ff. F.R. Allchin, *The Archaeology of Early Historic South Asia*, Cambridge, 1995.

[36] D.C. Sircar, *Select Inscriptions . . .*, Calcutta, 1965, p. 81.

Harappan period may have been because the earlier litterati, the *brāhmaṇas*, relied on the oral tradition. The invention of a script would only have come from the need for a written tradition and probably drew on existing scripts. According to one view, even the Aśokan edicts despite being engraved, judging by the speech breaks, suggest they were meant for recitation.[37] The recording of the Buddha's teaching eventually took the form of texts although the precise periods when various sections of the canon came to be written remains uncertain. The questioning of a script in pre-Aśokan times comes largely from the statement by Megasthenes that the Indians did not know the art of writing. But this statement contradicts Nearchos.[38] There has also been a substantial debate on whether the grammar of Pāṇini could have been composed in the absence of a script.

References to Indian traders in Iran and Mesopotamia during the sixth and fifth centuries BC establish the familiarity which some Indians had with Aramaic and the North Semitic script. A colony of Indians near Nippur is known, some of whom carried out military functions under their own chiefs, and an Indian woman is said to run a tavern in Kish.[39] A contract of the fifth century concerning a female slave has an endorsement in an unknown script, which, it has been suggested might be an early form of *brāhmī*.[40]

Familiarity with written texts is evident from the edicts, where the term *dhamma-lipi* carries the notion of a written text and not just a brief proclamation. Orders to inscribe appropriate rock surfaces and pillars is again suggestive of an established experience with writing. If the script had been invented in the early third century for purposes of administration, and for propagating ideas on social behaviour and beliefs, then it is unlikely that the major effort would have been to engrave on stone, infinitely more difficult than writing on birch-bark or cloth. If the purpose was to facilitate administration then presumably much more would have been stated about the administrative functioning than is actually done. The SEs belong more to this category but these are only two, and the Schism Edict refers to the making of multiple copies for the *saṃgha* and for the officials. Some of the edicts are addressed to the *ayyaputta/āryaputra*, the *kumāra* and the *mahāmattas*, but their contents include far more than merely matters of governing. Rather than being personal statements written in a conversational style, the edicts would also have been drafted in a

[37] K.L. Janert, 'About the Scribes and their Achievements in Aśoka's India', *German Scholars in India*, vol. I, pp. 141–5.

[38] L. Gopal, 'Early Greek Writers on Writing in India', *PIHC*, 1976, pp. 544–52.

[39] N.A. Dandamaev and V.G. Lukonin, *The Culture and Social Institutions of Ancient Iran*, Cambridge, 1989.

[40] G.V. Brobinsky, 'A Line of *Brāhmī*(?) Script in a Babylonian Contract Tablet, *JAOS*, 1936, 56, pp. 86–8.

more official language. They are likely to have been dictated to a writer who in turn conveyed them to engravers in various parts of the Mauryan domain. Engravers of inscriptions are seldom highly literate so small mistakes and local variants occur in these inscriptions.

Literacy would in any case have been limited at this time to some *brāhmaṇas*, Buddhist monks entrusted with recording the teachings of the Buddha, merchants, officials and some other professions requiring a modicum of writing. The edicts therefore were not intended to be read by ordinary people but to be read out to such gatherings. The inscription would then be symbolic of a statement of power in an oral society, all the more so in the south where no concessions were made to the local language. It may well be asked whether the idea of reading out a text did not come from readings by Buddhist monks to the laity. That some elements of a Buddhist Canon existed is evident from the Bhabra edict.[41] Recourse to writing would have helped in the centralization of state administration and communication with distant areas. Interestingly inscriptions in the Ganges plain do not occur in clusters in the same way as they do in the frontier areas in Karnataka and in the north-west. Where the edicts were in the vicinity of Buddhist monasteries, the monks would have read them out to the laity. Given the diversity of the empire, the fact that a body of texts were being propagated in every part would at least have encouraged the notion of a common ideology of persuasion.[42]

One of the fascinating aspects of the Aśokan pillars is that some of them came to be treated as a kind of historical palimpsest. What is thought to be the pillar from Kauśāmbi, now at Allahabad, carries a number of Aśokan inscriptions: the PEs I to VI, the Schism Edict and the Queen's Edict. It also carries the famous *praśasti* of Samudragupta as well as an inscription recording the visit of *Rājā* Birbal, presumably after Akbar had constructed the fort at the confluence. And there is an inscription by Jahangir giving his ancestry. In addition there are numerous short 'scribblings' as Cunningham called them, mentioning dates from the thirteenth century onwards.[43] There must have been some perception of the pillar incorporating the past that it comes to be treated as an agency of legitimizing the present. If this legitimation had arisen out of its being regarded solely as an axis mundi or a *lingam* then it would have been venerated but would not have carried further inscriptions on its body.

Important epigraphic evidence comes from the Aramaic and Greek

41 A.L. Basham, 'Aśoka and Buddhism: a Re-examination', *The Journal of the International Association of Buddhist Studies*, 1982, 5, 1, pp. 131–43.

42 R. Thapar, 'Literacy and Communication: Some Thoughts on the Inscriptions of Aśoka' (forthcoming).

43 A. Cunningham, Inscriptions of Aśoka, CII.I. London, 1879.

inscriptions which provide not only an insight into literacy, and the governing of the north-west, but also a further dimension to the discussion of the *dhamma* of Aśoka. The *dhamma* emerges not only as conceptually complex, enriched by his personal association with Buddhism and other belief systems of the time, but also as a policy reaching out to many dimensions of public life. Its significance as an ideology, both of the ruler and of his times, is thereby enhanced. The parallel concepts to the Prākrit inscriptions as well as the particular concepts of the Greek and the Aramaic, suggest meanings and nuances which would endorse the readings which have been made earlier in this book.

Archaeology

The evidence from archaeology is potentially a major source now on the Mauryan period. The archaeological activity in the last three decades has filled in some spaces largely with evidence of pre-Mauryan periods. For the Mauryan period excavations provide some data on settlements and the distribution of artefacts, although far more can be expected from future excavations.[44] Information on urban centres is relatively more accessible but of a limited nature.[45] A more broad-based study placing urbanization in the context of the archaeology of early historic south Asia, provides not only a useful summary of the archaeological data but suggests the possibilities of the emergent picture from archaeological sources.[46] Excavations pertaining to this period are almost entirely vertical and therefore useful for obtaining a stratigraphy of the site but of less help in reconstructing social and economic processes. There is therefore considerable need for more horizontal excavations.

The archaeological counterpart to the Mauryan period is included within the span of the Northern Black Polished Ware (NBPW) which occurs at an earlier date at some sites but is generally taken to have commenced by about 600–500 BC in the middle Ganges plain, diffusing and continuing until the second century BC. Frequently associated with this pottery are other artefacts such as punch-marked coins, terra-cotta figures, beads of particular kinds and the increasing use of iron. These provide a similarity of items across a large area although their locations include other regionally identified artefacts as well. They have been taken as evidence of the Mauryan period in their later levels, especially at sites in the peninsula where the pre-Mauryan cultures

[44] A. Ghosh (ed.), *An Encyclopaedia of Indian Archaeology*, Delhi, 1989, has a number of useful entries and one hopes that it will be up-dated soon. Most entries include references to reports of excavations.

[45] D.K. Chakrabarti, *The Archaeology of Ancient Indian Cities*, Delhi, 1995. A. Ghosh, *The City in Early Historical India*, Simla, 1973.

[46] F.R. Allchin, *The Archaeology of Early Historic South Asia*, Cambridge, 1995.

continue. Since the archaeological span is prior to the dynastic time bracket, there can be some disjunction in co-relating archaeological data with the chronology of the dynasty. The evolution of urban centres which date to the pre-Mauryan period become in some cases more important in the Mauryan period. The hierarchy of sites within an area is difficult to ascertain as there has not been much in the way of systematic explorations with this question in mind.[47]

The NBPW is now given an Indian provenance, originating in the middle Ganges plain. Apart from other factors its association is with what is being termed the second urbanization, set in the context of what is referred to by some as the Ganges civilization.[48] Its technical quality has been attributed to the constitution of the clay and the method of firing.[49] The NBPW reaches a high quality in the early Mauryan period although its use in the sixth century BC would be an acceptable date.[50] Being a luxury ware it has a wide distribution although the associated ware is often more informative on local connections. The quality of the ware gives it precedence, but in terms of numbers there is generally a greater use of other wares such as the Black-and-Red, Black slipped ware, Red wares, thick grey wares and other more localized pottery. The distribution of the latter tends to be more regionally defined.

As part of the potter's craft, terra-cotta figures of the elephant, horse, bull, ram, dog and *nāga* were popular. Models of carts, wagons and chariots occur in terra-cotta and in metal. Hand-modelled human figures are common at many places, especially representations of what might be mother-goddesses. The latter seem to occur in large numbers at many sites in the Ganges plain and could perhaps be identifiable with some religious intention.[51] This provides an interesting commentary on what constituted popular religious belief and worship in this period. A distinction between pre-Mauryan and Mauryan terra-cottas is based on the larger number of human female figurines and their greater ornamentation as well as some element of a possible Hellenistic touch.[52]

47 G. Erdosy, *Urbanisation in Early Historic India*, Oxford, 1988, is an attempt at such a study relating to the evolution of Kauśāmbi and its *umland.*

48 T.N. Roy, *The Ganges Civilisation*, New Delhi, 1983.

49 K.T.M. Hegde, 'Scientific Basis of the Technology of Three Ancient Indian Ceramic Industries', in B.M. Pande and B.D. Chattopadhyaya (eds), *History and Archaeology*, Delhi, 1987, pp. 359–62.

50 G. Erdosy in Allchin, op. cit., pp. 104–5.

51 S.C. Ray, 'Evolution of Hindu-Buddhist Art in the Gangetic Valley: a Study on the basis of Stratigraphic Evidence of Archaeological Excavations', in *Investigating Indian Art*, Berlin, 1987, pp. 273–90.

52 G.A. Poster, *From Indian Earth — 4000 Years of Terracotta Art*, New York, 1986. D. Desai, 'Terracotta Dancing-girls', *Marg*, 1985, 37, pp. 72–4.

Copper mirrors, dishes, ornaments of various kinds, and the usual arrowheads, antimony rods, nails and needles, occur at some sites. Iron objects suggest a more professional use. Weapons included caltrops, and household objects ranging from nails to axes and adzes. Iron hoes occur in larger numbers at Megalithic sites in the peninsula. Crucibles from Ujjain Pd. II and smelting furnaces point to iron working on some scale. Mauryan period workings at mines near Udaipur in Rajasthan have provided some striking results.[53] Silver and lead were the main products at Agucha and Dariba, and zinc was mined at Zawar (as it is to this day). Agucha has given C-14 dates going back to the third century BC and is in the vicinity of what is described as a Mauryan settlement. Dates for the mine at Dariba go back to the end of the second millennium, but the period for the most intensive work appears to be in the latter part of the first millennium. The timber revetment to the mine is thought to be perhaps the largest timber structure from antiquity. The evidence suggests a prodigious scale of lead/silver production in the Zawar area, which, it has been proposed, may well be tied to the demand for silver in the making of punch-marked coins. The technology of working the mines can be reconstructed from the remains, and points to sophisticated techniques.

A survey of ancient quarries in the vicinity of Chunar has been rewarding in terms of reconstructing the making of the pillars.[54] Incomplete monoliths cylindrical in form, suggesting the proto-type raw material for the working of the Aśokan pillars, were found together with evidence that the quarries were used in later periods as well. The choice of Chunar is explained by its closeness to the river which facilitated the transportation of these monoliths. The cylinders have marks which might be mason's marks or inscriptions. One carries a brief *kharoṣṭhī* inscription which might be of the Mauryan period. This, it is suggested, may point to quarry workers being from the north-west where there existed a familiarity with stone cutting and carving. But this also brings to mind the small presence of *kharoṣṭhī* registered by the engraver of some of the Minor REs in Karnataka. Possibly it was the engravers who came from the north-west.

The western plain was essentially wheat-growing although some rice was found at Atranjikhera in the *doāb*.[55] If this was locally cultivated rice, then it

[53] P.T. Craddock et al., 'The Production of Lead, Silver and Zinc in Early India', in A. Hauptman, E. Pernicka and G.A. Wagner (eds), *Old World Archaeology*, Bergbau Museum, 1989, pp. 51–69.

[54] V. Jayaswal, 'Evidence for Resource Exploration for Art Activities at Chunar', in R. Varma (ed.), *Art and Archaeology of the Vindhyan Region*, Rewa, pp. 133–44. P.C. Pant and V. Jayaswal, 'Ancient Stone Quarries of Chunar: An Appraisal', *Pragadhara*, 1990–91, no. 1, pp. 49–52.

[55] K.A. Chaudhuri, *Ancient Agriculture and Forestry in Northern India*, Bombay, 1977. R. Thapar, *From Lineage to State*, p. 29.

raises the possibility of the area being conducive to double-cropping. This in turn has a bearing on agriculture and has been used as evidence to suggest a fiscal crisis in the Mauryan economy requiring to be met with an enhanced revenue. Wet rice cultivation was concentrated in the middle and lower Ganges plain. It is thought to have been a staple in the peninsula together with millets, especially *rāgi*. The cultivation of cotton is indicated by the presence of cotton cloth at various sites.

Arrangements for irrigation were locally controlled as major irrigation works are sparse. Inscriptions mention some large scale irrigation works, a canal built by the Nandas in Orissa and the Mauryan dam on the Sudarśana lake in Saurashtra. The latter has yet to be conclusively identified,[56] but the dimensions given and the frequency of repairs suggest that the dam irrigated an area that was large but not extensive. Excavations at Kumrahar also revealed a canal connecting the palace with the river, doubtless used for transporting goods.[57] A canal lined with bricks and said to be of the Mauryan period was located at Besnagar from an early excavation. Small tanks and catchment areas are more common in the peninsula.

Mauryan expansion of trade and the facilitating of contacts between distant areas accelerated exchange particularly in small items such as glass, clay and shell beads, as also beads of agate, carnelian (including etched beads), jasper and lapis lazuli, ivory hairpins and combs, and ear-ornaments of bone. Silver and gold ornaments are more limited. It is likely that much of the silver was used in the making of punch-marked coins and silver was not widely available in India. Gold supplies were mainly confined to Karnataka and possibly the auriferous soil of some parts of the extreme north. It is thought that the diamond mines of the peninsula were also worked.

The earliest fortified settlements appear to have been those at Ujjain, Kauśāmbi, Rajghat, Rajgir and Campa.[58] The direction indicates an early route. Gradually other centres came to be fortified. Perhaps the most impressive were the wooden posts and nailed cross-beams from Pāṭaliputra. City sizes are difficult to determine even with relative precision in the absence of surveys. Literary sources often give exaggerated figures, more to emphasize the notion of an expansive settlement than to be accurate. City walls become essential and initially have a mud core with revetments of brick, rubble and stone and occasionally even wooden sleepers. Some have bastions, gateways with guard rooms or a moat. The wall was in part defence, in part flood control — where

56 R.N. Mehta, 'Sudarśana Lake', *JOI*(B), 1968, 18, pp. 20–8, is an attempt at locating the site and seems probable but not certain.

57 *Indian Archaeology — A Review*, 1954–5, p. 19.

58 Allchin, op. cit., p. 109. Ghosh, *An Encyclopaedia of Indian Archaeology*, II, p. 62.

the town was on a river bank — and in part a demarcation between town and country, although the last was by no means definitive.

Burnt bricks of a relatively large size are used for dwelling complexes. Wedge-shaped bricks are used for circular structures. Bricks introduce a notion of permanency and an attempt to control the weathering of structures. Room sizes tend to be small. Houses are fitted with wells, some brick-lined and some ring wells — a construction of large terra-cotta rings, or with soakage jars open at both ends and placed one on top of the other. Ring wells become a characteristic feature at many sites. Some varieties of wells are linked to drains.

These characteristics of urban centres enable a recognition of those that were more important and those that were marginal. In the north-west Taxila/Bhir Mound and Charsada (the ancient Puṣkalāvatī), remain small but are important. Bhir Mound was not a planned city but did have differentiated streets, lanes, drains and other features pointing to a civic organization.[59] Kandahar had earlier urban beginnings as a frontier town on the Indo-Iranian borderlands. The settlements at Ropar and Sugh in the Punjab were probably on the route to the Ganga-Yamuna *doāb*. In Rajasthan, Bairāṭ was a major Buddhist site at which excavations have provided evidence of an improvement in living conditions at what are said to be the Mauryan levels, as at some other sites. The Aśokan connection is further indicated by fragments of what seem to be Chunar sandstone pillars and an umbrella of stone with a Mauryan polish.[60] Excavations near Rupnath have provided evidence of a substantial improvement in living and the extensive use of artefacts in Mauryan levels.[61]

In western India, the port of Bṛghukaccha was associated with the manufacture of ivory and shell items and beads. Central Indian sites include the important centre of Ujjain as well as other sites such as Tripuri, Vidiśā/Besnagar, Maheshwar and Eran, some of which have a Chalcolithic history, but are in all cases pre-Mauryan settlements. Maheshwar was at the ford across the Narmada to Navdatoli and was on the route going south, the *dakṣinā-patha*. The route may have passed through Panguraria and Sannati. There will now be an increased interest in the possibility of Mauryan artefacts being found in the vicinity of Sannati.

Moving eastwards, there are traces of copper mining in Singhbhum and also some evidence of iron working, but more detailed excavation is required before the date of the working of these mines can be guaged. In the lower Ganges valley the port of Tamluk/Tāmralipti played a major commercial role

[59] A recent overview of the history and archaeology of the sites at Taxila is available in A.H. Dani, *Taxila*, UNESCO, 1986.

[60] *Indian Archaeology — A Review*, 1962–3, p. 31. D. Mitra, *Buddhist Monuments*, Calcutta, 1971, pp. 42ff.

[61] R.K. Sharma and S.N. Mishra, *Excavations at Kakrebta (Rupnath)*, Delhi, 1992.

and together with Chandraketugarh had links with coastal Orissa, Andhra and further south, and eventually with Sri Lanka. Mahāsthān is currently under excavation. In Orissa the extensive site of Śiśupālgarh has been partially excavated but its possibilities have not been adequately investigated. Orissa and Andhra have been the subject of an excellent study of secondary state formation in which the process is seen from pre-Mauryan to post-Mauryan times.[62]

The north-western Deccan carries traces of contacts with the north at sites such as Nasik, Prakash, and Bahal. In the south-eastern Deccan and in Karnataka, Megalithic settlements both precede and coincide with Mauryan expansion. The Mauryan presence is not evident as an agency of destruction or of change because the Mauryas seem to have been more concerned with acquiring the resources of this region rather than restructuring the economy. Dharanikoṭa/Dhānyakaṭaka in Andhra is associated with the arrival of the NBPW after extensive use of Black-and-Red Ware of the Megalithic variety, and a quantity of silver punch-marked coins. A wharf in alignment with a navigational channel points to maritime links, probably with the Ganges delta, and it would also have controlled the route along the Krishna valley leading to the area of the gold mines. Excavations at Amarāvatī indicate a settlement in the Mauryan period or perhaps even a little earlier, which makes it possible that the *stūpa* was initially built at the time of Aśoka.[63]

Nevertheless, the important sites of Brahmagiri and Maski in Karnataka, both locations of Aśokan inscriptions, show the continued predominance of the Megalithic culture ways. The importance of the sites in this area was enhanced by the fertility of the Raichur *doāb*. Nittur has Megalithic stone circles in the vicinity of the inscription and Udegollam is an early historical site. There is considerable uncertainty about the identification of a few sherds of possible NBPW further south in the peninsula.

A comparison of the distribution of archaeological sites associated with the Mauryan period and the Aśokan inscriptions, indicates that there were three areas which might be called areas of isolation at this time, where urban centres and inscriptions are absent. These are the lower Indus plain, the eastern part of central India (which remained an area of isolation for many centuries) and the far south.[64] Elsewhere Mauryan control established routes with emerging centres of exchange, some of an urban nature. With the break-up of the

62 S. Seneviratne, 'Kalinga and Andhra: the Process of Secondary State Formation in Early India', in H.J.M. Claessen and P. Skalnik (eds), *The Study of the State*, The Hague, 1981. *Social Base of Early Buddhism in South-East India and Sri Lanka*, Ph.D. Thesis, JNU, 1985.

63 I.K. Sharma, 'Early Sculptures and Epigraphs from South East India: New Evidence from Amarāvatī', in F.M. Asher and G.S. Ghai (eds), *Indian Epigraphy*, New Delhi, 1985, pp. 15–23.

64 F.R. Allchin, 'Patterns of City Formation in Early Historic South Asia', *South Asian Studies*, 1990, 6, pp. 163–73.

Mauryan empire, the larger cities became the nuclei of new states. The importance of Pāṭaliputra is clearly indicated by its being larger in size than the other cities of the time.

The archaeological evidence reinforces the argument that there appears to have been an improvement in the standard of living during this period at many sites and particularly those which evolve, or had evolved, into urban centres. This enhancement doubtless drew not only from new technologies but also from forms of administration, communication and exchange, which were part of Mauryan policy. Those sites which have Aśokan inscriptions and have been excavated, point to the presence of artefacts associated with the period, except however for the sites in central Karnataka which curiously have not so far registered the presence of northern artefacts although there is a heavy cluster of inscriptions in the area. This perhaps says something about the nature of Mauryan settlement and control in these parts. What is noticeable, although not unexpected, is that the cultures immediately prior to, and often even contemporary with the Mauryan are diverse from region to region, both in identity and in degrees of historical change. This not only endorses the argument that Mauryan society was indeed a multi-cultural society, but also requires us to view the possible divergencies in the relations between the Mauryan administration and the local people of a region.

Punch Marked Coins

These coins were discussed in some detail at a seminar, the proceedings of which have been published.[65] The coins appear in stratified levels at excavations often together with NBPW. The date of the NBPW has been taken back to the seventh century at some places and the dating on the coins in this publication has also been sought to be made earlier, some taking it back to 800 BC. General opinion however still adheres to the sixth century BC as the start of coinage. In any case they would have been in circulation prior to the Mauryas.[66] The symbols on the coins are suggestive of an indigenous origin although the notion of coined metallic money was probably known from west Asian usage. Pre-Mauryan literary evidence, with the exception of Pāṇini, does not confirm the use of coins, but is familiar with using weights of gold and silver with a designated value. Punch marked coins would have increased in number with the greater availability of silver and this may have required close connection with west Asia and Afghanistan, apart from the more sporadic mining in the subcontinent.

[65] A.K. Narain and L. Gopal (eds), *Chronology of the Punch-Marked Coins*, Varanasi, 1966.

[66] S.C. Ray, Stratigraphic Evidence of Coins in Indian Excavations and some allied issues, *Numismatic Notes and Monographs*, 1–14, Varanasi, 1959. See also M.K. Dhavalikar, 'The Beginnings of Coinage in India', *World Archaeology*, 1975, 6, pp. 330–8.

In the study of punch-marked coins the work of D.D. Kosambi remains the most challenging. Kosambi's papers on punch-marked coins, from various journals, were collected and published, thus bringing together his views on early Indian numismatics.[67] This makes available his substantial analysis of these coins and even if one may not agree with it on every count, it still directs attention to issues which need to be studied. He treated coinage as the necessary tool of trade and argued that it originated with traders. At a later stage the state appropriated the system. Coinage gives a clue to trade relations provided that the identification of coins with those who issue them can be ascertained. Where he identifies the symbols with certain Mauryan rulers there can be considerable difference of opinion. He uses his own identification to assert a debasement in the metal and therefore argues for a fiscal crisis in the later Mauryan period.[68]

Another view questions Kosambi's method of analysis and the early date of the coins.[69] Cribb dates the coins to the fourth century BC arguing that the association with the NBPW is chronologically uncertain. The date should be determined by dated coinage in the Chaman Hazuri hoard and by the reference to Alexander receiving talents of marked silver. An examination of the symbols suggests that there were local issues of varying weight which are rare in northern India and national issues with a standard weight found all over the subcontinent. The coins were developed in the north-west and were imitated in the Ganges towns. However the pre-Mauryan use of coins is suggested in other sources. The Nandas are said to have standardized weights and this is likely to have included coins.[70] Coins were a familiar item to Pāṇini,[71] which would date them to at least the fifth century.

Aśokan Pillars as Monuments

A major reassessment of the Aśokan pillars and their capitals was made by John Irwin in which he questioned a number of theories which have so far been taken for granted.[72] Irwin maintains that the pillars which are called

67 D.D. Kosambi, *Indian Numismatics*, New Delhi, 1981.

68 See the Appendix IV in this book.

69 J. Cribb, 'Dating India's Earliest Coins', in *South Asian Archaeology, 1983*, Naples, 1985, pp. 535–51.

70 Pāṇini II.4.21.

71 V.S. Agarwala, *India as Known to Panini*, Varanasi, 1963, pp. 259–74, 474.

72 John Irwin, 'Asokan Pillars: a Re-assessment of the Evidence', *The Burlington Magazine*, 1973, CXV, pp. 706–20; loc. cit., 1974, CXVI, pp. 712–27; 1975, CXVII, pp. 631–43; 1976, CXVIII, pp. 734–53. 'The Prayaga-bull Pillar: Another pre-Aśokan Monument', in H. Härtal (ed.), *South Asian Archaeology, 1979*, vol. II, Berlin, 1981, pp. 313–40. 'Origins of the Pre-Aśokan Pillar Cult at Prayaga (Allahabad)', *JRAS*, 1983, 3, 'True Chronology of the Aśokan Pillar, *Artibus Asiae*, 1983, XLIV, 4, pp. 247–65. 'Buddhism and the Cosmic Pillar', in G. Gnoli and L. Lanciotti (eds), op. cit. Some of Irwin's views have in turn been questioned by S.P. Gupta, *The Roots of Indian Art*,

Aśokan are not all Aśokan and some are pre-Aśokan. This is attested by PE VII where the king states that the edict is to be inscribed even on existing pillars. Irwin attempts to demonstrate this by using the evidence from archaeology. The pillars, according to him, were originally cult objects, some being regarded as the *axis mundi* and often associated with funerary tumuli, and therefore some remain uninscribed. They formed a sacred triad together with the tree, and the *stūpa*. Aśokan pillars therefore do not mark the beginning of monumental art but the culmination of an older tradition of setting up pillars, which was a religious tradition. With the exception of the Sārnāth pillar which shows a Perso-Hellenistic connection, the style of the other capitals is traceable to an earlier epoch when India was already familiar with the ancient Near East. The pillars were originally of wood and were placed directly into the earth. The pillar had associations with the sacrificial *yūpa*, and the *dhvaja*, and was symbolic of an established cult. The *dhvaja* was worshipped before battle because divinity was thought to reside in it.

Irwin discusses in detail the nine pillars around which there have been excavations. Of these, four were placed directly in the ground with no support in the fashion of the wooden pillars and these therefore could not remain upright and eventually fell. The other five were placed on a stone foundation and therefore survived for a longer time. Four of these were inscribed — Sārnāth, Topra, Rampurva (lion capital), Lauriyā Nandangarh — and the fifth is only a shaft at Gotihawa. The pillars have a bricked surround which was a *pradakṣinā-patha*. Irwin argues that the first group was earlier and the second group was later. The Vaiśāli pillar with a lion capital was also earlier as it seems to have sunk substantially into the earth suggesting that there was no foundation stone.

In discussing the chronology of the pillars his view is that the first edict issued was the Schism Edict, even though it would date to a later part of Aśoka's reign if it is linked to the Third Council at Pāṭaliputra. His contention that the Allahabad-Kosam pillar has always been located at Prayāga is plausible in terms of the method of engraving the edicts, but there is little convincing explanation as to why the edict addressed to the *mahāmattas* of Kauśāmbi should be inscribed on a pillar at Prayāga, particularly as it is uncertain whether the Ganga-Yamuna confluence was sufficiently sacred at that time to merit a pillar. The major monastic site, similar to Sarnath and Sanchi, was at Kauśāmbi and not at Prayāga and the contents of the Schism Edict would be relevant to a major monastery. Interestingly there is a strong association in the Buddhist tradition of dissenting monks with Kauśāmbi.[73]

Delhi, 1980, but the questioning has not furthered the debate in any essential sense.

[73] *Vinaya* I.337–57; *Kosambi Jātaka*, no. 428.

Discussing the capitals he argues that the lotus-and-palmette and the bead-and-reel designs are not Perso-Hellenistic but are ultimately derived from the Egyptian lotus which design came in various ways to Greece, Iran and India probably through Assyria, the Levant and Ionia in the mid-first millennium BC. The links with the Near East have however been questioned.[74] Irwin interprets the so-called 'honey-suckle' motif as a stylised lotus. The pillar for him is symbolic of that which separated heaven from earth in the creation myths. The elephant and the bull had Indian connotations, especially connected with fertility. The lion was heraldic and borrowed and to that extent represented new conceptions of royalty. The pillar then becomes the symbol of the divine role of ancient Indian kingship, a view not too distant from that of Coomaraswamy. It is not merely a Buddhist symbol but articulates the summation of all virtue. Aśoka's imperial vision is said to have been influenced by the Achaemenid example.

The connections between India and Assyria and the Levant are plausible since they would also relate to the issuing of silver bent bar coins in India and the evolution of the *brāhmī* script. But such connections may not have been influential beyond these similarities. That some pillars are pre-Aśokan and others set up by Aśoka also seems a convincing argument and the technical investigation of the actual setting up of the pillars points to the kind of excavation and analysis which needs to be carried out elsewhere where there are Aśokan pillars. That some were pre-existing and that some were earlier than others even during the reign of Aśoka would not create problems. His statement that not all the pillars attributed to Aśoka were cut and polished at Chunar would have to be further investigated particularly after the recent work at Chunar. This would include a discussion of the Mauryan style sculpture in Chunar sandstone found near Kauśāmbi and dated to post-Mauryan levels, which Niharranjan Ray maintains, reinforces his argument that the Didarganj *yakṣī* is post-Mauryan.[75]

But some major questions remain unanswered. Why were some pillars inscribed and not others? What conditioned the choice? If these pillars had the cosmic meaning which is imputed to them, then why are they limited to the Ganges plain? The texts which Irwin quotes, such as the *Ṛgveda* had a geographical context which was that of the north-west and the Punjab and the water-shed, an area which is devoid of pillars. The concentration in the Ganges plain is suggestive of a different tradition if we are to look for antecedents.

74 Allchin, op. cit., p. 239.

75 Niharranjan Ray, 'Maurya and Sunga Art', in *Indian Studies Past and Present*, 1964–5, VI, pp. 53ff. J.C. Harle, in *The Art and Architecture of the Indian Subcontinent*, Harmondsworth, 1986, p. 31 supports a date of the first century AD.

The pillars attributed to Aśoka in Hsüan Tsang's list are also largely in the Ganges plain. The inscriptions have no connection with the earlier cults of the Indradhvaja or such like and their contents tend to be practical concerns of administration, the welfare of the subjects, and social ethics as part of short discourses on *dhamma*, or alternatively are concerned with the functioning of the *saṃgha*. If Aśoka was resorting to traditional symbols in inscribing his edicts on pillars, the message he was conveying was not linked to the belief about the pillars. At most it could be said that in some cases Aśoka was drawing on the earlier associations with the pillars to legitimize his own message. This raises the question of whether he chose the pillars and pillar sites, which might be a partial explanation as to why they are confined to the Ganges plain, although of course the transportation of the newly cut pillars would have been a major consideration. There is little evidence of stone carving prior to the pillars, therefore the question of where the technique originated in India and how, remains as yet, unanswered. The function of pillars serving as imperial symbols, quite apart from their cultic or other significance, should not be ignored.

Certain other monuments and art remains pertaining to the Mauryan period have also been discussed. The Dharmarājika *stūpa* at Sarnath is now held to have an Aśokan nucleus.[76] The Lomas Rishi cave has come in for detailed consideration.[77] The list of Mauryan art remains has sought to be enlarged but the dating of many items still remains controversial.[78] Ring-stones and stone discs, associated mainly with urban centres have been described as Mauryan and on the basis of the reliefs carved on them, they are said to have possibly been votive objects in a religio-sexual context.[79]

Textual Sources

The *Arthaśāstra* of Kauṭalya

A three-volume study by R.P. Kangle has now become the standard work on the text, including as it does a critical edition, translation into English, and an introductory study.[80] Earlier English translations having been rather unsatisfactory, this is a substantial improvement. The notes which accompany the text are of considerable help in disentangling some of the more difficult passages. Kangle discusses the chronology of the text and is of the opinion that there is no convincing reason why this work should not be regarded as

[76] D. Mitra, *Buddhist Monuments*, Calcutta, 1971, p. 24.

[77] J.C. Huntington, 'The Lomas Rishi: Another Look', *Archives of Asian Art*, 1974–5, 28, pp. 34–56.

[78] S.P. Gupta, op. cit.

[79] Allchin, op. cit., p. 263.

[80] R.P. Kangle, *The Kauṭilīya Arthaśāstra*, Bombay, 1965.

the work of Kauṭalya, who helped Candragupta to come to power in Magadha.[81] He has elsewhere discussed more recent articles relating to various aspects of the *Arthaśāstra*.[82] Among these Burrow argues for differentiating between Cānakya and Kauṭalya.[83] An extensive bibliography on the *Arthaśāstra* is now available.[84] A more recent translation has re-arranged the text to make it more accessible to the modern reader.[85] But the justification for the re-arrangement is based on modern attitudes towards the administration of a state which takes the text outside its historical context. Why the text was arranged in the way it was originally, remains unexplained. There has also been an analysis of the text with a focus on political economy and some aspects of Marxist historiography.[86]

A detailed consideration of the chronology of the text which is a departure from the older form of argument is the study of T. Trautmann.[87] This includes the collation and analysis of various narratives concerning Cānakya/Kauṭalya and the differentiation between them in a variety of traditions. Turning to the text an attempt is made to arrange its various sections chronologically by using the statistical method with the aid of a computer. This involves listing the potential discriminators – the commonly used particles, such as *evam*, *ca*, *tathā*, *va*, and so on, the use of which in literary style helps identify and differentiate between the styles of various authors, if there is more than one. Sentence length and compound length were also used as discriminators. Trautmann's analysis suggests that there are three distinct books within and prior to the compilation of the *Arthaśāstra*, Books II, III and VII, which appear to have been composed separately. The composition and authorship of the other Books is less certain. There would then have been several authors and it would be incorrect to refer to Kauṭalya as the author of the entire text. *Arthaśāstra* was a category of literature like *Dharmaśāstra*, and would therefore have had antecedent texts, and others compiled in the early centuries AD.

Trautmann would date the compiling of the various texts into the *Arthaśāstra* at a date precluding the Mauryas and the Hunas and therefore of the early centuries AD possibly *c.* AD 250. Book II, entitled *Adhyakṣa-pracāra*, may have been the earliest. Books III and IV containing material akin to that of the *Dharmasmṛtis* probably pre-date Yajñavalkya. The elaborate doctrines of

[81] Ibid., p. 106.

[82] R.P. Kangle, 'Some Recent Work on the Kauṭilya *Arthaśāstra*', *JAS*, Bombay, 1968–9, 43–4, pp. 227–38.

[83] T. Burrow, 'Cānakya and Kauṭilya', *ABORI*, 1968, 47–9, pp. 13–17.

[84] L. Sternbach, *Bibliography of Kauṭiliya Arthaśāstra*, Hoshiarpur, 1973.

[85] L.N. Rangarajan (trans.), *Arthaśāstra*, New Delhi, 1992.

[86] Eva Ritschl and Maria Schetelich, *Studien zum Kauṭilīya Arthaśāstra*, Berlin, 1973.

[87] T.R. Trautmann, *Kauṭilya and the Arthaśāstra*, Leiden, 1971.

Book VII do not suggest a date prior to the Christian era. He further argues that although the existing *Arthaśāstra* may not be so old, the *śāstra* tradition which it contains probably pre-dates the *Dharmasmṛti* literature in view of the discussion on the relationship between the two categories.[88] The *rājadharma* section of Manu for example, could well have been drawn from an early *Arthaśāstra*. It may be suggested that this discussion has an added historiographical interest. Nationalist historiography maintained that the discovery of the Kauṭalya *Arthaśāstra* vindicated Indian civilization as having a rational and practical side as well. The inclusion of topics parallel to the *Arthaśāstra* in other texts such as Manu, or the *Mahābhārata*, indicates that this rational and practical side was more widespread than was earlier conceded.

Now that the Vedic corpus, the *Mahābhārata*, the *Rāmāyaṇa*, and many of the *Dharmaśāstras* are available in the form of data-bases for computers, the application of the statistical method is bound to increase. It does not supersede traditional scholarship but acts as a parallel investigation. Since the computer is largely an aid to the more mechanical side of the work, the discussion still draws upon references in various texts and a familiarity with the texts is all the more necessary to the reconstruction of the results of the computer analysis. Its potential also lies in the fact that the method can be further refined for more precise results. The introduction of this new technique of analysis in relation to the dating of the *Arthaśāstra* does require that those working on this particular subject should comprehend the technique and not set it aside as some do. This is a lacunae in a recent study which discusses the date of the *Arthaśāstra*.[89] Trautmann's method is dismissed because it is claimed that it cannot be verified in India, which is of course incorrect.[90]

That the *Arthaśāstra* was not a document describing the government associated with a single period is a widely held view. To the extent that it is a comment on how an efficient governmental system should be organized, it would inevitably refer to more than one period. If the present compilation dates to the third century AD then items, artefacts and concepts of earlier times are likely to occur in the discussion within the text. The identification of these would stretch from the earliest association in time of the text — the Mauryan period — to later times. To accuse scholars of arbitrarily using the evidence when they date passages by such identifications, is meaningless. Texts in the

[88] G.N. Dwivedi, *The Age of Kauṭilya*, Agra, 1966; J.D.M. Derrett, 'A Newly Discovered Contact between *Arthaśāstra* and *Dharmaśāstra*: the Role of Bharuci', *ZDMG*, 1965, 115, pp. 134ff.

[89] S.R. Goyal, *Kauṭilya and Megasthenes*, Meerut, 1985.

[90] The application of the statistical method to the Harappa script for example, a far more complicated procedure than the linguistic analysis of a text, was carried out entirely in India by I. Mahadevan and published by the ASI, *The Indus Script*, Delhi, 1977.

early period were constantly revised and updated and the *Arthaśāstra* was no exception. Thus in many such texts some sections are early, some are late and some early sections carry interpolated passages of a later date. Interpolations can have many reasons and take many forms including the foisting of names into manuscripts. Interpolations can suggest in some cases, the point in time when additions were made. Therefore if it is said that the *Arthaśāstra* was edited over time, this is not an attempt to 'explain away' interpolations. The freezing of texts in their original form becomes more characteristic of the post-Gupta period and suggests changed attitudes to the oral tradition and to literacy. As long as the text is not being quoted as an authentic, descriptive narrative, but as a normative text, then the question of its date gets subordinated to the concession to interpolation, and therefore it can best be used in a comparative sense with other textual sources.

There is also the need to consider who the authors of a text may be and to whom the text is addressed. The statistical method shows that it is not the work of a single author but a compilation. If Book II is the earliest, then it fits in with the initial attempts to establish a monarchy based on efficient revenue collection and a degree of centralization through administration. There is no concept of empire in the text, but the notion of government is very different from that of the earlier *janapadas* which preceded the Nandas and the Mauryas. This part of the text suggests that the state is also beginning to enter activities such as control over forests, over mines and semi-precious stones, over coined metallic money, and so forth, which was a departure from the earlier practices. It is precisely in the area of the state's control over economic resources that there is more agreement between Book Two of the *Arthaśāstra* and the *Indica* of Megasthenes.

If the *Arthaśāstra*, the Aśokan inscriptions and the Buddhist texts maintain that the *yonas* have a different social system, it does not mean that the *Arthaśāstra* is later, but that the system existed at the time of Aśoka and was being commented upon by the other texts. The nature of the comment would indicate whether they were speaking of a contemporary situation in emphasizing the difference. The use of various languages such as Prākrit, Greek and Aramaic by Aśoka and not Sanskrit, was because he intended a particular purpose through his edicts and this intention would not have been met by the use of Sanskrit. When the intention changes then later kings use Sanskrit. Royal inscriptions, largely votive, continue using Prākrit for some time after Aśoka. Initially these are a small part of the many brief votive inscriptions made at this time by ordinary people.[91] The *Arthaśāstra* is in Sanskrit because

91 R. Thapar, 'Patronage and Community', in B. Stoller Miller (ed.), *The Powers of Art*, Delhi, 1992, pp. 19–34.

it obviously has a very different function and belongs to the *śāstra* tradition which was in any case distanced from the Buddhist moorings of many of the Aśokan edicts. Daṇḍin in the *Daśakumāracarita* states that Viṣṇugupta composed six thousand *ślokas* for the Maurya to learn *daṇḍanīti*.[92] This passage has often been quoted with reference to the theory that the text may have been metrical in origin. What is more important for our purposes is the association with the Maurya, even at such a late date.

The *Indica* of Megasthenes.

A fresh survey of references to India in Greek texts has recently been made.[93] More specifically there have been a number of studies of the context in which Megasthenes was writing by various scholars of Greek and Classical history and these suggest that the text was not written in isolation from parallel texts at the time.[94] Megasthenes was viewing India through a Hellenistic perspective and Greek ethnographical writing. In two major articles, Zambrini made a detailed review of earlier scholarship on the subject and argued that there was a relation between the *Indica* and the *Aegyptica* of Hecataeus of Abdera and these have to be seen as polemical in the political tension between the Ptolemies and the Seleucids.[95] Megasthenes was in part locating his Indian experience in a Greek view of the world. Bosworth's study of both Arrian and the *Indica* leads him to maintain that Arrian is concerned essentially with the history of Alexander, therefore the *Indica* is a supplementary interest and has to be read alongside the major work.[96] Arrian's main interest is in the geographic and ethnographic details of the voyage of Nearchos. The *Indica* was propaganda in favour of Alexander but was not a polemic against Hecataeus who had made Sesostris the great world conqueror. He also suggests that Megasthenes may have been the representative of Sibyrtius who controlled Arachosia, rather than the ambassador of Seleucus and that his mention of visiting the court at Pāṭaliputra was probably not to repeated occasions of being at the court but to his single visit to Pāṭaliputra. Bosworth argues that it is more likely that Megasthenes visited India in *c.* 310, as the description of the Punjab and the Ganges plain seems earlier rather than later and prior to

[92] P. Peterson (ed.), *The Daśakumāracarita of Daṇḍin*, II, Bombay, 1891, p. 52.

[93] K. Karttunen, *India in Early Greek Literature*, Helsinki, 1989.

[94] O. Murray, 'Herodotus and Hellenistic Culture', *Classical Quarterly*, 1972, 22, pp. 200–13.

[95] A. Zambrini, 'Gli Indika di Megasthene', *Annali della Scuola Norm. Sup. di Pisa*, 1982, 3, 12, 1, pp. 71–149 and 1985, 3, 15, 3, pp. 781–853.

[96] A.B. Bosworth, *A Historical Commentary on Arrian's History of Alexander*, II, Oxford, 1995. 'The Historical Setting of Megasthenes' *Indica*', *Classical Philology*, 1996, 91, pp. 113–27. See also, 'Aristotle, India and the Alexander Historians', *TOPOI*, 1993, 3/2, pp. 407–24.

the loss of the Indus area to the Maurya. Candragupta, who is referred to as the king of the Prasii, is not said to be the only king ruling in India for there are other kings mentioned, as well as the autonomous cities. It should however be kept in mind that none of the authors who were supposedly quoting from Megasthenes were his contemporaries, therefore the quotations may well have been subjected to interpolations. Further, that Diodorus and Strabo are possibly closer to each other in what they say and that Arrian, perhaps because he is even later, not only paraphrases Megasthenes more evidently, but also makes an occasional statement which is not found in the earlier two.

It is interesting that the historiographical locating of Megasthenes has become part of a more analytical discussion among specialists of Greek sources of ancient history, examining the intellectual assumptions of those writing for Hellenistic society. This will help to clarify some of the ambiguities in the quotations from Megasthenes. Independent of this discussion I have argued that in his description of Indian administration and society and the seven castes, Megasthenes was clearly writing in the context of Greek and Hellenistic experience and ideas, and I have tried to reassess the statements from Megasthenes on the divisions of Indian society and on some aspects of economic arrangements.[97]

Megasthenes has little to say on the practice and worship of Buddhism, except for the possible general reference to renouncers as one of the categories included among the philosophers and sophists. Yet the Buddhists were among the sects which endorsed renunciation but nevertheless at this time lived on the fringes of urban settlements from where they obtained alms. Megasthenes does however mention more than once, the Indian gods whom he identifies with Herakles and Dionysus, generally believed to be references to Kṛṣṇa and Śiva. An attempt to change this identification to Indra and a tribal deity has not met with much support.[98]

Buddhist sources.

The *Aśokāvadāna* has received some attention. There is now an English translation of the first part of Przyluski's study *La Legende de l'Empereur Açoka*, which is an analysis of the northern Buddhist traditions concerning Aśoka as described in the *Aśokāvadāna*.[99] Subsequent to Przyluski the *Aśokāvadāna* has been edited with some reference to additional texts by S. Mukhopadhyaya and this edition

[97] R. Thapar, *The Mauryas Revisited*, Calcutta, 1988, pp. 32ff.

[98] A. Dahlquist, *Megasthenes and Indian Religion*, Uppsala, 1962.

[99] D.K. Biswas (trans.), *The Legend of Emperor Aśoka*, Calcutta, 1967.

[100] S. Mukhopadhyaya, *Aśokāvadāna*, Delhi, 1963. J.S. Strong, *The Legend of King Aśoka*, New Jersey, 1983. See also, *The Legend and Cult of Upagupta*, N.J., 1992. J.W.de Jong 'Notes on the Text of the Aśoka Legend', in G. Pollet (ed.), *India and the Ancient World*, Louvain,

has been used as the basis of a new study and translation by Strong.[100] The historicity of the legends from the *avadānas* has been discussed with reference to the Queen's edict possibly endorsing a weakening of Aśoka's control over the kingdom in his last years.[101] It is said that the edict was not engraved at the order of Aśoka since it opens with the statement, *devānampiyasa-vacanena*, suggesting that it was issued by the queen herself. But a similar opening statement occurs in the SEs and should more reasonably be interpreted as officials recording the orders of Aśoka rather than his losing control. An unpublished manuscript containing the legend of Kunāla as part of the *Aśokāvadānamālā* has also been discussed.[102] The complete text of the Lama Tāranātha's history of Buddhism in India has been translated afresh into English.[103]

The claim by various scholars that the date of the death of the Buddha should be advanced by about eighty to a hundred years, would make some difference to the interpretation of the evidence from Buddhist texts.[104] The changed date may suit events connected with the various Buddhist *saṃghas* as has been argued, but may not suit the chronological statements made about pre-Mauryan history, although it would not contradict the major historical processes in the Ganges plain associated with this period, such as state-formation and urbanization. Archaeological evidence supports, as we have seen, the start of urbanization at some sites in the sixth century BC with further changes in the subsequent century.

It has been argued that the sites associated with the life of the Buddha such as Lumbinī, Kapilavastu, Śrāvastī, Vaiśāli, Rājagṛha, Kauśāmbi and Sārnāth/Rajghat, could not have been urban centres this early.[105] Lumbinī was in any case not described as an urban centre in the narrative on the life of the Buddha. The settlement at Kapilavastu/Ganwaria has been dated to 800 BC with NBPW occurring in the time bracket 600–200 BC together with considerable evidence of structures.[106] Kapilavastu is described as the central town of the Śākyas but is not included among the *mahānagaras* in Buddhist texts. At Śrāvasti there is

---

1987, pp. 103–13.

101 G.M. Bongard-Levin, 'The Historicity of the Ancient Indian Avadānas: A Legend about Aśoka's Deposition and the Queen's Edict', *Indian Studies Past and Present*, Calcutta, 1971, pp. 123–41.

102 G.M. Bongard-Levin and O.F. Volkova, 'The Kunāla Legend and an Unpublished Aśokāvadānamālā Manuscript', *Indian Studies Past and Present*, Calcutta, 1965.

103 Alaka Chattopadhyaya and the Lama Chimpa, *Tāranātha's History of Buddhism in India*, Simla, 1980.

104 H. Bechert (ed.), *The Dating of the Historical Buddha*, I and II, Gottingen, 1991.

105 H. Härtel, 'Archaeological Research on Ancient Buddhist Sites', in Bechert, op. cit., pp. 61–89. H. Kulke, 'Some Considerations on the Significance of Buddha's Date for the History of Northern India', ibid., pp. 100–7.

106 K.M. Srivastava, 'Some Interesting New Finds from Kapilavastu, in B.M. Pande, op. cit., pp. 359–62. See Ganwaria in Ghosh, *Encyclopaedia*, p. 143.

an overlap between NBPW and PGW and a large variety of items suggesting that it was an exchange centre as early as Pd.I which is dated to the sixth century BC,[107] but given the overlap could have had earlier beginnings as a settlement. The *garh* area of Vaiśāli was under occupation from at least 500 BC, with an admixture of NBPW and BRW at the lowest level, although the structures are said to be later. Interestingly the NBPW at Ayodhya is being dated to the seventh century BC. The extensive site of Rajgir, both the earlier fort and the later settlement have produced NBPW and at one spot the settlement has been dated to 500 BC or earlier. Kauśāmbi, even with the revised dates, was clearly an urban centre in the sixth century BC. The settlement at Rajghat goes back to 800 BC with BRW, and urban characteristics are associated with the introduction of NBPW. In the absence of extensive horizontal excavations, the nature of urbanization for each site cannot be precisely guaged. On the basis of a comparative study of the sites of the Ganges plain it can be maintained that if the Buddha preached in the late sixth and early fifth century, some sites were urban centres and at others there was an initial change towards urbanization.

The evolution of urban centres requires a multiplicity of factors which, judging from the archaeological data of the Ganges plain, seem to have been present in the sixth century BC. Proto-urban settlements would require the support of a large agricultural base, and the possibility of double-cropping or of wet rice cultivation would have provided this. If the settlement was located on a route with potentialities for trade, as many of these early towns were, this would add to a tendency towards urbanization. In both these changes iron technology would have played a role even if it was not the major causative factor. Together with this, the emergence of kingdoms required a central settlement which would be the nucleus of political control and power. These are described in the texts as *rājadhānis* and as such would have attracted a larger population than other settlements. Population densities are evident in a comparison of pre-NBPW settlements with NBPW ones, where in one district which has been surveyed, the pattern is not only of an increase in the number of settlements but also larger numbers in most and in a few, a marked concentration of population. The latter are the recognisable urban centres.[108] The larger number of settlements would have provided the support of agricultural and other resources, particularly as their spread is in areas with arable land. The bigger settlements are along the Ganges which doubtless acted as a route. Environmental factors also determined the size and pattern of the settlement.

The early Buddhist texts show an awareness of some towns being urban

107 A. Ghosh, *An Encyclopaedia of Indian Archaeology*, II, p. 420.

108 Makkhan Lal, 'Summary of Four Seasons of Exploration in Kanpur District, Uttar Pradesh', *Man and Environment*, 1984, VIII, pp. 61–80.

centres at an early date and others becoming so later.[109] Kauśāmbi is of major importance both as a meeting point of routes and as the capital of the *janapada*, apart from developing into a monastic centre.[110] Rajgir is described as the old settlement of a hill fortress, Giribbaja, in the verse sections which are believed to be early, and the new settlement, Rājagaha, was a town at the foot of the hill built by Bimbisāra. In contrast, Pāṭaligāma is said to have been only a village in the lifetime of the Buddha and became the capital in the reign of Bimbisāra's great-grandson.[111] If the suggested later date is accepted then the main city providing the background to his teaching ought to have been Pāṭaliputra, which is not the city referred to in the Buddhist texts. Rājagaha declined with the rise of Pāṭaliputra. Incidentally, the *Mahābhārata* describes it as a flourishing town and the capital of Jarasandha, who is close in time to Brhadratha, which would make him earlier than Bimbisāra, although the date of this reference in the epic may be uncertain.[112] Vaiśāli is said to have many *caityas* dating to before the Buddha. Śrāvastī was a centre of exchange and commercially important. The towns associated most often with the Buddha were Śrāvastī, Rājagṛha, Kauśāmbi and Vaiśāli, conforming to a limited area in the middle Ganges plain. Banaras and Taxila are more frequently mentioned in the *Jātakas*. In the typology of towns, even in the Pāli Canon, there is a differentiation between the incipient urban centres and the well-established.[113] Kuśināra, although a capital of the Mallas is described as inferior and set in a forest. It carries the appellation of *nagara* as do the *mahānagaras* but is different, although it is not described as a *gāma*, as was Pāṭaligāma, thus pointing to the difference. The archaeological counterparts to these variants would also differ in this graded distinction of urban settlements.

The change to a *mahānagara* would have required mud walls and ramparts giving way to fortifications, therefore fortifications were not necessarily characteristic of the earliest period of urbanization. There is mention of the six *mahānagaras* or cities where the Buddha could have chosen to die, a list that is repeated more than once.[114] Obviously by the time that the Canon was compiled these cities had become major. There would therefore have been a difference between incipient or even early urbanism and mature urbanism. A comparison of the chronology of sites on the basis of archaeological artefacts with literary references can be misleading. A study of the pattern of settlements

[109] K.T.S. Sarao, *Urban Centres and Urbanisation as Reflected in the Pali Vinaya and Sutta Pitakas*, Delhi, 1990, pp. 213ff.

[110] *Vinaya Piṭaka*, I.337–57. *Kosambi Jātaka*, no. 428.

[111] *Vinaya Piṭaka*, I.226–230. *Dīgha Nikāya* II. 86ff. F.E. Pargiter, *The Purana Texts of the Dynasties of the Kali Age*, London, 1913, p. 22.

[112] Sabhāparvan, 19.1ff.

[113] K.T. Sarao, *Urban Centres and Urbanisation as Reflected in the Pali Vinaya and Suttapitakas*, Delhi, 1990.

[114] *Dīgha Nikāya* II. 146 and 169.

in an area surrounding an urban centre is a better gauge of the degree of urbanization.

With the juxtaposition of *gaṇa-saṅghas* and emergent kingdoms, the political change was evident. As *rājadhānis*, the early towns associated with this change were concentrations of power and recognized as such. As *nagaras* they introduced a different way of life. Even if they are not impressive in terms of their urban structures (and few cities were spectacular in this sense even in later times judging by the archaeological record) they nevertheless do represent a different complexity of governance, and of production, exchange and distribution, a complexity which becomes part of the historical context to the rise of Buddhism.

The archaeological correlation with the towns mentioned in the Pāli Canon is of less significance than the analysis of the Buddha's teaching as recorded in the texts which in terms of its historical context is associated with the coming of monarchies and urban society. The Canon describes a condition of established monarchies and mature urbanism which may not be evident from archaeology for the period of 600 BC. But this does not preclude the sixth century from being the period in which the urban change and the change to monarchy had been initiated. On the basis of the traditional reckoning the Buddha would have started his teaching in about 530 BC by which time the kingdoms had come into being. This would agree with Puranic chronology.[115] To the extent that the Buddha's teachings were receiving a hearing and gradually becoming popular, it can be assumed that this was in part related to these changes. The Middle Way was not just an alternative to Brahmanic ritual but also took cognizance of the newly emerging society, different from that visualized in Brahmanic ritual. Liberation from ritual, apart from its metaphysical concerns, was also a liberation from that which virtually destroyed wealth. This would have appealed to the *kṣatriyas* moving towards greater power through monarchical states, and who had prior to this begun to question the major sacrificial rituals as is evident from the early *Upaniṣads*,[116] and to the *seṭṭhis* wishing to invest wealth, both of which were situations evolving in the gradual change to state systems and to the introduction of commerce.

The compiling of the Canon is said to have occurred at the two Councils after the Buddha's death. By this time the urban context was well-established and was even more so when the Canon was converted from oral memory to writing. There was a time difference between the three events: the death of the Buddha, the compiling of the Canon and the writing of the Canon, and these events cannot be collapsed into a single period. The Bairat-Bhabhra

115 F.E. Pargiter, *The Purana Text of the Dynasties of the Kali Age*, London, 1913.

116 R. Thapar, 'Sacrifice, Surplus and the Soul', *History of Religion*, 1994, pp. 305–24.

Edict quotes the teachings of the Buddha which were obviously familiar and recognizable in an oral tradition and by the third century BC could well have been associated with texts such as the *Mahāvagga*, the *Nikāyas* and the *Suttanipāta*. For these teachings to have gained currency outside the middle Ganges plain may well have taken much more than a century, given the nature of communications at that time.

The Canon refers more frequently to the pre-Mauryan states such as Magadha, Kośala, and Vatsa, with their kings and their capital cities and to the Vṛjjis at Vaiśāli. If urbanization and state-formation evolved more or less at the same time, then these changes would have been initiated by the late sixth century. The historical context to the teaching of the Buddha is a situation of initial urbanization and a shift from chiefdoms to kingdoms, but prior to the emergence of large kingdoms or empire.[117] In fact the association in the early Buddhist texts is not even with the Nandas. There is unlikely to be a radical postponement of the historical processes linked to this period if the date is changed. But the evolution of Buddhism has to be seen as proceeding in stages. Allowing the Buddha a lifetime of half a century of teaching would in itself have witnessed the change from an initial urbanism to a more established form. The settings associated with his teaching were more often those of early urbanism. Much of the teaching was in parks and groves on the outskirts of urban centres.

It is argued that the figure 218 for the number of years between the *mahāparinirvāna* and the accession of Aśoka, is fictive since eighteen is a mythical number. If the figure from the Northern Tradition of 100 years is accepted then the *mahāparinirvāna* would date to 369/8, the period of Nanda rule. Some scholars basing themselves on the Northern tradition have suggested 386–4, which would of course again lead to 118 for the accession of Aśoka and coincide with the Nanda dynasty. Any date for the *mahāparinirvāna* subsequent to *c.* 400 BC would make the Buddha contemporary with either the Śiśunāgas or Nandas according to Puranic chronology. Even if a variant chronology based on a collation of the texts is considered, the rulers mentioned in such a chronology, such as Anuruddha, Nāgadasaka, Śiśunāga, do not figure in the early Pāli Canon and are mentioned briefly only in the Sri Lankan texts of a much later period, whereas the rulers prior to these are said to be contemporary with the Buddha.[118] The association is with Bimbisāra and Ajātaśatru, who, even allowing for exaggerated regnal years, preceded the Nandas. The *janapadas* mentioned in narratives

[117] R. Thapar, 'Ethics, Religion and Social Protest in the First Millennium BC in Northern India', *In Ancient Indian Social History: Some Interpretations*, New Delhi, 1978, pp. 40–62.

[118] H.C. Raychaudhuri, *Political History of Ancient India*, Calcutta, 1972 (7th Ed.), p. 201.

of the Buddha would have become part of the Nanda kingdom. Mention of the Nandas is late and marginal in the Buddhist texts, and this would be curious given that they would have been the pre-eminent political power during the lifetime of the Buddha, on the basis of this new reckoning.[119] The period of the Śiśunāgas and Nandas is associated with events after the death of the Buddha.

Mauryan Chronology

In a series of papers, Eggermont has continued his discussion on Mauryan chronology which he includes in the time-bracket of 317–186 BC.[120] He maintains that the original date for the *mahāparinirvāna* was 368 and this was later changed to 486 and then adjusted to 483 to accommodate Mahinda as the sixth *ācārya* and introduce the four-year interregnum prior to Aśoka's accession, with a final change in the twelfth century AD to 544. He also questions the length of Aśoka's reign of thirty-seven years according to the *Mahāvaṃsa*, arguing on the basis of expired and current years, that the correct length is twenty-seven years.[121] He has tried to make the calculation coincide with some readings of the *Purāṇas* where Aśoka's regnal years are given as twenty-seven. Eggermont largely accepts the list of the later Mauryas as given in this book, but disagrees with the idea that the empire after Aśoka was divided.

An attempt has been made by Guruge to reorganize the chronology of Aśoka's life with a consecration dating to 265 BC.[122] The Aśokan inscriptions have been rearranged, in terms of rock slabs and stone pillars rather than content, an arrangement which is historically unacceptable. Aśoka's conversion to Buddhism is dated to 262 BC, in the fourth year of his reign which does not conform to what the king himself states in the Minor RE. The Minor REs are dated to 255–54 and a year later Aśoka is said to have issued the bilingual Graeco-Aramaic inscription at Kandahar and this is prior to the issuing of the MREs, which, given the linguistic analyses that have been made of the Aramaic inscriptions, do not permit this inscription to precede the MREs. Aśoka's death is placed at 228 BC. There are some curious readings of the texts of the inscriptions to suit the new chronology. For instance, in an attempt to give less chronological weightage to the reference to the five Greek kings, the verb

119 F.E. Pargiter, *The Purana Texts of the Dynasties of the Kali Age*, Delhi, 1975 (rpt.), pp. 21ff.

120 P.H.L. Eggermont, 'New Notes on Aśoka and his Successors', *Persica*, 1965–6, II, pp. 27–70; 1969, IV, pp. 77–102; 1970–1, V, pp. 69–102; 1979, VIII, pp. 55–93.

121 This confusion over expired and current years, and mistakes of much more serious kinds occur in H. Alahakoon, *The Later Mauryas*, Delhi, 1980. See my review article in *The Sri Lanka Journal of the Humanities*, 1981, VII, 1–2, pp. 153–65.

122 A. Guruge, *Asoka, a Definitive Biography*, Colombo, 1994.

it is said, can be read both in the past and present tense; Aśoka therefore knew that some of the five were not alive at the time of issuing the inscription. If this was so he would either have referred to their successors or not mentioned them at all. One edict is read as Aśoka setting himself the quantitative target of increasing *dhamma* by exactly 150 per cent, which is not what the edict says. The author adopts his own classification and numbering of the edicts, which is most confusing.

Contemporaries of the Mauryan empire have received further attention. Among these the foremost are the Achaemenids.[123] There is now a detailed study of the social and economic history of this period[124] which provides both useful information as well as comparison with Mauryan studies. A recent discussion of the Seleucid state points to a more realistic assessment of Seleucid-Mauryan relations than previous works.[125] Megasthenes' *Indica* is seen as a legitimation of Seleucus' non-conquest of India and describes an apparently well-organized empire whose people are freedom-loving and should be left alone. Megasthenes may have viewed some aspects of Mauryan life from a Seleucid perspective. Looking northwards, a collation of the legends relating to the founding of the kingdom of Khotan and some linked to Aśoka, have been analysed and suggest that the legends associating Aśoka were meant to promote the prestige of the country rather than reflect historical events.[126] A recent translation and study of the Tibetan text, the *Li-yul Gyi lo rgyus*, establishes that Aśoka was believed to have visited Khotan, where in this version a son was born to him during the visit who was destined to rule Khotan, helped by the minister of Dharmaśoka.[127]

The reference to the five *yona-rājās* remains the bed-rock of ancient Indian chronology. Whatever fanciful turns may be given to the Sandracottos-Candragupta equation, the reign of Aśoka is pegged to the mid-third century BC. What is of interest is whether he had separate links with each of the five or did he know them by association, since there were both hostilities and close marriage alliances between the five. These particular five kings were part of a political network and the list therefore is not a casual one. The exchange of gifts at the level of the courts was a prelude to commercial

123 I. Gershevitch (ed.), *Cambridge History of Iran*, vol. 2, Cambridge, 1985. S. Chattopadhyaya, *The Achaemenids and India*, Delhi, 1974 (rpt.).

124 M.A. Dandamaev and V.G. Lukonin, *The Culture and Social Institutions of Ancient Iran*, Cambridge, 1989.

125 S. Sherwin White and A. Kuhrt, *From Samarkand to Sardis*, London, 1993.

126 G. Yamazaki, 'The Legend of the Foundation of Khotan', *Toyo Bunko*, 1990, 48, pp. 55–80.

127 R.E. Emmerick, *Tibetan Texts Concerning Khotan*, Oxford, 1967, pp. 15ff. Guruge's contention that there is no mention of Aśoka visiting Khotan (p. 389) is incorrect.

exchange. The port of Sopārā is likely to have been important in maritime links with coastal Arabia.[128]

The names and titles taken by Aśoka have been subject to further examination. On the basis of Indo-European roots it is thought that *devānampriya* means 'legitimate (child) of the gods', although it degenerates in meaning to a 'blockhead' in later times.[129] This is not the same as divine kingship for the gods are multiple and familiar to the humans and the legitimation is that of a special status conferred by the gods. Another argument maintains that Piyadassi was his personal name and Aśoka which occurs infrequently was a *biruda* bestowed on him by the Buddhist *saṃgha*.[130] If this was so then obviously he would have used this name when addressing matters relating to the *saṃgha*, which is not the case. It is more likely that, as the legends maintain, he was called Aśoka and adopted the name of Piyadassi, more appropriate to a king, when he began to rule.

There has been some criticism of the argument put forward by Bhandarkar, Smith, Przyluski, and myself that Aśoka may not have been married to Devī.[131] The earliest of the texts, the *Dipavaṃsa*, makes no reference to a marriage and mentions *samvāsa*. The later text, the *Mahāvaṃsa*, says that he obtained the daughter of a merchant and refers to *samvāsa*. The *Mahāvaṃsa ṭīkā*, still later, refers to the consent of the parents. *Samvāsa* means to cohabit but according to Guruge it is used in the sense of co-residence. But if the result is the birth of two children then obviously it has other connotations. He quotes the *Samantapāsādikā* as stating that Aśoka took the daughter of Devaseṭṭhi, where the word *aggahesi* also means to seize or to capture. It is frequently forgotten that such unions were common in royal families and did not carry moral censure. However the sons of these unions were often debarred from succession. A. Chattopadhyaya is right in her suggestion that Samghamittā could have married a nephew of Aśoka if it had been a cross-cousin marriage.

Aśoka and Buddhism

The virtual dichotomy between those who give priority to the edicts as a source for the activities of Aśoka and those who would accept the versions in the Buddhist sources, is made apparent in Guruge's biography where not only are the Buddhist texts privileged but among them the Sri Lankan Buddhist sources are given more credence.[132] It is tedious to go through what is described as the

128 R. Thapar, 'Epigraphic Evidence and some Indo-Hellenistic Contacts during the Mauryan Period', in S.K. Maity and U. Thakur, *Indological Studies*, New Delhi, 1987, pp. 15–19.

129 M. Hara, 'A Note on the Sanskrit Phrase, Devānampriya', *Indian Linguistics*, 1969, 30, pp. 13–26.

130 M.C. Joshi and J.C. Joshi, 'A Study in the Names of Aśoka', *JOI*, 1968, xvii, 4, pp. 415–24.

131 A. Chattopadhyay, 'Vidiśā Devī', *JOI*, 1970, xx, 2, pp. 115–20.

132 No wonder that President Premadasa of

bias of Indian historians and various mistakes in readings. These on investigation more often turn out to be those of Guruge's misreading of the primary and secondary sources. Since most of his criticisms are inconsequential I am discussing them in a lengthy footnote.[133] He provides us with his curriculum vitae of *devānampiya piyadassi* Aśoka, third emperor of the Mauryan dynasty' which is substantially an endorsement of the narrative of the Sri Lankan texts. Aśoka was the instrument of the establishment of Buddhism in Sri Lanka and has therefore to be presented as the greatest patron of Buddhism.[134]

Sri Lanka writes in his Preface to the book that 'From Dr Guruge's study the Pali sources of Sri Lanka emerge as being nearest to the truth'.

[133] Guruge is not above contradicting himself: at one point Aśoka is a Buddhist when he builds the Hell (107) but a few pages later is being converted through this agency (119); I am faulted for saying that Aśoka declared Sampadi the heir-apparent and the text quoted states that he was the Yuvarāja (275). My reference to Daśaratha is not to Przyluski but to the *Viṣṇu Purāṇa* (352) The list of later Mauryas is from the last section of the *Aśokāvadāna* as I have stated and not from the *A-yu-wang-ching* as Guruge maintains. Guruge confuses the abbot Yaśas with the minister and the latter obstructing Aśoka is referred to in the *Divyāvadāna*, XXVIII, 382ff. Guruge needs to read Przyluski more carefully. If he does so he will discover that I am not presenting a confusion of texts, but that Przyluski refers to a large number and my references in turn are to the specific text which he quotes and not just to his book. Fa-hsien states unambiguously that Gandhāra was where Dharmavivardhana, the son of Aśoka ruled: J. Legge, p. 31 (380). Guruge contends that Aśoka was never viceroy at Taxila, a view based on an erroneous understanding of the statement in the sources, for the *Aśokāvadāna* for instance, states that Bindusāra recalled Susīma and appointed Aśoka to govern Taxila. If this is unacceptable then it could equally well be argued that the Sri Lankan Pali sources invented the viceroyalty at Ujjain in order to give status to the initial missionaries to Sri Lanka. Hsüan Tsang maintains that Aśoka was viceroy at Taxila: Watters, I, 241. Khallata is not a name in this instance but a qualifier meaning bald-headed: *Divyāvadāna*, XXVI, 372–3. My statement that Aśoka was in Taxila prior to Ujjain does not mean that he went from Taxila to Ujjain but that he was in Taxila at an earlier period (379). There have been further discoveries of edicts in the last ten years but none of these date to the last years of Aśoka's reign (271). Jalauka is linked to Gandhāra because the two areas in contemporary sources are often a compound term: *Gandhāra Jātaka* 406; *Milindapanho* 327–8 (331). To argue that the Aśoka described in the *Rājataraṅgiṇī* was not the Mauryan king but a petty ruler of Kashmir, would be rejected by most historians (333). The story of the half *āmalaka* in the northern tradition cannot be rejected only because it is not confirmed in the southern Buddhist texts, for the latter have their own prejudices. Guruge states that the stories of Aśoka's conversion in the *Divyāvadāna* and in Hsüan Tsang are dissimilar whereas I have pointed out a similarity. On this Watters states that Hsüan Tsang probably condensed the story from the *Divyāvadāna* and the *Tsa-a-han-ching* as they agree closely in all the main incidents and differ in some particulars: II, 89 (381) Guruge states that I have misconstrued Eggermont's arguments in my discussion of Mauryan chronology (403) but curiously Eggermont in a more recent paper referred to above, agrees with me!

[134] Op. cit., pp. 452ff. The purpose of the book is made even more explicit not only in the statement that it was undertaken at the request of President Premadasa (519) but in the fuller explanation elsewhere: 'The historical tradition of Sri Lankan (sic) had commenced with the founding of the Sinhala nation by Northern Indian Aryans who had migrated into this island in several waves of immigration. This nation founded in a new country, separated by a strong

As in all sectarian literature, Buddhist texts have also to be viewed as emanating from a sectarian perspective. This is not to negate the value of this perspective but to be aware of the purposes of the authors, an awareness which is required even for using non-sectarian texts. Such an approach may well be uncomfortable for those who are adherents of the particular sects but is inevitable in any historical analysis. It has been pointed out repeatedly that the narrative of the life of Aśoka differs in the two traditions, the Northern Buddhist tradition and the southern Pāli Sri Lankan tradition. Not only is the projection of the individual not identical, but in the first the focus is more on him and his acts and in the second there is the added dimension of the Buddhist mission to Sri Lanka. The edicts provide a historically more reliable account of Aśoka's relation with Buddhism and the nature of Buddhism in the third century BC. At this time the Buddha was pre-eminent and the historical Buddha was more visible perhaps than the divine Buddha of later times.[135] The law of *dharma* as discovered by him placed some limitations on the supernatural powers that could be claimed for the Buddha, limitations which faded out in subsequent periods.

A new reading of the Schism Edict questions the view that Aśoka tried to unite the *saṃgha* and was a follower of the Theravāda.[136] The argument is that the Schism Edict does not deal with doctrinal differences, but with monastic practices and relates to the authority of the monastery. A similar reading maintains that this edict does not prove the historicity of the legend of the Third Council.[137] However the severity of the punishment — expulsion, would suggest that the matter concerned more than just monastic practice and discipline and may well have included doctrinal matters, although the king may not have been intending to intervene directly in the decisions of the major monasteries. Dissensions are referred to in the Pāli Canon, some associated specifically with the monastery at Kauśāmbi.

It has been argued that there were two Aśokas: one was the historical figure from the inscriptions and the other was the legend, and the legendary Aśoka

---

and rapidly expanding block of Dravidians from their fellow Aryans in the north of the subcontinent, had apparently felt the need to assert its cultural identity'. He goes on to say that a fully developed historical sense among Sinhala Buddhists brought about a national sangha.

135 A. Bareau, 'The Place of the Buddha Gautama in the Buddhist Religion during the Reign of Aśoka', in S. Balasooriya et al. (eds), *Buddhist Studies in Honour of Walpola Rahula*, London, 1980, pp. 1–9.

136 H. Bechert, 'The Importance of Aśoka's so-called Schism Edict', in L.A. Herns et al. (eds), *Indological and Buddhist Studies*, Canberra, 1982. See also N.A. Jayawickrama, 'A Reference to the Third Council in Aśoka's Edict', *University of Ceylon Review*, 1959, 17, pp. 61–72.

137 G. Yamazaki, 'The Lists of the Patriarchs in the Northern and Southern Legends', in H. Bechert, *The Dating of the Historical Buddha*, p. 320.

was the model for Buddhist writers.[138] Whether he was faced with the contradiction reflected in the model king as the *cakravartin* and the model Buddha as the *bodhisattva* as suggested, would depend on when these concepts became current and possibly both were post-Aśokan. The exercise of power may be viewed as incompatible with the ultimate Buddhist ethic yet royalty is beneficial for king and subjects. The temporal power of kingship had to be reconciled with the spiritual power of the *saṃgha*. Aśoka was attempting to resolve this contradiction. However, the distinction between the two Aśokas requires that the historical person be viewed as separate from the legend and assessed from the perspective of his thoughts and actions as depicted in his edicts, and in the context of his being at the helm of an empire. Even this study tends to use the legend as an entry point to the man, although it does so to a much more controlled degree than many others. The distinction between the two is pertinent to a historical view since the texts recording the legend are many centuries subsequent to the reign of Aśoka. The legend therefore already has a historiographical function. If the notion of the *cakravartin* is taken more literally then there remains the question of whether the concept had a political connotation during the time of Aśoka and of which he was aware, or whether it developed later, partly perhaps using him as a model.[139]

A more wide-ranging analysis of the role of the legend of Aśoka in Buddhist tradition and in the interaction of religion with the socio-political order, begins with an assessment of the historical Aśoka and then sets the legend in the context of various polities of south and south-east Asia.[140] This study has helped to shift the focus from primarily antiquarian concerns to a debate on the broader issue of the interrelations between the state and the *saṃgha*. The dichotomy between renunciation and conquest as projected in the institution of the *saṃgha* and the *rājā* is not an absolute dichotomy since the two are interdependent. One may argue that if the *saṃgha* helps imperial policy by being supportive, political authority also assists in aiding the *saṃgha* financially and in other ways. This interdependence is heavily underlined in the legends of the northern Buddhist tradition regarding the last years of Aśoka and the activities of his successor. State polity in the Buddhist tradition is opposed to the *kṣatriya vidyā* as defined in the *Arthaśāstra*, but the opposition is not as sharp as suggested by Tambiah. To the historian, the Buddhist model of kingship remains a partial and particular view and comes to be treated as such.[141]

138 R. Lingat, *Royautés Bouddhiques*, part I, Asoka et la Fonction Royale, Paris, 1989.

139 A.L. Basham, 'Aśoka and Buddhism . . . ', is of the view that it developed later else he might have referred to himself as such in the inscriptions.

140 S.J. Tambiah, *World Conqueror and World Renouncer*, Cambridge, 1976.

141 E. Lamotte, *History of Indian Buddhism*, pp. 233–4. R. Thapar, 'Religion and the Social Order', in *Contributions to Indian Sociology*, 1987, 21, 1, pp. 157–65.

Tambiah rightly points out that the *dhamma* was an efficacious ideology of pacification, political stability and security. It may also be said that it could have softened the thrust of Mauryan control especially in the peninsula. It is interesting that there is a considerable presence of Buddhism in the peninsula after the Mauryan rule, as also some visibility of Jainism in the south. The exhortation to the king to protect the *saṃgha* is a complex matter for it is the prosperity and property of the *saṃgha* which also requires protection and which in return guarantees the legitimacy of the protector, a relationship by no means unique to Aśoka and Buddhism, evident as it is in many situations of royal patronage to a religious order. Religions indigenous to India have imprinted the image of the ascetic on Indian thought. This in the past has been described as a life-negating principle, but as Tambiah shows, and other discussions would support it, the ascetic ideal far from being life-negating is in fact viewed as an alternative source of power, especially among orders of renouncers.[142] The ascetic/*saṃnyāsin* or renouncer/*bhikṣu*, is seen as being outside and above political concerns, although often the ascetic becomes the focus of movements in opposition to established authority. He deliberately contravenes social mores in order to terminate social obligations, nevertheless he is not relegated to low caste status as would happen with others contravening social norms, but is accepted as being outside the framework of caste society — a notion which is hinted at in Megasthenes' description of the philosophers.

Aśoka's relationship with Buddhism evokes therefore a range of interactions for that period, which have often been by-passed by historians and Tambiah's study underlines the need for looking afresh at the texts. That the legend was important to the Buddhist tradition has long been accepted and it has its own historiographical evolution in various Buddhist texts. Nevertheless, the historical Aśoka has to be viewed from a different stand-point. His ideas on *dhamma* borrow from the current debate but are set within an imperial framework. An attempt at uniformity at the ideational level is emphasized in the rock and pillar inscriptions. *Dhamma* as he defines it, was an ethical principle with an appeal to the broadest social spectrum. Moving away at one level from the usual hegemony of imperial systems, he was nevertheless endorsing a process equally important to imperial needs, namely, acculturation. This he sought to encourage through a policy of persuasive assimilation in which conforming to the ethical ideals of *dhamma* was encouraged. The cultural norm implicit in this was that of the Ganges plain and although

142 R. Thapar, 'Renunciation: the Making of a Counter Culture?', in *Ancient Indian Social History: some Interpretations*, New Delhi, 1978, pp. 63–104. 'Householders and Renouncers in the Brahmanical and Buddhist Traditions', in T.N. Madan (ed.), *Way of Life*, Delhi, 1982, pp. 273–98.

some concessions are made in the use of language, the message comes from a particular source.

If language lies at the boundary of the person wishing to communicate and those receiving the communication, then the social process of communicating becomes significant. The edicts are not to be examined only for the degree to which they reflect Buddhist ideas, because they also reflect the king's relations with his subjects and this varies in different parts of the empire. The universalistic ethic of the new sects was different from the *varna* framework of brahmanical norms. Renunciatory orders tended to cut across caste and clan and weaken these identities and where the orders were loyal to the state they provided a network of support across the empire. The search for uniformity was at one level the personal vision of an individual but its articulation related to his historical role.

The Mauryan Empire

A couple of monographs provide an overview of this period. The earlier one is a useful summary of the main events and some of the discussion around these.[143] The later monograph discusses society and economy in some detail and therefore provides a different focus.[144] The centrality of the economy as an aspect of state control is emphasized as also the importance of iron technology to the growth of urbanization.[145] The production of iron is recorded but that it was the sole catalytic agent in the creation of cities is now regarded as debatable. The working of the south Bihar mines which would be an obvious source of iron remains enigmatic and the extensive use of iron in the Megalithic sites of the peninsula largely precedes urban centres and the arrival of the Mauryas. Urbanization would have been accelerated by multiple factors apart from a change in technology and these factors included the establishing of administrative and commercial centres given the commercial expansion under the Mauryas. Much of the useful discussion in this monograph tends to get deflected by a wide use of sources some even of the pre-Mauryan period and others post-Mauryan. Admittedly the chronology of sources remains uncertain but perhaps a greater discrimination involving a comparison of different categories of evidence is now required.

In the discussion of the extension of agriculture the point that there was a

[143] S. Chattopadhyaya, *Bimbisāra to Aśoka*, Calcutta, 1977.

[144] G.M. Bongard-Levin, *Mauryan India*, New Delhi, 1985.

[145] This was initially argued by D.D. Kosambi and questioned by A. Ghosh, op. cit. and supported by R.S. Sharma, 'Iron and Urbanisation in the Ganga Basin', *IHR*, 1978, 1, pp. 1ff and V.K. Thakur, *Urbanisation in Ancient India*, Delhi, 1981, p. 65, and further questioned by N.R. Ray, 'Technology and Social Change in Early Indian History', *Puratattva*, 1975–6, 8, pp. 132–8.

multiplicity of forms in the working and ownership of land which would support multiple levels of development, is well made. That the description of Megasthenes seems to have carried the imprint of forms familiar from the Hellenistic kingdoms is now acknowledged and the practice in these areas may be responsible for some contradictions in the quotations from his account.[146] Diodorus writes of the absence of private ownership in land with cultivators probably paying a rent to the king in addition to one–fourth of the produce. Strabo refers to a *chora basilike* or royal lands and states to the contrary that the cultivators are given a wage as well as keeping one–fourth of the produce. Clearly there is a discrepancy here. Arrian speaks of the cultivators paying a tax on the land which they cultivate and makes no mention of royal ownership. Bongard-Levin draws attention to the differentiation between rent and tax.

The question of whether *śūdrakarṣakaprāya* in the *Arthaśāstra* II.1.1. should be translated as '*śūdras* and cultivators' or as '*śūdra* agriculturists'[147] has a bearing on the nature of agrarian arrangements as well as on the status of the *śūdra* where, as a cultivator it would have been better than as a labourer. It also relates to whether the major part of agricultural activity was that of slaves and *śūdra* labourers under state control as has been argued,[148] or whether there was a greater diversity of economic arrangements in which this was one among other systems. The *sītādhyakṣa*, supervising the cultivation of *sīta* lands, is required to use *dāsakarmakaras* and those providing labour in lieu of fines. The former were to be paid the abysmal sum of one and a quarter *paṇa* per month and given food.[149] But in the chapter on organizing settlements in rural areas, apart from the *śūdra* agriculturalists to be settled in villages, reference is also made to various other forms of tenancy. Mention is made of people from other professions who receive tax-free land. Furthermore some categories of tax-payers were to be allotted arable land for life. Assistance of various kinds was to be made available to cultivators, so as to enhance the income of the treasury, and such assistance was to be forthcoming especially to those who took the initiative to clear waste land and set up water systems for irrigation. Various categories of arrangements relating to the cultivation of land even on the *sīta* land are advised. Had there been an overwhelmingly *dāsakarmakara* or *śūdra* labour based cultivation by the state, throughout its territory and providing a sustained income, then the empire would probably have survived for a longer period. Such cultivation may have been unlikely in many areas such as the peninsula where the Megalithic settlements remain unchanged

146 R. Thapar, op. cit., pp. 32ff.

147 R.S. Sharma, *Śūdras in Ancient India*, Delhi, 1980 (rev. ed.), p. 163; R.P. Kangle, op. cit., vol. II, p. 55.

148 Ibid., p. 163.

149 *Arthaśāstra*, II.24.28.

during the Mauryan period. But some state controlled agriculture would have been carried out in the Ganges plain.

Bongard-Levin, in agreement with many other historians, does not subscribe to the view that there was a slave mode of production in the Mauryan period although he agrees that some slave labour is evident in both agriculture and craft production.[150] Slaves used in domestic work predominated over slavery for production. It could be argued that the use of the conjoint phrase, *dāsakarmakara*, referring to slaves and hired labour, makes it difficult to assess the amount of slave labour.[151] Megasthenes comments on the absence of slavery which I have tried to explain as an absence not of slavery in any form, but specifically, the predominant Greek form of the *doulos* which was the use of slave labour in production.[152] The *dāsakarmakara* were paid a minuscule amount but the fact of payment places this category in a status different from the *doulos*. The *Arthaśāstra* makes a distinction among the *dāsās* and refers to three categories: one that is permanently a *dāsa*; one who is kept as a pledge, the *ahitaka*; and the *ārya* who was temporarily enslaved but regained freedom after a stipulated time or a payment.

Associated with the theme of labour, the definition of *viṣṭi* frequently interpreted as forced labour has been questioned on the basis that in the *Arthaśāstra* it meant labour employed by the state or labour in lieu of taxes and not forced labour. It became forced labour in the post-Mauryan period.[153] The degree to which labour was forced (as was the case in a system of *corvée* where it was additional to the normal taxes), or alternatively was one among a list of regular taxes and therefore contracted for, probably varied according to context, as the references are not consistent in its description. Most of the references in the *Arthaśāstra* are of the latter kind, although at one point the king is advised to protect those cultivators who may be oppressed by *daṇḍa-viṣṭikara*, suggesting perhaps forced labour.[154] Megasthenes makes no reference to a labour tax for cultivators, and artisans are said to pay a tax/*phoros* to the state and render prescribed services/*leitourgai*. The meaning of the latter term was not forced labour but a service performed at one's own expense for a superior or for the state.[155] State oppression is in any case not limited to categories of taxation and can occur in other forms as well.

In addition to multiple forms of land working, Bongard-Levin also emphasizes the existence of the village community, said to emerge either from

150 Cf. D. Chanana, *Slavery in Ancient India*, Delhi, 1960.

151 R. Thapar, *From Lineage to State*, New Delhi, 1984, p. 83.

152 R. Thapar, *The Mauryas Revisited*, pp. 32ff.

153 G.K. Rai, *Involuntary Labour in Ancient India*, Allahabad, 1981.

154 *Arthaśāstra*, II.1.37.

155 R. Thapar, *The Mauryas Revisited*, pp. 32ff.

clans or from settlers moving to vacant lands, where the association of villagers enjoyed equal rights as owners of plots although as a self-governing unit it included other groups in the population. This argument seems to contradict that of multiple forms of land working and ownership. Information on the agrarian and fiscal economy of the Mauryan period and later, has also been gathered in another publication which is a useful addition even if it carries little theoretical discussion of the categories to which its refers.[156]

The concept of the 'tribe' remains opaque in most discussions of this period, in part because its modern usage covers such diverse situations that it does not allow for precision. For the Mauryan period it would seem to include in various secondary works, the forest dwellers, members of the *gaṇa-saṅghas* or those under the jurisdiction of self-governing cities and more generally what are referred to as 'tribal peoples'. One characteristic is that they are treated as peripheral groups and some are drawn into the mainstream whilst others remain outside. The occurrence of either one or the other would doubtless have depended on the degree of control which Mauryan administration wished to exercise in the area. This appears to become a pattern for state systems in the post-Mauryan periods and the relationship between the state and its 'tribal' peoples is a recurring theme, where the attitude of the former depends on the nature of resources controlled by the latter and the degree to which such resources are sought to be appropriated by the state. Even among the oligarchies, there is a difference between those of the Ganges plain which were absorbed into the imperial system and those of Rajasthan, Punjab and the watershed area which retained much of their identity in the post-Mauryan period. The reasons for the difference would have to do with the nature and importance of Mauryan interest in their habitat. The process of absorption was not simple as these groups would have required not only a change in political form but also a conversion to caste society. The preconditions to this would have differed in the oligarchies from the monarchies of the pre-Mauryan period.

A juxtaposition of Brahmanical and Buddhist sources does suggest a rather different view of caste in each. Whereas the former differentiate largely between *varṇas*, the latter seem to assess the hierarchy and ranking more in terms of *jātis* although mention of *varṇas* is also made. This has led to the debate on whether Megasthenes' description of the seven groups which constitute Indian society refer to *varṇa* or to *jāti*. A detailed discussion of the text relating to this and a return to investigating the possibilities of meanings in the Greek of that time, suggests that the reference was to the system of *jātis* rather than

156 N.N. Kher, *Agrarian and Fiscal Economy in the Mauryan and post-Mauryan Age*, Delhi, 1973. See also B.C. Sen, *Economics in Kautilya*, Calcutta, 1967.

varṇas, although there is a garbled inclusion of categories and rules derived from other sources as well.[157] Both Diodorus and Strabo use the word *meros* for the general divisions of Indian society and *genos* for the categories of birth, marriage and occupation. Arrian uses only *genos* and this may be because he tends to be paraphrasing Megasthenes to a greater extent than the earlier two.

A notable departure from the administration of the pre-Mauryan period lies in the description of how towns were administered. Allowing for a degree of exaggeration in the meticulousness of the *Arthaśāstra* in this matter, what does come through is the consciousness of urban living posing new and different problems from those associated with rural life. This is reflected not only in urban architecture, in the various offices located in the capital, in the markets of the city, but also in the precautions which are discussed to ensure the welfare of the urbanites. Among these is the concern for hygiene and medical aid, doubtless made necessary by the heavy concentration of population at a large city such as Pāṭaliputra.[158]

The emphasis on administration was necessary because of various factors: the extent of the territory under the control of a single state which was unprecedented, the need to rationalize taxation where the number of taxes still remain less than in later times but had to cover both agricultural and commercial activities, and the recognition of services not just as dues but sometimes even in lieu of taxes. Given the extent of the empire there could not be a directly controlled administration uniform throughout the territory. The inscriptions make mention of various categories of administrative divisions: as for instance, ***janapada***, ***pradeśa***, ***deśa***, and ***āhāra*** and the precise connotation of each remains problematic, particularly as these may be premised on varying considerations. Representation of Mauryan authority was accordingly ranked but doubtless drew both from those recruited at the capital as well as local potential in the provincial areas. In a section of the *Arthaśāstra* which could well be later, there is a listing of salaries.[159] These need not be taken as literal but point to an important aspect of the evaluation of various levels of administration. Where the clerk gets a salary of 500 *paṇas*, the minister gets 48,000 *paṇas*, a ratio of 1 : 96. The upper levels of the bureaucracy tend to be well paid and the difference with the lower levels is striking. The questions which remain unanswered are whether this trend was set by Mauryan administration and it may well have been, and whether salaries were paid in cash, which may not have been the norm. Such salaries would require the regular and systematic collection of revenue, an activity which characterizes

157 R. Thapar, *The Mauryas Revisited*, pp. 32ff.

158 D.V. Subba Reddy, *Glimpses of Health and Medicine in the Mauryan Empire*, Hyderabad, 1966.

159 *Arthaśāstra*, V.3.

state functioning. High office would then be conducive to the accumulating of wealth and ranks of kinsmen may well have closed in to make this more effective.

The question of the degree of centralization and the efficiency of communication as an aspect of administration has been analysed in terms of the nature of communication in the Mauryan empire.[160] Both Megasthenes and the Aśokan edicts speak of the construction of roads. Yet the *Arthasastra* does not mention any special service concerned with the fast delivery of messages. It has been estimated that a courier leaving Patna would have taken thirty days to reach Kandahar and much more to Karnataka. During the monsoon it would have been even longer. The deployment of troops, as for example those sent when Taxila rebelled for the first time, could not be accomplished in a hurry. Therefore troops would have to be posted permanently at strategic points and even important decisions would have to have been taken at the local level by the local administration particularly in the areas distant from Pāṭaliputra. This would imply that the local representative of the king was invested with power.

Fussman makes the further point that the inscriptions in *kharoṣṭhī* and in Greek and Aramaic would imply that the local officials were from the area and were not officers posted from Pāṭaliputra. Mauryan administration was not homogeneous in its recruitment or practice. The empire included a variety of tribes as well as erstwhile kingdoms and Arrian refers to autonomous cities. The edicts were not uniform because they were not directly transmitted by Aśoka but were sent to the provincial officials who passed them down to lower levels in the hierarchy. Fussman maintains that there was a central, absolute power dependent on the personal activity of the sovereign who relied on the army and on efficient officers; regional administration was of a non-systematic kind and there was greater liberty the further away it was from the centre. The centrifugal factors were the freedom of the high officials of the provincial administration, the continued existence of their powers derived from pre-Mauryan rulers and difficulties in communication. These factors explain the disappearance of the Mauryan empire.

Admittedly there has been in the past an overly emphatic description of the Mauryan state as rigidly centralized and controlled by a powerful bureaucracy and monarch. The recent trend of questioning centralized systems for early empires takes the Mauryan empire into consideration as well. However not all elements of centralization in the process can be discarded for there is also the fact of differing patterns in different areas. The Mauryan state is best

160 G. Fussman, 'Central and Provincial Administration in Ancient India: the Problem of the Mauryan Empire', *Indian Historical Review*, 1987–8, XIV, pp. 43–72. 'Quelques Problemes Asokéens', *Journal Asiatique*, 1974, pp. 376ff.

viewed from the perspective of two foci: one is the processes of state formation and the creation of the early state which occurred in the Ganges plain prior to the Mauryan period and which can be seen as occurring in some other areas even into the post-Mauryan period;/and the other is to observe the Mauryan system by providing a definition of empire.

The emergence of the state is a gradual process and not all areas which get demarcated as states go through an identical process. The early state focuses on a large redistributive system involving tribute and booty, and revenue from various sources including taxes and labour. Legitimacy which becomes an important component of the state requires consensus, coercive power and frequently an ideology which invokes the supernatural.[161] The mature state stretches these activities to a different level where legitimation, bureaucratization and control over economic resources become major items co-related with the size and the spatial distribution of the population. Together with these, social divisions, some of which take on class functions, become apparent.

With the evolution of an empire, the typology of the state changes and the structure of the state becomes more complex. It was previously argued that this complexity lay in the extension of centralized control, but in effect, the complexity lies in variations in control which have to be manifest in the system. I have attempted to examine the Mauryan state from this perspective.[162] The definition of an empire includes not only extensive conquest with a monopoly of force, but also territorial control which may not be of a uniform nature and domination over peoples regarded as culturally alien or at least different. Territorial conquest involves a frequency of wars since wars have an economic purpose as well: they are the agency for obtaining tribute, booty and loot as also prisoners-of-war to be used as slaves or labourers, and can result in the exploration of new kinds of resources. Thus if enhancing revenue is the motive then fertile agricultural land and trade routes are likely to be the prize of campaigns. Adjustments in administration become an on-going process if there are continual conquests. Thus roads have to be built in conquered areas and officers posted to these or at least local persons recruited to office. The expenses for this have to be offset by the tribute and booty. Therefore at some point an optimum territory would be the solution for any state and whatever is conquered in addition may be either deliberately or because of weakness, more loosely controlled.

The administration of Mauryan territory and economy may be seen as a

161 H. Claessen and P. Skalnik (eds), *The Early State*, The Hague, 1978. H. Claessen, 'The Internal Dynamics of the Early State', *Current Anthropology*, 1984, 25, 4, pp. 365–79.

162 R. Thapar, 'The State as Empire', in H. Claessen and P. Skalnik (eds), *The Study of the State*, The Hague, 1981, pp. 409–26. *The Mauryas Revisited*, Calcutta, pp. 1–31.

relationship between three categories of control: between the metropolitan state, the core areas and the peripheral regions. The metropolitan state would be the nucleus of the empire with a history of having evolved from an early state to a mature state. In the case of the Mauryas this would be Magadha which was an area of primary state formation and which had in the pre-Mauryan period become a hegemonic state in the Ganges plain. With the enlargement of Mauryan territory it may have brought into its ambit those parts of the Ganges plain with which it had interacted earlier. Resources and revenues would come to the metropolitan state and be distributed from here through channels of public expenditure, such as administration and the maintenance of an army. This area would be under a high-powered, centralized, bureaucratic control, being the nucleus of the empire, and may have approximated the pattern of government described in the *Arthaśāstra*. The text therefore may be said to relate not to an imperial system, but possibly to the functioning of a metropolitan state within such a system. This might also explain why Aśoka takes the title of *rājā-māgadhe*, seemingly simple but effectively powerful. The metropolitan state is juxtaposed with other categories of territories.

The core areas would be those which prior to their conquest were states, but had failed to develop into major states, such as Gandhāra and Āvanti, or else were areas of incipient state formation such as Kaliṅga or Āndhra.[163] These areas were not part of the metropolitan state, but were nevertheless governed by a hierarchy of officials. References to the different levels of the hierarchy as is apparent from the edicts suggests that the senior levels were familiar to both provincial and metropolitan administration. At the upper levels the administration was imitative of the metropolitan state but at local levels it would be more distanced. Core areas drew revenue from agriculture which required a certain investment and development on the part of the metropolitan state, even though much of this may have been local enterprise. The extension of *sīta* lands would in part be in such areas. Those who were deported after the Kaliṅga campaign are likely to have been settled on such lands.[164] These would be areas where there would be some restructuring of the economy with the introduction of multiple tenures ranging from the cultivation of *sīta* lands to privately owned lands. Such restructuring is suggested by the fact that the only two major irrigation works — the dam on the Sudarśana lake and the Nanda canal — are both in core areas. Varieties of privately controlled irrigation mechanisms were prevalent elsewhere. Core areas were also those which

163 On the process of state formation in the last two areas, see S. Senivaratne, op. cit.

164 D.D. Kosambi, *An Introduction to the Study of Indian History*, Bombay, 1956, pp. 185 and 218.

had a commercial focus with centres of exchange such as Taxila, Ujjain, Dharanikoṭa, Suvarṇagiri and were therefore on trade routes. Hopefully horizontal excavations in the future will provide more evidence on such centres. Trade routes acted as corridors connecting core areas and possibly the expansion of a kingdom such as that of Magadha was partly conditioned by the wish to control such areas, which is suggested by the points of maximum control in the subcontinent under the Mauryas. With the disintegration of the empire, the core areas often evolved into the mature states of later times.

The third category was peripheral regions where there had not been state systems previously and which had therefore been areas of isolation to begin with. They were located in the interstices of rich agricultural belts and trade routes. Their resources were frequently those which could be mined, such as iron or gold, or could be obtained directly, such as precious and semi-precious stones, timber and elephants, all much valued according to the *Arthaśāstra*. These areas therefore did not require bringing large tracts of land under cultivation or a major restructuring of the economy. Even the hierarchy of officials was probably more evident only at the senior levels where they worked in a supervisory capacity. Their prime function would have been accessing the natural resources and this the Mauryas do not seem to have regarded as necessitating a new imperial enterprise. Senior administrators in such areas may well have come from the north, since the language of administration in Karnataka for instance was not the local language but that of the metropolitan state. The large number of Aśokan inscriptions in this area are a contrast to the scant archaeological presence of artefacts associated with the Mauryas. Was this the result of enthusiasm on the part of the local Mauryan officials in having the edicts engraved at many places? That there was some variation in the contents of what was engraved seems apparent from the opening sentences of the Minor REs in Karnataka and the intrusion of some *kharoṣṭhī*.[165] It would seem that the existing channels of resource mobilization were tapped, but little attempt was made to change them and introduce systems from the metropolitan state. These were the regions inhabited by the forest peoples mentioned in the edicts and local tribes who had their own hierarchy of functioning under their own chiefs. Such areas would have been frequently associated with what I have elsewhere called, lineage-based societies.[166] The conversion of forest land and waste land to agricultural land would here be a more marginal and gradual activity as compared to tapping the existing resources. The administration would be relatively liberated from the control of the metropolitan state so long as the revenues and the resources reached the centre.

[165] Fussman, op. cit.

[166] R. Thapar, *From Lineage to State*.

Needless to say, core and peripheral areas were not permanently one or the other. Core areas did often develop into independent kingdoms but could occasionally lapse into regions of lesser importance. Peripheral areas more frequently, could develop into core areas of new kingdoms, given an investment in resources and the participation of the inhabitants in this investment. The latter was significant and initiated a cultural interaction as well. This it would seem, was well-understood by Aśoka and partially relates to his need to inscribe edicts which carry within them aspects of this interaction. One of the historical processes of change would have been the mutation of peripheral areas into core areas.

The distribution of population was not uniform as is evident from even an impressionistic view of the nature of archaeological sites in the different parts of the Indian subcontinent. The heaviest concentration was in the Ganges plain and around the hub of the core areas. A more limited density occurs in areas which were exceptionally fertile, such as the Raichur *doāb*. The peripheral regions were more sparsely populated with fewer concentrations.[167] An attempt was made to estimate the population of the Mauryan empire but it was based on what seem to be exaggerated numbers for the Mauryan army and resulted therefore in the figure of 181 million, which is excessive for that period.[168] Other methods of computing population using archaeological data suggest a much lower figure.[169]

In a reassessment of the decline of the empire, the policies of Aśoka could be viewed more dispassionately, and a further investigation made into possible administrative and economic problems. Aśoka's *dhamma* may well have assisted in acculturation without the usual upheavals associated with imperial systems. Given the availability of resources and the manner in which the imperial system exploited these, the cause for upheaval may have been more limited. However the coming apart of the empire in so short a time would be suggestive either of oppressive features or inefficiency or both. The Northern Buddhist tradition insisting on the revolt at Taxila may indicate that the attempts at acculturation were resisted in some places. The existence of a multiplicity of cultural perceptions and norms would also have tended to encourage local alignments and where the larger unity may have been distant. The legend about Aśoka building a vast number of *stūpas*, if taken literally would indicate a heavy drain on imperial finances. But the archaeological evidence suggests only a few and such as were hardly likely to seriously dent the Mauryan income. A comparative study with other ancient empires does point to the relatively small number of

167 Allchin, op. cit., p. 165.

168 J.M. Datta, 'Population of India in about 320 BC', *Man in India*, 1962, 42, 4.

169 Makkhan Lal, *Archaeology of Population*, Varanasi, 1984, pp. 40ff.

what might be called imperial monuments. Pāṭaliputra, built by Candragupta Maurya, was certainly in the tradition of an imperial capital. Curiously Megasthenes does not mention other cities with such monumental architecture.

Again if Greek and Latin authors are to be believed, the size of the standing army would have drawn away a substantial amount of imperial revenue. In the absence of conscription it would have been necessary to maintain a large regular force. Yet the figures quoted for the army do seem exaggerated and were intended to explain why Alexander did not campaign further into India. The Mauryas, having consolidated their strength in the Ganges plain and the north-west and controlling as they did the routes going south, had little need for further conquest. Whereas successful campaigns do bring in an income, nevertheless the maintenance of a large army quickly terminates the income. The forsaking of conquests by Aśoka was doubtless motivated by his reaction to the horrors of the Kaliṅga campaign, but possibly he was also nudged by the financially negative effect of such campaigns.

That the administrative system may not have been able to hold together the demands of empire has been stated often enough and has recently been discussed in some detail as we have seen. A properly efficient system for such a large territory requires a considerable revenue. It may be more appropriate to comment on this. If the senior bureaucracy received the emoluments that are suggested then these would have been a major item of expenditure. The junior levels of the bureaucracy, probably locally recruited would not have involved the same financial outlay. The question then is whether there was a sufficient tapping of resources and collection of revenue to generate the required wealth to maintain the army, the administration and the overall imperial system. The empire was short-lived and this may have been because it was primarily concerned with extracting revenue from existing resources and possibly not sufficiently with creating new revenue bases. To maintain the hegemony of the imperial system, it was not enough just to integrate other areas. A substantial reorganizing of the economy of these areas would also be required. Significantly, when the empire breaks up, the differentiations observed within the imperial system come into their own. Magadha continued as the nucleus of large kingdoms incorporating the Ganges plain even though the successor dynasties were unrelated to the Mauryas. The consolidation in the north-west was linked to the politics of states once regarded as Hellenistic but now more mixed. Successor states elsewhere in Orissa, Andhra and the western Deccan were virtually impelled by the break-up of the Mauryan state. The pattern of the erstwhile *gaṇa-saṅghas* is equally interesting for those in the Terai and north Bihar were assimilated into the monarchical system of the Ganges plain, whereas those in Punjab and Rajasthan reverted to their oligarchic forms. It is not therefore as if the Mauryas were succeeded by the Suṅgas and the system continued. There is a distinctive pattern in the way in which the Mauryan state comes apart and this pattern is a guide to post-Mauryan history.

BIBLIOGRAPHY

ADIKARAM, E.W., *Early History of Buddhism in Ceylon*. Colombo, 1946.

ADRADOS, F.R., 'Aśoka's Inscriptions and Persian, Greek and Latin Epigraphy', in S.D. Joshi (ed.), *Amṛtadhārā*. Delhi, 1984, pp. 1–15.

AGARWALA, V.S., *India as Known to Panini*. Varanasi, 1963.

Agni Purāṇa, Mitra (ed.). Calcutta, 1873–79.

Aitareya Brāhmaṇa, Agase (ed.). Poona, 1896.

AIYANGAR, P.T.S., *History of the Tamils to AD 600*. Madras, 1929.

AIYANGAR, S.K., *The Beginnings of South Indian History*. Madras, 1918.

Aiyangar Commemoration Volume.

ALAHAKOON, H., *The Later Mauryas*. Delhi, 1980.

ALLAN, J., *Catalogue of the Coins of Ancient India* (British Museum). London, 1936.

ALLCHIN, F.R., 'Upon the Antiquity and Methods of Gold Mining in Ancient India', *JESHO*, 1962, 5, pp. 195–211.

—— 'Patterns of City Formation in Early Historic South Asia', *South Asian Studies*, 1990, 6, pp. 163–173.

—— *The Archaeology of Early Historic South Asia*. Cambridge, 1995.

ALTEKAR, A.S., *State and Government in Ancient India*. Banaras, 1949.

ALTHEIM, F., *Weltgeschichte Asiens in Griechischen Zeitalter*. Halle, 1937–48.

ANDERSEN, P.K., *Studies in the Minor Rock Edicts of Aśoka*, I, Critical Edition. Freiburg, 1990.

Aṅguttara Nikāya, Morris and Hardy (eds). London, 1883–1900.

ANJARIA, J.J., *The Nature and Grounds of Political Obligation in the Hindu State*. London, 1935.

AŚVAGHOṢA, *Buddhacarita*, Cowell (ed.). Oxford, 1893.

AUBOYER, J., *Art et Style de L'Inde*. Paris, 1951.

BABELON, *Rois de Syrie* . . . . Paris, 1890.

BĀṆA, *Harṣacarita*, Führer (ed.). Bombay, 1909.

BANDHOPADYA, N.C., *Economic Life and Progress in Ancient India*.

BAREAU, A., 'The Place of the Buddha Gautama in the Buddhist Religion during the Reign of Aśoka', in S. Balasooriya et al (eds), *Buddhist Studies in Honour of Walpola Rahula*. London, 1980, pp. 1–9.

BARNETT, L.D., *Antiquities of India*. London, 1913.

BARRETT, D., *Sculpture from Amarāvatī in the British Museum*. London, 1954.

BARUA, B.M., *Asoka and his Inscriptions*. Calcutta, 1948.

BASHAM, A.L., *History and Doctrines of the Ājīvikas*. London, 1951.

—— *The Wonder that was India*. London, 1954.

—— 'The Rise of Buddhism in its Historical Context', *Asian Studies*, 1966, 4, p. 405.

—— 'Aśoka and Buddhism: A Re-examination', *The Journal of the International Association of Buddhist Studies*, 1982, 5, 1, pp. 131–43.

BEAL, S., *Buddhist Records of the Western World*. London, 1883.

BECHERT, H., 'The Importance of Aśoka's so-called Schism Edict', in L.A. Herns et al (eds), *Indological and Buddhist Studies*. Canberra, 1982.

BECHERT, H. (ed.), *The Dating of the Historical Buddha*. Gottingen, 1991.
BELOCH, B., *Griechische Geschichte*. 3 vols. Strassburg, 1893–1904.
BENI PRASAD, *The State in Ancient India*. Allahabad, 1928.
BENVENISTE, E., 'Edits d'Asoka en traduction grecque', *Journal Asiatique*, 1964, pp. 137–57.
—— 'Une inscription indo-araméenne d'Asoka provenant de Kandahar (Afghanistan)', *Journal Asiatique*, 1966, 254, Fas 3–4, pp. 437–70.
BEVAN, E.R., *House of Seleucus*. London, 1902.
BHANDARKAR, D.R., *Asoka*. Calcutta, 1925.
BHANDARKAR, R.G., *The Early History of the Deccan*. Calcutta, 1928.
BHATTACHARYA, S., *Select Asokan Epigraphs with Annotations*. Calcutta, 1952.
BIGANDET, P.A., *Life and Legend of Gautama*. London, 1914.
BISWAS, D.K. (trans), *The Legend of Emperor Aśoka*. Calcutta, 1967.
BLOCH, J., *Les Inscriptions d'Asoka*. Paris, 1950.
BONGARD-LEVIN, G.M., 'The Historicity of the Ancient Indian Avadānas: A Legend about Aśoka's Deposition and The Queen's Edict', *Indian Studies Past and Present*. Calcutta, 1971, pp. 123–41.
—— *Mauryan India*. New Dèlhi, 1985.
BONGARD-LEVIN, G.M. and VOLKOVA, O.F., 'The Kunāla Legend and an Unpublished Aśokāvadānamālā Manuscript', *Indian Studies Past and Present*. Calcutta, 1965.
BOSE, A., *Social and Rural Economy of Northern India*. Calcutta, 1942–45.
BOSWORTH, A.B., 'Aristotle, India and the Alexander Historians', *TOPOI*, 1993, 3/2, pp. 407–24.
—— *A Historical Commentary on Arrian's History of Alexander*. Oxford, 1995.
—— 'The Historical Setting of Megasthenes' *Indica*', *Classical Philology*, 1996, 91, 113–27.
BOUCHE-LECLERQ, *Histoires des Seleucides*. Paris, 1913–14.
Brahmāṇḍa Purāṇa. Bombay, 1906.
BRELOER, *Kautilya Studien*. Bonn, 1927–34.
BROBINSKY, G.V., 'A Line of Brāhmī(?) Script in a Babylonian Contract Tablet', *JAOS*, 1936, 56, pp. 86–8.
BÜHLER, G., *On the Origin of the Indian Brahmi Alphabet*. Strassburg, 1898.
—— *Indian Paleography*. Bombay, 1904.
BURCKHARDT, J., *The Age of Constantine the Great*. London, 1949.
BURGESS, J., *Report on the Antiquities of Kathiawar and Kacch*. London, 1876.
BURROW, T., 'Cānakya and Kauṭilya', *ABORI*, 1968, 47–9, pp. 13–17.
CALDWELL, R., *A Comparative Grammar of the Dravidian Languages*. London, 1875.
CHAKRABARTI, D.K., *The Archaeology of Ancient Indian Cities*. Delhi, 1995.
CHANANA, D., *Slavery in Ancient India*. Delhi, 1960.
CHATTOPADHYAY, A., 'Vidiśā Devi', *JOI*, 1970, xx, 2, pp. 115–20.
CHATTOPADHYAYA, Alaka and CHIMPA, Lama, *Tāranātha's History of Buddhism in India*. Simla, 1980.
CHATTOPADHYAYA, S., *The Achaemenids and India*. Delhi, 1974 (rpt.).
—— *Bimbisāra to Aśoka*. Calcutta, 1977.
CHAUDHURI, K.A., *Ancient Agriculture and Forestry in Northern India*. Bombay, 1977.
CHHABRA, B.Ch., 'Aśokan Pillar at Hissar, Punjab', *Vishveshvarananda Indological Journal*, 1964, p 3.

CLAESSEN, H., 'The Internal Dynamics of the Early State', *Current Anthropology*, 1984, 25, 4, pp. 365–79.
CLAESSEN, H. and SKALNIK, P. (eds), *The Early State*. The Hague, 1978.
—— *The Study of the State*, The Hague, 1981.
CODRINGTON, H.W., *A Short History of Ceylon*. London, 1939.
CONZE, E., *Buddhism, its Essence and Development*. Oxford, 1953.
COOMARASWAMY, A.K., *History of Indian and Indonesian Art*. London, 1927.
CRADDOCK, P.T. et al., 'The Production of Lead, Silver and Zinc in Early India', in A. Hauptman, E. Pernicka and G.A. Wagner (eds), *Old World Archaeology*, Bergban Museum, 1989, pp. 51–69.
CRIBB, J., 'Dating India's Earliest Coins', in *South Asian Archaeology*, 1983, Naples, 1985, pp. 535–551.
CUMMING, J. et al. (eds), *Revealing India's Past*. London, 1939.
CUNNINGHAM, A., *Inscriptions of Aśoka*, CII.I. London, 1879.
—— *A Book of Indian Eras*. Calcutta, 1883.
—— *Coins of Ancient India*. London, 1891.
—— *Ancient Geography of India*. Calcutta, 1924.
DAHLQUIST, A., *Megasthenes and Indian Religion*, Uppsala, 1962.
DANDAMAEV, N.A. and LUKONIN, V.G., *The Culture and Social Institutions of Ancient Iran*. Cambridge, 1989.
DANI, A.H., *Indian Palaeography*. Oxford, 1963, pp. 29–30.
—— *Taxila*, UNESCO, 1986.
DAS GUPTA, S.N., *History of Indian Philosophy*. Cambridge, 1923–49.
DATE, G.T., *The Art of War in Ancient India*. London, 1929.
DATTA, J.M., 'Population of India in about 320 BC', *Man in India*, 1962, 42, 4.
DE JONG, J.W., 'Notes on the Text of the Aśoka Legend', in G. Pollet (ed.), *India and the Ancient World*. Louvain, 1987, pp. 103–13.
DERANIYAGALA, S.U., 'Radio-carbon dating of Early Brāhmī Script in Sri Lanka', *Ancient Ceylon*, 1990, 11, pp. 149–68.
—— *The Prehistory of Sri Lanka*, II, Colombo, 1992.
DERRETT, J.D.M., 'A Newly Discovered Contact between *Arthaśāstra* and *Dharmaśāstra*: the Role of Bharuci', *ZDMG*, 1965, 115, pp. 134ff.
DESAI, D., 'Terracotta Dancing-girls', *Marg*, 1985, 37, pp. 72–4.
DEY, N.L., *Geographical Dictionary of Ancient and Medieval India*. London, 1927.
DHAVALIKAR, M.K., 'The Beginnings of Coinage in India', *World Archaeology*, 1975, 6, pp. 330–8.
Dīgha Nikāya, Rhys Davids and Carpenter (eds). P.T.S. London, 1890–1911.
DIKSHITAR, V.R., *Mauryan Polity*. Madras, 1932.
—— *War in Ancient India*. Madras, 1929.
Dīpavaṃsa, Oldenberg (ed.). London, 1879.
DIRINGER, D., *The Alphabet*. London, 1947.
Divyāvadāna, Cowell and Neil (eds). Cambridge, 1886.
DUPONT SOMMER, A., 'Une mouvelle inscription araméene d'Asoka trouvé dans la vallée du Laghman (Afghanistan)', *Academie des Inscriptions et Belles-Lettres*, 1970, pp. 158–73.
DUTT, N., *Early Monastic Buddhism*. Calcutta, 1941.

DWIVEDI, G.N., *The Age of Kautilya*. Agra, 1966.
EGGERMONT, P.H.L., *The Chronology of the Reign of Asoka Moriya*. Leiden, 1956.
—— 'New Notes on Aśoka and his Successors', *Persica*, 1965–6, II, pp. 27–70; 1969, IV, pp. 77–102; 1970–1, V, pp. 69–102; 1979, VIII, pp. 55–93.
ELLIOT, H.M. and DOWSON, J., *History of India as told by its own Historians*. Calcutta, 1953.
EMMERICK, R.E., *Tibetan Texts Concerning Khotan*. Oxford, 1967.
ERDOSY, G., *Urbanization in Early Historic India*. Oxford, 1988.
FALK, H., *Schrift im alten Indien: ein Forschungsbericht mit Ammerkungen*. Tubingen, 1993.
FERGUSON, J., *History of Indian and Eastern Architecture*. London, 1910.
FERGUSON, J. and BURGESS, J., *Cave Temples in India*. London, 1880.
FICK, R., *The Social Organization in North-East India in Buddha's Time*. Calcutta, 1920.
FILLIOZAT, J. and RENOU, L., *L'Inde Classique*. Paris, 1947.
FILLIOZAT, J, 'Studies in Aśokan Inscriptions', *Indian Studies Past and Present*. Calcutta, 1967.
FOUCHER, A., *L'art Greco-Bouddhique du Gandhara*. Paris, 1905–18.
—— *The Beginnings of Buddhist Art*. Paris, 1917.
—— *La Vieille Route de L'Inde de Bactres à Taxila*. Paris, 1947.
FRANKFORT, H., *Art and Architecture of the Ancient Orient*. Harmondsworth, 1954.
FUSSMAN, G., 'Quelques problemes Asokéens', *Journal Asiatique*, 1974.
—— 'Central and Provincial Administration in Ancient India: the Problem of the Mauryan Empire', *Indian Historical Review*, 1987–8, XIV, pp. 43–72.
GEIGER, W., *The Dipavamsa and Mahavamsa*. Colombo, 1908.
GERSHEVITCH (ed.), *Cambridge History of Iran*, vol. 2. Cambridge, 1985.
GHIRSHMAN, R., *L'Iran*. Paris, 1951.
GHOSH, A., *The City in Early Historical India*. Simla, 1973.
GHOSH, A. (ed.), *An Encyclopaedia of Indian Archaeology*. Delhi, 1989.
GHOSH, B.K., *The Hindu Ideal of Life*. Calcutta, 1947.
GHOSHAL, U.N., *Contributions to the History of the Hindu Revenue System*. Calcutta, 1929.
—— *The Agrarian System in Ancient India*. Calcutta, 1930.
—— *The Beginnings of Indian Historiography*. Calcutta, 1944.
—— *Studies in Indian History and Culture*. Bombay, 1957.
GILES, H.A., *Travels of Fa-hsien*. Cambridge, 1923.
GLASENAPP, H. VON, *Der Jainismus*. Berlin, 1926.
GNOLI, G. and LANCIOTTI, L. (eds), *Orientalia Iosephi Tucci Memoria Dicata*. Rome, 1988.
GOKHALE, B.G., *Buddhism and Asoka*. Bombay, 1949.
GOPAL, L., 'Early Greek Writers on Writing in India', *PIHC*, 1976, pp. 544–52.
GOYAL, S.R., *Kautilya and Megasthenes*. Meerut, 1985.
—— 'Brāhmī Script, an Invention of the Early Maurya Period', in S.P. Gupta and K.S. Ramachandran (eds), *The Origins of Brahmi Script*. Delhi, 1979.
GRUNWEDEL, A., *Buddhist Art in India*. London, 1901.
GUHA, B.S., *Outline of the Racial History of India*. Calcutta, 1937.
GUPTA, P.L., *A Bibliography of the Hoard of Punch-marked Coins in Ancient India*. Bombay, 1955.
GUPTA, S.P., *The Roots of Indian Art*. Delhi, 1980.
GUPTA, S.P. and RAMACHANDRAN, K.S. (eds), *The Origins of Brahmi Script*. Delhi, 1979.

GURUGE, A., *Asoka, a Definitive Biography*. Colombo, 1994.
HARA, M., 'A Note on the Sanskrit Phrase, Devānampriya', *Indian Linguistics*, 1969, 30, pp. 13–26.
Harivaṃsa, Kinjewadekar (ed.). Poona, 1936.
HARLE, J.C., *The Art and Architecture of the Indian Subcontinent*. Harmondsworth, 1986.
HÄRTAL, H., 'Archaeological Research on Ancient Buddhist Sites', in H. Bechert (ed.) (1991).
HEGDE, K.T.M., 'Scientific Basis of the Technology of Three Ancient Indian Ceramic Industries', in B.M. Pande and B.D. Chattopadhyaya (eds), *History and Archaeology*. Delhi, 1987, pp. 359–62.
HEMACANDRA, *Abhidānacintāmaṇi*, Böhtlinck and Rieu (eds). St. Petersburg, 1847.
HENNING, W.B., 'The Aramaic Inscription of Aśoka found at Lampaka', *BSOAS*, 1949, 13, 1, pp. 80–8.
HERODOTUS, *History*. Loeb Classical Library, London, 1921–25.
HERZFELD, E.E., *Archaeological History of Iran*. London, 1935.
HOFINGER, M., *Étude sur le Concile de Vaisali*. Louvain, 1946.
HORNER, I.B., *Women under Primitive Buddhism*. London, 1930.
HOWELL, J., 'Note on the Society's Excavations at Sannati, Gulbarga District, Karnataka', *South Asian Studies*, 1989, 5, pp. 59–62.
HULTZSCH, E., *Corpus Inscriptionum Indicarum*, vol. I. London, 1888–1925.
HUMBACH, H., 'The Aramaic Asokan Inscription from Taxila', *Journal of Central Asia*, 1978, I, 2, pp. 87–98.
HUNTINGTON, J.C., 'The Lomas Rishi: another Look', *Archives of Asian Art*, 1974–5, 28, pp. 34–56.
HUTTON, J.H., *Caste in India*. Cambridge, 1946.
HWUI LI, *Life of Hsüan Tsang* (trans. Beal). London, 1911.
Indian Archaeology — A Review, 1954–5, 1962–3, 1973–4.
IRWIN, John, 'Asokan Pillars: a Re-assessment of the Evidence', *The Burlington Magazine*, 1973, CXV, pp. 706–20, 1974, CXVI, pp. 712–27, 1975, CXVII, pp. 631–43, 1976, CXVIII, 734–53.
—— 'The Prayaga-bull Pillar: Another Pre-Asokan Monument', in H. Härtal (ed.), *South Asian Archaeology*, 1979, vol. II. Berlin, 1981, pp. 313–40.
—— 'Origins of the Pre-Asokan Pillar cult at Prayaga (Allahabad)', *JRAS*, 1983, 3.
—— 'True Chronology of the Asokan Pillar', *Artibus Asiae*, 1983, XLIV, 4, pp. 247–65.
—— 'Buddhism and the Cosmic Pillar', in G. Gnoli and L. Lanciotti (eds).
ITO, G., 'Asokan Inscriptions, Laghman I and II', *Studia Iranica*, 1979, 8, pp. 175–84.
I TSING, *A Record of Buddhist Practices*, Takakusu (ed.). Oxford, 1896.
JANERT, K.L., 'About the Scribes and their Achievements in Aśoka's India', *German Scholars in India*, vol. I, pp. 141–5.
Jātakas, Fausbøll (ed.). P.T.S. London, 1877–97.
JAYASWAL, K.P., *Hindu Polity*. Bangalore, 1955.
JAYASWAL, V., 'Evidence for Resource Exploration for Art Activities at Chunar', in R. Varma (ed.), *Art and Archaeology of the Vindhyan Region*. Rewa, pp. 133–44.
JAYAWICKRAMA, N.A., 'A Reference to the Third Council in Aśoka's Edict', *University of Ceylon Review*, 1959, 17, pp. 61–72.
JOLLY, J., *Recht und Sitte*. Strassburg, 1896.

JOLLY, J., *Arthaśāstra of Kauṭalya*. Lahore, 1923. .
JOSHI, M.C. and JOSHI, J.C., 'A Study in the Names of Aśoka', *JOI*, 1968, x, VII, 4, pp. 415–24.
JOSHI, M.C. and PANDE, B.M., 'A Newly Discovered Inscription of Aśoka at Bahapur', *JRAS*, 1967, pp. 96–8.
JOUGET, P., *Macedonian Imperialism and the Hellenization of the East*. London, 1928.
KALHAṆA, *Rājataraṅgiṇī*, Stein (ed.). Bombay, 1892.
KĀLIDĀSA, *Mālvikāgnimitram*, Suru (ed.). Bombay, 1892.
KANE, P.V., *History of Dharmaśāstras*. Poona, 1930–46.
—— *Kātyāyanasmṛtisāroddhara*. Poona, 1933.
KANGLE, R.P., *The Kauṭilīya Arthaśāstra*. Bombay, 1965.
—— 'Some Recent Work on the Kauṭilya Arthaśāstra', *JAS*, 1968–9, 43–4, pp. 227–38.
KAPADIA, K.N., *Hindu Kinship*. Bombay, 1947.
KARTTUNEN, K., *India in Early Greek Literature*. Helsinki, 1989.
KAUṬALYA, *Arthaśāstram*, Ganapati Sastri (ed.). Trivandrum, 1921–25. Trans. R. Shamasastry. Mysore, 1956.
KEITH, A.B., *History of Sanskrit Literature*. Oxford, 1928.
KERN, F., *Asoka*. Bern, 1956.
KERN, H., *Manual of Indian Buddhism*. Strassburg, 1896.
KHER, N.N., *Agrarian and Fiscal Economy in the Mauryan and Post-Mauryan Age*. Delhi, 1973.
KONOW, S., *Kauṭalya Studies*. Oslo, 1945.
KOSAMBI, D.D., *An Introduction to the Study of Indian History*. Bombay, 1956.
—— *Indian Numismatics*. New Delhi, 1981.
KRISHNA RAO, M.V., *Studies in Kautalya*. Mysore, 1953.
KULKE, H., 'Some Considerations on the Significance of Buddha's Date for the History of Northern Indian', in H. Bechert (ed.).
KURAISHI, M.H., *A Guide to Rajgir*. Delhi, 1939.
LAL, MAKKHAN, *Archaeology of Population*. Varanasi, 1984.
—— 'Summary of Four Seasons of Exploration in Kanpur District, Uttar Pradesh', *Man and Environment*, 1984, VIII, pp. 61–80.
LAMOTTE, E., *History of Indian Buddhism*. Louvain, 1958. Trans. 1988.
Lankāvatārasūtra, Suzuki (ed.). London, 1932.
LASSEN, C., *Indische Alterthumskunde*. Leipzig und London, 1858–74.
LA VALLÉE POUSSIN, L. DE, *L'Inde aux temps des Mauryas*. Paris, 1930.
LAW, B.C., *Some Ksatriya Tribes of Ancient India*. Calcutta, 1924.
—— *Geography of Early Buddhism*. London, 1932.
—— *Tribes in Ancient India*. Poona, 1943.
LAW, N.N., *Inter-State Relations in Ancient India*. Calcutta, 1920.
—— *Aspects of Ancient Indian Polity*. Oxford, 1921.
LÉVI, S., *Le Népal*. Paris, 1905–8.
—— *L'Inde Civilisatrice*. Paris, 1938.
LINGAT, R., *Royautés Bouddhiques*, part I. Asoka et la Fonction Royale, Paris, 1989.
LOHUIZEN DE LEEUW, J.E. VAN, *The 'Scythian' Period . . .* Leiden, 1949.
LÜDERS, H., *Das Würfelspiel im alten Indien*. Berlin, 1907.
Mahābhārata. Bombay, 1888. *BORI*. Poona, 1940ff.

MAHADEVAN, I., *The Indus Script*. Delhi, 1977.
—— 'Recent Discoveries of Jaina Cave Inscriptions in Tamil Nadu, in *Rishabhasaurabha*. Delhi, 1994, pp. 123–7.
Mahāvaṃsa. P.T.S. London, 1908.
Mahāvastu, Senart (ed.). Paris, 1882–97.
Majjhima Nikāya. P.T.S. London, 1888–99.
MAJUMDAR, R.C., *Corporate Life in Ancient India*. Poona, 1922.
—— *Ancient India*. Banaras, 1952.
MAJUMDAR, R.C. (ed.), *History and Culture of the Indian People*, vol. II, *The Age of Imperial Unity*. Bombay, 1951.
MALALASEKARA, G.D., *Dictionary of Pali Proper Names*. London, 1937–8.
MANU, *Dharmaśāstra*, Jolly (ed.). London, 1887.
MARSHALL, J., *Guide to Sanchi*. Calcutta, 1918.
—— *Mohenjo-Daro and the Indus Civilization*. London, 1931.
—— *Taxila*. Cambridge, 1951.
MCCRINDLE, J.W., *Ancient India as Described by Ktesias the Knidian*. London, 1882.
—— *Ancient India as Described by Megasthenes and Arrian*. Calcutta, 1877.
—— *The Invasion of India by Alexander the Great*. London, 1896.
—— *Ancient India as Described in Classical Literature*. London, 1901.
—— *Ancient India as Described by Ptolemy*. Calcutta, 1927.
MCPHAIL, J.M., *Asoka*. Calcutta, 1926.
MEHENDALE, M.A., 'What was the Place of Issue of the Dhauli and Jaugada Separate Edicts', *BDCRI*, 1953, 17, pp. 81–97.
—— 'North-western and Western Influence on the Versions of Aśoka's Minor Rock Edict', *JOI (B)*, I, pp. 240–4.
MEHTA, R.L., *Pre-Buddhist India*. Bombay, 1939.
MEHTA, R.N., 'Sudarsana Lake', *JOI (B)*, 1968, 18, pp. 20–8.
MENDIS, G.C., *The Early History of Ceylon*. Calcutta, 1948.
MEYER, J.J., *Das Altindische Buch von Welt und Staatsleben*. Hanover, 1925.
—— *Sexual Life in Ancient India*. London, 1930.
MITRA, D., *Buddhist Monuments*. Calcutta, 1971.
MOOKERJEE, R.K., *History of Indian Shipping*. London, 1912.
—— *Asoka*. London, 1928.
—— *Ancient Indian Education*. London, 1947.
MORELAND, W.H., *The Agrarian System of Muslim India*. Cambridge, 1929.
MOTICANDRA, *Sārthavāha*. Patna, 1953.
MUKHERJEE, B.N., *Studies in Aramaic Edicts of Aśoka*. Calcutta, 1984.
MUKHOPADHYAYA, S., *Aśokāvadāṇa*. Delhi, 1963.
MÜLLER, M., *History of Ancient Sanskrit Literature*. London, 1859.
MURRAY, O., 'Herodotus and Hellenistic Culture', *Classical Quarterly*, 1972, 22, pp. 200–13.
MURTI, G.S. and AIYANGAR, A.N.K., *The Edicts of Asoka Priyadarsin*. Madras, 1951.
NAG, K., *Les Théories Diplomatiques de l'Inde Ancienne*. Paris, 1923.
NANDA, R., *The Early History of Gold in India*. Delhi, 1992.
NARAIN, A.K., *The Indo-Greeks*. Oxford, 1957.
—— 'A New Version of the Minor Rock Edict I of Aśoka', *Bharati*, 1961–2, 5, 1, pp. 1–5.

Narain, A.K. and Gopal, L. (eds), *Chronology of the Punch-Marked Coins*. Varanasi, 1966.
Neogi, P., *Copper in Ancient India*.
Nikam, K.A. and McKeon, R., *The Edicts of Asoka*. Chicago, 1959.
Nilakantha Sastri, K.A. (ed.), *The Age of the Nandas and Mauryas*. Banaras, 1952.
—— *The Colas*. Madras, 1935–7.
Norman, K.R., 'Notes on the Bahapur Version of Aśoka's Minor Rock Edict', *JRAS*, 1971, pp. 41–3.
—— 'Notes on the Greek Version of Aśoka's Twelfth and Thirteenth Rock Edicts', *JRAS*, 1972, 2, pp. 11–118.
—— 'Notes on the Ahraura Version of Aśoka's First Minor Rock Edict', *IIJ*, 1983, 26, pp. 277–92.
—— *Collected Papers*, vols i–iv. London, 1990–3.
—— 'Aśokan Inscriptions from Sannati', *South Asian Studies*, 1991, 7, pp. 101–10.
Norman, K.R. and Allchin, F.R., 'Guide to Aśokan Inscriptions', *South Asian Studies*, 1985, 1, 43–50.
Ojha, G.H., *Bhāratīya Lipimālā*. Ajmer, 1918.
Oldfield, *Sketches from Nepal*. London, 1880.
Olmstead, A.T., *History of the Persian Empire*. Chicago, 1949.
Pande, G.C., *Studies in the Origin of Buddhism*. Allahabad, 1957.
Panini, *Aṣṭādhyāyī*, Böhtlinck (ed.). Leipzig, 1887.
Pant, P.C. and Jayaswal, V., 'Ancient Stone Quarries of Chunar: An Appraisal', *Pragdhara*, 1990–91, no. 1, pp. 49–52.
Paranavitana, S., *The Greeks and the Mauryas*. Colombo, 1971.
Pargiter, F.E., *The Purāṇa Text of the Dynasties of the Kali Age*. London, 1913.
Pariśiṣṭaparvan, Jacobi (ed.). Calcutta, 1883–91.
Parker, H., *Ancient Ceylon*. London, 1909.
Patanjali, *Vyākaraṇa Mahābhāsya*, Kielhorn (ed.), 3 vols. Bombay, 1892.
Periplus, *The Erythraen Sea*. Trans. McCrindle. London, 1879. Trans. Schoff. London, 1912.
Peterson, P. (ed.), *The Daśakumāracarita of Daṇḍin*. Bombay, 1891.
Pliny, *Natural History*. London, 1938.
Plutarch, *Life of Alexander*. London, 1914–26.
Poster, G.A., *From Indian Earth — 4000 Years of Terracotta Art*. New York, 1986.
Polybius, *Histories*. London, 1922–7.
Pran Nath, *A Study in the Economic Condition of Ancient India*. London, 1929.
Prinsep, J., *Essays on Indian Antiquities*. London, 1858.
Przyluski, J., *La Legende de l'Empereur Açoka*. Paris, 1923.
Radhakrishnan, S., *Indian Philosophy*. London, 1923–7.
—— *The Principal Upaniṣads*. London, 1953.
Raghavan, V., *Kalidāsa and Kauṭalya*. Nagpur, 1946.
Rai, G.K., *Involuntary Labour in Ancient India*. Allahabad, 1981.
Rāmāyana. Bombay, 1912–20. Baroda, 1960ff.
Ramesh, K.V., 'The Aśokan Inscriptions at Sannati', *Indian Historical Review*, 1987–8, xiv, 1–2, pp. 36–42.
Rangarajan, L.N. (trans.), *Arthaśāstra*. New Delhi, 1992.
Rapson, E.J., *Indian Coins*. Strassburg, 1897.
—— *Ancient India*. Cambridge, 1916.

RAY, H.C., *Dynastic History of Northern India*. Calcutta, 1931–6.
RAY, N., *Maurya and Sunga Art*. Calcutta, 1945.
RAY, N.R., 'Technology and Social Change in Early Indian History', *Puratattva*, 1975–6, 8, pp. 132–8.
RAY, S.C., 'Stratigraphic Evidence of Coins in Indian Excavations and some Allied Issues', *Numismatic Notes and Monographs*. Varanasi, 1959, 1–14.
—— 'Evolution of Hindu Buddhist Art in the Gangetic Valley: a Study on the Basis of Stratigraphic Evidence of Archaeological Excavations', in *Investigating Indian Art*. Berlin, 1987, pp. 273–90.
RAYCHAUDHURI, H.C., *Political History of Ancient India*. Calcutta, 1972 (7th edn).
RAY, Niharranjan, 'Maurya and Sunga Art', in *Indian Studies Past and Present*, 1964–5, VI, pp. 53ff.
RENOU, L., *La Civilisation de l'Inde Ancienne*. Paris, 1950.
—— *Religions of Ancient India*. London, 1953.
RHYS DAVIDS, T.W., *Buddhist India*. London, 1903.
—— *Buddhism*. London, 1907.
RICE, B.L., *Mysore and Coorg from the Inscriptions*. London, 1909.
RITSCHL, Eva and SCHETELICH, Maria, *Studien zum Kauṭilīya Arthaśāstra*. Berlin, 1973.
ROSTOVTZEFF, M.I., *The Social and Economic History of the Hellenistic World*. Oxford, 1941.
ROWLAND, B., *The Art and Architecture of India*. London, 1953.
ROY, T.N., *The Ganges Civilization*. New Delhi, 1983.
SALOMON, R., 'On the Origin of the Early Indian Script', *JAOS*, 1995, 2, pp. 271–80.
SANKARANARAYANAM, S., 'Ahraura Inscription of Aśoka', *IHQ*, 1961, 37, 4, pp. 217–24.
SARAO, K.T.S., *Urban Centres and Urbanisation as Reflected in the Pali Vinaya and Sutta Pitakas*. Delhi, 1990.
SASTRI, A.M., 'Fifty Years of Epigraphical Studies in India: a Brief Survey', *Puratattva*, 1994–5, 25, p. 27.
SCERRATO, V., 'A Bi-lingual Graeco-Aramaic Edict by Aśoka', *Series Orientale Roma*, 1964, XXIX, pp. 1–27.
SCHLUMBERGER, D. et al., 'Une Bilingue Greco Araméene d'Asoka', *JA*, 1958, pp. 1–48.
SCHLUMBERGER, D. and BENVENISTE, E., 'A New Greek Inscription of Aśoka at Kandahar', *Ep. Ind.*, 1967, 37, 5, pp. 193–200.
SCHLUMBERGER, D. and CURIEL, R., *Trésor Monetaire*. Paris, 1953.
SCHMIDT, E.F., *Persepolis*. Chicago, 1953.
SCHUBRING, W., *Die Lehre der Jainas*. Göttingen, 1926.
SCIALPI, F., 'The Ethics of Aśoka and the Religions Inspiration of the Achaemenids', *East and West*, 1984, 34, 1–3, pp. 55–74.
SEN, A.C., *Asoka's Edicts*. Calcutta, 1956.
SEN, B.C., *Economics in Kautilya*. Calcutta, 1967.
SENART, E., *Les Castes dans l'Inde*. Paris, 1896.
—— *Les Inscriptions de Piyadassi*. Paris, 1881.
SENEVIRATNE, S., 'Kalinga and Andhra: the Process of Secondary State Formation in Early India', in H.J.M. Claessen and P. Skalnik (eds), *The Study of the State*. The Hague, 1981.
—— *Social Base of Early Buddhism in South-East India and Sri Lanka*. Ph.D. Thesis, JNU, 1985.
SENGUPTA, P., *Everyday Life in Ancient India*. Bombay, 1950.

SHAKED, S., 'Notes on the new Aśoka Inscription from Kandahar', *JRAS*, 1969, 118–22.

SHARMA, I.K., 'Early Sculptures and Epigraphs from South East India: New Evidence from Amaravati', in F.M. Asher and G.S. Ghai (eds), *Indian Epigraphy*. New Delhi, 1985, pp. 15–23.

—— *Studies in Early Buddhist Monuments and Brāhmī Inscriptions in Andhra Pradesh*. Nagpur, 1988.

SHARMA, I.K. and VARAPRASADA RAO, J., *Early Brāhmī Inscriptions from Sannati*. Delhi, 1993.

SHARMA, R.K. and MISHRA, S.N., *Excavations at Kakrehta (Rupnath)*. Delhi, 1992.

SHARMA, R.S., 'Iron and Urbanisation in the Ganga Basin', *IHR*, 1978, I.

—— *Sudras in Ancient India*. Delhi, 1980 (rev. ed.).

SHERWIN WHITE, S. and KUHRT, A., *From Samarkand to Sardis*. London, 1993.

SIDDIQI, W.H., 'A Study of Aśokan Pillars: Re-erected by Firuz Shah Tughluq' (mimeographed), 1976.

SIRCAR, D.C., 'Fragmentary Pillar Inscription from Amravati', *Ep. Ind.*, 1963, XXXV, part I, pp. 40–4.

—— *Select Inscriptions bearing on Indian History and Civilization*. Calcutta, 1965.

—— 'The Ahraura Inscription of Aśoka', *Ep. Ind.*, 1965, 36, 5, pp. 239–48.

—— 'New Delhi Inscription of Aśoka', *Ep. Ind.*, 1970, 38, 1, pp. 1–4.

—— *Asokan Studies*. Calcutta, 1979.

—— 'Panguraria Inscription of Aśoka', *Ep. Ind.*, 1981, 39, 1, pp. 1–8.

SIVARAJAPILLAY, K.N., *Chronology of the Early Tamils*. Madras, 1932.

Skanda Purāṇa, Pausikar (ed.). Poona, 1893.

SMITH, V., *Asoka*. Oxford, 1924.

—— *Early History of India*. Oxford, 1924.

—— *History of Fine Art in India and Ceylon*. Oxford, 1930.

SRIVASTAVA, K.M., 'Some Interesting New Finds from Kapilavastu', in B.M. Pande and B.B. Chattopadhyaya (eds), *History and Archaeology*. Delhi, 1987, pp. 359–62.

STEIN, O., *Megasthenes und Kautilya*. Wien, 1921.

STERNBACH, L., *Bibliography of Kauṭilīya Arthaśāstra*. Hoshiarpur, 1973.

STRABO, *Anabasis*.

STRONG, J.S., *The Legend of King Aśoka*. New Jersey, 1983.

—— *The Legend and Cult of Upagupta* . . . New Jersey, 1992.

SUBBA REDDY, D.V., *Glimpses of Health and Medicine in the Mauryan Empire*. Hyderabad, 1966.

TAMBIAH, S.J., *World Conqueror and World Renouncer*. Cambridge, 1976.

TĀRANĀTHA, *Geschichte des Buddhismus in Indien*. St. Petersburg, 1869.

TARN, W.W., *Hellenistic Civilization*. London, 1927.

—— *Greeks in Bactria and India*. Cambridge, 1951.

THAKUR, V.K., *Urbanisation in Ancient India*. Delhi, 1981.

THAPAR, R., 'Renunciation: the Making of a Counter Culture?' in Thapar (1978).

—— 'Ethics, Religion and Social Protest in the First Millennium BC in Northern India', in *Ancient Indian Social History: Some Interpretations*. New Delhi, 1978, pp. 40–62.

—— 'The State as Empire', in H. Claessen and P. Skalnik (1981).

—— 'Householders and Renouncers in the Brahmanical and Buddhist Traditions', in T.N. Madan (ed.), *Way of Life*. Delhi, 1982, pp. 237–98.

THAPAR, R., *From Lineage to State*. New Delhi, 1984.
—— 'Epigraphic Evidence and some Indo-Hellenistic Contacts during the Mauryan Period', in S.K. Maity and V. Thakur, *Indological Studies*. New Delhi, 1987.
—— 'Religion and the Social Order', in *Contributions to Indian Sociology*, 1987, 21, 1, pp. 157–65.
—— *The Mauryas Revisited*. Calcutta, 1988.
—— 'Patronage and Community', in B. Stoller Miller (ed.), *The Powers of Art*. Delhi, 1992, pp. 19–34.
—— 'Sacrifice Surplus and the Soul', *History of Religion*, 1994, pp. 305–24.
—— 'Literacy and Communication: Some Thoughts on the Inscriptions of Aśoka' (forthcoming).
THOMAS, E.J., *The History of Buddhist Thought*. London, 1933.
TIMMER, B.C.J., *Megasthenes en de Indische Maatschappij*. Amsterdam, 1930.
TRAUTMANN, T.R., *Kauṭilya and the Arthaśāstra*. Leiden, 1971.
UPASAK, C.S., *The History and Palaeography of Mauryan Brahmi Script*. Nalanda, 1960.
VALAVALKAR, P.H., *Hindu Social Institutions*. Baroda, 1942.
Vaṃsatthapakāsinī, Malalasekara (ed.). P.T.S. London, 1935.
Vāyu Purāṇa, Mitra (ed.). Calcutta, 1879–88.
Vinayapiṭaka, Oldenberg (ed.). London, 1872–83.
Viṣṇu Purāṇa, Gupta (ed.). Gorakhpur, 1952.
VOGEL, J.P., *Buddhist Art in India*. Oxford, 1936.
WADDELL, L.A., *Discovery of the Exact Site of Aśoka's Classic Capital at Pāṭaliputra*. Calcutta, 1892.
WARMINGTON, E.H., *Commerce between the Roman Empire and India*. Cambridge, 1928.
WATTERS, T., *On Yuan Chwang's Travels in India*, 2 vols. London, 1904–5.
WINSTON, R., *Charlemagne*. London, 1956.
WOOLNER, A.C., *Asoka, Text and Glossary*. Calcutta, 1924.
YAMAZAKI, G., 'The Legend of the Foundation of Khotan', *Toyo Bunko*, 1990, 48, pp. 55–80.
—— 'The Lists of the Patriarchs in the Northern and Southern Legends', in H. Bechert (1991).
Yuga Purāṇa, Mankad (ed.). Vallabhavidyanagar, 1951.
ZAMBRINI, A., 'Gli Indika di Megasthene', *Annali della Scuola Norm. Sup. di Pisa*, 1982, 3, 12, 1, pp. 71–149 and 1985, 3, 15, 3, pp. 781–853.

INDEX

Ābhīra caste, 68
Achaemenid(s), 110, 126–9, 267–9, 278, 304
Actors and performers, 224
Adhikaram, E.W., 135
adhyakṣas, *see* Superintendents
Administrative divisions, 314
Administrative system, 320
Adrados, F.R., 276
Aegyptica [by Hecataeus of Abdera], 296
Aelian, 78
Agarwala, V.S., 289
Agents of the King, 107, 110, 111, 158
Agnibrahma, 24
Agoranomoi, 81, 107, 118
Agrammes, 12
Agrarian economy, 5
Agriculture, extension of, 310–11
Ahicchatra, 240–1, 269
Aitareya Brāhmaṇa, 141
Aiyangar, 132–3
Ajātaśatru, 302
Ājīvikas, 4, 18, 26, 27, 43, 139–40, 144, 154, 173, 178, 186–7
Akbar, 66, 144, 215
Alahakoon, H., 303
Alexander, 13, 14, 16, 20, 128–9, 138, 246, 296
Alexander of Corinth, 41, *see* Hellenic kings
Alexander of Epirus, 41, *see* Hellenic kings
Allahabad, 5, 228, 236
Allan, 121, 241, 243, 246–7
Allchin, F.R., 271, 272, 279, 282, 285, 287, 292
Altheim, 232
amissā, 155, 199
Amitrochates/Amitrochades, 17, 18, 20
Amarāvatī, 271, 274, 279, 287
amṭa-mahāmattas, 116
Ānanda, 25
Anantadeva, 226
Anderson, P.K., 271
Andhra(s), 124, 196, 317, 320
Aṅguttara Nikāya, 56, 235
Animals, treatment of, 69–71, 118, 150–2, 163, 173, 175, 177, 179, 198, 201–2, 225
Antigonus Gonatas of Macedonia, 41, *see* Hellenic kings
Antiochus I, 18, 20
Antiochus II, 20, 41, 123, 126, 130
Anulā, 47–8
Anuradhapura, 279
Aparānta, 47, 48, 77, 128, 229
Āpastamba Dharmasūtra, 155
Aramaic, 7, 21, 32, 128, 232
Aramaic inscriptions, 275, 276, 277, 281–2
Archaeological excavations, 11, 200, *see* Town planning, Coinage, Pottery, Terracottas
Archaeology, 282–8
Aria, 16
Ariṭṭha, 47, 135
Armour, 72, 75, 119
Army, 75, 118–20
Arochosia, 16
Arrian, 10, 57, 60–2, 65, 72, 75, 85, 87, 90, 102, 111, 112, 120–2, 129, 221, 234, 236, 296, 297, 311, 314
Art, 11, 76, 129, 205–6, 267–70
Arthaśāstra, 9, 10, 56, 62, 64–71, 74, 76–80, 85–91, 94–5, 98–100, 104–5, 107, 110, 112, 114, 115–20, 127, 144, 151, 154, 158, 159, 171, 204, 207–10, 218–25, 244, 247, 292, 293, 294, 295, 308, 311, 312, 314, 315, 317, 318
  dating of, 294
Artisans, 72, 91, 99
Asandhimittā, 23, 30, 51–3
Ascetic [*saṃnyāsin*], 309
Asher, F.M., 287
Aśoka, length of reign, 303
  two views, historical and legendary, 307–8
  and Buddhism, 305–10
Aśokan Pillars as Monuments, 289–92
Aśokārāma, 43
Aśoka's 'Hell', 29, 35, 238
Aśokasūtra, 21

Aśokāvadāna, 21–2, 28, 35, 184, 192–4, 200, 297
Aśokāvadānamālā, 298
āśramas, the four, 159–60
Aśvaghoṣa, 171, 218
Athenaeus, 17–18, 139, 141
Atranjikhera, 284
Avanti, 16
Ayodhya, 299
A-yü-wang-chuan, 35, 42
Ayyaputtaāryaputra, 280

Babylon, 129
Bactria, 219, 237
Bactrian Greeks, 11, 189, 190, 193, 195–7
Bahapur [New Delhi], 271
Bairāṭ, 5, 154, 229, 286
Balasooriya, S., 307
Bāṇa, 185
Banaras, 268
Bandhupālita, 182–3, 195–6
Barābar Caves, 5, 154, 173, 226, 229, 260 (trans. of inscription)
Bareau, A., 307
Barua, B.M., 12, 54, 97
Basham, A.L., 30, 32, 79, 142, 146, 151, 250, 268, 277, 281, 308
Bazira, 236
Beal, S., 6
Bechert, H., 298, 307
Benveniste, E., 274, 275
Besnagar, 268
Bevan, E.R., 129
Bhabra Edict, 37, 179–80, 229, 261 (trans.)
Bhadrabāhu, 17, 60
Bhandarkar, D.R., 117, 148–9, 219–20
Bharhut, 205–6
bhaṭakas, *see* Slaves
Bhavabhūti, 220
bherighoso . . ., 153, 202
bhikkhugatika, Aśoka as a, 148
Bhīlsā, 23
Bhir Mound, 286
Bhoja, 124
bhṛtakas, *see* Hired labour
Biṁbisāra, 26, 300, 302, 303
Bindusāra, 13, 17–21, 25, 33, 101, 132, 139, 191, 194, 245, 248
biruda, 198
Biswas, D.K., 297
Bloch, J., 18, 27, 31, 34–42, 49, 50, 62, 66, 70–3, 81, 90, 95–7, 102–10, 113, 116–18, 125, 127, 140, 147, 150–80
Bodhisattva, 308
Bodhi-tree, 30, 38, 47, 51, 160, 185
Bongard-Levin, G.M., 298, 310, 311; 312
Bose, A., 67, 89, 91, 92
Bosworth, A.B., 296
Brachmanes, 59
Brahmadeya grant, 67
Brahmagiri [Karnataka], 5, 132, 154, 229, 230, 233, 287
Brāhmaṇas, 218, 273, 281
Brahmanism, 140, 144
Brahmans, position of, 58–61, 96, 162, 167, 198, 200, 231
Brāhmī, 7, 132, 134, 242, 274, 275, 280, 291
  origins of, 278–9
Bramaṇaśramaṇa, 277
Breloer, 61
Bṛghukaccha, 286
Bṛhadratha, 182–3, 185, 192, 196, 201
Bricks, Mauryan, 76, 286
Broach, 77, 81–2, 128, 229, 231, 235, 237
Brobinski, G.V., 280
Buddha, advance of date of death, 298
  sites associated with life of, 298
  towns associated with, 300
Buddhism, 140–2
  and Aśoka, 2–3, 33, 144, 171, 179, 214–15
  and caste, 4, 5
  and *Dhamma*, 3
  and Missions, 46–9
  and routes, 80–1
  and slaves, 90
  and women, 86
Buddhist Councils, 41–2
Buddhist sources, 297–303
Buddhist texts as sectarian literature, 307
Bühler, G., 107, 121
Buner [near Peshawar], 271
Burckhardt, J., 145
Bureaucracy, Mauryan, 207, 222
Burgess, J., 231
Burrow, T., 293

caitya(s), 29, 300

Cakkavattisīhanādasutta, 8, 146
cakravartin, 8, 146, 308
Campā, 21, 285
Caṇḍālas, 92
Caṇḍāśoka, 29
Candragupta, 293, 297, 303
Candragupta Maurya, 3–4, 9, 12–13, 16–18, 33, 45, 60, 68, 121–2, 138–9, 144, 158, 160, 164, 190–1, 220, 224–5, 231, 248
Cankam, 278
Capitals (of pillars), 7
Cārūmatī, 30, 131
Caste, 4–5, 11, 56–7, 63, 68–9, 73, 92, 95–6, 98, 102–4, 117, 120, 138, 141, 143, 157
Cattle, 69–70
Catullus, 41
Ceylon, 12, 48, 82, 126, 131, 134–6, 202, 223, 237
Chakrabarti, D.K., 282
Chanana, D., 312
Chandraketugarh, 287
Charlemagne, 110–11, 145, 152
Charpentier, J., 45
Charsada [ancient Puṣkalāvatī], 286
Chattopadhyay, A., 305
Chattopadhyaya, Alaka, 298
Chattopadhyaya, S., 304, 310
Chaudhuri, K.A., 284
Chief collector, 99
Chitral, 276
Chunar, 274, 291
Cīna-bhūmi, 222
Cīna-paṭṭa, 219
City walls, 285–6
Claessen, H.J.M., 287, 316
Classical sources (Greek and Latin), 9–10, 11, 57, 81–2, 296, 320
Clement of Alexandria, 167
Coinage, 205, 233–4, 242
  Athenian owl, 242
  connection with West Asia, 288
  indigenous origin, 288
  kākiṇī, 247
  māṣaka, 247
  negama, 121
  paṇa, 74, 99, 119, 247
  punch-marked, 8, 11, 241–7, 282, 284, 288–9
  Seleucid coins, 242
  sigloi, 242–3, 246
  silver-bar, 11
Coḷas, 114, 124, 133
Communication within the Mauryan empire, 315
Computers, application of statistical methods to texts, 294
Coomaraswamy, A., 291
Coomaraswamy, A.K., 267–9
Conquest of the south by the Mauryas, 18
Constantine, 137, 145
Contact between the Mauryas and the West, 17–18, 125, 232, 237
Conversion of Aśoka to Buddhism, 33
Corpus Inscriptionum Indicarum, 6, 30, 41, 44, 81
Cotton cloth, 285
Council of Ministers, 99
Craddock, P.T., 284
Craftsmen, *see* Artisans
Cribb, J., 289
Cultivator, position of, 61
Cunningham, A., 281
Cunningham, Sir A., 6 (*see* CII), 44, 121, 130, 228–9, 232, 234–5

Dahlquist, A., 297
Dakṣiṇāpatha, 286
Dāmodara II, 184, 188
Dandamaev, M.A., 280, 304
daṇḍanīti, 296
daṇḍaviṣṭikara, 312
Daṇḍin, 219, 296
Dani, A.H., 245, 286
Darius, 20, 126–7, 128, 215, *see* Foreign contacts
dāsa, 312, *see* Slaves
dāsakarmakara, 311, 312
Daśakumāracarita, 224, 296
Daśaratha, 8, 30, 182–3, 185–7, 194–7, 226
Daśona, 183, 195–6
Dating of the Inscriptions of Aśoka, 31
Datta, J.M., 319
Deccan plateau, 11, 82–4
Decourdemanche, 244
Deimachus, 129–30
de Jong, J.W., 297
Delhi-Meerut, 5, 6, 230
Delhi-Toprā, 5, 6, 177, 230

Deraniyagala, S.U., 279
Derrett, J.D.M., 294
Desai, D., 283
Devadharman, 183
Devānampiya, 6, 222, 226, 305
Devānampiya Tissa, 24, 46–8, 126, 134–6, 202, 226
Devapāla, 30, 131
Devavarman, 182, 196
Devī, 22, 23
Dhamma, 2–3, 41, 51, 111, 116–18, 125–6, 128, 138, 143–8, 153–81, 197, 199, 273, 277, 282, 292, 304, 309, 319
  Aramaic for, 277
  Greek for, 276
Dhammā, 26
Dhamma-lipi, 280
Dhamma-mahāmattas, 49, 102, 117, 118, 123, 130, 133, 135, 154, 156–7, 161, 165, 168, 172–4, 176–7, 179, 189, 199, 216, 235
Dhammāsoka, 29
Dhamma vijaya, 48–9
Dhamma-yātā, 38, 160
Dharanikoṭa [Dhānyakaṭaka], 274, 287, 318
Dharma, 10, 181, 211, 236, 307
Dharmā, 21
Dharmaśāstra, 293, 294
Dharmasmṛti, 293, 294
Dharmavivardhana, 30, 186, *see* Kunāla
Dhauli, 5, 11, 164, 169, 176, 204, 230, 268
Dhavalikar, M.K., 288
Dhuṇḍirāja, 12
Dhvaja, 290
Didarganj *yakṣī*, 268, 291
Dīgha Nikāya, 8, 79, 146–7, 162, 300
digvijayin, 146
Dikshitar, V.R., 94, 148, 225
Diodorus, 10, 57–61, 65–8, 72, 89, 90, 98, 102, 111–12, 119–22, 311, 314
Diodotus, 245–6, 248
Dionysius, 129–30
Dīpavaṃsa, 6, 8, 14, 22, 25, 34, 38, 42, 44, 46–50, 146, 226, 305
Divyāvadāna, 9, 15, 21, 25–6, 30, 35, 50, 139, 154, 186–8, 190, 194, 199, 204, 229
Dotted Record of Canton, 14
Dupont Sommer, A., 275
Durga Prasad, 244
Dutt, N., 42, 43, 187
Dwivedi, G.N., 294

Eclipse, 15, 50–1
Economy under the Mauryas, 55–6, 142–3, 164, 205, 313
  fiscal crisis, 285, 289
Eggermont, P.H.L., 31–4, 36–8, 41, 44, 50–1, 160, 303
Emmerick, R.E., 304
Ephoroi, 111
Epigraphia Indica, 13, 22
Episcopoi, 111
Erdosy, G., 283
Eusebeia [Greek for *dhamma*], 276

Fa-hsien, 7, 18, 28–30, 47, 51, 188, 237
Falk, H., 279
Family, importance of, 164, 172, 178, 180
Famine, 7–8, 17, 68, 113, 233
Fazy, 50
Festive gatherings, 151–2, 206
Fick, R., 58, 73, 85, 92, 237
Filliozat, J., 60, 275
Fish, 71–2
Fleet, 14, 66, 226, 235
Forced labour (*Viṣṭi*), 61, 68, 89, 312
Foreign contacts, 124
  with Central Asia, 130–1
  with Ceylon, 134–6
  with the Hellenic world, 129
  with Iran, 126–9
  with Nepal, 131
  with Southern India, 132
Forests, 118
Fortified settlements, 285, 300
Foucher, A., 246–7
Fraser, P.M., 275
Fussman, G., 315

gahapati, 63
gāmabhojaka, 63–4
gaṇa-saṅghas, 301, 313, 320
Gandhāra, 12, 21, 31, 47, 48, 123, 126, 189, 193, 194 (Gandhāras), 124
Ganges, 11, 67, 81–2, 124, 132, 169, 205, 268
Ganwaria, 298
Garbini, G., 275
Gārgisaṃhitā, 191, 195

Gāvimatha, 5, 132, 154, 230, 233
Gedrosia, 16
Geiger, W., 8
Gershevitch, I., 304
Ghai, G.S., 287
Ghirshman, R., 110, 128
Ghosh, A., 268–9, 282, 285, 298, 310
Ghoshal, U.N., 64, 66, 201
Ghuggus [Chadrapur Dt], 271
Giles, H.A., 7, 28–30, 47, 51, 188, 237
Gilgit, 276
Girika, 35, *see* Aśoka's 'Hell'
Girnār, 5, 31, 37, 46, 70–3, 230
Gnoli, G., 275, 289
gopa, 109, 113
Gopal, L., 280, 288
Gorakhpur, 243
Goyal, S.R., 279, 294
Graffiti, 279
Greek inscriptions, 275, 276, 277, 281–2
Greek kings [*yona-rājās*], 273, 304
Greek texts, references to India, 296
Greeks, 167, 190, 197, 201, *see* Yona
Guilds, 73
Gujarra, 5, 231
Gupta, P.L., 11
Gupta, S.P., 289, 292
Guruge, A., 303, 305–6

Hara, M., 305
Harappa, 244
Harivamsa, 155
Harle, J.C., 291
Harprasad Sastri, 198–201
Harṣacarita, 185
Härtal, H., 289, 298
Hastināpur, 75–6, 205
Hauptman, A., 284
Hegde, K.T.M., 283
Hegesander, 18
Hellenic kings, contemporaries of Aśoka, 40, 130, 167–8
Hemacandra, 226
Henning, W.B., 7, 232, 275
Herdsmen, position of, 68
Herns, L.A., 307
Herodotus, 57, 125, 127
Highway, royal, 81–2
Himalaya, 48
Hired labour, 73, 89
Hofinger, M., 42
Hora, 71
Horner, I.B., 86
Houses, 93
Howell, 273
Hsüan Tsang, 6, 18, 24, 28–9, 35, 130, 133, 228, 233–7
Hsuan Tsang, list of Pillars, 292
Hultzsch, E., 81, 100, 104, 117, 128, 155 174, 226, 229–30
Humbach, H., 276, 277
Hunters, 72, 92
Huntington, J.C., 292

Indian traders in Iran and Mesopotamia, 280
Indrapālita, 182, 195–6
Inscriptions, 271–82
Interregnum, 25, 32–3
Iron objects, 284
Irrigation, 118, 285
Irwin, John, views on Pillars, 289–91
Isilā, 39
ithījhaka-mahāmattas, 102, 117
Ito, G., 275
I Tsing, 26, 148

Jabulpur, 234–5
Jaiminī Nyāyāmalavistāra, 63
Jaina, 3, 17, 45, 60, 138–9, 146, 187, 195, 226, 231
Jaina Council, 45
Jalauka, 30, 184, 188–9, 193
Jambai [South Arcot District], 278
Jambudvīpa, 28, 36, 196, 199
janapada, 295, 299, 302
Janapadakalyānī, 21
Janert, K.L., 280
Jātakas, 56, 58, 76, 85, 91–2, 101, 105, 107, 114, 153, 229, 235, 300
Jatiṅga-Rāmeshwar, 5, 132, 231, 236
jātis, 313
Jaugaḍa, 5, 164, 169, 176, 204, 231
Jayaswal, K.P., 63, 97, 106
Jayaswal, V., 284
Jayawickrama, N.A., 307
Jhansi, 5
Jolly, J., 218–19
Joshi, J.C., 305
Joshi, M.C., 272, 305

Joshi, S.D., 276
Judicial officers, 102–3, 113, 169, *see* *Rājūkas*
Junāgarh, 8, 13, 47, 128, 230
Justin, 12
Jyotiṣa-vedāṅga, 38–9

Kālidāsa, 191, 219, 221
Kaliṅga, 48, 77, 82, 90, 94, 131, 133, 164, 168–9, 203, 231–2, 317, 320
Kaliṅga War, 18, 33, 35–6, 40, 62, 133, 166, 168, 170, 274
Kālsi, 5, 11, 46, 62, 231–2
Kalyanov, 223–4
Kāmāśoka, 29
Kamboja, 94, 123
Kanakāgiri, 40, 236
Kandahar, 32, 84, 123, 128, 173, 226, 232, 260 (trans. of inscription), 271, 274, 275, 286
Kane, P.V., 64
Kangle, R.P., 292, 293, 311
karmakaras, *see* Hired labour
Karttunen, K., 296
Karūvākī, 30, 102, 178, 185
Kashmir, 47–8, 130, 131, 189, 193–4, 237
Kāśī, 77
Kauśāmbi, 6, 179, 228, 239, 285, 290, 291, 299, 300
Kauṭalya, 9, 12–13, 17, 77, 218–19, 225
Kennedy, 244
Keralaputra, 124
Kern, F., 39, 105, 146, 150, 159
Kern, H., 48, 149, 157
Kharoṣṭhī, 7, 128, 242, 272, 275, 276. 279, 284, 318
Khāśya, 25, 130
Kher, N.N., 313
Khotan, 193, 304 *see* Foreign contacts
Kielhorn, 13, 226
Killing of Aśoka's brothers, 25–7
Kingless states, 120–1, *see* Tribal republics
Kingship, Mauryan ideas of, 94
Kingsmill, 127
Konākamana, 51, 179, 233
Kosambi, D.D., 62, 128, 151, 204, 219, 310, 317
  views on coinage and Mauryan fiscal crisis, 289
Kosambi Jātaka, 290, 300

Krishna Rao, 218
Krishna valley, 274
Kṛṣṇa, 297
Kṣatriyas, 301
Kuhrt, A., 304
Kukkuṭārāma, 35, 53
Kulke, H., 298
Kumāra, 272, 273, 280
Kunāla, 22, 30, 52, 53, 101, 182, 185–6, 192, 194–7, 204
Kunālasūtra, 21, 192–3
Kuṣāṇa presence, 276

Labour, forced, 312
Laghman, 7, 123, 232, 271, 275
Lal, B.B., 75, 76, 93
Lama Chimpa, 298
Lama Tāranātha, history of Buddhism, 298
Lampaka (Laghman), 7, 123, 232, 271, 275
Lanciotti, L., 275, 289
Landownership, 63–7, 211–12, 311ff
Lanka, *see* Ceylon
Lassen, C., 41
Last years of Aśoka, 51–4, 187–9, 192
Lauriyā-Ararāj, 5, 232
Lauriyā-Nandangarh, 5, 11, 232
Law, B.C., 220
Legal system, 95–7, *see* Judicial officers Punishments
Lévi, S., 20, 30, 131
Licchavis, 94
van Lohuizen de Leeuw, 142
Li-yul Gyi lo rgyus [Tibetan text], 304
Liṅgam, 281
Lingat, R., 308
Literacy, 281
Lukonin, V.G., 280, 304
Lumbinī Garden, 49–51, 66, 179, 234, *see* Rummindei

Machiavelli, 210
Madan, T.N., 309
Madhurā, 77
Magadha, 13, 16, 37, 195, 210, 221, 233
Magas of Cyrene, 41, 45, *see* Hellenic kings
Magic spells, 70, 224–5
Mahābhārata, 114, 177, 200, 294, 300
Mahābhāṣya, 226
Mahābodhivaṃsa, 22

Mahadevan, I., 294
Mahādhammarakhita, 27
Mahājanapadas, 302
Mahāmantri, 98
Mahāmattas, 101–3, 113, 116, 157, 158, 166, 169, 178, 180, 222, 228, 230, 272, 280
Mahāparinirvāna, 302, 303
Mahāraṭṭha, 47, 48
Mahāsammata, 147
Mahāsthān, 7, 17, 68, 113, 233
Mahāvagga, 302
Mahāvaṃsa, 6, 8, 21–7, 30, 32, 34, 42–3, 46–51, 82, 127, 135, 203, 222, 237, 303, 305
Mahāvaṃsa ṭīkā, 305
Mahinda, 12, 22–5 (Mahendra), 28, 134–6
Mahinda's mission to Ceylon, 41, 45
Mahiṣa, 77
Mahiṣa-maṇḍala, 47 (map), 48
Maity, S.K., 305
Majjhima Nikāya, 28
Major Rock Edicts [MRE], 2, 5, 271, 275, 276, 303
  Ist, 70, 150, 198, 202, 250 (trans.)
  2nd, 46, 49, 70, 116, 152, 251, 273 (trans.)
  3rd, 31, 97, 105–6, 109, 127, 152, 167, 202, 251 (trans.)
  4th, 70, 153, 167, 251, 277 (trans.)
  5th, 27, 31–2, 49, 70, 96, 102, 117, 155, 156, 167, 252 (trans.)
  6th, 97, 102, 158, 216, 252 (trans.)
  7th, 159, 253 (trans.)
  8th, 37, 70, 160, 167, 226, 253 (trans.)
  9th, 71, 73, 162, 167, 253 (trans.)
  10th, 163, 254 (trans.)
  11th, 163, 167, 254 (trans.)
  12th, 102, 165, 189, 255, 273, 274 (trans.)
  13th, 15, 18, 20, 35–6, 40–1, 46, 48, 82, 90, 125, 134, 166–8, 202–3, 255, 273, 274, 277 (trans.)
  14th, 41, 169, 257, 273 (trans.)
  Kandahar III, 274
Makkhan Lal, 319
Mānsehrā, 5, 7, 123, 128, 233
Manu, 59, 65–6, 90–2, 168, 294
Marriage alliance, 20, 139
Marriages, types of, 87–9, 103
Marshall, Sir J., 7, 21, 75–6, 93, 200, 237, 268, 270
Maritime links, 287
Maski [Karnataka], 5, 6, 40, 132, 154, 233, 287
Mathura, 268, *see* Stone sculpture
Mauryan Chronology, 303–5
Mauryan empire, 197ff, 310–21
  centralization, 315
  centrifugal factors, 315
  decline, 197ff, 319–21
Mauryan state, 316
  and territory, 317–19
Mauryas, origin of, 12–13, 198–9
  chronology, 14–16, 303ff
Māyā, 59
McPhail, 233
Medical centres, 152
Megalithic settlements, 287
Megasthenes, 9–10, 11, 17–18, 57–70, 87–90, 98, 102, 105, 107, 111, 113, 119–22, 139, 158–60, 167, 206, 208, 221, 224, 234, 243, 280, 296, 311, 312, 313, 314, 320
  Indica, 295, 296–7, 304
Mehendale, M.A., 271, 273
Mehta, R.N., 285
Metals, 75, 142
Mines, gold, 272, 274, 285, 287
  copper, 286
  diamond, 285
  silver, lead, 284
Minor Rock Edict(s) [Minor RE], 2, 5, 36, 38–40, 102, 154, 166, 171–2, 199 (trans.), 259, 271, 272, 273, 277, 284, 303, 318
Mint, 147–8
Mishra, S.N., 286
Missi, 110–11
Missions, 125, 131, 133, 134
Missionaries sent by the Third Buddhist Council, 47
Mitra, D., 286, 292
Moggaliputta Tissa, 43, 45, 51
Mookerjee, R.K., 23, 31, 38, 148
Moreland, W.H., 66
Mudrārākṣasa, 12
Mukherjee, B.N., 275
Mukhopadhyaya, S., 297

Municipal work, 93, 99, 205
Murray, O., 296

Nābhaka tribes, 232
Nābha-panktis, 124
nāgaraka, 112–13, 115, *see* nagalaviyohalaka, 170
Nāgārjunī, 8, 186, 194
Nallamalai range, 274
Nanda canal, 317
Nanda, R., 272
Nandas, 12, 16, 94, 132, 144, 190, 198, 218, 220, 243, 302–3
Narain, A.K., 128–9, 191, 193, 272, 288
Nearchos, 280
Nemita, 25–6
Neogi, P., 75
Nepal, 232, *see* Foreign contacts, and Map; 48
Nigali-sāgar, 5, 179, 233, 261 (trans.)
Nigrodha, 34
Nikāyas, 302
Nilakantha Sastri, K.A., 48, 95–6, 108, 114, 242
Nirgranthas, 28, 42–3, 138, 140, 154, 178
Nirvāṇa, 277
Nittur [Bellary Dt], 271, 287
Norman, K.R., 271, 272, 273, 274, 275
Northern Black Polished Ware [NBPW], 239–41, 282, 283, 287, 288, 289, 298, 299
Numismatic evidence, 11, *see* Coinage

Ojha, G.H., 222–3
Oldfield, 131
Olmstead, A.T., 110
Omphis, 246
Orissa, 268
Ornaments, 285
Outcastes, 92
Overseers, 120

Pacifism of Aśoka, 198, 201–3
Padmāvatī, 30
Paila, 243
Pāladas, 124
Pali Canon, 301–2, 307
  mention of monarchies and urban society, 301
Pālkīguṇḍu, 5, 132, 233
Paṇas, 314
Pañcālas, 94
Pande, B.M., 272
Pande, G.C., 149, 152
Pāṇḍyas, 124, 133
Panguraria [Sehore Dt], 271, 286
Pāṇini, 129, 218, 226, 280, 288, 289
Pant, P.C., 284
Paranavitana, S., 272
Pargiter, F.E., 12, 13, 16, 32, 182–4, 195, 300, 301, 303
Parinirvāṇa, 13–16, 26, 39, 42, 44, 46, 134
Pariśiṣṭaparvan, 14, 16, 17, 68, 138, 184, 187, 195
Parkham, 268
Paropamisadae, 16
pāsaṃḍa, 276, 277
Pāṭaligāma, 300
Pāṭaliputra, 7, 9, 10, 17, 28, 46, 66–7, 81–2, 105, 114, 119, 122, 125, 135, 150, 156, 187, 191, 195–7, 206, 211, 230, 232–7, 269, 285, 288, 290, 296, 314, 315, 320
Patañjali, 226
Pātimokkha, 42
Periplus, 128, 229
Pernicka, E., 284
Peterson, P., 296
Philip Aridaeus, 242, 245, 248
Piggott, S., 229
Pilgrimage of Aśoka, 15
Pillar capitals, 291
Pillar Edicts [PE], 2, 5, 51, 123, 271, 275, 281, 290
  Ist, 173–4, 262, 273, 274 (trans.)
  2nd, 174, 262 (trans.)
  3rd, 175, 262 (trans.)
  4th, 103–6, 110, 176, 202, 263, 275 (trans.)
  5th, 31, 118, 177, 264 (trans.)
  6th, 95, 177, 264 (trans.)
  7th, 39, 44, 81, 102, 110, 117, 126, 140, 154, 177, 186, 189, 265, 275, 290 (trans.)
Pillars, location of, 290
Piṅgalavatsa, 26, 154
Piprahwa Relic Casket, 279
Pīṭha, 273
Pitinika, 124

Piyadassi, 6, 226–7
Pliny, 10, 18, 82, 125
Plutarch, 13
Polybius, 184, 190
Pollet, G., 297
Population, distribution of, 319
Poster, G.A., 283
Pottery, 11, 77, 205, 234, 239–41
pradakṣinā-patha, 290
prādeśika, 105–6, 109
Prākrit, 7, 134–5, 221, 295
Prayāga, 290
Precious metals and gems, 75–6, 86
Prinsep, J., 6
Propaganda, 154
Prostitutes, 88, 89, 112, 117
Provincial Administration, 100–1
Przyluski, J., 21–2, 27–30, 35, 42, 52–3, 184–6, 192–3, 200, 305, 306
Pseudo-Origen, *Philosophia*, 60
Ptolemy, 229–30, 237
Ptolemy II Philadelphus, 18, 41, 230, *see* Hellenic kings
Pugliese-Carratelli, G., 275
Punishments, 78–9, 99, 103–5, 127, 176, 200, 202
Purāṇas, 9, 12–16, 30, 32, 182–7, 191, 194–8, 222, 231, 236, 303
Puṣyadharman, 184, 192
Puṣyagupta, 13
Puṣyamitra, 182–5, 191–2, 196, 200, 206
Putta, 272

Qsyr [Aramaic for *dhamma*], 277
Quarries, Chunar, 284
Queen's Edict, 30, 44, 102, 178, 185 (trans.), 260

Rādhagupta, 25, 54, 97, 188, 194
Raghavan, V., 219
Raghuvaṃśa, 219
rāgi, 285
Rai, G.K., 312
Rājā, 308
Rājadharma, 294
Rājadharma Kauṣṭubha, 226
Rājagaha, 299
Rajagṛhȧ, 6, 42, 81, 188, 229 (Rajgīr), 240, 285, 299, 300
Rājā-māgadhe, 317
Rājatȧraṅgini, 13, 29–30, 130, 184, 188–9, 193
Rajghat, 285, 299
rājūka(s), 103, 105, 106–9, 118, 207, 272
Rajūla-Maṇḍagiri, 5, 234
Rāmāyaṇa, 226, 294
Rāmpūrvā, 5, 11, 75, 234
Ramesh, K.V., 273
Rangarajan, L.N., 293
Rank, O., 213
Rapson, E.J., 129, 242, 244
rāṣṭra, 272
raṭṭhikāni, 272
Ray, Niharranjan, 206, 291, 310
Ray, S.C., 283, 288
Raychaudhuri, H.C., 54, 66, 153, 198, 204
Renouncer [*bhikṣu*], 309
Revolt at Taxila, 21, 22, 101
Ṛgveda, 291
Rhys Davids, T.W., 56, 63, 80 (Mrs. Rhys Davids), 149
Rice, B.L., 199
Rice cultivation, 285
Riṣṭikas, 124
Ritschl, Eva, 293
Rock edicts, *see* Major Rock Edicts.
Romēdōte, 7, 22
Ropar [Punjab], 286
Rostovtzeff, 125
Routes, 80, 177, *see* Map, 83
Roy, T.N., 283
Rudradāman, 8, 13, 118, 230–1
Rummindei, 5, 49, 50, 66–7, 179, 233–4 (trans.), 261
Rūpanāth, 5, 40, 154, 234, 286
Rural administration, *see prādeśikas, rājūkus, yuktas, gopa, sthānika*

Sacrifices, 71, 140, 150–1, 198
Sahasrām Edict, 5, 38, 40, 82, 154, 235, 267
Śākyas, 12, 22
Salaries, 314
Śāliśuka, 183, 191, 195–6
Samantapāsādikā, 305
sambodhi, 37–8
Saṃgata, 183
Saṃgha, 2, 10, 37, 42–5, 49, 148, 150, 159, 178–9, 188, 192, 229, 280. 292, 298, 305, 307, 308, 309

Saṃghamittā, 22–4, 30, 47, 305
Saṃgham upāgate, 148, 154
Samprati, 30, 53, 183–4, 187–8, 192, 194–6
Samudra, 35
Samudragupta, 168, 203
Sanchi, 5, 11, 23, 76, 179, 205, 206, 235, 290
(Kākanāḍaboṭa), 269
Sandrocottus, 18, 20
Sankaranarayanam, S., 272
Sankisā, 7, 11
Sannati [Gulbarga Dt], 271, 274, 286
Sanskrit, 7, 221, 231, 295
Sarao, K.T.S., 300
Sāriputta, 26
Sarmanes, 59
Sārnāth, 5, 11, 179, 235, 269, 290, 292
Śāstra, 296
Sastri, A.M., 271
Śatadhanus, 182, 196
Śatadhanvan, 183, 196
Śatapatha Brāhmaṇa, 64
Satiyaputra, 124, 278
Sava-paṭhaviyaṁ, 272
Scerrato, U., 277
Schetelich, Maria, 293
Schism Edict, 34, 42–5, 159, 179 (trans.), 262
Schlumberger, D., 274, 276
Scialpi, F., 276
Script, 7
Script, invention of, 280
Seleucid-Mauryan relations, 304
Seleucus Nikator, 9, 14, 16, 17, 20, 139, 190 (Seleucids), 121, 125, 296
Sen, A.C., 23, 177
Sen, B.C., 313
Senart, E., 127, 149, 153
Seneviratne, S., 287, 317
Separate Edicts [SE], 271, 274
Ist, 273, 280
2nd, 273, 280
Separate Rock Edicts
Ist, 95, 100, 102–3, 113, 147, 169, 204, 230, 257 (trans.)
2nd, 100, 116, 170, 258 (trans.)
Set Mahet, 243
Seṭṭhis, 301
Settlements, pre-Mauryan, 286
Shahbāzgarhi, 5, 7, 123, 128, 236
Shaked, S., 275
Sharma, I.K., 273, 274, 287
Sharma, R.K., 286
Sharma, R.S., 310, 311
Sharma, Y.D., 93
Sherwin White, S., 304
Shi Huang Ti, 144, 215, 219
Ship-building and ships, 72, 85, 119
Siddāpur, 5, 40, 132, 154, 230, 236, 238
Sidersky, 50
Silk, 219
Sircar, D.C., 7, 22, 30, 48, 68, 101, 113, 118, 126, 128, 186, 226, 231, 271, 272, 273, 274, 279
Sisunāga, 302
Śiśupālgarh, 205, 240, 267, 287
Sīta lands, 311, 317
Sītādhyakṣa, 311
Sites of Mauryan finds, 248–9
Śiva, 297
Skalnik, P., 287, 316
Slave labour, 312
Slaves and Slavery, 73, 89
ślokas, 296
Smith, V., 16, 23, 32, 127, 148, 194, 196, 226, 232, 244
Sohgaurā, 7, 17, 68, 113, 236, 244
Soldiers, 74–5, 119
Somavarman, 183
Sopārā, 5, 82, 135, 236–7, 305
Sophagasenos (Subhāgasena), 184, 190, 210, 211
Sopheithes, 242
Spices, 86
Spies, 112, 208
śramanas, 59, 152–3, 157, 162, 167, 273
Śravaṇa-Belgola, 17
Śrāvastī, 6
Srivastava, K.M., 298
Standard of living, improvement of, 288
State, control of economy, 295, 310
State formation, 298, 302
Stein, A., 130, 188
Sternback, L., 293
sthānika, 109, 113
Stoller Miller, B., 295
Stone sculpture, 76, 141, 267
Strabo, 10, 58, 61, 65–6, 72–6, 77–9, 81, 85, 87, 90, 102–5, 108, 111, 113,

119–21, 125, 127, 129, 158, 160, 167, 234, 311, 314
Strong, J.S., 297
Stupa, 274, 290, 319
Subba Reddy, D.V., 314
Subhadrāṅgī, 21, 27
Sudarśana lake dam, 118, 231, 317
Sudatta, 27
Śūdra, 311
Sugatra, 27
Sugh [Punjab], 286
Sumana, 24, 34
Sumaṅgala Vilāsanī, 121
Śuṅga, 182, 192, 200, 205–6
Superintendents, 100, 112, 114, 116
Susīma, 25
Suttanipāta, 302
Suvarṇabhūmi, 47, 48
Suvarnagiri, 39, 145, 233, 236
Suyasas, 183, 185–6, 194–5
Svarga, 277

Taddei, M., 275
Takakusu, 26, *see* I Tsing
Tambapanni, 134, *see* Ceylon, and Map, 48, 134
Tambiah, S.J., 308–9
Tamil sources, 18, 132, 168
Tāmralipti (Tamluk), 46, 82, 131, 237, 286
Tāranātha, 9, 18, 25, 29, 36–7, 50, 130–1, 148, 184, 190
Tarn, W.W., 13, *see* Routes, Bactrian Greeks, 84
Tax, *see* Land ownership, Trade regulations, Rural administration, Urban administration
Taxes, 314
Taxila, 7, 12, 21–2, 27, 53, 75–6, 81–2, 101, 121, 128, 130, 139, 145, 192, 197, 204, 237, 240, 242, 244, 246–7, 268–70, 286, 315
Terracotta objects, 233–4, 241, 269, 282, 283
Textiles, 77, 86
Texts, interpolation of, 295, 297
  multiple authors, 295
Textual sources, 292–303
Thakur, U., 305
Thakur, V.K., 310
Thapar, R., 281, 284, 295, 297, 301, 303, 305, 308, 309, 311, 312, 316
Theragāthā commentary, 28
Third Buddhist Council, 41–5, 47, 148, 154, 172
Thomas, E.J., 32, 101
Timmer, B.C.J., 57, 79, 111, 121
Tissa, 27, 42, 46, 47
Tissarakhā, 30, 51–2, 185, 192
Titles of Aśoka, 180, 186–7, 222, 226–7
Tīvara, 30, 185
Tosalī, 145, 230
Town administration, 314
Town-planning, 93, 205
Trade, 5, 73, 77–80, 85–6, 235–6, 285
Trade regulations, 77–8, 85, 114
Trade routes to the West, 83–4
Transmigration of souls, 149
Trautmann, T.R., 293–4
Travel, 85
Treasurer, 98–9
Tribal people within the empire, 123, *see* Map, 124
Tribal Republics, 94–5, 102, 121, *see* Kingless states
Tribe, 313
Tughlak, Firoz Shah, 6
  shifting of Asokan pillars, 278
Tungabhadra/Tagabena, 18, 60, 82
Tuṣāspa, 48, 128, 231, 269, 277

Udegolam [Bellary Dt], 271, 287
Ujjain, 21–2, 27, 145, 187, 195, 231, 235, 237, 248, 285
Upaniṣads, 200, 218, 301
Uparāja, 27
Upāsaka (Aśoka), 46, 148
Urban administration, 112–15, *see* *nāgaraka*, *gopa*, *sthānika*
Urban centres, 299–301
  characteristics, 286
  mahānagaras, 298, 300
  nagaras, 300, 301
  rājadhānis, 299, 301
Urbanization, 298, 299, 302
  fortification, 300
  iron technology, 310
  second, 283
Usury, 78–9
Uttarapatha, 12, 25

Vaiśālī, 42, 299, 300
de la Vallée Poussin, 38, 153, 155, 186–7, 198, 203
Vālmīki, 226
Vamsatthapakāsinī, 8, 12, 13, 17, 21, 26
Vaṅavāsi, 47, 48
Vaṅga, 48, 77, 82, 131
Varaprasada, J., 273
Varma, R., 284
Varṇa, 310, 313, 314
Vatsa, 77
Vibhajjavāda, 43, 45
Vidiśā, 22–3, 235
Vigatāśoka, 21, 24, 27–8
Vijaya, 82, 134–5
Village administration, 67, 68
Village community, 312–13
Vinaya Piṭaka, 90, 300
Vīrasena, 184, 190–1
Virāṭa, 229
Viṣṇugupta, 218, 222–5, 296
Viṣṭi, 61, 68, 89, 312
Viśvakarman Bhauvana, 64
Vītāśoka, 21, 24, 27–8
Volkova, O.F., 298
Vṛhaspati, 184, 192
Vṛjjis, 94

Waddell, L.A., 129, 234
Wages, 74, 89, 99, 119, 208
Wagner, G.A., 284
Walsh, 243–4
Warder, A.K., 142
Warmington, E.H., 85–6
Watters, T., 24, 28–9, 35, 50, 130, 133, 228, 233–8
Weaving, 74, 88
Wells, the digging of, 70, 81, 152
Wheeler, Sir M., 230, 239
Winston, R., 110, 145, 151, 152
Winternitz, M., 220
Women, position of, 86, 91, 116–17, 175
Wood, use of, 76, 113, 221, 267
Wright, 131

Yajñavalkya, 293
Yamazaki, G., 304, 307
Yaśas, 50, 193, 194
Yerragudi, 5, 132, 154, 172, 234, 238
Yona, 47, 48, 123, 128–9, 130 (Yavana), 124, 189
Yonakamboja, 276
Yonarājā, 273
yukta, 97, 105–6, 109–10
Yūpa, 290

Zambrini, A., 296
Zodiac, 246

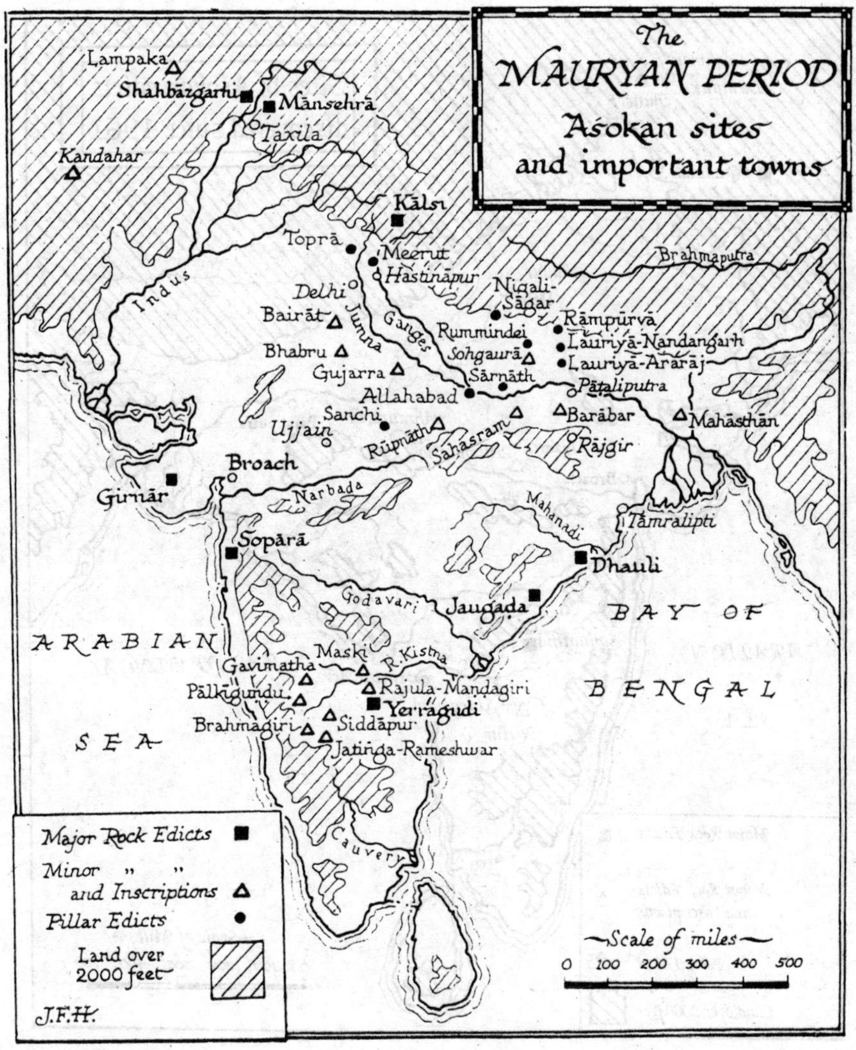
The MAURYAN PERIOD
Aśokan sites and important towns
Lampaka
Shahbāzgarhi
Mānsehrā
Taxila
Kandahar
Kālsı
Toprā
Meerut
Hastināpur
Delhi
Brahmaputra
Indus
Nigali-Sāgar
Bairāt
Jumna
Ganges
Rāmpūrvā
Rummindei
Lauriyā-Nandangarh
Bhabru
Sohgaurā
Lauriyā-Ararāj
Gujarra
Sārnāth
Allahabad
Pātaliputra
Sanchi
Barābar
Mahāsthān
Ujjain
Rūpnāth
Sahasram
Rājgir
Broach
Girnār
Narbada
Mahanadi
Tāmralipti
Sopārā
Dhauli
Godavari
Jaugada
BAY OF BENGAL
ARABIAN SEA
Maski
R. Kistna
Gavimatha
Rajula-Mandagiri
Pālkigundu
Yerragudi
Brahmagiri
Siddāpur
Jatinga-Rameshwar
Cauvery
Major Rock Edicts
Minor " " and Inscriptions
Pillar Edicts
Land over 2000 feet
J.F.H.
Scale of miles
0 100 200 300 400 500

Flyout]

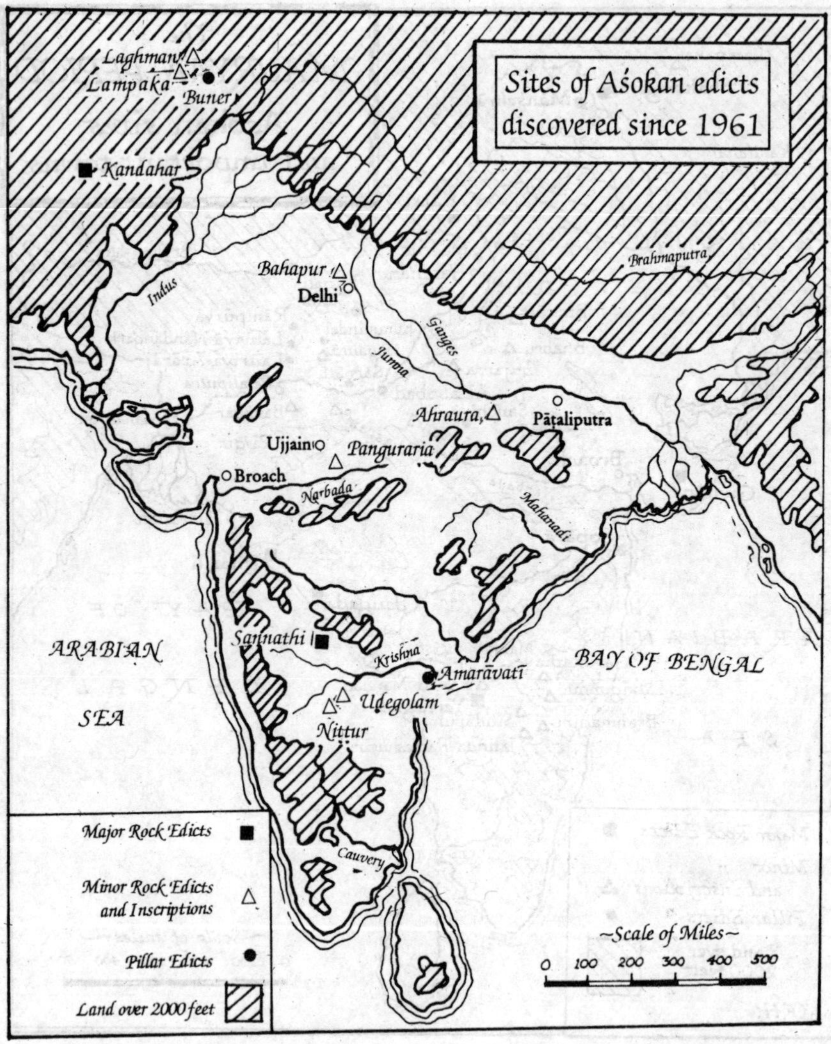

Sites of Aśokan edicts discovered since 1961

Laghman
Lampaka
Buner
Kandahar

Bahapur
Delhi

Indus

Brahmaputra

Jumna

Ganges

Ahraura
Pāṭaliputra

Ujjain
Panguraria

Broach

Narbada

Mahanadi

ARABIAN
SEA

Sannathi

Krishna

Amarāvatī

BAY OF BENGAL

Udegolam
Nittur

Cauvery

Major Rock Edicts ■

Minor Rock Edicts
and Inscriptions △

Pillar Edicts ●

Land over 2000 feet

~Scale of Miles~

0   100   200   300   400   500